KV-638-058

Advances in Human—Computer Interaction

Volume 2

Edited by

H. REX HARTSON
DEBORAH HIX

Virginia Polytechnic Institute and State University

ABLEX PUBLISHING CORPORATION
NORWOOD, NEW JERSEY

Copyright © 1988 by Ablex Publishing Corporation

All rights reserved. No part of this publication may be reproduced, stored
in a retrieval system, or transmitted, in any form or by any means, electronic,
mechanical, photocopying, microfilming, recording, or otherwise, without
permission of the publisher.

Printed in the United States of America

ISBN: 0-89391-428-2

ISSN 0748—8602

QUEEN MARY
COLLEGE
LIBRARY

Ablex Publishing Corporation
355 Chestnut Street
Norwood, New Jersey 07468

Contents

Preface

The preface to the first volume of this *Advances in Human-Computer Interaction* series stated the theme of the series: that the future of the development of interactive systems with quality human–computer interfaces is in the cooperating hands of behavioral scientists and computer scientists. Much has happened in the field of human–computer interaction in the relatively short time since that volume appeared. Many new ideas have emerged on both sides of this field. The field itself is much more established as a viable area of research and development. The result of new attention to the user interface is even showing up in the marketplace. Yet many of the same problems remain unsolved. One factor that has clearly emerged from the smoke and dust of the burgeoning effort in this field is the truth of this need for cooperation of roles—many roles—in solving the complex problems of human–computer interaction.

Although behavioral scientists and computer scientists have begun to reach toward each other, a gap still exists between their worlds. To some extent, the gap is caused by a lack of knowledge on each side of the needs and constraints of the other role. Also, there are genuine differences between the methods used by behavioral scientists to design and analyze interfaces and those used by computer scientists to design and implement software. Professional groups, such as the ACM SIGCHI, are starting to remedy this lack of information by promoting workshops, conferences, and other means for working together that foster mutual cooperation and education.

We believe cooperation between the roles is needed in all the major areas of current work, including *theory, modeling, methodologies, tools,* and *evaluation.* For example, behavioral science has a long-standing tradition of theoretical work based in cognitive and behavioral psychology. It would be valuable to see more application of *theory,* especially in the interface development process. It would also be useful to have more theoretical work based on developmental psychology (for example, see Whiteside & Wixon, in Chapter 2 of the first volume of this series).

There are user models, models of dialogue, control structure models—lots of disjoint *models* on both sides of the discipline. These models are helpful in understanding isolated issues and problems, but we need more integration of these models to help understand the broad picture.

Probably the one place where there is the most need for cooperative work is the area of development *methodologies.* Presently, software development approaches are separate from those for interface development. Given the reasonably well-established body of work that currently exists in software engineering methodologies, it is tempting to try to include interface development by simple extension of these approaches. But software engineering is not enough; the problems of interface development are significantly different from those of software development. On the other hand, interface development in a vacuum, without attention to the software component, won't solve the problem either. Each side of this issue has its own requirements and problems in the design and development domain. There is currently no integrated methodology to organize and guide designers through the activities of interactive system development over a complete, unified system life cycle.

The first *tools* (e.g., User Interface Management Systems, or UIMS) have been developed by computer scientists without much input from behavioral scientists. The result has often been tools that are primitive and hard to use, and generally not based on a solid understanding of the real problems of human–computer interaction. Similarly, some work on tools has been undertaken on the human factors side. Care must be taken that this effort is continued with a strong computer science input, especially with real-world connections to software engineering.

Finally, *evaluation* has long been accepted as an integral part of behavioral science, and lately is also finding acceptance in computer science. Many of the methods, however, are borrowed from earlier days before the testing of human–computer interfaces. The techniques need to be redirected and adapted. For example, controlled experimentation for point testing, while useful for testing hypotheses associated with human factors principles and design guidelines, is less suited as part of the system development life cycle. It is important to move evaluation into this life cycle, to include evaluation as a formative process rather than just as a summative process.

In addition to the importance of cooperation of roles, another theme of the first volume was diversity. Human–computer interaction is a very broad field, with ample room for different approaches and different perspectives. Once again, diversity is evident in the nine pieces of this second volume. The first chapter, by John Thomas, is an ambitious, carefully researched paper that takes a large step toward bridging the gap between human factors and the artificial intelligence aspects of computer science. It represents a broad new way of thinking about and relating these two fields. In the *theory* area, Mihai Nadin's chapter presents an unusual theoretical perspective on an approach to interface development using semiotics—the general theory and practice of signs and symbols. In particular, he explores the potential relationship of semiotics to interface design and evaluation. A *model* for generating responses to end-user errors is presented in the paper by Kemal Efe. This model, based on levels of program execution, allows the end-user to carry on a restricted dialogue with the system to determine the source of the error and possibly some information about how to correct it.

Some of the chapters span several of the five main research areas. The chapter by Andy Cohill, David Gilfoil, and John Pilitsis encompasses both the areas of *methodology* and *evaluation.* They propose a methodology for evaluating application systems and their interfaces along the dimensions of functionality, usability, performance, support, and documentation. Use of this methodology produces numeric scores that allow between-product comparisons and influence selection of application software packages.

Interactive *tools* for human–computer interface development are the theme of Tom Carey's chapter. His premise is that, by bringing together the developers of the tools with the users of the tools, one can help bridge the gap between the roles. He relates some real-world experiences with a dialogue design tool and offers some lessons about how these can be applied to the development of more tools. The paper by John Sibert, Dave Hurley, and Terry Bleser explores the development of a User Interface Management System (UIMS) *tool* based on an object-oriented paradigm, and presents some results of implementation of such a UIMS.

Spanning two areas, Tom Tullis' chapter describes an interactive *tool*—the Display Analysis Program—used for objective *evaluation* of the usability of an alphanumeric display format. This tool, based on a set of screen characteristics that influence human–computer interface usability, has been implemented and validated. The paper by John Whiteside, Dennis Wixon, and Sandy Jones details the broad, holistic *evaluation* of a wide range of systems, using a large variety of user types and tasks. User performance, compared among command-based interfaces, menu-based interfaces, and icon-based interfaces, produced some interesting counter-intuitive results. An *evaluation* of a specific type of human–computer systems—computer-based instruction (CBI) systems—is given in the chapter by Ted Shlecter. He presents several factors that affect CBI evaluation, including costs, learning increments, individual differences, and attitudes, and explores how CBI evaluation techniques might be applicable to other areas of human–computer interaction research.

It is with great relief at having brought this project to a close that we wish to acknowledge the help of several people who have stuck with us throughout the evolution of this volume. First and foremost, Pat Cooper, our tireless secretary, managed to organize, file, and keep track of the mountain of details needed to make this project happen. Ben Shneiderman gave continued encouragement when things got off to a slow start. Our Ablex editor, Barbara Bernstein was, as with Volume I, patient and cooperative throughout. And last, but not least, Jack Daniels and Glen Morangie provided late night companionship.

Rex Hartson
Debby Hix
Blacksburg, Virginia
January 18, 1987

CHAPTER 1

Human Factors and Artificial Intelligence

John C. Thomas

NYNEX
Artificial Intelligence Laboratory
White Plains, NY

INTRODUCTION

Artificial intelligence might be defined as programming computers to do things which, when done by humans, would show intelligence. *Human factors* may be defined as using what we know about the way people are to build systems that help make people happier and more productive. These two fields of knowledge relate to each other in at least five interesting ways.

First, artificial intelligence systems, if they are to be useful, must take into account a human factors perspective. This perspective is just as important as it is in conventional computer systems. However, the emergence of artificial intelligence in expert systems, "intelligent" tutors and help systems, and natural language dialogue systems presents a new set of problems for the human factors engineer.

Second, artificial intelligence provides new possibilities for the human interface to computer systems. For example, speech synthesis and speech recognition offer the human factors engineer new possibilities for presenting information to the user and getting information from the user. Much of the motivation of the Japanese Fifth Generation project was really to provide better human-factored interfaces to computers (although not necessarily stated in those terms). Reactions to the Japanese Fifth Generation project (e.g., ESPRIT in the European community and Alvey in the UK) have also tended to have a strong human factors flavor (J. Nielsen, personal communication, Sept. 17, 1985).

Third, human factors can provide useful guidance in how to develop an artificial intelligence system more efficiently. The de-

1

velopment of a system is, after all, a human activity, generally quite a complex one involving the interactions of numerous people and machines. To the extent that human factors expertise is effectively brought to bear, the development process itself can be made more efficient.

Fourth, in order to provide good human factors guidance, we must understand how people operate when they solve problems, create, learn, recognize and generate patterns, and comprehend language. But understanding these processes forms precisely the core problem for artificial intelligence. While it is probable that machines may ultimately carry out these activities in ways that are totally different from the ways in which people do them, there is also the possibility that a consideration of how people do these activities can lead to considerable insight into building artificially intelligent systems. While it is beyond the scope of this paper to prove the following point, it may help the reader to understand the author's bias. Artificial intelligence began making practical contributions when focus shifted from considerations of how to do learning, problem solving, and perception *in general,* to a consideration of building aids in particular, concrete situations. Similarly, I believe that cognitive psychology cannot answer questions about how people perform mental operations *in general.* People are incredibly flexible and can perform in a large number of ways, depending on their training, their early experience, their strategy, and the situation. By focusing on how people do and could operate in particular situations, we will simultaneously:

1. Provide solutions to real-world problems.
2. Provide a richer stock of metaphors for computer scientists.
3. Build better theories of human nature.

Fifth, the models that are developed in artificial intelligence and expert systems research, while not specifically built with the idea of modeling human behavior, can nevertheless provide useful contrast points for models of how humans actually do operate.

These topics will be discussed in turn; each contains references to relevant reviews and original research. Some future developments in artificial intelligence and expert systems will be predicted. Finally, a research program will be outlined.

The reader should be aware that what appears here is not a completely comprehensive review of the literature on artificial intelligence and human factors; rather, it is my personal reflection on the relationships between the two fields and key references to work that explores these relationships. The current work is certainly not a distillation of years of a comprehensive program of research (mine or anyone else's), because such a program of research remains to be done. The chief purpose of this chapter, then, is to stimulate investigators in both artificial intelligence and human factors to further explore some of the strong interactions I see between the areas.

HUMAN FACTORS CONSIDERATIONS FOR AI SYSTEMS

It is sometimes imagined that artificial intelligence is "the answer" to human factors problems associated with computers because it will allow humans to communicate with computers in the same ways that people communicate with people. I do not share this view (even assuming that it is feasible for machines to communicate in the same way that humans do). First of all, the manner in which people communicate with each other is seldom even appropriate for human–computer communication. To raise just one issue, human beings are identifiable by sight and voice, and are socially responsible for what *they* say. It is often far less obvious who is responsible for the data, rules, or conclusions of a machine. For these and other reasons, I prefer to conceptualize the computer as a *medium* of communication among human beings rather than as a communication *partner.*

Thus, an expert system, to take one example, is a complex and much more flexible way of communicating the ideas of an expert to a user than is a book. Note that it is not merely the ideas of the expert that are communicated, but also the ideas of the knowledge engineer.[1]

Even in cases where it might be appropriate for people to communicate via computers the same way they do with each other, it is seldom optimal. To illustrate this point, let us take the example

---

[1] The expert used in the development of expert systems is someone whose performance is much better than that of the novice. The expertise is based on extensive experience and is a verbalizable knowledge—not a sensory skill like wine-tasting, or a motor skill like riding a unicycle. Though verbalizable, the expert typically has not codified his or her knowledge. This is done with the help of the knowledge engineer who extensively interviews the expert. The goal of the knowledge engineer is to understand the expert's knowledge and code it in a neutral fashion. Clearly however, the resulting system will to some degree reflect the knowledge representations of the knowledge engineer and the developers of the languages or tools used to instantiate the program.

of spoken speech. Spoken speech between two humans is a compromise between the needs of the listener and the needs of the speaker. A human listener, for example, can distinguish different spatial locations and different voices. Yet, a single human speaker is only capable of speaking from one spatial location at a time and only in one voice quality at a time. Therefore, there is no way that the single human speaker can use all of the listener's capabilities for discriminating in these dimensions. We also know that people can listen at about twice the rate that they can typically produce speech. A machine speaker (synthetic speech) is under no such constraints, and we can imagine having the machine produce speech that has higher information transmission characteristics than human speakers can. Handwriting is a similar compromise; printed material is easier to read but harder to produce. It would be silly to insist that machines output handwriting rather than print because that is the way people typically write. In addition, computers are capable of real-time output of types that are impossible for humans to produce in real time, such as animation and resequencing of images from a video-disk.

Aside from the need for compromise on bandwidth, humans themselves have additional problems in working cooperatively and in communicating. Even speakers of the same native language sometimes have enormous communication problems. There is no reason to suppose that these will instantly disappear once humans have programmed enough of their knowledge into a computer for the computer to appear to carry on a conversation. Rather than attempting to have the computer act like a human, it may be better to analyze what is effective and ineffective about human–human communication, and then try to design the computer as a medium which supports the effective aspects of human–human communication while avoiding the ineffective aspects (cf. Thomas, 1980).

At a more immediately practical level, expert systems and other intelligent systems will *not* be exactly like humans. A typical natural language dialogue system works perfectly, provided the human being communicating with it is the inventor or a trained salesperson. Once a naive user interacts with it, that user may quickly run into a blind alley that is just as difficult to back out of as is the case for more traditional command or menu systems. The designers of natural language systems must keep in mind the lessons learned so often before:

- You must test out your interface with real users, and

- Human factors advice needs to be solicited throughout the development process.[2]

Consider this short section of output to a user from an expert system (Sleeman & Hendley, 1982, p. 111).

SYSTEM: WE ARE NOW CONSIDERING:
THE NEXT GROUP IS (C 0) WITH A PEAK (0 0).
THE NEXT GROUP IS (C H 2) WITH A PEAK (2 2).
THE NEXT GROUP IS (C H 2) WITH A PEAK (2 4).
THE NEXT GROUP IS (C H 2) WITH A PEAK (2 5).
THE NEXT GROUP IS (C H 3) WITH A PEAK (3 2).
THIS IS THE SOLUTION.
AN ARG WHICH WE HAVE RECONSTRUCTED FROM THE PARTIAL
ONE YOU GAVE IS THAT WHAT YOU INTENDED?:

Surely this output would be easier to read if it were in upper and lower case (Williges & Williges, 1984). Similarly, according to the work of Wright and Reid (1973), we would expect that there is probably some tabular or graphical way of presenting the data that is more immediately understandable. There is also the troubling apparent contradiction between "THIS IS A SOLUTION" and "WE ARE NOW CONSIDERING." While it may be argued that overlooking these fine points is acceptable in a research prototype, such features have an insidious way of surviving in products.

That is just one of many possible examples of some of the human factors points that may be overlooked even in rather good examples of expert systems. The main point is that having artificial intelligence or an expert system does not obviate the need for serious human factors study in order to make such a system usable. The success or failure of such systems in the real world will depend upon the extent to which human factors are taken into account empirically, seriously, and from the beginning.

It is important to use much of what we have already learned about the human factors of computer systems in the design of expert systems. To take a few trite and simplistic examples, screens should still be flicker-free and legible; error messages should still be understandable; the proper combinations of flexibility and support in furniture and terminals should still allow the user physical comfort. Software and documentation guidelines like "use short sentences; use words with only one part of speech; avoid negation" still make

---

[2] For a more complete outline of how to incorporate human factors into the development process, see Thomas (1985) or Carroll and Rosson (1985).

sense as objectives. This is not the place to explore less obvious examples, or discuss the details of such guidelines. However, a perusal of several references on computer–human interaction will reveal principles that are applicable to intelligent as well as more traditional interfaces (Engel & Granda, 1975; Miller & Thomas, 1977; Schneiderman, 1980; Thomas & Carroll, 1981; Thomas, 1983; Williges & Williges, 1984). (Of course, guidelines should always be used as a starting point and never as a substitute for empirical observations of real users using the real system in a real context.)

In addition, however, to following the advice given in the references above, "expert systems," "intelligent tutors," "adaptive systems," and other AI systems present a new set of issues. For instance, we can have a system that adapts to each particular user. At first blush, this seems like a good thing. However, such systems do raise a number of new issues. How do people adapt to an adapting system? Should the system adapt more slowly or more quickly than the person can learn? Are certain kinds of adaptation confusing? In some organizational settings, most of the information about how to use systems is learned from peers. What is the effect on this important source of learning, when every user ends up with a different system?

The second most commonly used source of information was a human consultant. This raises a similar problem, when everyone has a different system. Can the consultant keep track of all the variant systems? Is there a way for the system to quickly inform the human consultant of the ways in which it has adapted to this particular user? Clearly, research is needed to answer such questions.

In other cases, more than extensive research, we simply need a change in attitude on the part of systems designers of expert systems. It is already known that people can comprehend simple sentences with simple words more easily than complex sentences with complex words. Yet some systems designers may be tempted to use complex language to impress the user. This may have the unfortunate side effect of leading the user to believe the system has much more intelligence than it really does. The explicitness and politeness of messages issued by systems can also influence the behavior of the user (Richards & Underwood, 1984). This, in turn, can influence the difficulty that a natural language dialogue system, or speech recognition system, would have in dealing with the human input.

To the extent that the system itself uses words, syntax, and implied intelligence within the scope of what it can really handle, one would expect that there would be a tendency for users to keep their inputs to the system within these bounds as well. In addition, there may be various kinds of meta-comments that the system could make that would help the user keep the dialogue going along lines the system could handle.

As an example taken from what appears to be one of the *better* tutors (and one of the very few with any empirical work associated with it), consider the potentially misleading implications for a naive user of the prompts of the calculus tutor below (Kimball, 1982, p. 285).

SYSTEM: WHAT SHALL WE DO TO SOLVE IT?
USER: SUB

It seems clear that the user was not really free to reply in natural English here, but restricted to a few known methods. Later, we see: (p. 286)

SYSTEM: WHAT SHALL WE DO TO SOLVE IT?
USER: HELP
SYSTEM: I SUGGEST YOU TRY INTEGRATION BY PARTS.
SYSTEM: WHAT SHALL WE DO TO SOLVE IT?
USER: PARTS
SYSTEM: INTEGRATION BY PARTS!

There are some subtleties here. But what is the meaning of "what shall we do" when a computer is addressing a human being? What is the meaning of an exclamation point! Is the computer excited at the prospect of doing integration by parts? Is the computer excited that the student took its hint? Of course, whether the net effect of such conventions on learning is positive or negative is an empirical question. But, in the absence of any empirical evidence, it would seem highly questionable to have the system subtly imply that it is capable of cooperation and emotion. In a study by Chin (1984), users who believed they were communicating with a person used about twice as much reliance on context as those who believed they were communicating with a computer program (although everyone was actually communicating with another person). Greater reliance on context would presumably make the natural language understanding task for the program more difficult.

As another example, consider the interaction between a student who seems to have no notion at all of how to solve quadratic equations and a tutor which uses expressions that belie its "true" intelligence (at least as I perceive it) (from O'Shea, 1982, p. 313).

> *SYSTEM:* CONSIDER THE EQUATION X TIMES X + 18 = X TIMES
> 9 GUESS THE ANSWERS.
> *STUDENT:* WHAT HAPPENS IF I CANT
> *SYSTEM:* PLEASE TYPE IN A NUMBER OR TYPE STOP IF YOU
> WISH TO STOP

It may be picky, but I believe words are important in teaching! In what sense is this sytem capable of asking a student to "consider" an equation? Apparently, this introduction does give the student the wrong mind set about the capabilities of the system. The idea of a truly intelligent partner, however, is contradicted by the system's next response. What does it mean to ask a student to "guess" at the answer? In fact, guessing is exactly what the student appears to be doing for the rest of the dialogue presented!

The student successively guesses as solutions to the above equation 1,2,3,4,5, and 6. When the student finally reaches 6, which happens to be the second possible solution (we gather the student has already guessed the "first" solution, viz., 3), the system responds:

> *SYSTEM:* WELL DONE (Sic) YOU HAVE GOT BOTH THE ANSWERS
> CONSIDER THE EQUATION X TIMES X + 18 = X TIMES 19 GUESS
> THE ANSWERS
> *STUDENT:* 3
> *SYSTEM:* NOPE KEEP TRYING
> *STUDENT:* 6,12,2,3

Note that the student's first two guesses are the two guesses that worked the previous time. Either the student has misread this as the same equation (not seeing the "1" in "19"), is not motivated, or is deeply confused about mathematics). Under all three hypotheses, the behavior of the tutor is beside the point.

> *SYSTEM:* NOPE KEEP TRYING
> *STUDENT:* 4,5,6,7,8,9,10
> *SYSTEM:* YOU ARE NOT TRYING TO THINK OF ANY RULES TO
> HELP YOU WE WILL LOOK AT ANOTHER EXAMPLE TRY TO FIND
> A RULE. . . ."

So . . . the system did not really want the student to be guessing after all. Why not make that clear at the beginning? And I certainly do not agree that the student is not using a rule. It seems clear that much of the student's behavior is governed by a rule: Choose successive integers. If the student is seriously trying, the comment made by the tutor could be quite demoralizing.

The point of these examples is *not* that these are bad tutors; rather, good ones were chosen to make the point that one needs to take care in the implications of what the system says. A further point is that even having the tutor "adapt" within some bounds is not the same as doing iterative design. That is, while both of these tutors "learn" on the basis of their performance, they are not going to stop using misleading language on the basis of their adaptation. For that, the philosophy of iterative design is needed (Carroll & Rosson, 1985; Thomas, 1983).

NEW POSSIBILITIES IN HUMAN FACTORS FROM AI

While artificial intelligence is not the answer to all human factors problems, it is true that advances in computer software that have sometimes been labeled "artificial intelligence" do provide the human factors designer with an additional array of possibilities. The human factors professional who is aware of new I/O technologies such as speech synthesis, speech recognition, handwriting recognition, and new visual representations is clearly in a better position to make reasonable design decisions.

In addition to new I/O technologies, AI also provides the possibility of limited communication in some sort of natural language. AI can also be used to manage the interaction more intelligently. For instance, AI offers the possibility of adaptive interfaces, online tutors, and advice-givers. In the sections below, some references will be given to relevant research and reviews in these areas.

Speech Synthesis

The various basic methods of getting computers to talk are well documented in Witten's (1982) *Computer Speech.* We should at least distinguish unlimited text-to-speech conversion systems, which are capable of reading aloud any text stored in the computer, from resynthesized speech systems, which essentially are sophisticated ways of recording human speech inside a computer at a greatly reduced bit rate. For a given cost, the latter systems give much better quality speech, but at the price of limited flexibility and high start-up costs. They are typically preferred in situations where there are only a limited number of messages that need to be recorded.

Text-to-speech systems, however, can be used to make text audible without human intervention. They are useful when greater flexibility is desired or where only a few users are interested in particular pieces of text, so that having a person read the text aloud would not be economically feasible.[3]

Commercially available devices are described in recent issues of *Speech Technology*. A more comprehensive review of some of the human factors issues in using synthetic speech is given in Thomas, Rosson, and Chodorow (1984), McCauley (1984), Pisoni (1982), and Simpson, McCauley, Roland, Ruth, and Williges (1985).

There are now several commercially available speech synthesis devices that produce speech that is clear under certain combinations of conditions of users, tasks, and conditions. Generally, unlimited text-to-speech conversion is useful for four separate reasons:

- Speech is available remotely.
- Speech provides an alternative interface for people who cannot get the needed information visually.
- Speech provides an additional information source when the visual channel is overloaded.
- Speech provides a highly attention-demanding channel.

First, because of the near ubiquity of the telephone, speech systems mean that computer information (which is quickly including most printed material) is available nearly everywhere. If and when the proper dialogue structures can be worked out, this opens up a great number of interesting possibilities. Rosson (1985) describes the simulation of a system that would allow a traveller to access information via telephone on entertainment, transportation, hotels, and food. Subjects varied in their ability to deal with such an interface, but they typically viewed it as a very desirable facility. Because of the current quality of unlimited text-to-speech conversion and the limitations of a 12-key pad with no visual guidance, though, some subjects found it difficult to navigate efficiently through the data base.

There are a number of people who cannot read because they are too young. A very large number of people (easily a billion according to the 1986 World Almanac) can understand spoken, but not written, language. Speech synthesis offers both a method of aiding these people to learn to read and a way to access written information in the interim. In addition, there are people in situations (e.g., running a lathe, wiring) where reading is less convenient than listening. The extreme case of this, of course, is severely visually impaired people,

---

[3] For a description of a particular research system, the reader is referred to Thomas, Klavans, Nartey, Pickover, Reich, and Rosson (1984).

for whom audio output can be a tremendous benefit (e.g., Hirsch, 1981).

Speech also provides additional channels of information to the person who is overloaded (e.g., a pilot) or who needs lots of stimulation for maximum benefit (e.g., entertaining games, computer-aided instruction, computer-aided design systems, new users needing help) (cf. Wickens, Sandry, & Vidulich, 1983). Finally, speech can be heard even when the user was not preattending to the channel. This makes it useful for warnings and alarms.

Speech Recognition

Unfortunately, many people still believe that speech recognition is pure science fiction. This is not so. Provided that careful attention is paid to human factors, useful speech recognition devices already exist for certain applications. If one is willing to train the system on individual speakers and the application allows discrete utterances (not necessarily single words), then one can recognize several hundred utterances at any one time. It should also be pointed out that this does not mean the total vocabulary is only a few hundred words. By using contingent branching to different vocabularies, the total number of recognizable utterances can be considerably expanded. However, as the number of distinct vocabularies grows, the amount of training time increases, as do the restrictions on what the user can do at any one time.

This type of system is a discrete utterance, user-trained system. In contrast, the situation in which a human being who has not trained the system walks up and speaks continuously and has the machine translate the speech into correct text is still 5 years away (as it has been for the last 30 years). Nevertheless, the former type of system, with user training on discrete utterances, can be useful when fast input is required, and particularly if the user's hands and eyes are busy elsewhere (e.g., industrial inspection). Such a system could also be used in conjunction with a pointing device to make a very user-friendly editor in which operators are specified in speech (delete, move,—to here, insert) and operands are indicated by the pointing device (cf. Bolt, 1984).

An important issue for discrete utterance speech recognition systems is what kind of feedback to give the user. In what medium should the feedback be given? How quickly should the feedback be given? For a data entry task, Schurick, Williges, and Maynard (1985) found that visual feedback was superior to synthetic speech, and that immediate feedback was best. Conceivably, the answers could be different in the case of text entry or editing, but empirical work is needed in this area.

In studying the human factors of new technologies like speech recognition, one good technique is to simulate the system before it is implemented. This has been dubbed "Wizard of Oz" by Kelley (1984). Gould, Conti, and Hovanyecz (1983) used this technique to simulate a speech recognition machine. The value of various proposed restrictions (speaking with pauses, moderate vocabulary size) on speech recognizers could be assessed before implementation.[4]

Handwriting Recognition

As pointed out in Carroll and Mack (1984), problems for new users tend to tangle. Problems with a keyboard, for instance, may interact with difficulties in attempting to understand the conceptual structure of the interface. Learning to use a new interface and a keyboard at the same time form a very difficult combination, so that some trainers often separate the two. The difficulty with applying such a technique in teaching office principals to use a tool is that the user will not get any useful work done until both the keyboard and the conceptual interface are mastered. An alternative is provided by the possibility of recognizing ordinary handwritten input (Tappert, 1982).

Knowledge-Based Systems

The growing power of computers makes feasible the implementation of knowledge-based systems that incorporate many of the ideas that have been developed in cognitive science over the last 30 years. The possibility of such systems means that online help systems could be made potentially more helpful. In order to be truly "intelligent" aids, the system must infer what the user is trying to accomplish. This is a difficult task (Pollack, 1985). Somewhat easier is the intelligent tutor (Sleeman & Brown, 1982; Johnson & Soloway, 1983). Here, the system is attempting to teach the user something and hence has an a priori preprogrammed instructional goal. In this context, it is easier to provide useful guidance based on a knowledge of what the user should know, what the system is trying to teach the user, and what the user already knows (as evidenced by past

---

[4] Again, see McCauley (1984), Simpson et al. (1985), Schurick et al. (1985), and Williges, Schurick, Spine, and Hakkimen (1985) for recent research and guidelines for speech recognition.

behavior). This type of system provides one more example of how new developments in AI make new choices possible for the human factors professional.

Novel Representations of Data

Representation is a powerful determiner of the ability of a person to solve problems (Carroll, Thomas, & Malhotra, 1980), or to form new concepts (Goldsmith and Schvanaveldt, 1984). New computer tools incorporating sophisticated and novel algorithms, for instance, are being applied to many fields, including molecular biology (Pickover, 1984), speech (Pickover, 1983a), and education (Pickover, 1983b). With the increasing availability of computer graphics and the computer power to present meaningful images, a new set of tools for human factors engineers is available.

One dimension along which representations differ is their degree of abstractness. Problem solving can be delayed by having too concrete a representation of a problem or too abstract a representation. Rather than being limited to a single representation, modern computer systems allow the possibility of multiple representations simultaneously. For instance, the SPIRE system developed for speech research at MIT allows one to picture simultaneously text, phonemes, waveforms, and Fourier components. Another excellent example of an interface allowing multiple representations is STEAMER, a simulation-based training system used in the U.S. Navy (Hollan, Hutchins, & Weitzman, 1984). A similar multiple-representation interface in another domain, that of a space station life-support subsystem, is described by Malin and Lance (1985).

Traditional speech spectrograms typically are either "narrowband," with a relatively fine discrimination in frequency but poorer discrimination in time, or "broad-band," with finer time discriminations but poorer discrimination in the frequency domain. With the speeds of modern computers, there is no reason not to have a dial that can be used to vary the bandwidth.

Even a cursory examination of the history of science shows a strong correlation between the development of new representations and progress (reflecting in the real world the experimental evidence cited above). Yet there have seldom been attempts to design representations consciously based on what we know about human capabilities. (See, however, Bolt, 1984, for some interesting possibilities.)

When human capabilities in perception, memory, decision making, and problem solving are viewed in the light of "ideal" performance on many tasks, there appear to be many problems. Perhaps this is because we now operate in a world substantially different from the one in which we evolved (Thomas, 1977). In any case, given that we know something about what these capabilities, limitations, and biases are, we should be able to design systems whose operating characteristics compensate in some sense for these capabilities, limitations, and biases in order that the overall performance of the human/computer system would be closer to optimal (Remus, 1984). One principle that could be used is to provide stimulation over more channels. If properly done, this should allow for easier pattern recognition by human beings (see, e.g., Buxton et al., 1985). Such general considerations, however, are always subservient to an understanding of a person's actual and desired behavior in specific situations.

Adaptive Systems

The possibility now exists for adaptive[5] interfaces and adaptive training (Benyon, 1984; Alty, 1984; Smith & Connally, 1984). There are reasons to suppose that such systems could be more effective than static systems. For example, one line of reasoning is that there are individual differences in style, ability, and background, and that much of what very good human teachers or therapists do is modify the approach to suit the particular individual. To the extent that a computer system can do the same, it will tend to be a better tutor and/or system than one that does the same for everyone. Beyond this, the system could monitor and improve its performance based on which tutorial techniques work (Kimball, 1982; O'Shea, 1982). O'Shea in particular presents empirical evidence that the tutor actually became more efficient both in terms of computer time and student performance (though the latter was not statistically significant).

One can also imagine that an adaptive interface could alter the order of choices in a menu, optimize abbreviation schemes to minimize keystrokes, highlight often-chosen items, or change defaults in command systems. It may seem as though it is obvious that such adaptiveness would be good. As pointed out in Branscomb and Thomas (1984), however, there are certain counter-arguments. What happens when a person is trying to adapt to a system at the same time the system is adapting to the person? It could become quite

---

[5] *Adaptive* means that the system will change its behavior in a deep way, depending on the user's behavior.

confusing for the user (cf. Maskery, 1984). In addition, much of the learning that people do in the field is from peers. If the systems of the two peers were different, it might be harder to get appropriate advice.

There seems to have been little empirical work that pins down the advantages of intelligent or adaptive computer-aided instruction. There is also little work that specifies when it is most likely to be useful in terms of various users or applications, and very little empirical investigation of the details of how such systems should be implemented (e.g., see the review by Eberts & Brock, 1984).

One example of some evidence to show improvement from being adaptive is in an indexing system (Furnas, 1985). The basic problem addressed here is that users seldom spontaneously agree with each other or with the system designer about what constitutes the "name" for an item. A possible solution is to allow numerous predefined synonyms (Furnas, Landauer, Gomez, & Dumais, 1984). Making the scheme adaptive makes it even more efficient. Aside from comparative evaluations, empirical studies in this area have the potential to help show major conceptual deficiencies in the possible structure of the systems themselves (Pollack, 1985; Thomas, 1975) even before the system is actually implemented.

Some conceptual analysis has been done of various possible styles of teaching and their relation to Intelligent Computer Aided Instruction (ICAI) (Elsom-Cook, 1984). However, here again, empirical work specifically testing various possibilities seems scant. The best work does illustrate a degree of use of the iterative design principles described by Carroll and Rosson (1985).[6] A more detailed review of various advice-giving strategies is given by Carroll and McKendree (1986).

A major exception to the general lack of empirical demonstration in this area is work at Carnegie-Mellon University (Reiser, Anderson, & Farrell, 1985), in which they compared three groups who learned LISP. One group used a private human tutor; a second group worked on its own, with a teaching assistant available; and a third group used a computer tutor. The groups were comparable in final performance. The computer tutor was nearly as good as the human tutor in terms of mean time it took students to learn (15 hours versus 12 hours, respectively) and much better than the group that was on its own (27 hours). In a second test, the computer tutor taught students faster and to a higher final performance level than the standard classroom teaching situation.

---

[6] See, e.g., Feigenbaum (1979), and Brown, Burton, and de Kleer (1982).

USING HUMAN FACTORS TO SPEED THE DEVELOPMENT
OF AI SYSTEMS

The people who develop AI systems are people. In building AI systems, they use a variety of computer and noncomputer tools. If human factors is "using what we know about the way people really are to help build tools that help make people happier and more productive," then we can apply that knowledge to help make AI system-builders more productive.

In this section, three examples will be given of how human factors principles can make AI system building more products. First, based on my own experience in attempting to develop an unlimited text-to-speech conversion system, I will explain how human factors helped make the process more efficient. Second, I will explore the development of expert systems and describe how consideration of certain principles of psychology can help select experts, guide the construction of the proper environment, and help in the dialogue used to extract expert knowledge. Third, I will describe an earlier study in which we simulated an expert system using the "Wizard of Oz" technique.

Speech Synthesis

I have already mentioned that speech synthesis is one example of how AI can help the human factors expert by providing new methods of human computer interaction for potential use. Let us now turn the tables. How can we use human factors principles to help the development of a better speech synthesis system?

There are several ways in which a consideration of human factors can help make the development of speech systems more efficient. First, we can use existing knowledge, particularly knowledge that is already in a form that can be used by a computer. Thus, for instance, we rely on an online dictionary and a parser (Thomas et al., 1984). In addition, we have tried to analyze what additional information must be added to the system. Unfortunately, the system builders adapt very quickly to the synthetic speech. Naive listeners must therefore be brought in often, to check on the progress of the synthesizer. Thus, the main additional source of information is the perceptions of these naive listeners. This is one of the slowest subprocesses of synthesis development.

In the typical perceptual experiment, several subjects are each asked to make many judgements, and the outcome is a small number of bits of information. This seems odd because the subjects have thousands of bits of information in their heads about speech perception. In our recent experiments, we have been exploring alternative methods of obtaining information from subjects in a more efficient way. For example, rather than simply asking subjects which of two intonation contours they prefer, we have outlined a method whereby they could "play" a sentence with the intonation they believe is most natural by playing the keys of a piano to trigger the playout of words. In this way, subjects would be giving timing and pitch information at much higher information rates.

Another labor-intensive part of our attempts to build a speech synthesis system is in developing the library of stored control parameters. We use diphones in our library because of the strong interactions between adjacent phones. Basically, a diphone specifies the main perceptible features of the frequency spectrum from the appropriate portion of one phoneme to the appropriate portion of the next. In cases where perceptual data indicate that coarticulation (the tendency of nearby speech sounds to influence each other) extends in a perceptually important way over more than a diphone-sized segment, we use larger units or build rules to account for these longer segments. The advantage of using diphones is that more natural sounding speech can be created; the disadvantage is that there are many more diphones than phonemes or even allophones (phonetic variants of phonemes). Our diphone library contains 1400 diphones, while systems commonly have 100 to 200 allophones. This is why it is important to make the creation of the diphone library efficient.

An investigation into the problems of attempting to build a diphone library reveals that one major problem is that speech is a series of highly transient events. One hears something, and then it is gone. Although one can hear that something is amiss, it is generally difficult to locate the problem temporally or even to characterize the perceived problem. For this reason, we feel a major breakthrough that is needed is better visual representations for speech. Visual representations are stable and can capture the temporal and frequency characteristics of speech events. The sonogram does this but suffers from several limitations. For instance, some subtleties that our research showed to be important, such as nasalization of vowels are difficult to see. In addition, the sonogram is insensitive to phase and makes no attempt to build in what we know about the auditory system. For this reason, we have developed several alternative representations of speech (Pickover, 1985). Preliminary empirical work indicates that such representations highlight certain similarities of speech much more clearly than the traditional spectrogram.

Expert System Development

There are several ways that human factors work can aid in the development of expert systems. We can break these into three categories: selecting the right experts, providing the right setting, and using the best information extraction techniques. Research specific to all three areas needs to be carried out, and human factors professionals should have a background to do collaborative research in these areas. In the absence of such research, some general principles can be cited.

A major psychological problem in attempting to develop an expert system is that the expert cannot really think aloud. To use this term is probably misleading. Thinking is a complex, not very well understood process that certainly goes on at many levels simultaneously. When asked to think aloud, the most one can hope for is a stream of verbal behavior that bears some relevance to the underlying processes. Thinking aloud has its own set of communicative goals. One can never make these disappear so that one is directly looking into the expert's mind. (See especially Schoenfeld's 1983 work.) By proper selection of the expert, providing the right setting, and cross-checking conclusions, however, one can hope to develop a system that will help novice with a larger proportion of the cases.

Obviously, one must choose a person with expertise. It may not be quite so obvious that equally expert people may differ considerably in the degree to which they are conscious of the processes they go through. Mozart and Coleridge are both cited as examples of people who sometimes had compositions appear as a whole. In contrast, Beethoven and Poe are claimed to have been relatively more deliberate. We could well imagine, then, that Beethoven and Poe would represent easier experts upon whom to base an expert composer or writer. Clearly one must choose experts capable of some degree of verbalization. To an extent, this is a characteristic of the problem domain itself. It would be difficult to build an expert system for wine tasting or riding a unicycle. Generally, one would like a potential application area to pass the "telephone test." The expert should be able to communicate with a novice over the telephone and lead the novice through the problem solving process. Even within a domain, however, you may find one expert who uses visualization, one who often derives things from first principles, and another who uses specific rules. The "rules" person will probably be easier to emulate using existing technology. This is *not* to say that the expert will initially be self-aware of those rules. The best way to find out about general rules is to ask about specific cases, i.e., tap into episodic memory first. It may even be that the rules are actually *developed* by the expert during the knowledge engineering process. The important point is whether the system so developed proves to be a useful tool, and not the epistemology of rules.

One also wants to choose an expert who is willing to admit to possible gaps, errors, or inconsistencies. An expert who is too concerned with reputation, or too perfectionistic, will tend to bias verbal reports more than one who is open and willing to treat knowledge engineering as a joint exploration. Making such judgements about people requires considerable clinical practice and expertise, but one can reveal something by seeing how experts react to compliments. Do they deny these or explain them away? This could indicate that acceptance, approval, or being right is an issue with them. How do they react to questions like: "With the wisdom of hindsight, how else might you have handled that case?" If they refuse, even this obliquely, to admit to any errors, appearing right may be more important than learning to be right. Of course, in making these comments about choosing among top experts, I recognize you may be very lucky just to find sufficient amounts of time from *any* expert! You may not have the luxury of choosing a nondefensive expert.

The degree of defensiveness that the expert exhibits will also be influenced to a considerable amount by the atmosphere provided by the knowledge engineers. To the extent that the knowledge engineers are willing to be open, open-minded, and willing to admit error, they will tend to produce an atmosphere in which the expert will also be willing to be more open. A perusal of standard texts in interviewing may be of some use here (e.g., Stewart & Cash, 1974). To provide an optimal atmosphere, however, one must do more than simply appear to be open (Ellis & Harper, 1961); one needs to learn to be open enough to listen to what is really being said. This may be a problem for the experienced software engineer who may be tempted to recode the expert's domain in terms of known algorithms. Such a tack will not only destroy rapport; it may also result in implementing an elegant but totally inadequate solution. Remember what the expert is!

Cognitive psychologists have developed a number of techniques to cross-check hypotheses about knowledge structures. One important fact is that knowledge tends to be context-dependent. It is quite possible for an expert to sincerely believe that he or she "always" does such and such when considering the rule in the context of a particular case. What one must try to encourage the expert to do is consider an entirely different type of case and see whether a diferent rule applies. One can also treat rule-checking as a creative process, by asking such questions as: "can you imagine what would have to be true about the world for this *not* to be the appropriate action?" For a further discussion of some of the issues involved in extracting knowledge from an expert, see Kidd and Cooper (1985). The importance of using many concrete cases is even more central if we take the position of Winograd and Flores (1986). From that framework, one would have to view an expert system, not as a distillation of rules that the expert actually uses, but as a complex communication medium used to facilitate sharing experiences. From such a framework, I would imagine that concrete case histories should be available as back-up for the novice; even taped interviews and the ability to efficiently scan real records would help the novice. None of this discussion is meant to imply that current builders of expert systems are unaware of these issues, or that the efficiency of building expert systems has not risen tremendously over the last few decades (e.g., Pundit, 1984).

Dialogue Simulation Studies

As early as the mid-'70s, work in our labs (Thomas, 1974; Malhotra & Sheridan, 1976) illustrated that one could simulate a desired natural language interface by using a human being at the other end. Doing so gives insight into the value of the application, the needed vocabulary, and the types of dialogue structures that are useful. We discovered in this work, for instance, that, while many business and computer words could theoretically occur as multiple parts of speech, in practice, real business people typically used them in only one way (e.g., file, record). We also found that the metalanguage— that is, the dialogue about the dialogue—was absolutely critical for the user and the system to keep converging toward a goal.

Thus, it was recommended that an "expert system" in any area also needed to at least be an "amateur" in psychology and communications, provided one is providing a natural language front-end. The system must have an understanding of what to do when the user says "Huh? Back up." or introduces a sentence with "Now, . . .". Such comments simply cannot be ignored or countered with the standard, "I'm sorry. I don't understand. Could you rephrase that?" Until natural language dialogue systems deal adequately with such metalanguage, they will not be natural language dialogue systems. An additional unsolved issue is the question of commitment. If I say something, I am an identifiable and unique individual who can be held accountable. In a computer system, the expertise of many individuals is simultaneously brought to bear on the task at hand. In fact, it is essentially this quality of the computer—to focus multiple *human* experts on a task—which accounts for its apparent power as a tool. Unfortunately, the converse of this is that responsibility and commitment are not clear. We must develop ways of dealing with this issue.

INTELLIGENT MECHANISMS IN HUMANS

In discussions of artificial intelligence, it is often pointed out that having planes flap their wings is not the best way for those machines to fly. On the other hand, many early aviators might have lived longer if they had paid more attention to the cross-sectional areas of the wings of birds. Sometimes it is wise to copy nature as is; sometimes one is better off to start afresh. In most cases, one can borrow selectively and then modify natural solutions to be more ideally suited to the artificial.

Not only are plane wings similar in shape to bird wings; birds and modern jet-liners are alike in other ways as well. Their control centers are in front, and they are piloted largely by a reliance on visual cues; their piloting mechanisms require good three dimensional abilities; they are controlled by using control surfaces that alter air flow; their energy comes from oxidizing hydrocarbons; their oxygen supply comes from the air they travel through; they must have special systems for taking in energy and for releasing wastes; they have special landing gear which is retracted during flight; and they use star positions and landmarks to navigate.

In any case, the point is not that artificial intelligence systems must be built like humans (even if they could). The point is *certainly* not that AI systems will or can be "intelligent" in the human sense. Indeed, I view software only as a sophisticated way for people to communicate (cf. Winograd & Flores, 1986). Nevertheless, human mechanisms are an excellent source of ideas for AI researchers. We must not make the error of assuming that similarity of mechanisms for doing a task implies the equivalence of two entities (human beings and software!) that are by their very nature completely different.[7] However, humans do have ways of dealing with many

---

[7] This would be like serving "airplane under glass" for dinner!

of the unsolved problems of artificial intelligence. It at least seems worthwhile to examine these solutions before dismissing them out of hand. My attitude here is fairly close to that expressed by Charniak and McDermott (1985, pp. 6–7). I would claim the potential for using human solutions as a starting point becomes even more plausible when these solutions also bear a resemblance to the solutions of more microscopic systems (e.g., genetics) and more macroscopic systems (e.g., business firms). Let us examine a few specific examples.

The Problem of Knowledge Reorganization

A number of systems for learning have been proposed (Feigenbaum, 1961; Quinlan, 1986; Mitchell, 1984; Rumelhart & McClelland, 1986). One of the major problems with such systems is that, if they go down a nonoptimal path of learning, it is difficult to totally reorganize. The work on bugs in children's learning indicates that this is a problem with humans as well. Beyond a certain point (that is, age), it also becomes difficult to learn to speak another language or acquire the highest level of expertise in athletics.[8] Apparently, we learn (by modifying) what we know, and totally reorganizing that knowledge becomes difficult. Partly this is because we must continue to live during the learning phase; total reorganization might be possible, but may well result in gambler's ruin (schizophrenia?) during the period of reorganization. How do people (partly) solve this problem?

One method of partial solution is to provide safe environments. This is what is done during therapy when one is encouraged to build entirely new behavior patterns. Artificial reinforcement is provided until the new behavior patterns are sufficiently well learned that they are useful in the real world (Rimm & Masters, 1974). Another type of safe environment is provided by games wherein totally new behavior patterns can be tried out with relatively minor consequences in the real world. Similarly, a pilot's first experiences are with simulators and/or instructors who can instantly take over and recover from errors.

Despite these mechanisms, there seems to be a real difficulty with total readjustment of an individual's nervous system. The only way to totally readjust is to die! That is, the nervous system of the individual human being may have a limit on the extent to which

---

[8] Separating motivation from capacity becomes difficult in such cases. Adults often avoid situations that would "force" them to learn the language.

it can adapt to a totally new environment. Therefore, beyond a certain point, it is necessary to literally start over by training a new organism. The child can then learn the accumulated wisdom of many generations of people quickly, in succinct form, and use this distillation of hopefully useful information as a springboard for further discovery. Perhaps something similar must ultimately be used during iterative design. At some point, a prototype may have to be thrown out and a totally new system built. If a new, incompatible operating system is installed, some method of communicating data and programs must be provided. Note that in the human case, this "cutover" takes years, and that we can communicate (via written language) with many generations.

Learning from Failures

It is clear that people tend to remember for long periods of time certain critical events that violate their expectations, especially when there are very large consequences. For example, people who were minding their own business and had something traumatic happen will tend to replay the event many times in their minds, trying to figure out what they did wrong. Holland (1975) has pointed out that this is generally adaptive for a system that has to learn. It appears possible that similar mechanisms may occur at lower biological levels as well.

Certain genes, for instance, produce proteins that interact with an expected environment in certain ways to produce chemicals that feed back to a gene that inhibits intrachromosomal duplication. When the environment changes so that the gene no longer has the desired effect, the inhibition of intrachromosomal duplication stops and the gene that produced the original protein now undergoes an intrachromosomal duplication in which thousands of copies of the gene are made. Effectively, this means drastically increasing the mutation rate. The chances are greatly increased that one of the new copies will be a modification of the original gene and will now produce a modified protein that will react appropriately in the modified environment to produce the desired effect. Such a mechanism could also be incorporated into a computer system that needs to "learn" from its mistakes.

To make this notion of modification more concrete, let us examine the application of this principle to a game-playing machine. In the case of a game-playing machine using a linear polynomial of weighted features, suppose that the machine expected a good position with a high degree of certainty. Now suppose that, instead, the position proved to be a very bad position. At this point, the computer should attempt to add a set of new features to its feature set and "replay" the game until it found a new feature that differentiated the old from the new set. The possibilities for new features should begin by taking old features and modifying them. The particular old features that would be a good starting point for finding reasonable new features would be those that changed value drastically just prior to, or at, the big shift in evaluation. Such a scheme implies that the machine needs both a semantic memory (that is, an abstract representation of how to play the game—its feature set, their weightings), and an episodic memory (that is, a very detailed memory of everything that went on during the play). Episodic memory would soon require tremendous storage. But not every event need be stored in detail in episodic memory. Only traumatic events—events that accompanied a sudden shift in the evaluation function—would need to be stored in detail so that these events could be replayed with variant programs until one was found that worked.

Psychologists may recognize that this describes quite closely what people in fact do. Shank (1984) pointed out that machines trying to comprehend stories should probably also concentrate on "failures of expectation." Riesbeck (1984) describes a system that uses failure as a clue to reorganize.

Similar principles could apply to a speech recognition machine. Suppose the speech recognition machine worked by a linear combination of weighted features. The machine should keep an exact representation of each speech event until it determines that it has made the correct recogniton. When it has failed to make a correct recognition, it should store both the exact waveform representation and its evaluation of that waveform along with the correct interpretation. Now it should start storing all additional examples of the word (or other unit) with which it has had trouble. When enough examples are stored, it can make an intelligent choice about a new feature that will discriminate these difficult words. Where should these new features come from? Modifications of old features. A heuristic place to begin is by combining those old features of the word in question with features that differentiated the signals coming right before the word in question. What this amounts to, in essence, is capturing coarticulation effects.

Depression

Drastic change in a person's environment often causes a temporary depression. Such depressions have different symptoms from so-called endogeneous depressions which seem to have a more biochemical, genetic component. They are also somewhat different from neurotic depressions, although the normal post-change depression can often be exacerbated by neurotic beliefs. In any case, one would surely think that all depression is bad and not something that one should model in an artificial intelligence system.

Instead, I propose that a short period of depression—that is, a relative lack of initiative and action—following a major change is an adaptive response in which humans engage, one which probably should have an analogue in artificial intelligence systems. Again for concreteness, imagine a speech recognition system. It is humming along nicely, doing 98% correct recognitions, when suddenly its entire world changes. Not only does its performance drop precipitously; the long range measures it takes of its acoustic inputs shows a major shift. What is the intelligent response? Is it to keep on making a large number of recognition errors? A better response may be to observe passively the environment and extract new invariances. If possible, this should be coupled with following a ritual, called "having a training session," for the new user and/or background noise that is causing the problem.

Similarly, when we humans have large changes such as marriage or the death of a close family member, we are given prearranged scripts (rituals) to follow until we have had a chance to develop new evaluation functions that are appropriate to the changed environment. Any initiatives on our part at the very beginning of a new entry into an environment will be based on our knowledge of the past and, to some extent, inappropriate. It is more useful to follow rituals and do some passive observation first.

Social Psychology and Committee Architecture

A fair amount of research on team effectiveness, small group behavior, and social psychology is potentially relevant to considerations of parallel architecture. Most parallel architectures discussed today have two major limitations. First, every processor is the same. Second, everything has to be specified, either by a program or by a set of rules that holds for all elements. Such an architecture is valuable for limited kinds of problems, like matrix manipulations, and may even be representative of how people solve certain problems (e.g., mental rotation; Funt, 1983). However, let us examine the parallels to human groups.

If we imagine a human organization in which every decision is made at the top and everyone is treated as having the same abilities and everyone has essentially the same job, we have an organization that is very ineffective for dealing with most kinds of tasks and certainly for any task whose structure changes dynamically over time.

Instead, in the most productive companies, what one finds is a diversity of people with a diversity of skills and a diversity of assigned tasks. A considerable amount of overhead in companies is spent in deciding who is good for what tasks, in training, and in determining fair rewards for performance. Each person has some degree of flexibility and local control in decision making. Greater local control may also improve parallel computation in computers (cf. O'Leary & Stewart, 1985).

Within the broad guidelines sketched, there are two common kinds of organizations: hierarchial and committee. In the hierarchies, there is still considerable freedom for decision making at each level. The decision making model of Yetton and Vroom (1973) actually offers quite a good model of what type of decision making (democratic, consultative, authoritative) is reasonable under what conditions. These same conditions (ignoring motivational considerations) could be applied to decision making in a multiple-processor system at the hardware level or a multiple expert system at a software level.

In human organizations, unlike computer organizations, no attempt is made to choose perfect individuals, that is, error-free components. Obviously, all people make mistakes. The organization is structured to minimize the effect of these errors by using redundancy, and by counseling—giving diagnostic feedback to people so they can avoid making the same mistakes in the future. In contrast, we try to make sure that only perfect components are used in computer systems. However, there are already exceptions to this. If a diskette track is bad, we just avoid using that track. If a network link is down, we just try another path. In telephone and onboard aviation systems, we use redundancy. So far, we do not generally build self-correctable components that can use feedback about what is wrong to correct their performance—at least not at the hardware level. However, we can easily imagine doing so. A group of CPUs operating in parallel could be under the direction of a supervisory piece of hardware. The systems could give overlapping results, so that the supervisor would know when something was wrong and could give special tests to determine which component was malfunctioning and how. At that level of complexity, it might be simplest at this point to bypass that component rather than try to fix it.

Another architecture that organizations sometimes use is the interdisciplinary committee or team. Here we try to use various sorts of experts. We assume each expert is good at particular sets of problems, and that they all have some meta-knowledge that lets them know for which kinds of problems they are best suited.

In the future, one might well expect to see diverse kinds of processors working together in this type of structure. Even now, one can, for instance, buy a personal computer and enhance it with coprocessors of many varieties: a floating point processor, a digital signal processor, or a string comparator, for instance, can all be added. Presumably, each type of processor is best on certain kinds of operations. One could now imagine building some method for determining who does what for overall efficiency. Just as in the case of an interdisciplinary team, there may be some task structures which will mean that not every processor will be spending all of its time doing what it is best suited for. There are a number of other interesting mechanisms that humans use to learn complex things that could provide the basic outline for solutions to problems in artificial intelligence. These include roleplaying, the distinction between games and work, humor and exaggeration, making things into binary opposites like "good" and "evil," and the use of "over-inference" systems (Thomas, 1977). Space does not permit a discussion of all these mechanisms, but the examples above should provide a hint of how a closer examination of human characteristics could prove useful to researchers in artificial intelligence. Again, this is *not* meant to imply any essential similarity between what human beings are by nature and what software is by nature. These parallels are to be taken in the spirit of metaphors used in idea-generation techniques like Synectics (Stein, 1975).

Other things being equal, there is one additional advantage when one models an AI approach on the way people do it. If people and machines carry out tasks in similar ways, it will be easier to explain how the machine works, and it will be easier for people to maintain and modify the computer system. On the other hand, if the machine carries out tasks in ways similar to the way people do them, it might induce people to attribute to the computer human powers or even feelings that it does not possess. Care should be taken to avoid such destructive attributions.

As a final note, we should make clear that we are discussing normative aspects of human behavior. We do not necessarily want AI systems to model errors that humans make due to carelessness and inattention. Researchers should keep an open mind, however, about whether certain types of human error and human creativity are merely two sides of the same coin.

AI AS A SOURCE OF IDEAS FOR HUMAN FACTORS

Just as there is no logical necessity that the way people do things will turn out to be the way computers should do them, there is no necessity that the way someone invents for a computer to solve a problem is like the way people do it. But, just as the way people do things forms a valuable source of ideas for computers, so, too, AI systems provide an interesting source of hypotheses about how people *might* do things.

One of the advantages of programming a model is that it forces a hard look at details that might otherwise be overlooked.[9] Of course, metaphors from computers have been applied to human behavior before.

Even though the typical outcome of serious empirical work is that the computer does *not* form a good model for how people operate, the exercise of making the comparison is valuable. For example, it makes sense to use "bits" when talking about information processing machines. It turns out that a "chunk" is a closer (though harder to define!) approximation to what people use as a unit of thought. Nevertheless, it is doubtful that the notion of a "chunk" would have been developed if the attempt had not been made to explain human information processing capabilities on the basis of bits. Understanding the relationship between bits and chunks deepens our appreciation of both concepts. Indeed, AI models and concepts have become so enmeshed in our thinking about cognitive psychology that, when reading a recent important book in psychology (Anderson, 1983), it is difficult to tell when an AI program is being described and when human cognition is being described.

More specific examples in which AI models have served as comparison points for human behavior include Thomas (1974), Johnson et al. (1981), and Funt (1983). These studies compare human performance with computer models in problem solving, diagnosis, and mental rotation, respectively. In particular, the computer modeling work of Newell and Simon (1972) produced a paradigmatic shift in the methods and thinking of investigators in the area of problem solving.

While such comparisons are often valuable starting places, there are several dangers investigators should strive to avoid. One danger, not unique to computer modeling, is that we tend to design ex-

---

[9] Such issues are dealt with more fully elsewhere (Reitman, 1965; Newell & Simon, 1972). They are only alluded to here for completeness and because useful theory is so sorely needed in the cognitive aspects of human–computer interaction.

periments and interpret results in ways limited to our world view. At some point, we may have to play this game or forego using the power of mathematical models and simulations to make predictions about situations we cannot actually observe. If we limit ourselves prematurely in the analysis of a real situation, we may overlook critically important variables in that real situation because we do not yet know how to incorporate those aspects. This danger is not limited to computer modeling and psychology. Economists, for instance, do not know how to measure how "good" a tomato is. Instead, they equate for purposes of calculating the Gross National Product a vine-ripened tomato you buy from a farmer for 49 cents and a rock-hard, ethyl-chloride-ripened tomato you buy at the supermarket for 49 cents, of which only 10 cents goes into growing the tomato. Typical oversimplifications in psychology that seem particularly prevalent in computer modeling are:

1. Ignoring motivation (!),
2. oversimplifying or ignoring individual differences,
3. ignoring the social context, and
4. ignoring the ability of humans to escape the experimenter-defined context, and create their own.

The second danger (which is uniquely true for computer modelers of human thought) is the ontological confusion between the model and the thing modeled. No sane rocket engineer insists that there is no difference between a rocket engine and a model of that engine. No sane meteorologist would equate a tornado with a model of a tornado. No musician would say that a score *is* a live performance, or even that a CD ROM reproduction *is* a live performance. Mysteriously, some few computer scientists seem to *equate* human thinking with their models of that process. This would be an ontological error even if such models were far more accurate and robust than they are today. Such an error is not just a philosophical oddity; equating a human being's thinking with a computer program could easily lead to social injustice. Human beings are ends; computers are *tools* to those ends.

FUTURE PREDICTIONS AND RESEARCH PROGRAM

The Future of Expert Systems and AI

Human factors research in artificial intelligence systems has tended to lag behind the existence of such systems. However, as illustrated by the references to the "Wizard of Oz" technique, this is not a necessary state of affairs. For this reason, I will risk a look ahead at some of the future developments likely in artificial intelligence. Obviously, trying to predict the future in this area is very tricky, even though I will limit the discussion to the area of expert systems. Within the next several decades, I believe at least eight major problems with expert systems will be solved, resulting in the widespread use of much better expert systems. These predictions are not necessarily the most important ones from the standpoint of artificial intelligence or expert systems. These are the ones I find interesting from the perspective of the relationship of human factors to artificial intelligence and expert systems.

1.   Every expert system will have an "expert psychologist" in it. This means that the system will know something about having different viewpoints, communicating differently depending upon a person's current state of knowledge, something about how quickly new information can be assimilated by people. In addition to making the system better in the sense that it could communicate information to people more effectively, it provides a necessary step for enabling the system to learn from people by knowing the kinds of limitations they have and knowing how to cross-check information.

2.   Expert systems will be able to communicate with each other and resolve differences when two or more perspectives are needed on a problem. Essentially, some form of "committee problem solving" will be implemented. Point one above would be a useful step toward solving this problem.

3.   Expert systems will be able to handle associations as well as rules and conditions; they will have reasonable ways of combining absolutistic and probabilistic data. Both types of systems exist today. In a sense, combining them is a special case of point two above. An example of how one might at least use various methods, depending upon the state of knowledge, is outlined by Hayes-Roth (1984). See also Zimmer (1984) for an approach to combining qualitative and quantitative data and reasoning.

4.   Expert systems will be built with rules largely induced from existing cultural archival data bases, such as dictionaries. For instance, one could imagine building an expert letter-to-sound system for use in a text-to-speech system. The traditional expert system way to do this would be to have a knowledge engineer work with one or more linguists (although, in this case, any fairly sophisticated native speaker might be considered an expert). Alternatively, one could use a very large existing online dictionary. A program could induce regularities in the dictionary of correspondences between

letters and sounds, run this set of rules against the dictionary, pick up exceptions, and use this as the basis for deriving a more sophisticated set of rules which could be rerun against the dictionary. When successive run-throughs stopped giving improvements in the performance of the rules, this might indicate that all words that were not given the correct pronunciations would need to be stored as exceptions. As more publishing is done via online computer systems, the possibility of making expert systems from encyclopedias, newspapers, and other types of compendia becomes even more intriguing.

5. Some expert systems will have nonverbal interfaces for joint computer/person control. For instance, an expert system computer operator could have a perceptual/motor interface that could apprise the operator of states of actions taken by the expert system. The operator and the system might together push on a joystick whose position would determine where the operating system parameters should be set in a multidimensional space. The expert could push harder toward what is believed to be correct depending upon its degree of certainty.

6. Expert systems will be able to induce rules from behavioral patterns even in domains where knowledge is nonconscious. This is similar to point four above, but more difficult. Visualize the following as an example. A decision maker is presented with all data relevant to the decision online. The decision itself is recorded online, as well as any intermediate actions and information retrievals. It is not far-fetched to suppose that a monitoring program could begin to induce invariances from these transactions; to induce, in other words, the rules by which the expert decision maker operates. After a large body of evidence accumulates about a particular combination of conditions, the expert monitor could suggest a rule to the expert and ask what the exceptions to the rule are. If the expert asserts that there are no exceptions, the system itself could make these decisions and inform the decision maker. This would presumably leave the expert more time for the more difficult decisions whose bases would be more difficult to capture in rules, or for decisions in which offline information sources must be consulted. Such a system raises a number of human factors problems, as well as potential social issues. Nevertheless, the net result, if properly implemented could well be a more satisfied human decision maker, who spends less time making routine decisions and a more productive one.

7. Knowledge-based systems will be part of many human–computer interfaces. There are many ways in which such

systems could be used. I am using *interface* here in the broadest possible sense. The system could even build a model of patterns of use and anticipate which data would be retrieved by the user. If such a model were accurate, the system could use the model for anticipatory staging to lower overall system response time.

To take an example closer to the user's interface, let us imagine that the system notices common command sequences. Beyond a threshold determined by some combination of frequency of command sequence and the number of keystrokes potentially saved, the system could put a representation associated with the most common command sequences in a menu area. This has the potential to save the user quite a number of keystrokes. However, it raises a number of additional human factors issues. What should the threshold be in terms of frequency of use and number of keystrokes saved? Does it depend on how fast a typist the user is? Does it depend upon how much real estate is available on the screen? How should a command sequence be represented in the menu area? While such a feature would save keystrokes by definition, would it actually improve productivity?[10]

8. Expert systems will be incorporated into tools for system design—and, in particular, the design of the user interface. This is really a special case of point seven, but warrants separate discussion. Human–computer interfaces will often still be designed and developed by numerous individuals and small groups without much access to human experts in human factors or interface design. While guidelines and textbooks on the subject may be of some help, probably the most effective method of improving the quality of interfaces is to provide a set of tools that allow the designer to have more fun, be more productive, and end up with better interfaces. One can imagine a tool set that helps one from the beginning to the end of development: from establishing marketing requirements, goal specification and elaboration, idea generation, building preliminary mock-ups, formal testing (helping to keep track of results and analyzing them), prototyping, finding trouble spots, and helping to make fixing trouble spots easier, all the way through collating user reactions to the product in the field and feeding them back to the system designers (cf. Malhotra, Thomas, Carroll, & Miller, 1980; Branscomb & Thomas, 1984).

Even short of tools to carry out the complete development process,

---

[10] It might not, because the experienced user might be able to think about something different in parallel with issuing a standard set of keystrokes; while the system might potentially be more valuable for a novice user, the system would have insufficient data on the novice to make reliable inferences about command sequences.

however, AI tools for programmers will continue to evolve. One side-effect of this will be to make it easier to modify code and therefore engage in iterative design.

In the next few decades, we will see, not only a growth in the number and variety of systems that mimic the routine aspects of what people do; but also the emergence of systems that help people do things more intelligently. At least some of these will be designed from a careful analysis of what it is that people do not do well today. Such systems can be thought of as ones that amplify human intelligence.

One direction that such systems could take would be based on the proposition that a person's reaction depends upon the totality of stimuli reaching him or her. Now, it is true that those stimuli to which we consciously attend have a greater effect on our behavior than those to which we do not consciously attend. Most instrumentation and computer interfaces—and, for that matter most work environments—totally ignore the peripheral stimuli to which people are exposed (except insofar as they may be unsafe or highly distracting). However, if we imagine that we could modify, not only, say, the CRT screen the person is attending to, but the entire visual, auditory, and tactile array surrounding the person, we could construct environments to help facilitate task concentration by having everything point back to the task at hand. For tasks that relied on occasional use of pieces of information, we could have these pieces of information or obvious gateways to them always present. For tasks that required divergent thinking we could have irrelevant stimuli from many different domains to help generate ideas (Thomas et al. 1977).

A Research Program for Human Factors in AI Systems

One of the main theses of this paper should now be clear to the reader: AI systems, like other systems, will only be successful to the extent that they are grounded in good human factors as well as good computer science. Many existing AI systems would have profited enormously from having had what is already known about human factors applied to them. Nevertheless, a great deal of additional research is needed to deal specifically with new issues in human–computer interaction. In the section below, I will suggest a few of the areas that require new research. These ideas are organized in four sections: issues that cut across technologies, issues specific to a particular technology, methodology, and theoretical work.

Issues that cut across technologies. For each of the new technologies that AI might allow (e.g., expert systems, adaptive interfaces, ICAI, speech synthesis, speech recognition, handwriting recognition, face recognition, speaker identification, problem solving, natural language front ends, robotics), two kinds of issues arise that human factors people must concern themselves with. The first set of issues is *what* to do, and the second is *how* to do it.

Just because a new technology is developed does not necessarily mean that it solves any real problem. What combination of users, tasks, situations, and systems provides real value? How can the value be measured? Does the AI system have positive or negative impacts on the larger context in which it operates? To illustrate some of these questions more concretely, let us examine them in terms of speech synthesis.

First of all, users in various situations differ in their acceptance of synthetic speech. At one extreme, a visually impaired programmer who is only able to work via speech synthesis will frequently use the system, and because of this practice and motivation will find current speech synthesis quite acceptable. At the other extreme, we might expect that it would be quite a while before speech synthesis could serve as the voice of an actor. A person who is working on an assembly line 8 hours a day, getting directions from synthetic speech, will soon learn to adapt to any peculiarities of the speech. An office principal who has a choice of whether or not to use a system with speech synthesis at all may not accept a system at the same level of quality.

Apart from situations, there are very large individual differences in the ability to perceive synthetic speech correctly. It has been suggested that age and native language are two variables that may be important in this regard. However, these certainly do not account for all of the variance. In addition to individual differences, the properties of the signal itself make huge differences in the intelligibility of synthetic speech. Syntax, semantics, and word frequency all have effects. It would also be useful to be able to quantify, in terms of savings or productivity changes, the actual value of synthetic speech in particular situations.

The above issues point to a set of research questions. How can we predict on the basis of an analysis of situations, the value of speech? How do we predict which individuals will do particularly well with speech synthesis? What guidelines can we provide regarding word use, syntax, and semantics to maximize intelligibility? How do people adapt to synthetic speech? How can we use this knowledge to make adaptation more rapid? What is special about speech output and what are the implications of that for an interface that uses speech? Answers to such questions do not obviate the need for studying specific situations; they can usefully point out possibilities, however.

Questions specific to technologies. Every technology raises issues about feedback. However, the nature of these issues is somewhat different for different technologies. For instance, it has been suggested that a limited natural language interface should not use language that is appropriate to a greater intelligence or humanity than the system in fact possesses. Is this really true? What is the best way to keep the user operating within the bounds of what is understandable by the system? Is there a specific training method that will help differentiate the acceptable constructions from those that are unacceptable? Is there a way to give the user a general set that will be useful; e.g., instructions to keep in mind that the system is only a computer?

Methodology. There are many methods for studying human factors questions (e.g., Hirsch, 1981). These can generally be adapted to issues in AI. In addition, however, there are a few specific methodological points to be made. One point is to emphasize again the utility of the "Wizard of Oz" simulation. This technique allows one to use human beings to simulate systems that do not yet exist.

The utility of iterative design (a/k/a rapid prototyping) cannot be overstressed in this area. While it is a useful design principle for any human–computer interface, it is even more essential when one is exploring new technologies. Space does not permit a full discussion of iterative design in this chapter. However, it might be useful to make clear what is *not* meant by iterative design. Iterative design is not inviting in a few friends with similar backgrounds, having them use the system, and then explaining why you did things in the way that initially confused them. Nor is iterative design using the system yourself to finish building the system. That is not necessarily a bad idea, but it should not be misconstrued as having anything to do with ensuring the system has good human factors.

Another methodological issue that is particularly troublesome in the field of artificial intelligence is how to generalize from small systems to big systems. For many reasons, it is desirable to test out ideas in a small system. The issue is, what happens when one then uses these ideas in a full-scale system? For example, one might be interested ultimately in a system that allows one to find information from the entire Encyclopedia Britanica via natural language queries. Suppose that, in order to study how to do this, one builds a system that allows one to ask natural language questions concerning dinosaurs. First, one must do some conceptual analysis. What will be different about *this part* of the system once it is incorporated into the entire encyclopedia? For one thing, there exists a much greater potential for confusion about particular words. Suppose that we would like the system to ignore minor misspellings. The user types in tritops for triceratops. It is fairly obvious in the context of dinosaurs what is intended. But in the context of the entire encyclopedia, it is far less obvious. Does the person want to find out about triceps muscles, trichinosis, tripartite government—or perhaps they really mean treetops? These possibilities mean either that a disambiguating dialogue must ensue, that the user must specify topic first, or that much stricter criteria must be applied before a misspelling is accepted.

At a deeper level, most of what is contained in the encyclopedia about dinosaurs is a set of fairly independent facts. We would probably not find users asking questions like, "How important was sexual selection in the evolutionary history of the triceratops compared with the defensive advantages?" But just such a question might be asked with respect to killer bees. In this case, choosing the particular domain of dinosaur information means that certain kinds of AI questions as well as certain interface questions may be finessed. This does not mean one should not limit the prototype domain, but that one should analyze what it means to do so, and then, insofar as practical, simulate the system that will exist beyond the boundaries of the limited domain.

In the case at hand, for instance, one could attempt to use an algorithm to correct misspellings, but use the entire dictionary rather than just those words that have to do with dinosaurs. This will give a more realistic assessment of how much one can automatically correct. One could add some material (even if purely speculative) about cause and effect to the dinosaur data base, and then give users tasks that require asking questions of that nature.

In a similar vein, one can have a human being monitoring the dialogue between a user of a part system and that system. When the user asks a question or does something which the part system cannot handle, the human monitor can step in and get the dialogue back into the portion of the overall system that is currently implemented. Of course, such excursions from the working system should be carefully noted and later studied. But again, the general point is that it is a good strategy to study *part* of what could be a useful overall system. This is a different philosophy from studying a *toy* system, where there is no growth path to a real system and no attempt made to understand what the implications of such growth might be. It should also be noted that going from prototype to fielded system effectively requires up-front consideration of a whole host of additional issues beyond human factors: maintenance, integration with existing hardware and software, political and organizational issues, cost/benefit analysis, etc.

Theory. It has sometimes been argued that nothing is as practical as a good theory. In the domain of human–computer interaction, there are few theories. Probably the most extensive is the keystroke model of Card, Moran, and Newell (1983). Other interesting efforts include the work of Reisner (1984), Carroll (1985), and Polson and Kieras (1985).

While the most comprehensive to date, the keystroke model still has major gaps (Thomas, 1984), such as concentration on error-free performance and not dealing adequately with motivation or learning. One might question the benefits of a good theory. To some extent, these are addressed in Card, Moran, and Newell's (1983) book. It might be useful to outline briefly some of the benefits of a good theory before outlining needed developments in theory.

A difficulty with attempting to apply human factors to new technologies is that, even if one applies the principles of iterative design, unless one starts with some generally accurate notions of how human beings operate, the chances of converging to a good interface are slim. In the absence of a comprehensive theory, the interface designer may still find useful some overall principles on which to base interface design, even though it must be recognized that this only improves the batting average and can never substitute for empirical work or even for a real theory.

An example of such a principle might be that people can take in more information when it is presented over more channels. Such a principle obviously needs to be intelligently applied or it is worthless. That is, using multiple channels can certainly be used to further confuse a user. This does not invalidate the principle, however.

Another example of such a principle might be to allow direct manipulation. Again, using such a design principle does not automatically prove that direct manipulation is best under all circumstances and no matter how badly implemented. It merely seems like a good principle to consider applying, all other things being equal. In addition to research on specific systems, further research is also needed on proposed principles such as these to determine where they are generally valid.

The benefits of a real theory (as opposed to such ad hoc principles) would be enormous. They could help tell us the dimensions along which it is relatively safe to generalize; they could help separate out variables which must be controlled; they could allow us to make reasonable predictions in areas where experimentation is impossible. One only needs to look at the progress of physics to see the potential for a good theory. It could turn out, of course, that the nature and goals of physics and human factors are so different that theory turns out to be useful only in physics.

One of the things which seems odd about the current state of theory in psychology is that there are scores if not hundreds of minitheories; that is, theories that are fairly good within very limited domains. What is mainly missing is a way of integrating these minitheories. The careful reader may have noted that this is precisely the problem I mentioned with respect to expert systems in point two of the section on "The future of expert systems and AI." Indeed, I believe the first really comprehensive and fairly accurate theory may well be an expert system developed from the input of many expert psychologists in these minidomains. Building a system from numerous experts with different ways of thinking goes beyond simple expert systems. Blackboard architectures may provide a starting point, but it would still be quite a challenge. Such a theory will not only make predictions across a variety of domains; it will also be more accurate within limited domains like human–computer interaction. The reason for this is that splitting up human behavior into small subdomains does not work terribly well, because there are strong interactions across the subdomains. What the clinician knows about anxiety is important in determining how people react to computers; so is what the social psychologist knows about group behavior; so is what the psychometrician knows about individual differences. The ideas about knowledge structures and processes offered by AI may provide a medium for experts in these areas to communicate effectively for the first time. Conversely, building a communications medium that would support such diverse viewpoints would perforce require an expansion of the conceptual frameworks of AI.

ACKNOWLEDGEMENTS

I would like to thank Amy Aaronson, John Carroll, Richard Halstead-Nussloch, Robert Mack, Jane Schurick, Jakob Nielsen, and Ted Selker for helping me to find relevant references and for their comments on earlier drafts of the manuscript. I also thank the reviewers for

their excellent and thought-provoking ideas as well as Candee Walls
for her excellent secretarial help.

REFERENCES

Alty, J.L. (1984). Use of path algebras in an interactive adaptive dialogue
system. In B. Gaines (Ed.), *Proceedings of INTERACT '84.* Amsterdam:
Elsevier.

Anderson, J.R. (1983). *The architecture of cognition.* Cambridge, MA: Harvard University Press.

Benyon, D. (1984). Monitor. A self-adaptive user interface. In B. Gaines
(Ed.), *Proceedings of INTERACT '84.* Amsterdam: Elsevier.

Bolt, R.A. (1984). *The human interface: Where people and computers meet.*
Belmont, CA: Lifetime Learning Publications.

Branscomb, L., & Thomas, J. (1984). Ease of use: A system design challenge.
IBM System Journal, 23(3), 224–235.

Brown, J.S., Burton, R.R., & de Kleer, J. (1982). Pedagogical, natural language
and knowledge engineering techniques in SOPHIE I, II, and III. In D.
Sleeman & J.S. Brown (Eds.), *Intelligent tutoring systems,* London:
Academic Press.

Buxton, W., Bly, S.A., Frysinger, S.P., Lunnery, D., Manxur, D.L., Mezrich,
J.L., & Morrison, R.C. (1985). Communicating with sound. In L. Borman
& B. Curtis (Eds.), *Proceedings of the '85 Computer Human Interaction
Conference.* New York, NY: ACM.

Card, S.K., Moran, T.P., & Newell, A. (1983). *The psychology of human–computer interaction.* Hillsdale, NJ: Erlbaum.

Carroll, J., Thomas, J., & Malhotra, A. (1980). Presentation and representation
in design problem solving, *British Journal of Psychology. 71*(1), 143–155.

Carroll, J.M. (1985). *What's in a name?* New York: Freeman.

Carroll, J.M., & McKendree, J. (1986). *Strategies for on-line advice-giving
and help.* (IBM T.J. Watson Research Report. RC-11984), Yorktown
Heights, NY: IBM. (Also in *CACM,* January 1987.)

Carroll, J.M., & Mack, R.L. (1984). Learning to use a word processor: By
doing, by thinking, and by knowing. In J. Thomas & M. Schneider
(Eds.), *Human factors in computer systems.* Norwood, NJ: Ablex Publishing Corp.

Carroll, J.M., & Rosson, M.B. (1985). Usability specifications as a tool in
iterative development. In R. Hartson (Ed.), *Advances in human–computer interaction.* Norwood, NJ: Ablex Publishing Corp.

Charniak, E., & McDermott, D. (1985). *An introduction to artificial intelligence.* Reading, MA: Addison-Wesley.

Chin, D. (1984). An analysis of scripts generated in writing between users
and computer consultants. *Proceedings of the National Computer Conference,* 637–642.

Dixon, N.R., & Maxey, H.D. (1968). Terminal analog synthesis of continuous speech using the diphone method of segment assembly. *IEEE Transactions on Audio and Electroacoustics, AU16,* 40–50.

Eberts, R., & Brock, J.F. (1984). Computer applications to instruction. In F. Muckler (Ed.), *Human factors review: 1984.* Santa Monica, CA: The Human Factors Society.

Ellis, A.E., & Harper, R.A. (1961). *A guide to rational living.* North Hollywood, CA: Wilshire Books.

Elsom-Cook, M. (1984). Design considerations of an intelligent teaching system for programming languages. In B. Gaines (Ed.), *Proceedings of INTERACT '84.* Amsterdam: Elsevier.

Engel, S., & Granda, R. (1975). *Guidelines for man/display interfaces.* (IBM Tech. Rep. TR-00.2720) Poughkeepsie, NY: IBM.

Feigenbaum, E.A. (1961). The simulation of verbal learning behavior. *Proceedings of the Western Joint Computer Conference, 19,* 121–132.

Feigenbaum, E.A. (1979). Themes and case studies of knowledge engineering. In D. Michie (Ed.), *Expert systems in the micro electronic age.* Edinburgh: Edinburgh University Press.

Funt, B.V. (1983). A parallel-process model of mental rotation, *Cognitive Science, 7*(1), 67–93.

Furnas, G.W. (1985). Experience with an adaptive indexing scheme. In L. Borman & B. Curtis (Eds.), *Proceedings of the 1985 Conference on Human Factors in Computing Systems.* New York, NY: ACM.

Furnas, G.W., Landauer, T.K., Gomez, L.M., & Dumais, S.T. (1984). Statistical semantics: Analysis of the potential performance of keyword information systems. In J. Thomas & M. Schneider (Eds.), *Human factors in computer systems.* Norwood, NJ: Ablex Publishing Corp.

Goldsmith, T.E., & Schvanaveldt, R.W. (1984). Facilitating multiple-cue judgements with integral information displays. In J. Thomas & M. Schneider (Eds.), *Human factors in computer systems.* Norwood, NJ: Ablex Publishing Corp.

Gould, D., Conti, J., & Hovanyecz, T. (1983). Composing letters with a simulated listening typewriter. *Communications of the ACM, 26*(4), 295–308.

Hayes-Roth, F. (1984). The knowledge-based expert system: A tutorial. *Computer, 17*(9), 11–28.

Hirsch, R.S. (1981). Procedures of the Human Factors Center at San Jose. *IBM Systems Journal, 20*(2), 123–171.

Hollan, J.D., Hutchins, E.L., & Weitzman, L. (1984). STEAMER: An interactive inspectable simulation-based training system. *The AI Magazine, 5,* 15–27.

Holland, J.H. (1975). *Adaptation in natural and artificial systems: An introductory analysis with applications to biology, control, and artificial intelligence.* Ann Arbor, MI: University of Michigan Press.

Johnson, P.E., Duran, A.S., Hassebrock, F., Moller, J., Prietula, M., Feltovich, P.J., & Swanson, D.B. (1981). Expertise and error in diagnostic reasoning. *Cognitive Science, 5*(3), 235–283.

Johnson, L., & Soloway, E. (1983). PROUST: Knowledge-based program understanding. (Tech. Rep. No. 285). New Haven, CT: Yale University, Department of Computer Science.

Kelley, J.F. (1984). An iterative design methodology for user-friendly natural language office information applications. *ACM Transactions on Office Information Systems, 2*(1), 26–41.

Kidd, A.L., & Cooper, M.B. (1985). Man–machine interface issues in the construction and use of an expert system. *International Journal of Man–Machine Studies, 22,* 91–102.

Kimball, R.A. (1982). Self-improving tutor for symbolic integration. In D. Sleeman & J.S. Brown (Eds.), *Intelligent tutoring systems.* London: Academic Press.

Malhotra, A., Thomas, J., Carroll, J., & Miller, L. (1980). Cognitive processes in design. *International Journal of Man–Machine Studies, 1*(12), 119–140.

Malhotra, A., & Sheridan, P. (1976). *Experimental determination of design requirements for a program explanation system,* (IBM T. J. Watson Research Report RC-5831). Yorktown Heights, NY: IBM.

Malin, J.T. & Lance, N. (1985). An expert system for fault management and automatic shutdown avoidance in a regenerative life support subsystem. *Proceedings of the Instrument Society of America First Annual Workshop on Robotics and Expert Systems* (pp. 185–193), Instrument Society of America.

Maskery, H.S. (1984). Adaptive interfaces for naive users—An experimental study. *Proceedings of INTERACT '84.* Amsterdam: Elsevier.

McCauley, M.E. (1984). Human factors in voice technology. In F.A. Muckler (Ed.), *Human factors review.* Santa Monica, CA: Human Factors Society.

Miller, L.A., & Thomas, J.C. (1977). Behavioral issues in the use of interactive systems, *International Journal of Man–Machine Studies, 9*(5), 509–536.

Mitchell, T.M. (1984). Toward combining empirical and analytical methods for learning heuristics. In A. Elithorn & R. Banerji (Eds.), *Human and Artificial Intelligence.* Amsterdam: North-Holland.

Newell, A., & Simon, H.A. (1972). *Human problem solving.* Englewood Cliffs, NJ: Prentice-Hall.

O'Leary, D.P., & Stewart, G.W. (1985). Data-flow algorithms for parallel matrix computations. *Communications of the ACM, 28*(8), 840–852.

O'Shea, T.A. (1982). Self-improving quadratic tutor. In D. Sleeman & J.S. Brown (Eds.), *Intelligent tutoring systems.* London: Academic Press.

Pickover, C.A. (1983a). *The use of vector graphics system in the presentation of alternative representations of synthetic speech data.* (IBM T.J. Watson Research Report RC-10084), Yorktown Heights, NY: IBM.

Pickover, C.A. (1983b). *The use of computer-drawn faces as an educational aid in the representation of statistical concepts.* (IBM T.J. Watson Research Report RC-10234), Yorktown Heights, NY: IBM.

Pickover, C.A. (1984). Spectrographic representations of globular protein breathing motion. *Science, 223,* 181.

Pickover, C.A. (1985). *On the use of computer generated symmetrized dot-patterns for the visual characterization of speech waveform and other sampled data.* (IBM T.J. Watson Research Report, RC-11110), Yorktown Heights, NY: IBM.

Pisoni, D.B. (1982). Perceptual evaluation of synthetic speech, *Speech technology, 1*(2), 10-n23.

Pollack, M.E. (1985). Information sought and information provided: An empiricle study of user/expert dialogues. In L. Borman & B. Curtis (Eds.), *Proceedings of the 1985 ACM Human Factors in Computing Systems.* New York, NY: ACM.

Polson, P.G., & Kieras, D.E. (1985). A quantitative model of the learning and performance of text editing knowledge. In L. Borman & B. Curtis (Eds.), *Proceedings of the 1985 ACM Human Factors in Computing Systems.* New York, NY: ACM.

Pundit, N. (1984). A progress report on some AI projects. In L. Chase & R. Landers (Eds.), *AI: Reality or fantasy.* Washington, DC: The Information Industry Association.

Quinlan, J.R. (1986). The effect of noise on concept learning. In *Machine Learning II,* R. Michael Ski, J. Carbonelli & T. Mitchell (Eds.), Los Altos, CA: Morgan Kaufman.

Reiser, B.J., Anderson, J.R., & Farrell, R.G. *Dynamic student modeling in an intelligent tutor for LISP programming.* IJCAI. Los Altos, CA: Morgan Kaufman.

Reisner, P. (1984). Formal grammar as a tool for analyzing ease of use: Some fundamental concepts. In J. Thomas & M. Schneider (Eds.), *Human factors in computer systems,* Norwood, NJ: Ablex Publishing Corp.

Reitman, W.R. (1965). *Cognition and thought.* New York: Wiley.

Remus, W. (1984). The impact of cognitive processing limitations on decisions made using a computer based managerial workstation. In H.W. Hendrick & O. Brown, Jr. (Eds.), *Human factors in organizational design and management.* Amsterdam: North-Holland.

Richards, M.A., & Underwood, K.M. (1984). How should computers and people speak to each other? *Proceedings of IFIP Interact '84, I,* 33–36.

Riesbeck, C.K. (1984). Knowledge reorganization and reasoning style. *International Journal of Man-Machine Studies, 20,* 45–61.

Rimm, D.C., & Masters, J.C. (1974). *Behavior Therapy: Techniques and empirical findings.* New York: Academic Press.

Rosson, M.B. (1985). Using synthetic speech for remote access to information. *Behavioral Research Methods, Instruments, and Computers, 17,* 250–252.

Rumelhart, D.A., & McClelland, J.L., & PDP Research Group (1986). *Parallel Distributed Processing.* Cambridge, MA: MIT Press.

Schneiderman, B. (1980). *Software psychology.* Cambridge, MA: Winthrop.

Schoenfeld, A.H. (1983). Beyond the purely cognitive: Belief systems, social cognitions, and metacognitions as driving forces in intellectual performance. *Cognitive Science, 7*(4), 329–363.

Schurick, J.M., Williges, B.H., & Maynard, J.F. (1985). User feedback requirements with automatic speech recognition. *Ergonomics, 28*(11), 1543–1555.

Shank, R. (1984). Keynote address. Artificial intelligence in the Information Industry: Ideas into Action. Hyannis, MA, July 19. Washington, DC: Information Industry Association.

Simpson, C.A., McCauley, M.E., Roland, E.F., Ruth, J.C., & Williges, B.H. (1985). System design for speech recognition and generation. *Human Factors, 27*(2), 115–141.

Sleeman, D., & Brown, J.S. (1982). *Intelligent tutoring systems.* London: Academic Press.

Sleeman, D., & Hendley, R.J. (1982). ACE: A system which Analyses Complex Explanations. In D.H. Sleeman & J.S. Brown (Eds.), *Intelligent tutoring systems.* London: Academic Press.

Smith, L.L. & Connally, R.E. (1984). Artificial Intelligence and an adaptive training concept. In H.W. Hendrick & O. Brown, Jr. (Eds.), *Human factors in organizational design and management.* Amsterdam: North-Holland.

Stein, M. (1975). *Stimulating creativity, Volume 2: Group procedures.* New York: Academic Press.

Stewart, C.J., & Cash, W.B. (1974). *Interviewing: Principles and practices.* Dubuque, IA: William C. Brown.

Tappert, C. (1982). Cursive script recognition by elastic matching. *IBM Journal of Research and Development, 26,* November.

Thomas, J.C. (1974). An analysis of behavior in the hobbits-orcs problem. *Cognitive psychology, 6,* 257–269.

Thomas, J.C. (1977, August). *Cognitive psychology from the viewpoint of wilderness survival.* Paper presented at the American Psychological Association, San Francisco. (Available as IBM T.J. Watson Research Report RC-6647), Yorktown Heights, NY: IBM.

Thomas, J.C. (1980). The computer as an active communications medium. *Proceedings of the 18th Annual Meeting of the Association for Comutational Linguistics.* (pp. 83–86). ACL.

Thomas, J.C. (1983). Psychological issues in the design of data base query languages. In M.E. Simes & M.J. Coombs (Eds.), *Designing for human-computer communication.* London: Academic Press.

Thomas, J.C. (1984). Goodness (human factors) does not equal degree (quantification). *Contemporary Psychology, 29*(2), 119–120.

Thomas, J.C. (1985). Organizing for human factors. In Y. Vassilou (Ed.), *Human factors and interactive computer systems.* Norwood, NJ: Ablex Publishing Corp.

Thomas, J.C., & Carroll, J.M. (1981). Human factors in communication, *IBM Systems Journal, 20*(2), 237–263.

Thomas, J.C., Rosson, M.B., & Chodorow, M. (1985). Human Factors and synthetic speech. In B. Shackel (Ed.) INTERACT '84. Amsterdam: Elsevier.

Thomas, J.C., Klavans, J., Nartey, J., Pickover, C., Reich, D., & Rosson, M.B. (1984). *WALRUS: A development system for speech synthesis* (IBM T.J. Watson Research Report RC-10626), Yorktown Heights, NY: IBM.

Thomas, J.C., Lyon, D., & Miller, L.A. (1977). *Aids for problem solving.* (IBM T.J. Watson Research Report RC-6468), Yorktown Heights, NY: IBM.

Wickens, C.D., Sandry, D., & Vidulich, M. (1983). Compatibility and resource competition between modalities of input, central processing, and output: Testing a model of complex task performance. *Human Factors, 25,* 227–248.

Williges, B.H., & Williges, R.C. (1984). Dialogue design considerations for interactive computer systems. In F.A. Muckler (Ed.), *Human factors review.* Santa Monica, CA: The Human Factors Society.

Williges, B.H., Schurick, J.M., Spine, T.M., & Hakkimen, M.T. (1985). Speech in human–computer interaction. In R.C. Williges, & R.W. Ehrich (Eds.), *Human computer dialogue design.* Amsterdam: Elsevier.

Winograd, T., & Flores, R. (1986). *Understanding computers and cognition.* Norwood, NJ: Ablex Publishing Corp.

Witten, I.H. (1982). *Principles of computer speech.* London: Academic Press.

Wright, P., & Reid, R. (1973). Written information: Some alternatives to prose for expressing the outcomes of complex contingencies. *Journal of Applied Psychology, 57,* 160–166.

Yetton, P.W., & Vroom, V.H. (1973). *Leadership and decision making.* Pittsburgh, PA: University of Pittsburgh Press.

Zimmer, A.C. (1984). A model for the interpretation of verbal prediction. *International Journal of Man-Machine Studies, 20,* 121–134.

CHAPTER 2

Interface Design and Evaluation— Semiotic Implications

Mihai Nadin

The Ohio State University

Knowledge and experience from several disciplines (psychology, sociology, communication theory, graphic design, and linguistics, among others) are used, or should be considered, in this still new field of human activity identified as interface design. The implicit acknowledgement of the interdisciplinary nature of interface design is symptomatic for the ability to differentiate between general and specific requirements peculiar to the use of computers by various users, as well as for understanding the need to translate this differentiation in a design appropriate to the functions desired. After an expensive and prolonged trial and error phase, researchers and industry indeed acquired a more appropriate apprehension of the complex nature of interface design and of procedures to evaluate it (before and after implementation on computers).

WHY SEMIOTICS? WHAT KIND OF SEMIOTICS?

The input from various specialized fields of knowledge made possible rapid but partial progress of interface design. While we know how to cope with complexity in particular situations, we do not know yet how to assemble successful specialized interfaces in a system which can be approached by the user at a higher level than that of each component. The ideal towards which the field is moving— emulation of human communication, with special emphasis on interactive natural language user interface—requires not only the use of paradigms and empirical findings from the various fields dealing with different aspects of human being and its social existence, but also an integrative methodology. Interdisciplinarity and integration

45

should go together. This integrative methodology can be seen as a bridge between all the disciplines from which interface design has borrowed concepts and findings, as well as between them and computer science, whose spectacular progress made the design of interface a rather critical element of the progress of computer technology and its applications. Semiotics, a relatively new discipline, built on an impressive history of interest in its object and method, provides the bridge mentioned above.

Semiotics, the general theory and practice of signs, studies everything that is interpreted by human beings as a sign, and defines the circumstances under which interpreting something as a sign allows for its better understanding, or for an improved use of it.

People communicate among themselves, or, to use the word "communicate" loosely, with machines, using signs, some of which belong to the stabilized system of so-called natural language, others to the shared conventions of gestures, sounds, colors, or synthetic languages. People learn available sign systems and generate new signs for various purposes. Any type of knowledge is shared by means of language (the most complex sign system we know) complemented by specialized signs such as those found in mathematics, logical formalism, diagrammatic representations, and in musical or engineering notation. Scientific and speculative theories, as well as art works, are similarly expressed. Whether people regard computers as mere sophisticated tools or as machines embodying a certain degree of human intelligence (in hardware and the programs driving it), they agree that, in order to use them effectively, human computer interaction should be provided which does justice to the user and takes advantage of the computer's potential. Everything supporting this interaction makes up the entity called interface.

This interaction is not physical, as with tools designed and used before computers, but symbolic. That is, it takes place through the intermediary of shared representations, i.e., signs of intended actions, or of feedback signs designed for specific purposes. Accordingly, the underlying thesis of this chapter is that, since the user interacts with computers by means of signs, the design of interfaces can advance by applying the principles and empirical findings of semiotics. The reason for a semiotic approach lies in the very nature of interface design; therefore, requirements intrinsic to the subject should guide in identifying what kind of semiotics can be useful, as well as what can be expected from such an endeavor. Let us first identify the appropriate semiotic framework.

In order to apply semiotics, we have to adopt one of the many definitions of the sign which have been advanced. Known definitions fall into two categories:

1.   Pertinent to natural language. A sign is adopted as a paradigm with the understanding that every other sign is structurally equivalent. The Swiss linguist Ferdinand de Saussure advanced the definition of sign as the unity between a *signifier* (the actual sign embodied in material form, such as words or shapes) and the *signified* (what the sign is supposed to mean). Artificial intelligence researchers are quite comfortable with this model.

2.   Pertinent to local structure. Each type of sign and each sign operation can be described in a logical system. The American scientist and logician Charles S. Peirce (1839–1914), and pioneer of the computer (cf. Ketner, 1984), advanced the definition of sign as "something that stands to someone for something in some respect or capacity" (Peirce, 1932, p. 135).

Arguments in favor of one or the other definition can be produced, but, since computers are *logical* machines, a logical conception of the sign and its functioning in different contexts is more appropriate to the subject. Design in general, and interface design in particular, are not reducible to the model of natural language (or any other sign system). On the basis of Peirce's definition, this diagramatic representation (not the only one possible) can serve as an operational model.

Figure 1 should be read as saying that only the *unity* between

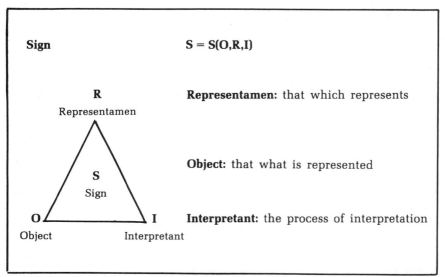

Figure 1.   Sign definition in Peirce's semiotic.

the three components represent a sign, i.e., that signs are identified as such only through their representation, and that, where we interpret a sign, we become part of it for the time of that interpretation. Let me explain this through an example. Icons in the user interface paradigm are *representamina.* Like the icon of the file, calculator, or clipboard, every other icon represents an object with which the user is familiar from previous experience. The *representamen* of the clipboard (the drawing resembling the object clipboard that we use in school, in the office, or on other occasions) is interpreted by the user as being the computer equivalent of a stationary item. Only when the user establishes the relation between the drawing that represents the clipboard (representamen), the physical item clipboard (object), and the understanding of the function of the computer-simulated clipboard (interpretant) can we speak of constituting a sign.

The sign can be constituted according to the intention of its designer, or quite independently of it. Design of icons as part of interface design requires that we understand under which circumstances the intended or accidental user will correctly constitute the sign, i.e., interpret it according to a desired intention. Once the kind of semiotics suitable for better interface design is identified, we know what to expect from its application. Prescriptive tools will become available. Such tools help designers avoid errors when a given activity is to be modelled in a user interface supporting the most efficient interaction between computers and users. The basic prescriptive rules which semiotics provides refer to the coherence of the repertory of signs used, as well as to the consistency of sign operations applied to the repertory chosen. Second, semiotics offers tools for quantitative and qualitative evaluation through the basic semiotic principles of appropriateness of representation and stability of the dynamic sign system. The vocabulary of semiotics is less important than the awareness of how people constitute and interpret signs and use them as tools for new developments. As a metadiscipline describing signs, in particular language, by using language and other signs to constitute its own corpus of knowledge, semiotics is less a descriptive theory and more a methodology for improved interpretation and evaluation of how people communicate, represent things, express themselves, and constitute new models and theories. For this reason, it is necessary to explain how semiotics, within the adopted definition of the sign, deals with such activities. Once these explanations are provided, examples will be introduced.

SIGN AND CONTEXT

The functioning of the sign in the context it was constituted in (in our case, on the screen of a computer using a well-defined visual convention, i.e., resemblance between the representamen and the object represented) is expressed through the concept of *semiosis* (sign process). This describes how given signs preserve or change their meaning, how the change of context affects their interpretation, and how the three fundamental functions of signs are obtained (see Figure 2).

1.   If, when using a sign, the emphasis is on the relation between the representamen and the object represented (which is the case of icons in user interface, in the use of pictograms in airports, etc.), we actually confine ourselves to the function of representation.

2.   There are circumstances under which the emphasis is on the formal qualities of the representamen, interpreted almost independently of the relation to what it represents. This is the case with artistic expression, sometimes pursued by overzealous interface designers right up to the computer screen. (I remember the bee on the initial Intran system, flying in a strange fog while the computer was "resting." The bee turned into a cursor once the system was started, and the cursor into a hand once a graphic program was chosen.)

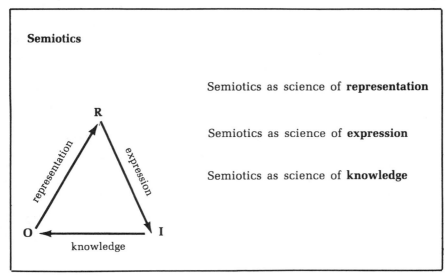

Figure 2.   Sign functions.

3. If the user of a sign integrates representation and expression, and tries to derive from the sign specific or general knowledge of the object, the cognitive function is accomplished. Computational biology, astronomy "on the chip," computational physics, linguistics, etc. are examples in which a representation—let's say the DNA model—its expression (in computer graphics-adequate form), and the theoretic explanation it makes possible constitute a new body of knowledge.

Based on these concepts, we can further explain the semiotic levels at which sign processes (semioses) take place, levels that are undoubtedly familiar and important to those working in computer science (see Figure 3).

Letters, characters, words, and commands are just examples of representamina. They have a precise syntax which in turn supports the semantics (as a necessary but not sufficient condition). Even such words as "if," "the," "and," or some artificially produced sequences represent objects, i.e., concepts with a precise logical meaning. Whether images, sequences of letters or numbers, time sequences, touch sensitive areas, temperature sensitive sensors with attached functions, etc.—all have a syntax, which can be prescribed as rigidly as the system requires, on whose basis the intended semantics is built and the expected pragmatics is obtained. The relation between the semiotic levels is far more complicated than the diagram shows; insofar as in dynamic situations there is an interdependence between them, the borderline becomes fuzzy. This semiotic distinction, successfully applied in formal logic and then taken over in computer science terminology, is useful in defining structures. Once such structures are designed (the desktop metaphor, to be discussed later on, is an example), we have to modify/amend

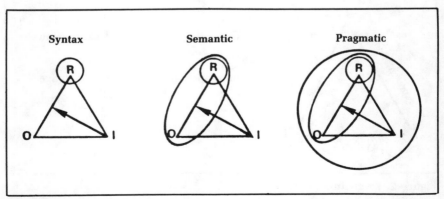

Figure 3.   Semiotic levels.

them by considering the dynamics of sign processes. No sign can be considered independently of its relation(s) to other signs, be these similar (such as words in a given language) or different (words, images, sensory perceptions, etc.). The interdisciplinarity of semiotics is a consequence of the fact that sign processes are heterogenous by their condition, and that, in order to understand how different kinds of signs constitute interpretable strings or configurations, we have to acquaint ourselves with each different kind, as well as with the principles governing human or machine interpretation of such strings or configurations.

DESIGN AND SEMIOTICS

Design comes about in an environment traditionally called *culture* (currently identified as *artificial* through a romantic distinction between natural and artificial) and acts as a bridge between scientific and humanistic praxis. Along this line of thinking, Herbert Simon (1982, p. xi) stated, "Engineering, medicine, business, architecture, and painting are concerned not with how things are but how things might be—in short, with design." There is no human activity that does not contain some design component. Quite a few attempts are made to put together a unified design theory. The concept is very broad, while the forms embodying design are becoming narrower and narrower, i.e., more specialized. This is also the case with interface design. But no matter how specialized design becomes, there are certain common elements which make products remote in function share design qualities socially identified as appropriate, good, useful, aesthetic, efficient, etc. Due to the role of computers in supporting and improving human activity, it becomes crucial to identify means for improving design quality, and eventually to develop computational design. Automatic programming is certainly one step in this direction. Progress in the design of interface will follow once we better understand the nature of design and the specific elements of human–computer interaction.

One way to achieve this goal is to look at design principles as semiotic principles—in other words, to consider design as an activity through which designers structure systems of signs in such a way as to make possible the achievement of human goals: communication (as a form of social interaction), engineering (as a form of applied technical rationality), business (as a form of shared efficiency), architecture, art, education, etc. In the case of genetic engineering, the DNA model became the basis for a new field of research and a new industry. The same can be said about computer science, which has as its domain the processing of a precise type of sign—the *symbol*—according to the rules of Boolean logic. Programming languages are *designed* languages; programs are designed too. Computers, with their designed architecture and operating systems which specify the sequence and structure of data processing, reflect our acquired knowledge of the human beings who conceive and produce them. Haber and Myers (1982, p. 23) noted, "Human beings have their own architectures and operating systems that determine how they process information." The organizational principles of the human being as sign producer and sign interpreter, and the organizational principles used in designing computers, should be carefully considered when we design the entity/ies through which users will interact with computers. Everything we know from semiotics about how people devise, interpret, and use signs can and should be used in the design of entities through which interaction will take place. As already stated, this interaction takes place not at the level of physical (or biological or chemical) reality, but through the intermediary of sign sequences (letters, words, icons, programs, interrupt messages, calls of routines, etc.). With our new tools, we no longer interact directly—as with the hammer, the screwdriver, or the plough—with whatever we wanted to change or use—but indirectly, using the mediating function of commands, programs, and expert systems. Accordingly, the breakdown of a tool is primarily a conceptual problem (in a given social context) and not one of physical relevance.

INTERFACE DESIGN: SCIENCE OR ART?

While it is true that the interaction between humans and tools became fashionable in the "computer age," the concept of interface is actually a product of human culture (seen as an artifact environment). It is in this respect that Simon (1982, chapter 1) regarded "the artifact as interface" and "the environment as mold." Design of interface is not just concerned with users and computers, but also with human-to-human relations, especially in the context in which our relation to tools, human contact, and interinfluence become more and more indirect, mediated through entities to a large extent programmed. Signs fulfill the function of *intermediary, go-between,* and *medium.* Some signs can be very precise: mathematical formalism, instructions for booting/rebooting a system, E-mail addresses, passwords. Others are less critically defined: contents of log-in/log-out files in time-sharing systems, names of passed parameters in complex programs, E-mail paths, the place a document occupies on a multiwindowed screen. The designer of an interactive editor has to look in both directions: to the architecture and operating system of the computer and the "architecture" and "operating system" of the user. The two are rather different. While, at the computer end, the designer will assume uniformity and homogeneity (at least for a line of products, and until the succession of improved versions starts), at the user's end there is no such thing as a *general* or *abstract* user. This makes the designer's task quite complex and explains why the computer community is so frequently frustrated.

Schneider and Thomas (1983, pp. 252–253) pose two questions that express the feeling of that community: (a) Why isn't the design of computer interfaces more like science? (b) Why can't the people who design interfaces be more like engineers? These concerns stem from the recognition of the role interface design plays in the human use of computers. In the past (of timesharing and expensive hardware), interface, although important, was less critical. With computer technology becoming cheaper and expanding to more segments of society (especially in the personal computer environment), and in view of the diversity of utilizations of this quasi-universal tool, interface design issues (together with networking) acquire more importance.

If a science of interface design for computers or any other kind of machine is conceivable, then this science will have to integrate in its body of knowledge semiotic concepts and experimental data regarding the human use of signs. On the other hand, computer scientists and engineers should have no problem in understanding the nature of interface design as science *and* art; as information engineering and design; as communication and expression. Despite the diversity of signs and sign processes used in interfaces, these all fulfill the basic function of intermediary between users and computers. Their meaning is determined by what we actually do with computers. The contingency of each mediation—its *likelihood, relative predictability,* its *dependency* on and *conditioning* by other factors—that is, the contingent nature of each interface, is a reflex of design's dual nature as science (in respect to scientific principles of design applied to computers) and art (in respect to a particular, original way of designing). In suggesting attention to semiotics, I do not intend to reduce everything to semiotics, but to point to underlying processes taken for granted for a long time, but not yet integrated in a methodology for improved design interface. The fact that there is more than one answer to the question of efficient interface with a system seems to worry those inclined to accept only one answer to an engineering problem. Such people forget that programming, while a very rigorous activity, allows for the use of creative algorithms and their creative interpretation. Two programs for the same application can be as original and innovative as their authors. The scientific nature of logic reflected in the scientific nature of the computer, as well as the scientific foundation of semiotics, implies the art of reasoning and allows for an *art of computing* expressed in elegant, balanced, optimized codes. The late recognition of the fact that computers are basically sign processing devices (see "the concept of symbolic computation"), and not merely number crunchers, was not just a matter of terminology. It made possible progress in our design of computers and implementation of understanding (intelligence) algorithms.

All that we understand or know, we know through the intermediary of signs and *in* signs. (Gibsonians of all shades and nuances will of course disagree.) And all that we apply from our knowledge is semiotic in nature. This observation may seem banal. But for a society still trying hard to explain that there is nothing in a computer which was not previously put there by those who built it, wrote programs for it, or stored data in it, it makes sense to clarify where knowledge comes from and how it comes.

REPRESENTATION

At the beginning of the computer age, which means not only the abacus, but also Babbage's analytic engine or Peirce's logic machine, representation was kept very close to the Boolean logic which was supposed to operate on the represented items. In truth, black and white feats or similar simplified representations (in two-valued logic) of the basic repertory of signs called "yes" and "no," or "one" and "zero," sufficed. More was difficult to handle. Leibniz noticed so much ahead of his time that a language of zeros and ones, while very handy in view of its reduced repertory, was complicated, since it entailed very complicated sign operations applied to the repertory. He hoped that semiotics (which he anticipated) would come up with precise rules for generating not only the equivalent of sentences from natural language, but also mathematical formulae, music, as well as universal ethical principles.

Today we use several layers (assemblers, compilers, interpreters) and operating systems to coordinate the flux of activities that users require as an intermediary between zeros and ones of machine language and high level human reasoning involving the use of language and other sign systems. In order to provide the user with efficient means for reaching his goals in using a system, we try to make it transparent to the user. Interface helps in this endeavor. The specifications according to which they are designed determine the degree of transparency assigned to particular groups of users. Representation of objects, action, data, process status, etc. is a matter of the relation between the representamen and what is represented (the generic object in the sign definition from Figure 1). Representation, and the consequent interpretation of this representation, can take three forms (see Figure 4).

Let us discuss the implications of choosing one of these fundamental modes of representation. Based on a relation of resemblance between the object represented and the iconic representation, the use of icons implies recognition, i.e., a shared environment. Users familiar with the object represented have no difficulty in associating the icon with some object they have used before. However, if they have no prior experience with whatever is represented, if the experience is different from the one intended, or if the convention of resemblance is not carried through uniformly, interpretation is affected. When the *Metaphor for User Interface Design* was introduced at the Xerox Palo Alto Research Center, the intention was "to make computer systems accessible to many people and to make computer

Representation

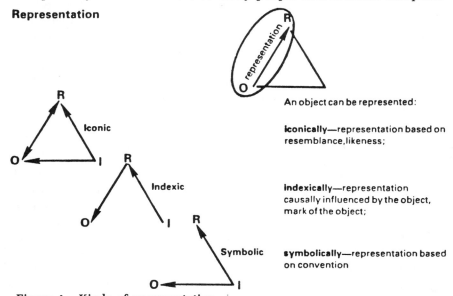

An object can be represented:

Iconic

iconically—representation based on resemblance, likeness;

Indexic

indexically—representation causally influenced by the object, mark of the object;

Symbolic

symbolically—representation based on convention

Figure 4.   Kinds of representation.

systems do many more things for people" (cf. Goldberg & Robson, 1979, p. 157). The first goal demanded simplicity, and was later achieved, to a certain degree, by using the simplest form of representation, i.e., iconic. The second required complexity (of available programs first of all). In order to find the optimal compromise, designers of the system opted for filtering templates for implementing software interfaces between various groups of users and a complex computing system. Filtering templates make possible the display of graphic representations. They are invisible layers which support the iconic interface which was afterwards, with direct participation of semiotics (the concept of icon), implemented in Xerox's Star Workstation (cf. L. Tesler, personal communication, Cupertino, December, 1983).

Among the indexical representations used in interface are account number/name, passwords, and memory management (how the user learns about available memory or memory limitations). In the UNIX operating system, there are quite a few indexical signs. In the attempt to implement an iconic version of UNIX, designers noticed the difficulty in dealing with such representations. However, indexical signs proved very important for identifying "break-ins." The entire computer security issue brought the topic of indexical signs into the design of interfaces, supposed to be friendly to the legitimate user and impenetrable to information thieves. The symbolic level of representation makes use of high level conventions, such as those of natural language and of logical or mathematical formalism.

The need to establish a coherent level of representation and to avoid changing the convention emerges as a precise normative requirement to be observed when interfaces are designed and evaluated. What this means in concrete terms will be explained when examples are given of actual interfaces and work done.

CONCEPTUAL AND PERSONAL MODEL

Based on these elements, I shall introduce a generalized concept of interface and then apply it to a computer system on which I worked as consultant for the Apple Computer Corporation. First, I should point out that interface, no matter what kind, specifies the optimal set of signs for the interaction between two entities, be they animate or inanimate. In a limited sense, user interface specifies the action the user is supposed to take in order to access different parts of a system according to the design of the conceptual model which is the basis of that particular system (see Figure 5).

In the case of computers, Meyrowitz and van Dam (1982, p. 323) ascertained that user interface, together with the conceptual model, constitute the interactive editor. According to this conception, user interface contains the input devices, the output devices, and the interaction language. In what follows, this view will be contradicted, since I consider the interactive editor itself an interface. Moreover, *every* point of contact between the computer and the user will be integrated in the extended model of user interface, from product design to service (support, documentation, tutorials, seminars, packaging, etc.). What makes things a bit more complicated in comparison to the most common social forms of interfacing through the intermediary of natural language is that *user interface is part of the computer system.* As we know, it participates in, and sometimes supports, process interfacing among different components of the system. Top level interaction with the user through the formal programming language also falls in the sphere of user interface activity.

In the spirit of accepted language theory (in particular, generative grammars), language can be understood as a generative mechanism given as a grammar to be applied to a vocabulary (or, more generally, a repertory) and rules to generate valid expressions. The personal user model, reflecting the way users perceive interface under given operating conditions, is an interpretation of the interface sequence of operations. It is formed in a long process which sometimes starts with tutorials, at other times with reading instruction manuals, and not infrequently with simply trying commands or operations based

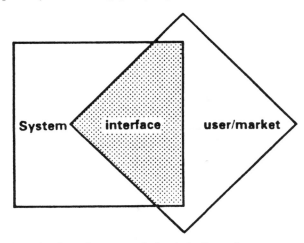

Figure 5.   Constitutive elements of the interface sign.

on prior experience while looking for some online documentation (help facility, error messages, or menus, in the case of menu driven machines). In each of these cases, the user tends to extend what he or she already knows. In doing so, his or her semiotic competence suggests two assumptions:

1. uniformity of rules
2. consistency of the representation convention adopted.

These two assumptions are actually semiotic principles derived from empirical observations regarding the way people with a certain competence act when faced with new sign systems or with new languages. Although operationally different, the conceptual model—obviously anticipating the user model—has to integrate these two requirements. In order to give an idea of how semiotic methodology can be applied, I shall concentrate on a common example: the so-called office system computer. The premise for considering a computer's interface from a semiotic viewpoint is that it represents a *complex sign system;* specifically, it represents a system we interpret as an emulation of *the office.*

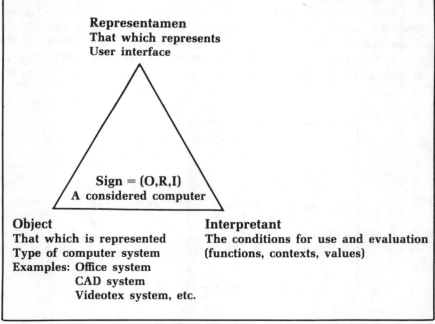

Figure 6.   Applied sign definition to computer.

Figure 6 helps in defining the elements of the basic semiotic entity, i.e., the sign, as constituted in the computer context. I have already mentioned that user interface makes transparent in three ways (iconic, indexic, symbolic representation) whatever can be accomplished with the help of computers. The syntax of user interface, although usually influenced by the semantics (the applications available), is independent of the program's syntax. This is not the case with the applications, although the user does not necessarily know this. Sometimes we notice that interface designers impose syntactic rules which make more sense to programmers than to users. Dennis Wixon, in his helpful comments to a previous version of this chapter, presented the opposite position, according to which the issue is to "decrease the distance between it [computer] and its users, much as the hammer is an extension of the arm." If computers were only such extensions, the use of semiotic concepts would not be justified. In fact, they are extensions of our minds, for which reason we have to avoid imposing on the user conventions as rigid as those required in programming. The interpreter should be aware of conditions for use and evaluation as dictated by the activity to be performed (word or data processing, planning, designing, communicating, etc.) and not by the applications available. In other words, users should have enough freedom to do what has to be done in a way which will not make them servants of the machine. If, in the process of constituting the unity *interface–applications–conditions for use and evaluation* represented by the diagram in Figure 6, one or the other of the elements imposes requirements affecting their reciprocal relation (e.g., interfaces not transparent enough for the applications they represent, applications difficult to use or inappropriate to the desired activity), the need to improve the general design of the machine should be recognized. Videotex applications provide an example of this situation. Despite all the investment made in the United States, videotex did not succeed because, among other reasons, the user interface did not adequately represent the applications (electronic banking, shopping, mail, travel schedules, etc.) and the conditions for use (via telephone lines) made it cumbersome.

Some examples of well-constituted semiotic entities nevertheless prevail in the computer market. Without going into detail, I would like to mention office systems offered by Xerox and Wang, workstations produced by SUN and Apollo, graphics machines from Raster Technologies and Silicon Graphics. In these and other cases, attention was given not only to technical performance (speed, memory), but also to how this desired performance is made available to users working under different conditions and needing to accomplish work often not anticipated by system and interface designers, or not entirely understood by them.

LISA—AN ABANDONED OFFICE SYSTEM

The constitutive elements of the office system for which I did consulting work (together with graphic designer Thomas Ockerse) were the desktop metaphor (representamen using iconic representation of applications appropriate to an office system), conditions for use as defined by office work requirements in the context of improved productivity, augmented communication, and integrated activity. The *pragmatics* results not only from the functions made available (word processing, ledger, listing, etc.), but also from the recognized need to integrate them. Everything used in this representation of the office constitutes part of a *repertory,* while the rules of usage, as applied in the process of interfacing, define the grammar of the interface language. Once the product becomes available, the final result that the designer and user look for is not the value of true or false, as in formal logic, but *meaning.*

This requires one more definition of semiotics: Semiotics is the logic of meaning. As such, it approaches the logical laws of sign processes conveying a certain meaning to an intended interpretant (i.e., the *process* of interpretation in which various users become involved, the use of the system). In order to design the interface (representamen = that which represents), the *low level protocol* has to be established. We came to the conclusion that an office is the unity of the *environment, tools, supplies,* and *activities* which make possible the pragmatics defining the specifics of each particular office. There is no such thing as a universal office. There are different types of offices, and when a computer is identified as an office system (IBM's, DEC's, Wang's), this identification opens the door to interpretation and different uses. The list to follow, a low level protocol description, presents an office as our society considers one to be. Once a decision for specialization (insurance, financial planning, law practice, medical, etc.) is made, under the assumption that the production of a specialized computer or the implementation of a specialized software package is justified, the description becomes more specific. In other contexts (the European market, Far Eastern office activity, etc.), the low level protocol will look slightly different (see Figure 7).

The semiotic condition of metaphors is that of expressive ab-

ENVIRONMENT	ACTIVITIES	TOOLS	SUPPLIES

physical space
  – architectural
  – interior
space filled w.
  objects (rugs,
  furniture, plants,
  pictures, tools . . .)
lighting
  – natural
  – artificial
human interactivity
  – w. personnel
  – w. clients
communication
environment
controlled environment
  – w. specified areas
  – w. rules inside
    outside
  – w. rules for
    legal entity
    public environ-
    ment
	typing
	editing
	dictating
	formatting
	accounting
	payrolling
	  – employees
	  – sales
	  – expenses
	calculating
	financial modeling
	cutting/pasting
	representing
	planning
	tracking
	  – inventory
	  – schedules
	analyzing
	preparing tasks
	developing tasks
	meeting
	presenting
	serving
	informing
	communicating
	answering questions
	telephoning
	advising
	controlling (quality)
	filing
	retrieving
	listing
	reporting
	centralizing
	keeping records
	inventorizing
	recording
	performing
	cheating
	hiding
	working in private
	pretending
	entertaining
	living
		furniture
		  – desk(s)
		  – chair(s)
		  – shelving
		  – storage cab.
		  – supply cab.
		  – file cabinets
		  – safe
		machines
		  – copy
		  – dictation
		  – shredding
		  – binding
		  – typewriter
		  – calculator
		  – paper cutter
		stapler
		scissors
		letter opener
		rulers
		straight edge
		protractor
		desk lamps
		clock
		telephone
		trays
		  – in/out
		  – letters
		waste basket
		tape dispenser
		file organizer
		desk organizer
		clipboard
		rolodex (open card
		  files)
		business card file
		hole puncher
		light table
		magnifying glass
		postage scale
		desk pad/blotter
		calendar
		telephone books
		dictionaries
		secretary's
		  handbook
		thesaurus
		copy stand
		numbering/date
		  stamp
		rubber stamps
		stamp pads/stamp
		  ink
		decorative-pictures
		objects
		  – plants
		  – rugs
			pencils
			  – black
			  – colored
			pens/markers
			  – black
			  – gray
			  – colors
			erasers
			liquid paper
			glue
			paper
			  – plain
			  – graph
			  – colored
			  – tracing
			carbon paper
			acetate sheets
			spread/ledger
			  sheets
			stationery
			invoice forms
			billing forms
			memo pads
			telephone
			  pads
			labels.
			stickers
			file folders
			binders/cases
			tape cassettes
			rubber bands
			clips/paper
			  clips
			tapes (clear/
			  masking)
			string

Figure 7.   The office environment.

stractions. They are generated, for poetry or science, by way of selecting characteristics according to an intention which the metaphor makes explicit. A desktop as such is not a metaphor, but a working surface. The desktop becomes a metaphor once it is selected to represent the office environment. Behind the desktop metaphor, there is actually another layer which implements a more general model, the layer of windows, a filtering template used for displaying graphic representations (text or pictograms, diagrams, etc.). Windows are components of the repertory and can vary in size. The possibility of arbitrarily overlapping windows facilitates the analogy of paper on an office desk. Obviously, not every system is designed to support covered windows (tiled window managers do not); i.e., the desktop metaphor, as any other metaphor, requires that the designer of an interface which implements desktop conventions use a system that can support it well. Raster display is a necessary condition.

The Lisa machine, which Apple developed using or adapting previous results obtained by Xerox, was supposed to fulfill the goals of user friendliness ("accessible to many people") and complexity ("do more things for people") by providing a very transparent user interface and an integrated, multitasking computing environment. The advantages of implementing Alan Kay's covered window model (accommodating several large displays which could not fit together side by side, making better use of screen, maintaining familiarity with the convention of overlapping paper on a desk) were to be augmented by a mode-free environment. Since a graphics interface was considered, the list in Figure 7 was soon turned into a visual representation of the office.

SYNTAX OF INTERACTION

After defining interface as representamen and specifying its elements with the aid of low level protocol description, and after defining the type of representation (iconic, indexical, or symbolic), we have to relate these to the computing environment, to the integration language. Larry Tesler (1981) explained what this means from the perspective of the user we considered: "How do I do this?" "How do I get out of this mode?" as opposed to seeing on the screen what is available, choosing with a pointing device (which moves a cursor wherever the cursor is needed), and switching from one application to another. Since this issue is critical for interface design, let me explain it briefly and give an example.

User interface consists of input and output devices and interaction language. The latter consists of a repertory (constitutive elements which can be put together to form meaningful commands) and the equivalent of a grammar (rules to be applied). We can input character strings, commands, and coordinates. We can receive the same as output, as well as formatted text or data (or both). The syntax of interaction languages can be prefix, postfix, or infix. Once we adopt a conceptual model for the user interface, we implicitly adopt an adequate syntax for the interaction language. The two aspects are interrelated. Until the Palo Alto Research Center unveiled its then original iconic interface (the Alto ᴿ station) and the Smalltalk environment (Thacker, McCraight, Lampson, Spronll, & Boggs 1979; Tesler, 1981), the main type of command was the prefix. Basically, a prefix syntax command specifies first the verb (operation) and then the object of the operation (example: edit; file to be edited). The postfix syntax command does just the opposite, allowing first for the selection of the object (file) and then for the desired operation (append). It requires a subject-oriented interface language; i.e., it makes possible a visual language, i.e., a graphics interface. The infix command implies the existence of several operands, each action being virtually connected to such operands.

Let us consider the way the world of typography is emulated on computer-driven typesetters as an example (the Mergenthaler OMNITECH 2000 to be precise) that points to the inherent constraints of a prefix system (see Figure 8).

The pragmatics of the emulated world, on which the culture of the printed medium relies quite extensively, determined the functions of the new machine and consequently its interface: What used to be the composing stick was turned into a sequence defining the font (■T#sp), size (■S##sp), lead (■L#sp), and measure ■M##sp (in picas and points). The text to be typeset immediately follows ■M##sp, the highlighted specifications; hardware (the stick) becomes a software specification. Pagination requires a formatting command, quite opaque to the user (defining page area, zero position, negative area, etc.). Obviously, the change from the technology of linotype (hot type) and letterpress to the technology and interface of the digital typesetter is impressive. Desktop publishing, which was supposed to become a Lisa function, shows not only how technology has changed, but also how changes in interface (from the abovementioned awkward prefix commands on the Mergenthaler to the more direct specification of today's systems) facilitated access to more complex computing for more people.

ᴿ Registered trademark, Xerox, Inc.

Figure 8.   Computer emulation of typographic environment.

   The infix command implies the existence of several operands that are established through user interface design. Since the sequentiality of computer string processing is a structural given—and natural language is sequential—the first, and still most common, design interfaces use the sequential paradigm. The relation between the user and the computer is established during the typing in of strings (text or abbreviations) for names (commands) and for operands, sometimes as close to natural language as possible, at other times according to other conventions. Intuitively following the semiotic principle of feedback, the designers of such interfaces made sure that the commands are echoed on the output device (screen, in this case) before or after being processed by the editor. The interface design becomes more and more critical when online activities are performed. The old, hot metal typesetter was an online device. Each key command ended up in the mechanical selection of the appropriate mold; the hot metal was poured in the mold and the result was a line. Norpak's IPS-2 system (which supports a Telidon alphageometric system) duplicates the real world of design and typography, moving beyond the infix structure (to a mixed environment in which infix and postfix commands coexist, with a drawing tablet that allows for the actions connected to some of the available operands). Interface preserved some basic tools: compass, pantograph, ruler, triangle. But the end products (image on an editing screen as opposed to newspapers at a delivery station) are obviously different. There is also a limit to the emulation, clearly illustrated in the way people interface to a newspaper as opposed to the selection pad of a teletext-videotex-television device.
   Up to this point, we have examined different ways a strategy of imitation is pursued and interface designed to make the imitation clear to the user. The limitation imposed by the postfix syntax on the interface adopted for Lisa can be partially overcome by the introduction of function keys, the use of macros, better emulation of natural language, design of "intelligent" editors, etc. The postfix command opened the way for multiple choice of strings and/or visual images (graphics interface which is mainly iconic). But, to date, less has been made known about the semiotic characteristics and limitations of such interfaces. In the process of semiotic evaluation of the postfix syntax and its use, conceptual limitations as well as experimental findings were considered. Adopting the postfix syntax was only one more step in the direction of better understanding the perspectives for improving interface over the course of time. For instance, frequently the basic distinction object–action (reflecting the noun–verb distinction in natural language) is not

clear–cut. People also tend to transform nouns into verbs (and vice versa). Moreover, and for reasons implicit in the semiotic structure of such interface, selection and response times sometimes increase over the time of operation itself (opening or closing a file is the most obvious example). In what follows, particular aspects of the office system interface design will be more closely considered.

The following model was used in evaluating the interface specifications (see Figure 9):

Since the desktop metaphor and the iconic representation were chosen for the object (of action), the specification of the action had to use a graphic form, too, but a different type. The user should not be put in the confusing situation of an undifferentiated representation of objects and actions. Because actions are difficult to represent in static pictograms (they can be represented in animated sequences), representations of actions were not iconic, but symbolic (through words). These words are displayed in pop-up menus and organized according to main categories corresponding to the state of the machine (after booting, once the application was started, before and after editing, etc.). Since window sizes can be changed and both characters and full bitmap graphic operations are supported, the interface had to be designed so as to preserve the realism of the convention. Once the window size is changed, the user sees only a portion of the document and not a sized–up/down image.

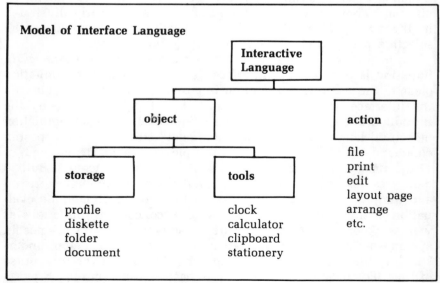

Figure 9. Model of interface language.

Interface design requires *semiotic consistency;* i.e., it becomes a matter of uniformly using whatever means of representation are considered adequate.

Although every effort was made to ensure consistency, later on, during an evaluation in which design principles were applied to see how successful the designer had been, it became evident that the clear-cut conceptual distinction between actions and objects was really quite fuzzy. Instead of documenting the successful parts—in the meantime acknowledged by their widespread use in interfaces designed for other systems—I prefer to discuss the critical aspects and what means semiotics provides for evaluation and redesign.

The type of representation chosen (iconic, indexical, or symbolic) influences the user's interpretation. The following representation of the Lisa calculator visualizes this idea (see Figure 10).

Recognizing that the squares on an icon called *calculator* are "real" buttons which have to be "pressed" (not on the screen, but

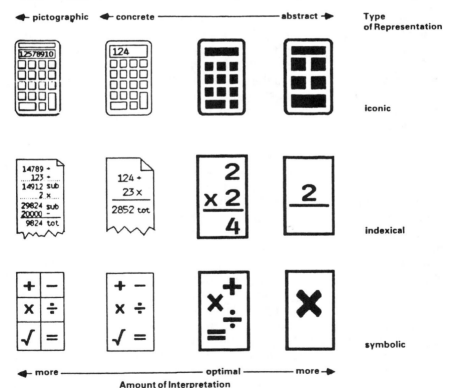

Figure 10.   The relation between representation and interpretation.

via the mouse button) involves an interpretation different from what the pictogram of a stack of paper suggests—and again, different from the convention of a clipboard which holds the last item cut or copied, but which cannot be edited. The LED–type of display and the numbers displayed are a kind of convention–over–convention. The user is confronted with a real calculator and a representation (iconic) of a pocket calculator. This is a difficult semantic situation, similar to the one we face if some of our words were at the same time the objects they denote! Figure 10 presents the visual analysis a designer should go through to evaluate options that might prove better than the initial one.

The easiest and most direct interpretation is the one resulting from information sufficient to facilitate recognition. After semiotic inconsistency, the second issue is whether icons should be presented with the names of the items they represent. Recognition memory is better for iconic representation. However, the recognition of tasks, such as how to use the calculator, seems to imply that dual coding (images and words) is sometimes confusing, because users will typically wonder why they need a label underneath an image they recognize. Is there something they might not understand?

Computers such as Xerox Star, Intran, and later Macintosh added the interactive editor formatter to the postfix command that is part of the interface language: "What you see is what you get." While this is a welcome quality, soon to be adopted by other computer designers, it has the drawback which Brian Kernighan identified as "What you see is *all* you've got." In the opinion of several interface designers, it is uninformative and gives no clues to what influences a certain format, why some changes are not possible, and why there is no consistency between formatting capabilities or between the different applications used. The filtering templates used in such an interactive editor formatter are as important as the input messages in the prefix commands. On most available systems, the semantics of the templates is confusing and not consistent with the visual representation of the objects, locations, or the pop-up menus of actions (based on a computing environment such as Smalltalk and supported by a pointing device connected to the cursor or current position independent manager). Another limitation affecting the use of visual language results from the aliasing condition of raster graphics (which supports the window model). It can be compensated for either by increasing the density of pixels (which results in the need for computer memory and increased response time) or by using multiple bits per pixel (grey-scale displays). This is not only a hardware issue. The higher the quality of images, the better the possibilities to generate a visual language for the interface and to support high quality applications.

HUMAN–COMPUTER COMMUNICATION

An office is not a collection of files, typewriters, calculators, etc. That is, it is not a collection of hardware but an *environment* where communication (exchange of documents, for example, storage and retrieval of data, planning, etc.) is necessary, and interconnection should be possible. This explains why office systems successful in supporting individual office work but not communication have not made it in the market. As far as the semiotic evaluation of the Lisa is concerned, it failed on the market due to severe communication limitations, among other reasons. Apple was aware of some of the limitations. Produced under market pressure and unveiled before the product was actually finished, from the perspective of technology and interface, Lisa claimed an integrated environment within which communication among applications was possible. From the beginning, this communication was limited and difficult to accomplish. The user learned from the manuals that information could not be switched between all the programs, and that sometimes only one-way communication was possible. This was confusing, to say the least. What was worse was the reality that the system performed below these specifications. When trying to use the clipboard as a communication go-between, the user frequently experienced crashes which destroyed a file. Communication with the outside world was possible through the *LisaTerminal* (sic!) within which editing possibilities were kept to a minimum. The emulation of terminals used for electronic mail (especially DEC) was considered sufficient. Implementation of this emulating function was primitive. Local Area Networking was not provided; consequently, while data was processed electronically, it had to be exchanged through hard copy obtained on a rather slow printer. Against the background of these communication limitations (to which incompatibility with other systems should be added), the price tag of $10,000.00 came as a further shock. Nevertheless, I claim that it was not the price but the communication limitations that undermined the product. Later on, when the price was slashed and communication facilities only slightly improved, Lisa—which did introduce very important computing concepts—did not make a recovery in the market.

At this point, it is useful to suggest that more attention be paid to the semiotics of communication pertinent to computer interface.

There are people who question the subject. "Do people want or need to communicate with computers any more than they want or need to communicate with a typewriter?" is a question Dennis Wixon obliged me to consider. Actually, there is no such thing as man-machine communication; this is a way of speaking, a way of anthropomorphizing machines. Communication is the semiotic activity that brings user and designer together by the intermediary of the language(s) they use. Once the user accepts a language, he or she will apply it according to the rules the designer embedded in the interface, and *their* communication, mediated by a certain machine, will take place. The point is not that the user is at the mercy of the designer. After all, aren't we all at the mercy of our parents, who brought us to life in a language we could not choose? Rather, the designer and user, as parts of a given culture, share established conventions and participate in the establishment of new sign systems, if such become necessary. Programming languages are just such systems, i.e., languages which support precise functional activities and make possible new tools, which are cognitive in nature. The field of human factors in computer systems, "an unruly mixture of theoretical issues and practical problems" (Norman, 1983, p. 1), developed as a result of the difficulties computer scientists and engineers face when considering the relation between the systems they build and their potential users. Psychological concepts were brought into the picture first, and previous observations on the interaction between humans and various tools and machines were applied, not unsuccessfully, to a technology very different from any previous one. What was less considered was the fact that signs and sign processing represent the common underlying principle both of human interaction with computers and of the computer, "a member of an important family of artifacts called symbol systems" (Simon, 1982, p. 28). Since the technology upon and for which we build interfaces changes very rapidly (some that we are aware of, some to be discovered), semiotic principles provide a foundation for a more comprehensive specification of interface design (user and process interfaces), and for the evaluation of interfaces currently in use.

INTERPRETATION OF INTERFACE

We know that signs are constituted of structural components in a limited number of ways. For instance, major structural components of visual signs are shape, contour, color, and texture. If an object is distinct enough, shape alone may be sufficient for recognition (an observation that interface designers using visual representations sometimes apply). I shall exemplify this by referring again to the calculator (see Figure 11).

Pictographic representations are very concrete, almost so concrete that, if the context changes and the user is presented with a different pictogram (let's say one of the solar battery calculator), he or she will have difficulties in "using" the sign. The semiotic level is reached when the conventionality of the sign becomes evident. (Convention here means *as convened, agreed upon,* and accordingly shared in a given social context, in a culture.) Once the convention is recognized, the next step in interpretation is associating sign and function. Only at this moment does the user integrate the component of an interface's repertory in what the designer intends the language to become. Obviously, understanding what an icon represents, as opposed to what it pictures, is essential for designing user interface language. Once this is understood and consistently applied, we can decide upon one type of interface or another, or upon a mixture of representations. Regardless of our choice, what is important is understanding the different sign processes (different "grammars") that characterize the three fundamental types of representation. Words can be used as well; and at the extreme of the symbolic representation, one can add the word *CALCULATOR,* or some abbreviation.

Evolution of a Sign Representation

Symbols may evolve from pictographic representations.
As the symbol becomes more abstract,
it also becomes more recognizable.

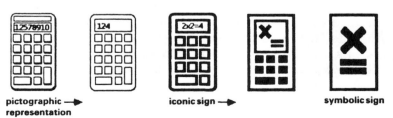

pictographic ➡
representation   iconic sign ➡   symbolic sign

Figure 11.   Evolution of a sign representation.

MACINTOSH (OR: REINVENTING LISA
IN THE MAC ENVIRONMENT)

The initial step in designing a user interface is to determine the operations and the entities on which operations will be performed. If template filters should be used, the identification must consider object/location as opposed to action/structure. Editing filters are in fact devices that perform the basic semiotic operations (substitution, insertion, omission) according to specifications from the user or the system. The same holds true for viewing filters (used to specify areas of a document to be viewed and to generate viewing buffers). The editing and viewing filters are semiotically equivalent; functionally, they are sometimes identical (screen editors), disjoint, partially overlapping, or properly contained in one another. This is part of the pragmatics of the interface, and necessarily relies on hardware specifications. From a semiotic perspective, which emphasizes the unity between function (interpretation, content, use), syntax, and semantics, there is only one way to proceed in approaching interface: as part of the system, not as a delayed addition to it. Despite its qualities, the Apple IIC (one among several possible examples) shows what happens when an interface concept (the use of the mouse) is adopted primarily for marketing purposes. The same holds true for the Macintosh computer in its initial stage—a product celebrated by quite a few but which, despite its qualities, was considered a hybrid between an office system and a dignified toy. Let us examine some of the reasons for this ambivalent evaluation. As with the phased-out Lisa, emulation was the semiotic strategy used. One might argue that, for the sake of realism, a certain *overdesign* of the interface (emulation of details) makes the Macintosh's very small screen (management of a reduced number of pixels) seem continuously too busy.

Figure 12 exemplifies what kind of representation was adopted: sometimes reminiscent of the tool (typewriter) whose functions the computer can fulfill; at other times, new functions; and finally, icons of pencils, brushes, and paint cans, or of forms already available. More than one convention was implemented here, the quality of the interface consisting of directness but not consistency. What also surprises is the way tools are introduced under the cutesy name of *Goodies,* a mixture of necessary and less necessary elements (see Figure 13).

Moreover, the finder—a remarkable device used in a contradictory way—almost turns into a hidden collection of toys. It is not that computers—especially the PC category—should make users lose

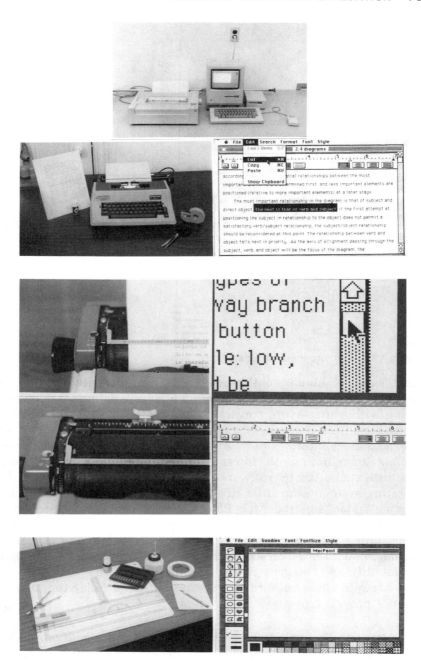

Figure 12.   Macintosh emulation of typing and drawing.

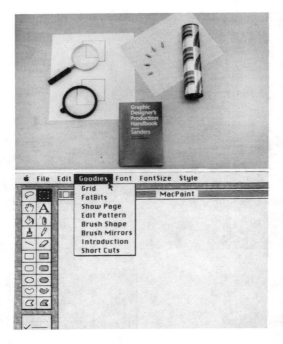

Figure 13. The semiosis of Goodies.

their sense of humor, childishness, or ingenuity. Rather, it is a question of evaluating options within a precisely defined framework. Living within the severe constraints which the development of the initial Macintosh (128K RAM memory) posed should have made the designers of its interface more aware of what is necessary and what becomes a frustrating user interface option. For as long as Macintosh was little supported by software developers, the weaknesses of the operating system were little noticed. Later, this situation changed; the "fat" Mac and the Mac Plus solved some critical problems. Nevertheless, each improvement seemed quite accidental because Apple failed to understand the need for a comprehensive *design language© within which scope, changes and improvements maintain the identity and integrity of the product.*

In view of the semiotics of the interface, the following characteristics proved critical for the system:

1. directness or simplicity (which the Macintosh designers stretched almost to the extreme with visual representations that are sometimes excessive in their details);

© Copyright Mihai Nadin, 1979.

2. consistency or uniformity, observed within applications but *not* among them. The degree of integration is actually less than some believe and Apple advertises. However, a certain modularity is noticeable;

3. permissiveness, unfortunately not clear to the user how far an application goes, and not entirely complemented by what is known as "forgiveness" in the case of mistakes (the UNDO function)—not every operation can be UNDO-ne, but this the user finds out after the fact;

4. operationality, i.e., a set of qualities referring to computing time, uniformity of speed, file management, etc.

Clearly, these characteristics are related. While Macintosh is a very fast machine (assembler programmed), in its initial stage it had poor file management and consequently seemed slow (psychological differential) at times. When the user switched from the mouse functions to the keyboard, this structural shortcoming became even more evident. Some operations, "cut and paste" for instance, do not follow the prefix mode.

The new Macintosh Plus offers the enhanced speed, storage, and expandability which the specifications of its user interface design require for meaningful use of the conventions it is based on. In fact, the evolution is towards what *Lisa offered before the Macintosh* became a product, especially the multitasking capability, plus a much better communication capability, despite the limitations of Appletalk. Even the input and output devices were improved. The MacPlus has a keyboard with numeric keypad, four cursor control keys, and a new port (SCSI, the *scuzzy* interface) for high transmission speed connections of peripherals, which can further expand the complexity of tasks for which users might choose this machine. The long learning process, at the end of which semiotic implications were recognized and actually used in *Macintosh's* improved interface design, does not stop here. There are other companies which use the advice of designers aware of or applying semiotics to their own work. Aaron Marcus and Associates is one such design firm whose methods incorporate semiotic principles. Aaron Marcus (1983, pp. 63–70 and 1983, pp. 103–123) has written about his work, and I encourage the reader to consult the respective articles.

TRANSLATING SEMIOTIC REQUIREMENTS INTO DESIGN

Part of the desktop metaphor, and certain elements of iconic representation convention, have in recent years been assimilated in the design of interfaces for new machines competing for their share of the market (Amiga, Atari ST, and a whole bunch of "generic" computers). I see nothing bad in this trend, provided that, in the process of imitating a successful approach, designers attempt to understand what made this approach necessary. Generally speaking, the design procedure is exactly the reverse of the interpretive process the user goes through when dealing with user interface language. Only after the appropriate functions are determined is it useful to consider how those functions translate in computing content and memory-related issues (i.e., semantics) and, furthermore, how this content will be represented. If the pragmatics of the system leads to the conclusion that visual representations (for example, icons) are justified, design should be considered only in the greater context of the design *language* system. I would insist that interface language be, in principle, formal, which means that the language should function according to a logical structure that the user is familiar with or can easily grasp, and which, while adhering to the spirit of computing logic, should not contradict so-called natural logic (cultural background as the environment of human logic). Of course, voice input devices—a subject impossible to ignore when predictions present this alternative as almost available—do not make this task easier. In the course of using a given interface, the user acquires a progressively higher level of competence (learns the editor), and, accordingly, user performance in operating a system improves (use of short-cuts, for example). In respect to this, a certain influence, quite often overlooked, is exercised by the type of computing environment: stand–alone (becoming more pervasive in the market), distributed, or timesharing. The constraints each type imposes on the design of the interface should also be accounted for when the sign representing the system is constituted, not after everything else has been defined. Many computers, especially stand–alone units, are offered with all kinds of "cosmetic" interface contraptions added under marketing pressure and offered by various OEMs. This quite often affects the user's performance and adds to the confusion already disseminated by the rather chaotic computer market. No interface language is an entity in itself, even if it enters the market with the backing of the largest companies. In one form or another, they all refer to everyday language(s), the so-called natural language, to the language of gestures, of trademarks, etc. In extension of user interface (documentation, tutorials, seminars, support, etc.), this aspect is even more obvious. While the conceptual model of a system is the *premise* for the coherence of interface language, there is actually nothing that guarantees such coherence. Knowing that the user is in fact represented by a divided cognitive structure, in which sequence and configuration (i.e., time-related and space-related perceptions and activities) are not homogenously supported by the brain, we should be able to design interfaces in such a way as not to affect the balance of these two basic cognitive modes.

Interface engineers might find this distinction irrelevant to their work. But experimental data fully support the fact that switching from a sequential mode (operation of keyboards) to a configurational mode (using painting devices, digitizing tablets, etc.) affect the user and his or her performance. In a good interface design theory, the observation that interfaces represent what we know about computers and the humans using them might prove useful. For instance, knowing how people learn proved important at Xerox Park, where the user interface "transparency" of interface is a cognitive quality supporting sign processes within the general framework of the theory of learning. Comprehending a specific system of signs means to identify the structure of that system. The "transparency" of interface is a cognitive quality supporting an emotional component. As long as we have human beings in mind when we talk about the user, emotions cannot be simply discharged as irrelevant. In order to be made more apparent to the user, interface languages should use (a) *concrete* representations of objects and storage, and (b) operation representations that relate *directly* to actions. Concreteness and directness must be expressed as clearly as possible.

Engineers require that we operationalize these terms; otherwise, the requirement of concreteness and directness remain quite obscure. To make concrete representations of objects and storage, one can start with almost photographic images of the respective items. Directness of actions can be achieved by animated sequences. Whether, in the end, the interface will keep the photographic image or simplify it in a realistic rendition is less important. However, the level of concreteness should be uniformly maintained.

The wastebasket on the *Lisa* user interface has an elegant slant lid. No other object represented on the desktop has a similar visual accent. The icon of the computer is called *Preferences.* Actually this is not the representation of an object, but of actions to be

Wastebasket   Profile   Clipboard   Preferences   Diskette

Figure 14.   The syntax of Lisa icons.

performed: setting conveniences, selecting defaults, connecting various devices. While, during the design stage, concreteness was not a goal, directness was, supported by the use of the mouse as a pointing device. Evaluation of what is actually implemented allows for improvements. The framework for evaluation is set by identifying requirements—even those difficult to formalize and render operational—which ensure the quality of human–computer interaction. The examination of the syntax of the icons in Figure 14 already suggests ways to operationalize aspects of concreteness and directness.

As already stated, user interface contains the so-called input and output devices and the interaction language as it is developed from/ with the conceptual model of a given system, plus extensions (documentation, tutorials, seminars, support, etc.). Obviously, the design of such components (keyboards, tablets, light pens, painting devices, printers, etc.) integrates product design considerations, ergonomy, psychology, marketing, etc., but not always communication requirements. The unity of hardware–software, and their reciprocal influence, is also important. Very few systems available today, as far as I know, were designed to integrate such diverse components. Dealing with the pointing device (mentioned in the previous paragraph as important in achieving directness) as an independent component (there are manufacturers which specialize in "mice") is against the spirit in which this interface component was conceived. There is nothing wrong with specialized manufacture-of—"mice" (or, for that matter, of hard disk units, or other interface components)—if a unifying and integrating design which is faithful to the initial concept serves as a premise. But this is rarely the case. The three-button mouse (e.g., on the Apollo workstation or on VAXSTATION 100) is functionally quite different from the one-button mouse. But it was uniformly integrated in the user interface. The syntax of clicking— once, twice, three times—introduced by Apple affects directness. It is not an extension but a new dimension, complicating the user interface.

USER FRIENDLY: A FUNCTIONAL QUALITY

Ease of use and learning are frequently identified with user friendliness. This is accomplished when the interface is clear, displays conventions familiar to the user, allows the user to infer from the use of one application to another; when the system is reliable and responsive; when help is provided but does not become excessive, and is provided in adequate formats corresponding to the user's level of expertise. Hence, friendliness is not only an interface issue. Unreliable or slow systems are not friendly even if the interface is pleasant. The Xerox 6085 office system is an example at hand. It apparently uses the successful iconic interface of the Xerox Star, while simultaneously imposing upon the user rules of operation (e.g., moving icons, copying, printing, etc.) which, after Lisa and Macintosh, are anachronic. The system is slow. Consequently, the appearance of friendliness and the slick product design turn into teasers. The quality of typography and, for computers with color capabilities, color considerations affect friendliness, too. Rudimentary icons in color, such as the ones used on the Amiga, make clear that without maintaining the quality of design, the iconic interface can degenerate. One critical area—also evident in the Amiga—involves error messages. Errors make the user, even the expert, quite uneasy. The way errors are represented to the user affects performance and the learning curve. Using the appropriate word or image, or their combination, is an important semiotic requirement. Usually, an alert file stores these messages; but it is the routine of the alert manager designed to display them. And this particular routine is usually designed with little understanding of error message semiotics.

Error messages, often anthropomorphized, should be integrated in the user interface language and reflect the degree of integration of the available software. The problem is that, since the software comes from different developers, who receive only system specifications, error messages are improvised without any consideration of the interface requirements. A recent analysis of error messages in the major programs available for the IBM-PC—5 years after its introduction, and with three million machines sold—shows that they constantly deviate from the convention of the user interface. In the case of programs trying to emulate the desktop metaphor in the IBM-PC environment, error messages pertinent to the Macintosh are simply taken over (the icon for a crash, the message referring to the sequence "select object before action," corresponding to the postfix syntax of the interaction language).

An important conclusion resulting from the observations discussed and exemplified above is that, while underlying principles are relatively independent of technology, semiotic principles, as they refer to sign processing, become technologically dependent when applied. This reflects the law according to which the pragmatics of the sign is context sensitive (Nadin, 1981, p. 215). There is no way to avoid the consequences of this law. Efforts in the direction of better programming (sometimes for the sake of programming) or higher technology (sometimes for the sake of technology) are quite impressive. Programming and technology are interwoven. Design weaves them together, and precise design concepts, uniformly applied, ensure the unity of the computer. As mentioned above, interface issues are issues of interpretation (pragmatics) as related to the various types of signs used in interface. Recognition of the object represented is based on two complementary processes:

1. recognizing parts of the object in relation to each other and to the whole, and arriving at some inference based on their interrelationship;
2. recognizing the whole, and inferring from the whole to the parts.

A product's look and functionality are a continuation of user interface, and are related to every other interface of the system. In the course of product design, the formal and the functional qualities should be achieved, while considerations of semiotic unity of the interface are observed. User friendliness refers to physical and mental aspects of working with a computer, programming it, or simply using some of its routines.

Usually, designers know what their computer is supposed to provide; that is, they know what the expected product can be. They also know, or are able to determine, who is going to use the computer (be interested in the product) and what his or her background is. At the system level, the following relations can be established in view of the intended user friendliness (see Figure 15).

Within a given conceptual level, which takes into account the multiple interconditioning of user interface, it is possible to avoid both settling at an arrogant level (if you don't understand it, too bad!) or a primitive form of friendliness (which ends up offending the user). There is no such thing as universal friendliness. This becomes clear at the conceptual level, which shows that each user will form his or her own model when using a given computer (see Figure 16).

Should interfaces entirely specify a course of action (friendliness by holding the user's hand through every step), or provide a free environment in which each user is able to decide his or her own sequence? The question has no clear cut answer. In my recent work on a project entitled *Design Machine,* this issue was brought up by the community of designers for which we want to build a computer able to support not only production, but also conceptual, creative work. Simulation in software of design work showed us that basic

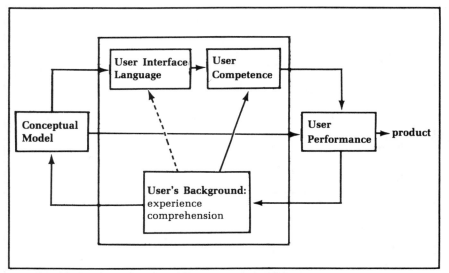

Figure 15.   Systems view of the structure of interface elements.

design tools are necessary, but that they have to be conceived as versatile, as "soft" as possible (cf. Nadin, 1986).

The model developed by each particular user (influenced by manuals, guides, tutorials, etc.) is the product of "learning" the system or being "taught" how to use it. Generally speaking, the user employs interface according to the semiotic interpretation given to the interface. This interpretation is based on the user's model. Preconceptions influence this model; so do other semiotic contexts: cognitive skills, emotional factors, aesthetic characteristics, etc.

CATEGORIES OF USERS

The common representation of *the user* distinguishes the novice from the veteran. This is a linear representation, very comfortable, but not necessarily appropriate (see Figure 17). It implies that a novice will sooner or later become an expert, a supposition that is far from confirmed. It also implies that, once initiation is over, the expert must work with the limitations inherent in the system that made it approachable to the novice, i.e., accept the help that later turns into a hindrance. A more complex model is necessary, one that considers the knowledge the user accumulates from working with various computers as an important characteristic of the dynamics of the interface. Although experience is important, a semiotic

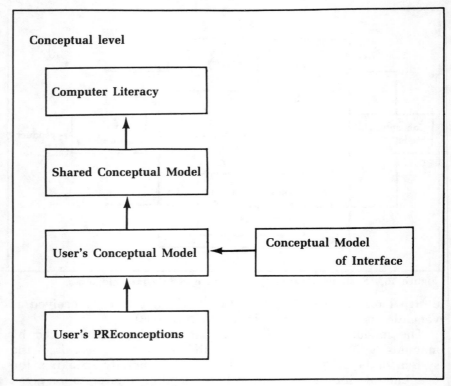

Figure 16.   Conceptual level.

Simplified User Model   Naive   Experienced

Figure 17.   Simplified user model.

property of computer-aided activity is that, in order to understand and use sign systems, a user has to bring into the activity not only specialized knowledge, but also comprehension skills gained from culture and general education. Computer literacy is only part of this comprehension. The *improved user model* is supposed to help the interface designer evaluate his choice of signs (see Figure 18).

   The distinctions *naive, competent, experienced,* and *expert* are not easily quantifiable. Intuitively, designers tend to identify such distinctions through the use of certain idiomatic expressions (words), or by giving up images (deemed primitive). Lisa was designed not just as an office system addressing secretaries, accountants, graphic designers, and other professionals, but also as a computer tool which could support a fair amount of development work. The distinction

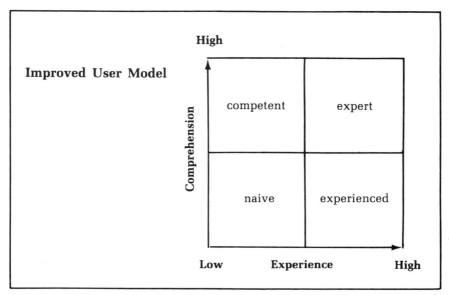

Figure 18. Improved user model.

between the office system environment and the workshop actually reflected the distinction between user and programmer. The desktop metaphor and iconic convention were carried over to the workshop environment only to a very small extent *(Preferences* and *Editor).* Once in the workshop, the programmer faced conventions familiar to professionals acquainted with a programming environment: FILEMgr, SYSTEMMgr, Edit, Run, Debug, Pascal, Basic, Quit? (at the top of the tree). The cursor functions only for Edit and for setting Preferences. A letter confirms each command selection. The tree of successive options goes no deeper than two more layers. The change in the set of signs used (from icons and menus to actions specified in technical terms, from windows to separate process commands, etc.) corresponds to the change of expected user, but in a way in which jargon takes over the interface concept. For some reason, the computer community developed a scientific vocabulary and a stock of almost private expressions—opaque to the nonexpert and humorous (or intended to be so). We know how this semiosis came about. We also know that the energy and inventiveness of young and very young computer developers contributed to a special stratum in our technological culture. In the workshop, friendliness takes the form of options which in the office system would sound threatening—*Kill Process, Scavenging*—or questions which sound worse than what they are—*What?* or the abrasive *Do you really want to. . . .?*

Interface designers could avoid the discrepancy noted here if they considered the users from the perspective of the expected comprehension and assumed experience, as reflected by their professional language (a subset of the natural language they use) and their ability to infer from one environment to the other, from one program to the other. In view of this, the two-dimensional matrix can be improved, first of all by involving other qualities which, after the introduction of more "intelligent" systems, have proven essential in computer use and are more and more acknowledged in computer culture. Imagination, to give just one example, plays an important role in programming, as well as in running programs or adapting programs to new functions. The multidimensionality of such matrix representations corresponds to the user's intellectual and emotional qualities (see Figure 19).

An immediate practical application of this representation is in designing interfaces for the handicapped. The way people with impaired hearing and vision and those with physical handicaps interpret signs belonging to language and other systems of expression has to be considered when interfaces meant to support their access to computers are designed. Although some research has been done, more is necessary. We know, for instance, that the deaf have prob-

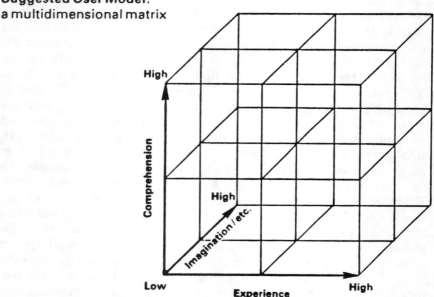

Figure 19.   Suggested user model.

lems in dealing with time and time-related representations. Accordingly, interface has to be conceived as an expression of space relations. Audio components of user interfaces, on the other hand, help people with impaired vision. In this case, every quality of sound can be used, the pattern of sound sequences becoming part of the language. The semiotic concept of appropriateness applies in such cases.

COMPUTERS, USERS, AND COMMUNICATION

Signs are used predominantly for communication. They are means to represent our problems: mathematical signs for mathematical problems, 3-D representations for architectural problems, natural languages or formalisms (diagrams, vectors, matrices, etc.) for describing social problems. Computers are basically used for problem solving, a fact that should be carefully considered when communication issues are approached. As opposed to other tools, the computer is a "universal" problem solver once the problem is presented in a computable form (see Figure 20).

This model was devised after viewing computers from the semiotic perspective, i.e., after considering how people interact with each other through the intermediary of the messages they exchange. Bühler (1933), in his impressive semiotic study of social communication which, unfortunately, scientists outside his field know little of, and Jakobson (1960), in his research of linguistic processes, made

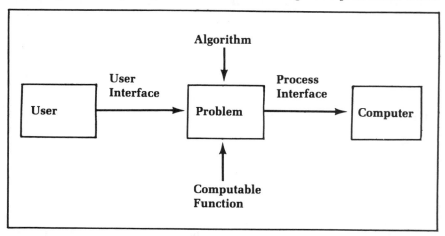

Figure 20.   Semiotics of the user-computer relation.

contributions which help us better understand the nature of communication.

Examining this model (see Figure 21), (to which Calude and Marcus (1985) brought their contribution), we can identify several functions, to which I add their implications for the user–computer relation.

1. the function of communication—actually the function of maintaining communication, identified as the phatic function
2. the expressive function—relating addresser and the message
3. the metalinguistic function—dealing with the functioning of the code(s) used (expressing both the addresser–code and addressee–code relations)
4. the pragmatic function—dealing with the context and the way it influences communication (relation between addresser, addressee, and context)
5. the connative function—representing the attitude of the addressee towards the message (imperative messages are quite different from optional or query messages)
6. the design function—reflecting the way the addresser and addressee (in particular) relate to the medium
7. the referential (or cognitive) function—dealing with the meaning of the message
8. the formal (poetic) function—pertaining to the message's formal qualities (syntax error, for instance, is but an indication of this function).

Looking at a symmetrical communication structure, we have to

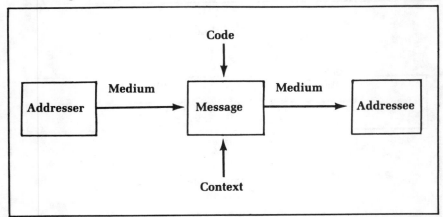

Figure 21. Communication in the semiotic concept (cf. Buhler-Jakobson).

consider specific situations related to the three basic segments identified in order to obtain optimal design: user–computer, computer–computer, computer–user. Examining Figures 20 and 21, the reader will notice the line of thought pursued: The message is the problem to be solved with the computer's help; the context and the code are represented by the computable function which describes the problem and by the program as based on some known or newly developed algorithm. A minimal requirement is that communication be maintained (the phatic function). This minimum proves quite complex (ever heard of crashing?) and involves the relations among user–computable function, computable function–program, program–computer, user–computer. Some computable functions describe a given problem better than others. But not all are equally computable; and if in principle they are computable, then some limitations in the hardware may affect the response time. And since each system comes with specifications impossible to avoid, whether the given system can accept the program becomes an issue. And if it can, how effectively? Finally, the messages meant for the user (and "issued" by the computer) should be concise, precise, and understandable—conditions easier to claim than to implement. I shall refer here only to the connative function, from among the others, mainly because interface issues are concerned with the type of problems a system is supposed to assist the user in solving. Two different forms of "intelligence" are evident: the "intelligence" built (wired) in the hardware, and the "intelligence" of the program. Several design decisions are expected in regard to error handling (interface and compiler, or interface of an environment like LISP or PROLOG), feedback to the user (how? what? why?), type of processing (effective, virtual), etc. The referential function is difficult to approach because, while the computer is a Boolean machine, the relation between the concrete problem and the computable function can be described in modal, not binary, logic. The expressive function, influenced by the same two-valued logic, reflects the state of the art in deterministic thinking, hopefully to be improved by the use of fuzzy logic or of the logic of vagueness. Zadeh (1984) is the best source for more information on this matter. Looking from the computer to the user, we see a slightly different picture in Figure 22. Obviously, the referential function of this segment is the same as the metalinguistic function of the user–computer segment. Two interesting aspects relate to the expressive function:

1. As a Turing machine, the computer can deal with the com-

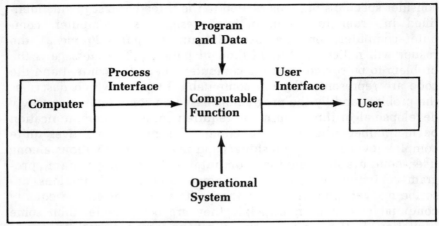

Figure 22.   Computer-user relation.

putable function step by step (one thing at a time); i.e., no
evaluation of the entire function is possible.

2.   Moreover, the computer evaluates only a limited part of the
generally infinite function, which brings into discussion the so-
called approximation of the infinite by the finite (in computer
terms, the evaluation of algorithms by machines).

Recently, artificial intelligence concepts (Reichman-Adar 1984,
pp. 157–218) have suggested ways to improve this function. The
problem to be approached in this respect is the presentation of a
computable function in machine language. Operationally satisfactory
definitions for computable functions are far from being a trivial
issue. The designer of interface (process interface in this case) should
be aware of the semiotic implications of this issue. We can refer
to compiler-related aspects as a particular case pertaining to the
same segment of communication (see Figure 23). Very relevant here
is the metalinguistic function, since what actually goes on is "translation" (from programming language to machine language). We refer
to three semiotic aspects of such translations: Is it faithful? How
complex is it? How efficient is it? Although the user is not distinctly
referred to in this segment, the formal (poetic) function is very
important. The programming language influences the way the search
for syntactic errors takes place and, in the case of more advanced
systems, the so-called level of gravity (permissiveness of the system).
Some languages better support this function by allowing a higher
level of gravity (that is, although a program may have some errors,

it is "accepted" in the processing phase). More recently developed programming languages provide an improved formal function.

The last segment to be considered concerns the computer user (see Figure 24). Basically, this segment deals with the way the results of computing (finite subset of the range of the computable function used) are made available/communicated to the user (assuming that the program was accepted and run and that the data was compatible with the software requirements). Semantic considerations are prevalent in this segment. The user ignores the metalinguistic function if the program performs well. In a debugging mode, this function becomes very important. As I have already shown, interface designers treat application environments and programming and debugging environments as though they were totally independent.

In short, the model presented here introduces normative concepts which interface designers should observe. It also suggests that evaluation should take place more systematically, submitting by explicit requirements a set of criteria derived from the semiotic perspective on which this model is built. Some requirements are already known (some even observed!); others have not been adopted in design interface. What is perhaps more important, the model explains the interrelation between the requirements, making clear that a system with high performance and low permissiveness—to mention one example—undermines the purpose of a user friendly interface. The vocabulary used in explaining the semiotic implications is of marginal importance. I do not suggest that designers learn this vocabulary, but that their understanding of what is explained by using

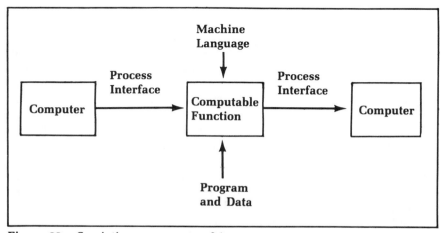

Figure 23. Semiotic components of inner computer processes.

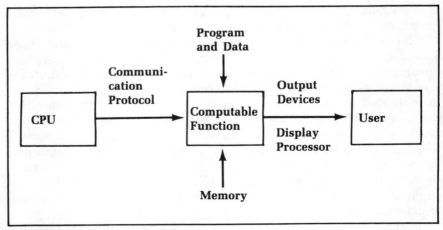

Figure 24.   Semiotics of output.

these concepts can be improved. Entrenchment in jargon—and this holds true also for the computer jargon ("computerese")—annihilates the spirit of interdisciplinarity that we all agree upon.

ACCOUNTING FOR THE USER'S COGNITIVE CHARACTERISTICS

If we intend to deal with a user as concretely determined as possible, we have to incorporate results of cognitive studies of humans in the knowledge used for improved interface design. Some human characteristics are fuzzy: attention, response, adequacy of sign interpretation, to name a few. Others, while perhaps significant in work with tools different from computers, only marginally affect interaction between user and computer: endurance, sociability, exercise of physical strength, to name a few in this category. Attention should be given also to affordance parameters, reflecting environmental requirements and a better understanding of the relation human being–environment. Partially, ergonomic considerations cover such affordance parameters. In each of the above cases, semiotics is involved mainly in the way people externalize their opinions and beliefs and in how they express themselves and make their expressions understandable to others. In a matrix characterizing the future user, we should also deal with how human beings form their representations, beliefs, ideas, doubts, i.e., the internal semiotic characteristics of thought processes and emotions. Cognitive scientists agree with semiotic theories concerning the semiotic nature of thinking as well as the semiotic implications of feeling. One aspect of immediate practical relevance can be given as an example.

Whether the distinction left–right hemispheres of the brain can be sustained or not—an issue very much on the minds of psychologists and cognitive scientists—we cannot ignore the semiotic observation that signs can be structured in sequence (arrays of symbols) or configuration (e.g., visual constructions). The two modes in which we perceive and organize information are reflected in the characteristics of their interpretation. As far as we know, human beings process symbolic information mainly sequentially. Computers function the same way. Configurational systems of signs are processed by human beings in a parallel way. In the first case, a predominantly analytical dimension is apparent; in the second, a synthetic dimension. In sequential processing of signs, there is a dominant attempt to differentiate; in configurational, integration dominates. Time is related to sequence (our time representations are sequential), while space is related to configuration (see Figure 25). The two modes are interrelated, interfere with, or try to suppress each other; under certain circumstances, they enhance each other. To involve the user in a homogenous environment, i.e., to avoid abrupt switching from one mode to the other, is a minimal requirement almost consistently ignored by interface designers. Even when the designer provides a pointing device (e.g., a mouse), one type of user will rely on emulating keys in order to avoid swift changes that in several tests have proven exhausting (Patterson, 1983, pp. 75–82). A second requirement, reflecting the fact that users are so different, is to give the user a choice of dominant mode. Cooperation or interference between the basic cognitive modes takes place through both hardware and software (see Figure 26).

Physical properties (of the keyboard, display, printer, pointing device, etc.) are but an extension of the properties of the system in its entirety. While aesthetic and functional criteria are difficult to encode, they influence the design of the interface. No matter how attractively the mouse is designed, if the user is forced to switch often from pointing (configuration semiotics) to the keyboard (sequence semiotics), the design is inappropriate. To provide a really user-friendly interface means to make possible not everything, only what is acceptable. Aesthetic and functional acceptability, as well as cultural adequacy, are becoming ever more critical qualities once computer technology matures. Only a superficial designer, who targets the lower level of the market, thinks that cultural adequacy is reducible to emulation of characters used in foreign languages. Unfortunately, almost nothing is ever attempted beyond this. (IBM

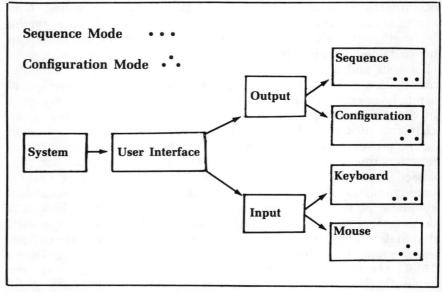

Figure 25.   Sequence vs. configuration.

is a rare exception, AT&T a promising challenger, with impressive
user interface accomplishments, especially on systems designed for
internal use or switches). Typically, designers approaching interface
issues, particularly communication aspects, are obsessed with quantitative aspects or make decisions based on intuition. Neither can
be ignored, but to reduce interface issues to quantity is unacceptable.

An example of how this direction should be pursued is given by
the Vivarium Project, a curriculum-driven project seeking to teach
children about animals and initiated by Alan Kay. In her paper,
Allison Druin (1986, p. 2), a former student of mine, currently a
graduate student in the MIT Media Lab, asks: What will the next
generation of computer learning tools be? From among many semiotic aspects of the Vivarium, Allison Druin (1986, p. 2) concen-
trates on one alternative (the furry computer called Noobie) to the
traditional terminal: "a soft and inviting environment, which sur-
rounds the child, and looks like a five-foot version of the squeezable
input device . . . what emerged was the idea of a tactile computing
environment in which the child would sit and create animals in
the actual input device." We notice here several ideas relevant to
the approach: the "universal" tool can be adapted to various tasks,
not only through its application programs—which is the dominant
strategy today—but also through an interface design adapted to the

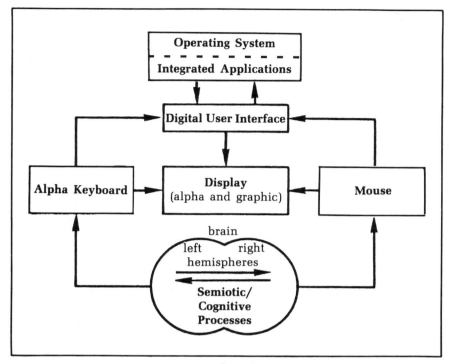

Figure 26.   Integrating sequence and configuration.

cognitive characteristics of the activity that the computer will support. Adaptation of the tool to the problem will take place through
the intermediary of different interfaces that are part of the system
and that simultaneously connect the system with other environments: the user, other systems of education such as toys, stuffed
animals, drawings, animation, entertainment. (It is no accident that
the Henson Group is involved in this project.) Programs are abstract
entities which obey formal rules. Applications, such as editing a
document and retrieving from a database, cause an abstract entity
(document, database) approachable through appropriate interface to
have a concrete reality: Documents receive names; information can
be ordered and formatted according to needs.

In short, using a computer means to make the abstract concrete.
As opposed to typewriters, a word processing program is *all* the
typewriters which can exist. A database program has the same
characteristic. The designers of the Vivarium understood this semiotic peculiarity of computer tools, extended the limit to which
the abstract program is made concrete, and integrated even the

terminal and input devices. Indeed, the study of animals by children cannot be reduced to an exercise in typing on the typical keyboard, or to a display, no matter how sophisticated, on a CRT screen. There is more to the experience of such a class. There is the sense of touch, the sense of proportion, sound, etc. Correspondence to the real world will be ensured through an improved convention of likeness. This treatment of interface makes several channels of interaction necessary.

PRESENT AND FUTURE

The different ways users interact with interface devices is very important and should be accounted for in design specifications. But while we understand how the machines we build work, and even manage to find out why their functioning sometimes seems "irrational," we only partially understand processes in which our thinking and emotions are involved. Some progress has been made in understanding behavioral aspects; cognitive processes have been extensively and intensively researched, too. The results are frequently applied in the design of interfaces. The following aspects are routinely observed: message from user to computer, feedback, and computing and return of results. But, as was already mentioned, interfacing goes well beyond these and extends to everything a user will come in contact with when using a system and getting output from it (on CRT display, slide, film, hardcopy, etc.). Two attitudes regarding how interface should be approached can be identified:

1. Emulate the current human way of thinking and acting on the computer. ("It is important that the formal computer procedures do not prevent the user from changing his representation of the problem or task environment necessary to reach the best solution."*)
2. Challenge the user with a totally new language, thus with a totally new way of thinking and acting.

In both cases, a better understanding of what languages are, how they are used, and how they work is necessary. Our expectations are reliability, with tolerance towards the user if possible, self-sufficiency, ease of use, and adaptability. All relate to the semiotic qualities of interface language. We can distinguish between as many

---

* This is a quotation whose source I no longer know.

languages, as many senses, as we have; and this distinction encouraged the Vivarium concept. A "taste" statement can go as a
mixture of, or succession from, sour, bitter, sweet. . . . hot, warm,
cold . . . or can represent an example of a touch-interpreted statement. The same holds for smell. Programs to take advantage of this
have been written or seriously considered. Van Dam (1984, p. 646)
confirmed this when he stated, "The computer interface may eventually metamorphose into a total sensory environment." This being
the case, we have to prepare ourselves for the challenge of the task
by understanding the specific semiotics of each sensory environment
through paying attention to general semiotic principles.

The main system of signs are the visual and the verbal (natural
language). In reality, the distinction is less obvious, and influences
between both are very important. Another distinction is between
natural and formal languages. A suggestive representation can be
given as a matrix (see Figure 27). Voice input devices, or other I/
O features (heat sensitive, touch sensitive, for instance), will of
course require a more sophisticated matrix which is not just multidimensional but also reflects influences between the different components. The distinction of visual–verbal first of all refers to possible
forms of representation. The distinction of natural–formal refers to
the logical structure and thus to the nature of language (cultural
vs. artificial). The matrix takes combinations into consideration, too.
Formal verbal languages may prove difficult for people to read or
write in. Such languages require special training and a competence
level demanded by specialized fields (mathematics, symbolic logic,
language programming, dance, music, etc.). Reading text written in
a programming language, or a musical score, or a choreographic
laba-notation is difficult. Formal visual languages may prove difficult
to "write" in but can be read more easily (not necessarily with
precision). Research has recently approached such languages and
the attempts to resuscitate visual modes based on pictographic representation or to improve such forms of visual representation (e.g.,
diagrams, charts, lists, etc.). Although controlled by grammar, natural
languages are easier to write in because this grammar is not as
rigidly specified as the grammar of formal languages. On the other
hand, it is harder to be specific, precise, and to avoid ambiguity in
natural language. In the cultural environment, this is an advantage
evidenced by qualities which are usually not duplicated in formal
languages. This is not to say that natural language is easier to use,
as so many assume. Bar-Hillel (1970) maintained that natural languages are essentially pragmatic-free. Whether something fundamental has changed since 1970 in respect to our understanding of

the pragmatics of formal languages, or to the way such languages are used, is a matter of controversy. Nevertheless, the pragmatics of natural languages is far more difficult than the pragmatics of any other language (formal included). What we address here are issues of language use in two different environments: one in which the user is comfortable, since it is the environment of his or her everyday life; and the second, in which the user faces something less familiar, in which interface should play a mediating role. "The ideal situation," as van Dam (1984, p. 646) described it, in tune with many computer scientists and/or science-fiction writers, "would be to interact with the computer as if it were a helpful human being, perhaps chatting in natural language."

Progress in better emulating natural languages (English basically) is to be expected, but the use of natural languages can become possible only on computers applying the logic of such languages. In reviewing this paper, Tom Carey tried to convince us that there is no reason why multi-valued logic cannot be simulated. Interface is a trade-off in which amount and type (of signs used) are the fundamental parameters. Norman (1983, p. 1), who introduced a remarkable quantitative method for trade-off analysis, makes the basic

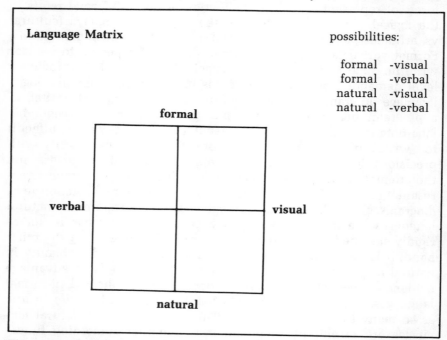

Figure 27.   Language matrix.

statement: "Any single design technique is apt to have its virtues along one dimension compensated by deficiencies along another." Maybe Figure 28 will explain the kind of trade-off implicit in the semiotic decision involved in the design of interfaces:

In the Programmer's Hierarchical Interactive Graphics System (also known as PHIGS), goals specific to rendering visual presentation of information require a semiotic structure which supports interaction. As a toolset, the system permits model building and manipulation. Its transformation pipeline starts with visual primitives (modeling of coordinates) on which operations corresponding to viewing (from world coordinates to viewing coordinates, according to the photographic camera metaphor), clipping, and mapping are applied. The workstation independent elements are interfaced with workstation dependent elements. The organization of data is multilevel. Obviously we have here an implementation of a formal language in which the predefined grammar applies to images. As an interactive graphics interface, it supports a semantics specific to images and not to natural language statements. PHIGS is an integrated, interdisciplinary approach to interface which considers the contribution of each component. Semiotics coordinates the relation between everything that participates in interfacing. Product design, software engineering, hardware, ergonomics, etc.—highly specialized fields—should each in turn be evaluated and integrated in the comprehensive language of the product using PHIGS. Of course, semiotics has to provide the necessary means required. Recent

Natural Language	Formal Language
general	specific
unlimited vocabulary	limited vocabulary
indefinite grammar	predefined grammar
intuitive structure	logical structure
easily acquired competence	difficult to acquire competence
difficult to obtain performance	easy to attain high performance/ easy to learn

Communications Characteristics of Formal Languages

write	select	read
understand system	read system	model system
concrete knowledge	intuition	intuition
have purpose	have purpose	indefinite purpose
syntax error	semantics error	semantics error

Figure 28. Natural vs. formal languages.

contributions (cf. Winograd and Flores, 1986; Lakoff, 1987) concerning conception of the mind and understanding of computers suggest alternative strategies for designing computer systems. It seems that the maturing of technology and difficulties in accounting for failures affecting people's use of computer technology made the need for improved understanding of human–computer interaction more critical than at any previous time.

FINAL REMARK

In concluding one of the most passionate debates of the CHI '86 ACM-SIGCHI Conference on Human Factors in Computing Systems (Boston, April 1986)—the one between Stu Card and Don Norman— moderator Richard Pew noted that it explored whether "systematic effort applied to interface design is a worthwhile effort." This chapter contributes to an affirmation without ignoring that "design through natural evolution" (comparable to the natural evolution of our use of various signs) brings its own contribution. Method helps intuition if it is not transformed into dictatorship. Intuition augments method if it does not instill anarchy. In every moment of our semiotic existence, method and intuition complement each other.

ACKNOWLEDGEMENTS

The author is grateful to Leif Allmendinger, Thomas Ockerse, Richard Zakia, and Harvey Carapella for valuable comments and for providing some of the figures used here. In addition, the author thanks his students from the class, "Semiotics of Computer-Aided Human Activity", held at The Rochester Institute of Technology in Spring, 1984, during his tenure as William A. Kern Institute Professor in Communications, and "Computer Graphics-Graphics Design Issues," Autumn 1984, RISD. The reviewers, Dennis Wixon and Tom Carey, as well as the editors, Rex Hartson and Deborah Hix, provided criticism and questioned many of my views. If the chapter improved and is at the level of their expectations, I gladly share with them in the credit it deserves. Shortcomings are, of course, my responsibility.

REFERENCES

Bar-Hillel, Y. (1970). Communication and argumentation in pragmatic languages. In Y. Bar-Hillel (Ed.), *Pragmatics of natural languages.* New York: Humanities Press.

Bühler, K. (1933). Die Axiomatik der Sprachwissenschaft. *Kant Studien, 38,* 19–90.

Calude, C., & Marcus, S. (1985). Introduction to the Semiotics of Man–Computer Communication. In M. Nadin (Ed.), *New elements in the semiotics of communication.* Tübingen: Gunter Narr Verlag.

Druin, A. (1986). *A Vivarium project* (MIT Media Laboratory Working Papers). July. Cambridge, MA.

Goldberg, A., & Robson, D. (1979). A metaphor for user interface design. *Proceedings 12th Hawaii International Conference System Sciences, 6*(1), 148–157.

Haber, R.N., & Myers, B.L. (1982). Memory for pictograms, pictures, and words separately and all mixed up. *Perception, 11,* 57–67.

Jakobson, R. (1960). Linguistics and poetics. In T. Sebeok (Ed.), *Style and language.* Cambridge, MA: MIT Press.

Ketner, K.L. (with the assistance of A.F. Stewart) (1984). The early history of computer design. Charles Sanders Peirce and Marquand's logical machines. *The Princeton University Library Chronicle, XLV* (3), 187–225.

Lakoff, G. (1987). *Women, fire, and dangerous things. What categories reveal about the mind.* Chicago/London: The University of Chicago Press.

Marcus, A. (1983, July). Graphic design for computer graphics. *IEEE, 3*(4) 63–69. Los Alamitos, CA: True Seaborn.

Marcus, A. (1983). Designing iconic interfaces. *Nicograph 83,* pp. 103–122. Tokyo: Seminar Notes.

Meyrowitz, N., & van Dam, A. (1982). Interactive editing systems. *Computing Surveys, 14*(3), 323.

Nadin, M. (1981). *Zeichen und Wert* [Sign and value]. Tübingen: Narr Verlag.

Nadin, M. (1986). Design machine. Columbus: Art and design technology research notes.

Norman, D.A. (1983). Design principles for human–computer interfaces. Human Factors in Computing Systems CHI '83. *Proceedings.* New York: ACM.

Patterson, M.L. (1983, November). Graphical interface design considerations. *Computer Graphics World, 6*(11), 75–82. Tulsa, OK: Pennwell Publications.

Peirce, C.S. (1932). *The collected papers of Charles Sanders Peirce* (C. Hartshorne & P. Weiss, Eds., Vol. 2). Cambridge, MA: Harvard University Press.

Reichman-Adar, R. (1984). Extended person-machine interface. *Artificial Intelligence, 22,* 157–218.

Schneider, M.L., & Thomas, J.C. (Eds.). (1983). Introduction: the humanization of computer interfaces. *ACM Communications 26*(4), 252–253.

Shannon, C., & Weaver, W. (1947). *The mathematical theory of communication.* Urbana, IL: University of Illinois Press.

Simon, H. (1982). *The sciences of the artificial.* Cambridge, MA: MIT Press.

Tesler, L. (1981). The Smalltalk environment. *Byte,* August, p. 90.

Thacker, C.P., McCraight, E.M., Lampson, B.W., Spronll, R.F., & Boggs, D.R. (1979). *Alto: A personal computer* (Report CSL-79-11). Palo Alto, CA: Xerox Palo Alto Research Center.

van Dam, A. (1984). Computer graphics comes of age [interview]. *ACM Communications, 27*(7), 646.

Winograd, T., and Flores, F. (1986). *Understanding computers and cognition. A new foundation for design.* Norwood, NJ: Ablex Publishing Corp.

Zadeh, L. (1984). Coping with the impression of the real world [interview]. *ACM Communications, 27*(4), 304–311.

CHAPTER 3

The Problem of Levels and Automatic Response Generation in a "Let's Talk About It" Strategy

Kemal Efe

Computer Science Department
University of Missouri–Columbia

THE PROBLEM OF LEVELS

Because most computer users are not familiar with how their systems work beyond their terminal screen, there is a problem of levels in error message generation in interactive software systems. The problem of levels arises when an error occurs at a program execution level lower than that of the user. The problem is that the error messages are generated by lower level operations unknown to the user. To illustrate the problem of levels, consider an airline reservation clerk who uses a software package on the job. To find out who is booked on flight 173 from Heathrow on October 1, 1986, the clerk might type a command such as

Listbookings (Heathrow, 173, 10/1/86)

In response to this command, an error message such as

1) Buffer area is full, can not complete the creation of file 173100186.TEMP. Reset buffer to 256 records

is issued by the system. This message will not make much sense to the user whose intention is to see a listing of passengers booked on a certain flight. What buffer area is being talked about? Why did the system have to create a file called "173100186.TEMP"? The "friendly" system even told the user what to do to fix the error:

"Reset buffer to 256 records." But how does one "reset" the buffer? To answer these questions, the user needs to know the following

The heart of the reservation package is a database management system. When the system was being set up, the management decided to keep all of the bookings in monthly files. That is, all of the bookings made during a month would go into a special set of files designated for that month, irrespective of their destination, date, flight number, ticket number, etc. The management would keep these files to use in its trend analysis and other high level management decisions.

Given this requirement, the system designer sets up the system so that the command

Listbookings ("airport," "flight-number," "date")

searches for the records with matching keys for the specified airport, flight number, and date. Those records are stored in a temporary file which has a name reflecting the flight number and date; hence the file name "173100186.TEMP." This temporary file is stored in a special buffer for the screen display program to go and find it.

The size of that buffer was originally set to 250 records, since all of the planes that the company deals with take at most 250 passengers. After using this system for many months, the management was alert to see that, among 250 bookings, there were up to 10 last-minute cancellations in most of the flights. To utilize these unused seats, the management decided to make up to 260 reservations for each flight. Should more than 250 passengers turn up, they could provide alternative flights for some passengers.

In the case of the above message, there were 256 bookings. The system did not complain while the bookings were made. The trouble occurred while putting those 256 records into a buffer with a maximum size of 250 records.

The situation described here is imaginary and it does not represent any real system. Nevertheless, it represents the general flavor of messages generated by many actual systems. For example, the message below is generated by 4.2BSD UNIX while formatting files on the terminal (see Lewis & Norman, 1986, for a more detailed discussion of this message).

2) Longjmp botch: core dumped.

Another actual system signals the following message as a response to a print command

3) Error creating file.

The problem with these messages is that, among many other things, they are signalled by a lower level operation which is invoked by the user command. In the case of message (2) above, the user commmand invokes a lower level command, called "more" for screen display of the formatted file. "More" gets into trouble of some unknown nature, and crashes, signalling this message. In the case of message (3), the "print" command invokes another command to create a temporary print file. But the memory is full and print file can not be created.

Figure 1 illustrates this concept schematically. The user types the command Pi, which invokes lower level processes such as Pj. Pj may in turn invoke other lower level processes, and so on. An error is detected at the lowest level by Pl and Pl signals an error message.

For the system operator, a message like "longjmp botch," generated by operation Pl, may be just the information needed to fix

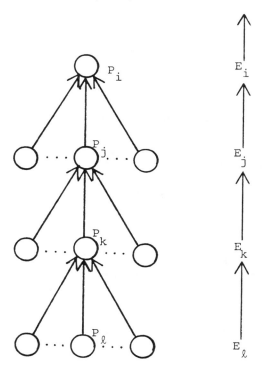

Figure 1.

the error. For the user, however, an error message generated by lower level operations cannot be expected to make sense. As far as the user is concerned, the command the user issues is an indivisible operation. That is, the user is not aware of the existence or the purpose of lower level processes. Furthermore, although the combined effects of lower level operations may amount to the user command, there is a distinction between the user's intention and the intention of individual operations in the lower levels. For example, the user's intention is to print a file, while a lower level operation invoked by "print" command attempts to create a temporary print file. Despite this distinction in intentions, the error message generated by "create" command is designed on the assumption that the user intended to create a file.

It is possible for low level operations to generate messages that make sense in the user's level of intention? The answer is almost always "no," unless the lower level operation "knows" the user's intention, or the message says

4) There is a difficulty in carrying out your command. I cannot explain to you what it is. Call the operator.

The difficulty in error message generation in such cases is due to the fact that a lower level operation may be invoked by many different commands serving radically different user intentions. In this sense, a more realistic representation of a system may be the one shown in Figure 2 rather than Figure 1. Figure 2 shows two levels of intentions, but there may be many such levels in general. An operation at level i may invoke many processes at level i–1. Conversely, a process at level i–1 may be invoked by many different operations at level i. When designing an error message for a low level operation, it is difficult to find the magic phrase which is informative and makes sense in the context of every possible user intention.

"LET'S TALK ABOUT IT" STRATEGY AS THE ANSWER

The problem of levels in response message generation was also recognized by other researchers (Draper, 1986; Lewis & Norman, 1986), who proposed a "Let's Talk About It" strategy (LTAI) as a possible solution, although they did not discuss how to implement such a method. In this strategy, the system first generates a message

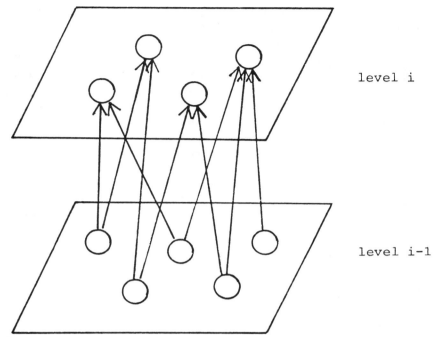

level i

level i-1

Figure 2.

at the highest level of intension, indicating that there has been a difficulty. Lewis and Norman (1986, p. 428) comment:

> Let the user be given tools to explore the problem to whatever depth is desired. Let the user be able to trace down the levels, to see where the original mismatch occurred, how that level was reached, and the state of system at each level. The programmer can explore in detail: The experienced user can explore until the basic problem is clear, and the uninterested can remain uninterested. . . . This kind of constructive interaction with the system has the possibility of solving the levels problem along with the error message problem.

The purpose of this chapter is to describe how an LTAI strategy can be implemented. The original research on the problem of levels was performed while the author was at Leeds University, England, as part of a project in designing user oriented operating system interfaces for computer networks (Efe & Hopper, 1981; Efe, Miller, & Hopper, 1983). However, the basic concepts involved in error message generation are applicable to any interactive software. In-deed, to test the results of this research in an application different from the originally intended area of operating systems, a prototype system was designed which simulated a desk calculator. The following is a typical dialogue that the system is capable of carrying out: Suppose the user typed the "+" command, forgetting that there is only one value in the memory. The system initially generates the message

System: I can not add two values, because there is only one value

The user can initiate a dialogue to trace down the levels of program execution by typing "why?"

User: Why?
System: To add two values I needed to get the two values, but there is only one value.
User: Why?
System: To get the two values I needed to get the first value, which I did.
User: Then?
System: Then I needed to get the second value, but there are no more values.
User: OK

The user has the option to quit this dialogue at any stage by typing "OK." Assuming it is required to trace down the levels as far as possible, the message "That is all" indicates that the level of error has been reached. This will be illustrated later in a longer version of the above dialogue.

One might convincingly argue that, in the case of "+"operation, there is no need to generate error messages: a default value of zero may be used for the second operand. This is indeed the case for most desk calculators. However, the purpose of the implemented system is not to fix errors, but to report them. It is designed to test if the LTAI strategy works the way the theoretical research indicated it would.

In the later sections of this chapter, examples are given through the desk calculator program, how it is designed, and how do various mechanisms for error message generation work. But the designed system of error message generation is not a special purpose program for the desk calculator. It is a general purpose mechanism which automatically generates error messages, or carries out dialogues, for any interactive software for which a system description is provided. System descriptions take the form of a declarative data base which describes the operations allowed at each level of the system, and their interrelationships represented as an invocation tree with accompanying tables. Detailed discussion of the system description is given in the section on "System Description." Figure 3 shows the invocation tree for the "+" operation as it is implemented in the desk calculator program. Such invocation trees are also automatically constructed from formal specifications of interactive user packages, which are needed in any case for other purposes.

WHY AUTOMATIC MESSAGE GENERATION

To explain the motivations for automatic generation of error messages, it may be appropriate to consider the alternatives first. Let us reconsider the question: "Is it possible for low level operations to generate messages that make sense in the user's level of intention?" The answer given earlier was "no," unless the lower level operation "knows" the user's intention or unless a noninformative message like (4) is generated. The option of generating messages like (4) may be necessary under certain circumstances as will be discussed in the Summary section. The immediate question is, how can lower level operations "know" the intention of the user?

One method may be just to follow and extend the most common approach to message generation in the existing systems: when an error occurs at the user's level of intention, one of the messages among a prepacked set is signalled. The detailed organization of the mechanism may vary among systems; the set of error messages may be kept in an indexed table where an index is chosen depending on the error which occurred, or the set of messages may be distributed over a program, each message being signalled to the user by the failing operation itself.

This method may be extended to message generation by low level operations by turning on a flag to indicate the calling operation, every time a low level operation is invoked. By inspecting the states of flags, the low level operation will "know" who the caller is and the intention of user. In this method, suppose an operation Pj immediately below the user level may be called by n different user level operations. Then, n different error messages may be designed for each error that may occur while Pj is running. One of these messages may then be signalled, depending on the states of flags.

This method serves the purpose, but it has serious limitations. First of all, referring back to Figure 2, each level-i operation may be called by many operations in the higher level, and in general

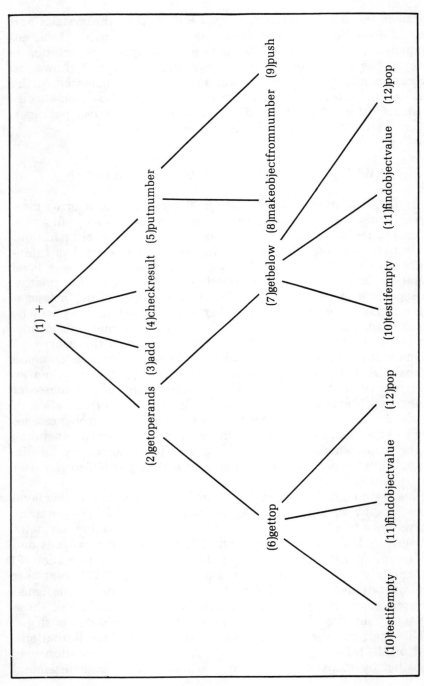

Figure 3.

there may be many levels of intentions. Consider a situation where an operation Pk may be called by m different operations, each of which may be called by n different operations, each of which may be called by k different operations, etc. It is not difficult to see that the number of situations in which a low level operation Pk can be called quickly reaches exponential proportions (for three levels, there are mxnxk possibilities for each error which may occur while Pk is running). When it is necessary to distinguish between these situations, as in the LTAI strategy, the number of distinct flag states and message packages becomes prohibitive.

The second disadvantage of this method is that, supposing the system designer took the challenge of designing such a mechanism, it will work only for the particular software package for which it is designed. To implement the same mechanism for a different product, the system designer needs to start from scratch.

In the proposed model, error messages are constructed automatically from the description of the application package being used. Hence, the problem of designing and maintaining a large number of messages is eliminated. Also, the response generator needs to be designed once, and it can be used for any application package as long as a formal description of the package is provided. Provision of the system description is needed in any case, at least as a guideline while it is being built. Finally, the use of the proposed model provides uniformity in the style of response messages among the application packages that use it.

In various examples in the rest of this chapter, the desk calculator program is used. Therefore, a brief description of this program is given below. In the next section, the response generation mechanism is described in detail, and the theoretical issues involved in implementing this model are identified. The following sections discuss these issues in detail, giving examples from the desk calculator implementation. The conclusions include the discussions of remaining problems for future research.

THE DESK CALCULATOR PROGRAM

The program designed to test the LTAI strategy simulates a desk calculator with two memories; (a) a stack as a work space for storing temporary results until they are assigned to a variable, and (b) an array with 26 memory locations for the main memory which holds the variables "A" to "Z." All of the calculations are carried out by using the values on top of the stack. The top of the stack contains the "current" value that is most recently calculated or input from the terminal. The user can save this value into the memory by assigning it to a variable. In this case, the stack is popped and the next value becomes the "current" value.

The operations that the user can perform are given below. On the left is the system designer's view of the system functions, while on the right is the novice user's view of the same set of operations. This difference between the system designer's view and that of the user exists because the user is not familiar with the internal details of the program.

=	Assign to variable or top of stack the value below it.	Assign to Most Recent (MR) variable the MR value before it.
+	Replace top 2 values by sum.	Add two MR values.
-	Replace top 2 values by below-top	Subtract MR from Next-MR (NMR)
*	Replace top 2 values by below*top	Multiply MR with NMR
/	Replace top 2 values by below/top	Divide NMR by MR
°	Replace top by its negative	Negate MR
s	Replace top by its sine	sine(MR)
c	Replace top by its cos	Cos(MR)
l	Replace top by its log	Log(MR)
t	Replace top by its tan	Tan(MR)
x	Replace top by its exp	Exp(MR)
p	print top	print MR
P	print entire stack	print all values
e	erase top	erase MR
E	erase entire stack	erase all values
W	wipe memory array	erase all variables

Variables are denoted by a single upper or lower case letter preceded by %. %A and %a are not distinguished. The variables %P and %E are set to pi and e, respectively. All operations are postfix, and inputs is in reverse polish notation. The user does not know of the system stack or the memory array. All the user knows is that, by default, operations are carried out on the most recent values that are computed or that are input from the terminal. To be able to use less recent results, the user should get rid of the more recent ones, either by assigning them to variables or by erasing them.

The novice user is told that one can either enter values and commands one at a time, or enter several of them in one line. It is, however, recommended to enter them one at a time until the user is an expert user. For example, to calculate B*X+C for X=2, B=3, C=1, one would type the following steps:

```
2                         ; input x
3                         ; input b
*                         ; find B*X
1                         ; input C
+                         ; find (B*X)+C
p                         ; print the result.
```

It is expected that the user will eventually discover the post-fix notation to write a "program" calculating this expression as:

```
2, %X, =, 3, %B, =, 1, %C =    ;  initialize variables
%B, %X, *, %C, +, p            ;  calculate B*X+C
                               ;  and print result.
```

THE MESSAGE GENERATION MODEL

As noted earlier, an error message signalled at any level of the system is designed on the assumption that the receiver is the caller of that operation. There is, of course, nothing wrong with this assumption, if the command is activated by the user. The trouble occurs when the user is not the caller of that operation. Based on this idea, in the proposed model, lower level operations do not signal any messages to the user. The user only ever receives messages from an operation Pi which the user has invoked, or, in the case of a dialogue in the LTAI strategy, messages are generated by the highest level operation being traced by the user.

Conceptually, this mechanism works as follows: referring back to the invocation tree in Figure 1, when a lower level operation Pl detects an error, say El, it signals this error to its caller, Pk. Pk receives this error signal, interprets its significance for its own purposes, and if necessary signals another error to its caller Pj, and so on. Eventually, the error signal propagates up to the user command Pi, which generates a message for the user. Now this message will make sense to the user, because it is generated by the user command Pi.

In the case of LTAI strategy, an error message will be generated by a low level operation after the user has traced down to this level, and has been told the purpose of that operation. By repeating the process of telling the user about intention of low level processes and the cause of error at that level, it is expected that the error messages will make sense to the user all the way down to the lowest level of intention.

This outlines the basic idea behind the model described here. Figure 4 shows the basic components of this model. In order to keep the mechanisms of error propagation and message generation independent of the application program, these processes are implemented separately as an independent unit. This unit constitutes the "message generator." The message generator performs the same routine no matter what application package is used. Therefore, it is also possible to time share it among many application packages, as long as a system description is provided for each package.

The context stack is used to store currently active operation names. At the bottom there is always a command invoked by the user. Newer operations are pushed as they are invoked by higher levels. An operation is popped from the stack after its successful completion. Thus, the context stack provides a means of monitoring the system's state, and is used in message generation in order to determine the exact path in the invocation tree, where the error has occurred.

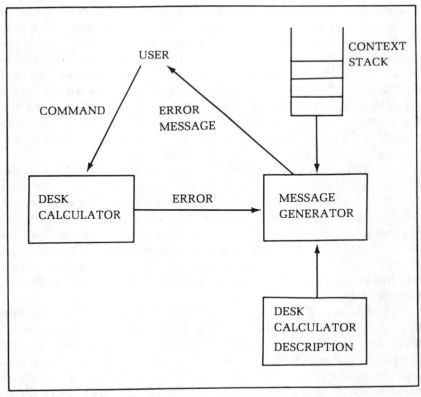

Figure 4.

The system description consists of three modules. The first of these modules contains a set of invocation trees, one tree for each user command. The second module is a table of pieces of text which informally describe what each operation is supposed to do. The entries in this table are indexed according to index numbers associating the command names in the invocation trees. For example, the entries for the index numbers in the invocation tree of Figure 3 are shown in Figure 5. The third module is another table that contains text informally describing error conditions, one entry for each error. Figure 6 shows these entries for all possible error conditions in the invocation tree of Figure 3. All of these data structures are constructed from formal system description supplied for the programmer. This issue is discussed in detail in the section on "Error Handling and Propogation."

To illustrate how these mechanisms work in the LTAI strategy, suppose the user has typed the "+" command, forgetting that there is only one value in the calculator's memory. The first thing "+" does is to push its name in the context stack. Then, "+" invokes its lower level operations (immediate children in the invocation tree) in the order prescribed by its algorithm (shown left-to-right).

```
 1. add two values
 2. get the two values
 3. find sum of two values
 4. check the validity of result
 5  store the value to workspace
 6. get the first value
 7. get the second value
 8. prepare value for storing
 9. store the value to workspace
10. check if workspace is empty
11. interpret the value
12. dispose the value in workspace
```

Figure 5.

error	phrase
onlyone	there is only one value
nomore	there is no more value
empty	workspace is empty
NIL	the value is nil
toobig	the result is too big
toosmall	the result is too small
novalue	there is no value in workspace

Figure 6.

This is repeated for each operation called, all the way down to the lowest levels. When an operation completes its task successfully, it pops its name from the context stack before terminating. An operation is considered successful when all of its children in the invocation tree have terminated successfully.

When an error is detected in the lowest level of program execution, the current state of the context stack is preserved. The set of nodes in the context stack constitute a path in the invocation tree, from the root down to the terminal node where the error has occurred. This path is called the "error path." In the case of "+" operation, an error is detected inside "getbelow" by the operation "testifempty." "Getbelow" is called by "getoperands," which is called by "+." The context stack in Figure 7a shows the nodes in the error path when this error occurs.

The error detected by "testifempty" is "empty," but, before generating a message, this error is converted into another error in the

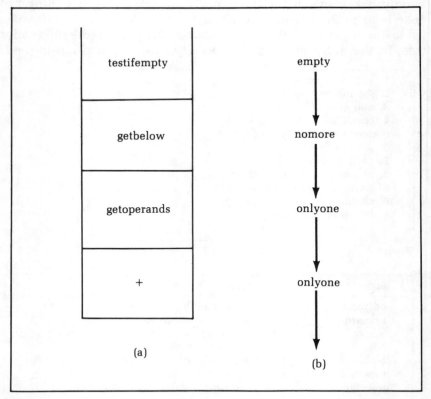

(a)

(b)

Figure 7.

user's level of intention. The mechanism of error conversion will be discussed in the following section. For the error case considered here, the following are the stages in error conversion. In the context of "getbelow," the error "empty" corresponds to the error "nomore." Therefore "empty" is converted into "nomore." Similarly, in the context of "getoperands," the error "nomore" corresponds to "onlyone," and, finally, in the context of "+" the error "onlyone" corresponds to itself (i.e., it is preserved). This is the error in the user's level of intention that is used in message generation.

In the implementation of the message generation mechanism, the names of exceptions are inserted into a list every time they are signalled to higher levels. The first exception inserted into the list corresponds to the lowest level operation, and the last one corresponds to the user command. The last exception name, together with the user command at the bottom of the stack, determine the initial error message generated. Figure 7b shows the list of exceptions corresponding to the operations in the error path for the error case considered here.

In generating a message from an error, a basic template is used. The template for highest level exceptions is in the form:

I CAN NOT <operation>, BECAUSE <error>

The "operation" and "error" are replaced by pieces of text explaining the operation invoked, and the error signalled. These are found in the tables for operation and error descriptions, i.e., modules 2 and 3 in the system description. For the error case considered here, the message obtained would be:

I can not add two values, because there is only one value.

Once the user is signalled an error message, the user can start a dialogue by typing: "why?" During a dialogue, a pointer T is used to indicate the "current" operation name in the invocation tree. In constructing a response message, the "current" operation name pointed by T is used as the "focus" of dialogue. That is, the error message first tells the purpose of the "current" operation, and then the error detected in the context of that operation. Initially, T points to the root of the invocation tree. Therefore, the message generated uses the root of the invocation tree as its context in its initial message.

During a dialogue, the user can type one of "why?" or "then?" to change the focus of dialogue, i.e., to move the pointer T between the nodes of the invocation tree. Every time T moves to a new node, a new message is generated in the context of the new node.

Figure 8 illustrates the possible pointer movements in a binary tree, depending on the user query, discussed below.

Why?: Moves the pointer T to the leftmost child of the node pointed to by T. If T is pointing to a terminal node that is in the error path, then T remains in its original place. In this case, a response of *"that is all"* is printed. If, however, T points to a terminal node that is not in the error path, then the effect of "why?" is the same as the effect of "then?" described below.

Then?: Moves the pointer T to the right sibling of the node pointed by T, subject to following exceptions:

1. If there is no right sibling, T moves to the right sibling of the parent of node pointed to by T. If the parent has no right sibling, then the parent of parent is considered, and so on. If none of the ancestors has a right sibling, then T remains in its original place. In this case, a message of "THAT IS ALL" is printed.
2. If the node pointed to by T is one of those in the error path, the effect of "then?" is same as the effect of "why?" above.

Depending on the user query, a certain template is used in the message constructed. These templates are as follows:

In the "why?" template, the "parent-op" refers to the parent of the node pointed to by T. "Current-op" is the node pointed to by T. Vertical bars represent different options in the message generated. If the node pointed to by T is in the error path, then "BUT <error>" option is used. Otherwise, no error has occurred in the operation

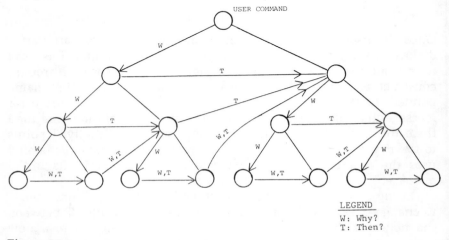

Figure 8.

why?:
> TO <parent-op> I NEEDED TO <current-op>, | BUT <error> |
> | WHICH I DID |

Then?:
> THEN I NEEDED TO <current-op>, | BUT   <error> |
> | WHICH I DID |

pointed to by T, and therefore the "WHICH I DID" option is used. Similar comments are valid for the "then?" template. Below, a dialogue is given to illustrate the use of these templates, together with the invocation tree of Figure 3 and other description modules in Figures 5 and 6.

User: why?
System: to add two values I needed to get the two values, but there is only one value
User: why?
System: to get the two values I needed to get the first value, which I did
User: then?
System: then I needed to get the second value, but there are no more values
User: then?
System: to get the second value I needed to check if there is any value in the workspace, but workspace is empty
User: then?
System: that is all.

In the first two messages, the "why?" template is used. The third message uses the "then?" template. In the fourth message, the "why?" template is used, although the user asked "then?" This is because the pointer T was pointing to an operation in the error path before the user asked "then?" Therefore, the effect of this query is same as the effect of "why?"

For any given error, there are many different dialogues possible, depending on the user queries. The number of different dialogues is equal to the number of distinct paths between the root of the invocation tree and the terminal node where the error has occurred. The actual path followed during a dialogue depends on the sequence of "why?" or "then?" queries that the user types. For example, if an error occurs in the rightmost terminal node in the tree of Figure 8, 10 different dialogues are possible, since there are 10 distinct paths from the root to this node. In general, it is well known from graph theory that the number of distinct paths in a graph increases as an exponential function of the number of nodes in it. For example, by adding one more level (i.e., 16 nodes) to the graph of Figure 8, the number of distinct paths from the root to the rightmost terminal node increases to 260. Generating such a large number of dialogues would only require adding 16 new lines of explanatory text for the new operations, and a proportional number of error text lines.

As can be seen from the above discussion, error detection, propagation, and formal system description are central to the implementation of the proposed model. The following sections discuss these issues in detail.

ERROR HANDLING AND PROPAGATION

In this section, error handling is considered as part of a system design discipline for software reliability. In a system consisting of many levels of procedure calls, the notion of "atomicity" of operations becomes a fundamental design concept. That is, as far as higher levels are concerned, the internal details of low level operations are irrelevant. A higher level operation only needs to know the input parameters needed by the lower level operations, and the results they return.

More formally, earlier researchers in software engineering characterized an atomic operation as follows: an atomic operation is one which does not communicate, during its execution, with other processes defined at the same level of abstraction. Performing an atomic operation causes no indirect state change as a side effect of its execution. An atomic operation is not aware of the existence of any other active processes, and no other process is aware of its activity. The reader may refer to Best (1980) for a detailed discussion of atomic operations.

With this formalism in mind, the notion of levels of intentions readily corresponds to that of levels of abstractions in software engineering terms. This concept is represented in a similar way to that in Figure 2. This time, a plane represents a level of abstraction. The circles at a plane represent atomic operations in this level, and the arrows between atomic operations represent mappings between two levels. As can be seen, many atomic operations at level i-1 may be "fused" into a single atomic operation at level i. Alternatively, a command at level i-1 may be called by many operations at level i.

When a command is received at the i'th level of abstraction, the system first determines the corresponding set of atomic operations in the lower level. Then these subcommands are activated in the order that is specified in the command definition. This is repeated at every level of abstraction, all the way down to the lowest level.

In this formalism, the notion of error is completely eliminated. Instead, one talks of an "exception." This is because the term *error* implies a mistake or negligence by the programmer that will cause the program to crash. An exception, on the other hand, implies a potential error that is anticipated by the programmer. The term *exception handling* refers to taking care of potential errors in a program in a systematic way. Errors cannot be tolerated in programs, whereas exceptions are inevitable facts of life.

In order to devise mechanisms for exception handling, it is necessary to better understand just what an exception is. In general, the term exception refers to an object state inconsistent with the purpose of a computation. It is important to realize that an *exceptional state* of an object is defined in relation to an operation applied to this object. No object state can be said to be exceptional in isolation. Without exception handlers, an atomic operation is a "partial" function whose behavior is defined for only a subset of input states. An inconsistent state of an object with respect to an operation is then a state for which program behavior is undefined. The purpose of using exception handlers is to make programs "total" functions by specifying back-up operations that are carried out if the primary operation cannot be activated because of state inconsistencies.

To detect exceptional conditions, the states of the objects used in an operation must be checked before the operation is activated. Thus, the definition of an atomic operation must include a set of routines for testing the states of the objects used during its execution. These test routines do not contribute to carrying on system functions, but are used solely to ensure that objects are in the right state for operations. They can be thought of as filters which pass an operation only if all the objects used in its execution are valid. Similar routines may also be activated after execution of an atomic operation, in which case the purpose is to ensure the validity of the result returned.

The test routines are not aware of the existence or purpose of higher levels, because they are defined independently of any command context. Therefore, they cannot judge the significance of their own results for the higher levels. For evaluating the results of test routines, command definitions include a set of interpretation rules. These interpretations depend upon the command semantics. Consider as an example a routine for checking the state of a stack. If the result returned by this routine is "empty," this might cause an exception in the context of a POP operation, while in the context of a PUSH operation it would be considered as a normal state.

As noted above, command definitions may also include definitions of alternative operations to be run when an atomic operation fails; i.e., it cannot be executed, either because the object states are not consistent with the purpose of operation, or because one of its constituent atomic operations fails. These alternatives may involve calling a back-up operation, or conveying the exception to the higher level. Thus, handling an exceptional object state means considering it as a valid state for the activation of a back-up operation and carrying out the execution accordingly. This is true even if the back-up operation decides to halt the execution. If no back-up operation is specified, then the exception is conveyed to the higher level, possibly as a different exception. This process continues until a back-up operation is found or the end-user is reached.

In light of this discussion, a formal specification of a command at level "i," including exceptional conditions, is given by a function, "R," as:

$$C = R \{ A, T, I \}.$$

Here, A is the set of atomic operations included in the command C. This set includes both primary atomic operations and the alternatives which are activated upon an exceptional condition. T is the set of test routines used in this command. A certain subset of T is associated with each member of A. I is the set of interpretations which decide whether a result returned by a test routine indicates an exception or not. R provides a set of regulations by which A, T, and I are put together. It defines the overall effect of the command.

Based on this philosophy, the mechanism of exception handling that serves as a basis in response generation is as follows: When a command is received at an abstraction level "i," test routines are activated to test the states of the objects involved. Then the results of test routines are interpreted in the context of the command. If all the interpretation results are positive, then the command itself is activated. When the command finishes executing, a final test-interpretation is made on the results returned by it. If all the interpretations yield positive outcomes, then it is concluded that the operation is completed successfully.

If an exceptional object state is detected, then an exceptional operation table is consulted. This table contains a list of all the anticipated exceptions and the corresponding back-up operations to be activated. Hence, a generic form of an exception handler looks like:

```
Call Pj
    except when
        e1 : Q1

        e2 : Q2

            •

            •

        en : Qn
    end except
```

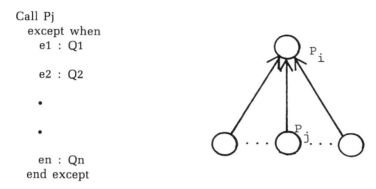

Here, Pj is one of the operations called by Pi. Various exceptions that may be signalled by Pj are e1, e2, . . ., en. The corresponding alternative operations for these exceptions are Q1, Q2, . . ., Qn. Any of these alternative operations may either consist of a procedure call, having a structure similar to the one above, or a statement such as

$$signal \ (e')$$

which causes Pi to resignal an exception e' to its caller. By repetitive resignalling of exceptions, an exception at the lowest level of abstraction can be propagated to the user's level.

Some programming languages, such as ADA or CLU, provide mechanisms to implement this exception-handling methodology. For other programing languages, it is possible to simulate this mechanism using the language features provided. In the desk calculator program, written in PASCAL, the above exception handling mechanism was simulated using CASE statements.

As can be seen from the discussions so far, the tasks of propagating exceptions, managing the context stack, and constructing the exception list are carried out by the application program itself. In case of an error, the context stack and the exception list are passed to the message generator, to be used in a dialogue with the user. The task of error propagation does not constitute any extra burden on the programmer's part, since reliable programs must contain mechanisms for dealing with errors anyway. Nevertheless, the tasks of maintaining the context stack and constructing the exception list are extra tasks that need to be carried out by the application program.

To release the programmer from the burden of writing extra codes for these tasks, it is possible to modify the compiler so that it is done automatically: For every procedure in the system, the compiler can insert a PUSH statement, as the first executable statement, that will push the name of the procedure to the context stack. Similarly, a POP statement can be inserted as the last executable statement of every procedure. This takes care of the task of maintaining the context stack. To construct the error list, the compiler again can insert appropriate code, so that, every time an exception is signalled to the higher level, the name of exception is inserted onto the exception list. Once such a compiler is implemented, the message generator becomes compatible with any program that is compiled by that compiler.

SYSTEM DESCRIPTION

As far as the response generation mechanism is concerned, the purpose of program descriptions is to specify the construction of higher level operations in terms of the lower level operations. These specifications may be viewed as a description of the algorithm of the system, though in the simplest possible way. An excellent survey of various program specification techniques can be found in Berg, Boebert, Franta, and Maher (1982). The applicability of such specifications in software development has also been investigated (Parnas, 1972). Because of the atomic nature of operations, the application of these techniques in an interactive program becomes straightforward. Without taking the space to review these techniques, we give below a list of the requirements they must satisfy for application in the problem of message generation:

1. Descriptions must provide sufficiently precise and complete information, including no more detail than essential.
2. Descriptions of low level operations must be independent of the higher levels of intension. This is necessary since any low level operation may be called by many higher level operations.
3. Descriptions must also include specifications of exceptional object states in relation to the operations defined on abstract objects, and specifications of mappings between a lower level exception and its higher level counterpart.

The first of these requirements needs no justification. The second and third requirements are directly related to the exception-handling model described above.

The proposed program description technique reflects the leveled structure of programs. There are as many levels of specification as there are levels of procedure calls. For example, the desk calculator program contains four abstraction levels. In the first level, there are 20 primitive atomic operations and 3 test routines used on the objects defined at this level. Higher abstraction levels are constructed from these primitive operations. As far as the message generation mechanism is concerned, the implementation details of the level–1 operations are not of any particular interest. What is important, however, is the type of objects they use as input parameters or deliver as results, and particularly the exceptions they signal. Therefore, the lowest level specifications only contain this information. The generic form of a level–1 specification is:

```
op-name ( input-types ) → { output-types | exceptions }
/* English description of effect */
```

Here, *input-types* refers to the types of objects required as input parameters. Zero or more parameters may be specified. *Output-types* refers to the types of results returned. The special case of a procedure returning no value is indicated by "OK" as the output parameter, which means a successful termination. *Exceptions* refers to the list of possible exceptions signalled. The execution of an operation terminates either by returning the expected results specified in *output-types,* or by signalling one of the exceptions specified. The second line informally describes what the operation is supposed to do. To illustrate this description method, the set of level–1 operations used in the "+" operation is given below:

Level–1

```
pop ( STACK ) → { OBJECT | empty }
/* dispose the value in workspace */

findobjectvalue ( OBJET ) → { REAL | NIL }
/* interpret the value */

add ( REAL, REAL ) → { REAL }
/* find sum of two values */
```

Test routines:
   < testifempty (STACK) > → { OK, empty }
   /* check if workspace is empty */

   < checkresult (REAL) > → { OK, toobig, toosmall }
   /* check the validity of results */

Level–2

Descriptions in level–2 or above consists of a first line, similar to those in level–1, followed by the description of the effect of the operation being specified. The effect description consists of a list of lower level operations called by the operation being specified. Test routines of Level-1 will be used in the construction of higher levels, along with Level-1 operations, as necessary. However, the results of these test routines may be interpreted in different ways, depending on the purpose of calling operation. This facilitates the conversion of an exception into another exception in the context of a higher level operation. For example, in the "getbelow" operation below, the "testifempty" operation may return an exception of "empty." The "getbelow" operation converts this into "nomore" (depicted as empty(nomore)) and signals it when this exception occurs. On the other hand, in the context of "gettop" operation, the exception "empty" is propagated without conversion.

   putnumber(REAL, STACK) → {OK}
     /* store value to workspace */
     1. makeobjectfromnumber(REAL) → {OBJECT}
     2. push(OBJECT I STACK) → {OK}

   gettop(stack) → {REAL I empty}
     /* get the first value */
     1. <tesifempty(STACK)> → { OK, empty }
     2. findobjectvalue(stacktop) → {REAL}
     3. pop(stack) → {OK}

   getbelow(stack) → {REAL I nomore}
     /* get the second value */
     1. <testifempty(STACK)> → { OK, empty(nomore) }
     2. findobjectvalue(stacktop) → {REAL}
     3. pop(stack) → {OK}

Another property of these specifications is that some of the exceptions specified for level–1 operations may be omitted in higher

levels. For example, the specification of "pop" in level–1 states that
an exception of "empty" may be signalled by this operation. However, this exception is omitted in the context of "getbelow" above,
because the test routine "testifempty" checks for the possibility of
this exception anyway. If the result of "testifempty" is "empty,"
execution of the rest of the operations is "getbelow" will not start;
hence, "pop" will not return the exception of "empty." Descriptions
in higher levels are similar to those in level–2.

Level–3

```
getoperands(STACK) → {REAL, REAL | novalue, onlyone}
   /* get the two values */
   1. gettop(STACK) → {REAL | empty(novalue)}
   2. getbelow(STACK) → {REAL | nomore(onlyone)}
```

Level–4

```
+(stack) → {REAL | novalue, onlyone, toosmall, toobig}
   /* add two values */
   1. getoperands(STACK) → (REAL,REAL | novalue, onlyone}
   2. add(REAL,REAL) → {REAL}
   3. checkresult(REAL) → {OK | toosmall, toobig}
   4. putnumber(REAL) → {STACK}
```

This method of specification can be used for recursive procedures
as well. Consider an operation "erase," which erases the top element
in the stack. This operation may be used in another operation,
"eraseall," which erases all of the elements in the stack. Specifications for "erase" and "eraseall" are given as:

```
erase(stacktop) → { OK | novalue }
   /* erase most recent value from workspace */
   1. <testifempty(STACK)> → { OK, empty(novalue) }
   2. pop(STACK) → { OK }

eraseall(stack) → { END | novalue }
   /* clear the workspace */
   1. erase(STACK) → { OK | novalue }
   2. pop(STACK) → { OK | novalue }
   2. eraseall(STACK) → { END | novalue(END) }
```

Here, the "erase" operation signals "novalue" if the stack is empty,
and erases the top element if it is not. Inside "eraseall," "erase" is
invoked recursively. The first time "erase" is executed, the exception

"novalue" terminates the execution. If, however, the exception "novalue" is signalled after the first time, then the exception "novalue" is treated as an expected result, depicted as "novalue(END)."

SUMMARY AND FURTHER RESEARCH AREAS

The problem of levels in error message generation is important, since messages generated by lower level operations often give very little help to the user. Based on Lewis and Norman's (1986) recommendation, a model has been developed that enables the user to trace down the levels of program execution to find out the source of error. The proposed model is essentially based on two concepts: (a) atomic operation, which is the foundation of a technique to locate, detect, and handle exceptions; and (b) error abstractions, which can be used to tailor the semantics of exceptions to the user. Based on these concepts, implementation of a prototype message generation system has been described. However, there are important problems that require further research as discussed below.

One of these problems is the development of generalized protocols for user–computer dialogues in a "let's talk about it" strategy. In the prototype system designed, a dialogue can be achieved based on changing the focus by using two different types of queries, "why" and "then?" However, no experimental data is provided to test the preferability of alternative or additional protocols.

Another important problem is how to handle messages received from the lower level system on which the user's application package is embedded. In a real implementation, it may be necessary to suspend these messages, or alter or map the meaning of these messages to the user level, or generate a message as in (4). The online decision of which course of action to select, as well as the implementation of the selected course of action, are important problems.

Another important problem closely related to error message generation is the one with partially executed commands. Conceptually, the set of lower level operations invoked by the user command serves an intention as a whole. In case of an error, the intention may have been served only partially, and it may be necessary to undo the partial effects caused by lower level operations. Provision of tools to undo the effet of partially executed commands would be an invaluable aid to the user.

Finally, online help facilities are needed which enable the user to find out how to fix the system, once the basic problem is clear, so that the error will not occur again. The user should be given the option to start a dialogue, through which the system can suggest alternative courses of action to reach the intended goal. An attempt at online generation of explanation text about what the system can and cannot do is reported in Glasner and Hayes (1981). However, much more research is needed before a satisfactory set of tools is provided to the user of interactive software.

ACKNOWLEDGEMENTS

The airline reservation example in the opening section of this chapter is due to Paul Blackwell. This chapter is reprinted by permission of the Association for Computing Machinery, Inc., which appeared in *Communications of the ACM, 30*(11), November, 1987.

REFERENCES

Berg, H.K., Boebert, W.E., Franta, W.R., & Maher, T.G. (1982). *Formal methods of program verification and specification.* Englewood Cliffs, NJ: Prentice-Hall.

Best, E. (1980). *An operational characterization of the atomicity of activities* (Tech. Rep. 147). Newcastle-upon-Tyne, England: Computing Lab, University of New Castle-upon-Tyne.

Draper, S.W. (1986). Display managers as the basis for user-machine communication. In D.A. Norman & S.W. Draper (Eds.), *User centered system design* (pp. 339–352). Hillsdale, NJ: Erlbaum.

Efe, K., & Hopper, K. (1981). KIWINET/NICOLA approach: Matching the OS responses to users. *Proceedings of the Sixth ACM European Regional Conference on Systems Architecture, Westbury House* (pp. 393–402).

Efe, K., Miller, C.D.F., & Hopper, K. (1983). The KIWINET/NICOLA approach: Response generation in a user friendly interface. *Copmputer,* September, pp. 66–78.

Glasner, I.D., & Hayes, P.J. (1981). *Automatic construction of explanation networks for cooperative user interface* (Rep. No. IJCAI–81). Computer Science Dept., Pittsburgh, PA: Carnegie-Mellon University.

Lewis, C., & Norman, D.A. (1986). Designing for error. In D.A. Norman & S.W. Draper (Eds.), *User centered system design* (pp. 411–432). Hillsdale, NJ: Erlbaum.

Parnas, D.L. (1972). A technique for software module specification with examples. *Communications of the ACM, 15*(5), 330–336.

CHAPTER 4

Measuring the Utility of Application Software

Andrew M. Cohill
David M. Gilfoil
John V. Pilitsis

AT&T Technology Systems
Springfield, NJ

ABSTRACT

A methodology for evaluating applications software is proposed, using five different categories of criteria. Three of the categories, functionality, usability, and performance, are tailored for each class of applications software. The other two categories, support and documentation, have generic criteria that can be applied to all types of application software. After a software package has been scored according to the criteria of a category, statistical analysis is used to convert the raw data to a numeric score that can be used to make between-product comparisons. The methodology has been used to evaluate word processing packages and data base management systems.

INTRODUCTION

The rapid drop in the cost of computing hardware has created a corresponding increase in the amount of software available. But having more software packages from which to choose also makes the choosing more difficult. When there were only a few word processing packages available, evaluating the relative merits of them was a simple task. The 1985 DataPro Report on Microcomputer Software (1985) listed 234 word processing packages, which makes picking one more difficult.

The notion of measuring the characteristics of software has been studied for many years. Boehm, Brown, and Lipow (1976) lists an extensive set of checks for software that focus on code measurements like portability, reliability, efficiency, testability, and modifiability. McCabe's (1976) cyclomatic complexity measure is well known because it is independent of program length, and provides a better analysis than mere counting of lines of code of types of statements.

These and other types of measures have been automated (see Basili & Reiter, 1979) to provide more rapid feedback on the progress of a software development project and to highlight individual effort on that project. But these efforts address only one side of the quality issue in software: *manufactured* quality. For manufactured hard goods, analogous measures of quality have been available for many years. In the physical world, measuring the fit and finish of a product is facilitated with tools like calipers, rulers, and destructive and nondestructive testing techniques that use a myriad of devices that measure physical size and dimension.

The fact that similar measures are now available to measure software may indicate that the science of software development is beginning to mature. But measuring the manufactured quality of software and the achievement of high manufactured quality in software, or in any kind of product, does not indicate the usefulness or *utility* of that product. A well-engineered product is not an automatic guarantee that anyone will want to *use* it.

Economists have long been familiar with the notion of utility. Kotler (1980) notes that users see products as multiattribute objects, where the attributes are relevant to that product class. The measure of utility, in this situation, is the expectation by users that they will be satisfied by the product. For each attribute, there is some minimum level of satisfaction that must be met in order for the user's idea of utility to be met (Kotler, 1980). If, for a product class (like software), attributes can be identified, it then becomes necessary to develop some quantitative method for measuring the utility, or efficacy, of these attributes. Without that, the act of choosing by end users becomes a probablistic event (Brems, 1968). Users of software who do not have a formal method for comparing the attributes of several packages are guessing. It is likely that they are responding to exogenous factors, like external packaging or cost, that have no direct bearing on the utility of the software itself.

King (1967) discusses the idea of a *utility number*, which is an overall measure that can be used as a basis for the comparison of product ideas. It would be derived from human judgements which are aggregated as an overall measure (King, 1967). But overall measures of utility are rarely seen in connection with the evaluation of software. Nearly every computer periodical regularly carries evaluation reports. They offer useful information but suffer from some flaws. The magazines rely on the opinions of the reviewers, who have widely varying evaluation techniques and review styles. There is rarely a standard format for the presentation of data, and the reviewers often discuss minor features and problems in great detail. The attributes used for each evaluation differ from reviewer to reviewer, and often the same reviewer will use different attributes to evaluate similar software packages. The evaluations sometimes reveal more about the reviewer than the product. One is left with the feeling that, if the evaluation had been done on another day, the review would have been entirely different.

To evaluate software, what is needed is a standard set of attributes that can be mapped onto a standard scale of measurement. Only then can users engage in an "evaluation function" which is cognitively oriented, based on making a decision through conscious and rational processes (Kotler, 1980). But the problem is more complicated. King (1967) considers utility to be a subjective concept. Users must have a way of evaluating products for their particular application. There must be a way of adapting a standard measure of utility to fit the task or user environment. One way of doing this is to weight the attributes used in the evaluation process, where the weights represent information about the needs of the user.

It is important to recognize, though, that, just as measures of manufactured quality say nothing about the utility of software, measurements of the utility of software say nothing about the manufactured quality. A product with a very high utility index may in fact be riddled with poorly designed subroutines, unnecessarily complex functions and procedures, and be very inefficient in execution and the use of system resources. A comprehensive evaluation of one or more pieces of software would include measuring both manufactured quality and utility.

Some of the benefits that might accrue from measuring the utility of software applications are listed below.

> Increased User Satisfaction—Using a rigorous evaluation before choosing software will increase the likelihood of obtaining software that suits the task environment and the user population.
> Increased Sales—Software manufacturers that embark on a program of evaluating their own software products against

those of competing companies may be able to identify ways to market the advantages of their product more effectively.

Decreased Development Costs—The same software manufacturers, in reaching a better understanding of the differences between their product and the competition, may be able to target development more effectively by enhancing features that will differentiate their product more.

Decreased Product Returns—Satisfied users may be less likely to return software, reducing costs for everyone in the software distribution chain.

Decreased Training Costs—Satisfied users will be less likely to change from one piece of software to another, which will reduce the requirements for training people to use new packages. Higher quality software may also require less training.

Increased Productivity—High quality software may enable work to proceed more quickly, or offer better information that reduces the amount of interaction with the system in obtaining it.

OVERVIEW OF THE METHODOLOGY

Demand by internal clients at AT&T led to the development of the methodology that is described in the rest of this chapter. The primary goal of the project was to develop a formal evaluation methodology that provided better information on available software products. This methodology is not user oriented but product oriented. Some may view this as a limitation. However, we were not interested in making decisions for the user, but to provide the user with intelligently collected information represented in a format that is easy to read and easy to understand.

It seemed unlikely that a single data collection process would be suitable for the diverse user populations that exist, so a system of weighting the information was developed. This weighting process allows users to adapt the basic data to specific requirements for their task environment. However, it is the responsibility of the user to determine how to apply the weights. This can usually be facilitated by the use of task analysis and function allocation analysis. We found that our users were often unaware of the complexity of their own work (at a task and subtask level), and that asking them to participate in the weighting process gave them a better appreciation for the application of a formal methodology in the evaulation process despite initial reservations about the time and cost of the work.

We defined three criteria for a system that measures the utility of software.

1. A set of standard attributes that are used as the basis of comparison between similar software packages.
2. A numerical measurement process that provides consistent and reliable data.
3. A weighting procedure that adapts the numerical information to the specific needs of the end users of the software.

In the development of the software evaluation methodology, we chose five attributes to be part of the measurement process.

- Functionality—What can the product do?
- Usability—How easy is the product to use?
- Performance—How much can the product do?
- Support—How well does the vendor support the product?
- Documentation—Is the documentation adequate?

For each attribute, we developed a set of criteria that are used in the actual measurement process. The kind and type of measurement we used are different for each attribute or criteria class. We also devised a weighting system that can apply user-weighting information both within a criteria class and between criteria classes. Both the criteria and the weighting are discussed in more detail later in this chapter.

Before the process of evaluating software packages can begin, an application area must be selected. There is no shortage of application areas; thumbing through one of the popular computer magazines reveals advertisements for word processing software, spreadsheets, communications packages, statistical software, project management tools, graphics packages, and data base managers, to name a few.

Once a selection has been made, the evaluation can begin. Figure 1 illustrates the two-phase process we developed and used.

Each package is analyzed, listing the functions that it offers to the user. The function lists from all the packages are combined into a master "functional capability" list. This represents the set of all functions (or features) that can be performed. Some functions may

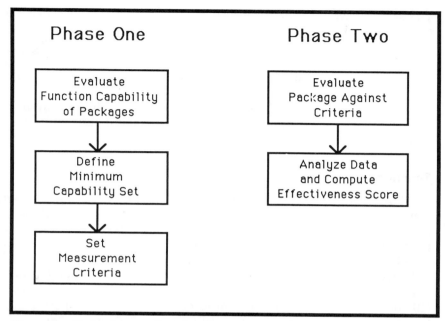

Figure 1. Two phases of evaluation.

be performed by just one or two of the packages, while it may be possible to do other functions with all of the packages.

Once this functional capability list is complete, a minimum capability set is derived from this set. The minimum capability set represents the minimum number of functions that must be available in a package in order to perform useful work. Any packages that do not offer the minimum capability set can be eliminated from the evaluation immediately.

The minimum capability set may also be used in the development of usability and performance criteria. After this work is complete, phase one of the evaluation methodology is finished.

Phase two of the methodology measures each application package against the five criteria classes. Once the data are collected, the raw scores are analyzed and reduced, yielding an effectiveness score in each of the five criteria classes and an overall effectiveness score. The overall score is the average of the individual scores.

Weighting can be applied in either portion of phase two; individual criteria can be weighted before the raw score is computed, and the effectiveness scores can be weighted after data reduction and analysis. The weighted scores conform to the idea of utility measures as described in the introduction.

THE EVALUATION CRITERIA

There are five criteria classes covered by the evaluation system. Each one covers a different area of concern about the application being evaluated.

Functionality

The functionality of a software product refers to what the product can do (functional capability). A methodology adapted from Roberts and Moran (1983) is used here to measure functionality. Their basic premise is that the functionality of an application package is measured by how many tasks it can perform.

Phase one of the methodology begins with the development of a master list of tasks for an application package. Roberts and Moran (1983), for example, examined nine commercial and experimental text editors to develop a taxonomy of about 220 tasks. This work was later validated by Borenstein (1985). The functionality list that we developed for the evaluation of data base management systems included nearly 400 items. It is important to note that the list of tasks should only include tasks that can actually be performed by an existing software package. Developing a "wish list" of tasks that are not available (or perhaps even possible) can distort the evaluation process and result in unrealistically low scores.

A sample subset of tasks taken from a recent evaluation of base management system packages is provided in Figure 2. The database functional capability list was developed by polling several experienced users of database management systems. These included an end user, several applications programmers, and several data base administrators. The list was then reviewed by another set of users for completeness and overlap of items. Less than 10% of the items were changed during the review.

After developing the master list of tasks, as depicted above, each application package is evaluated with respect to its capability to perform each task on the list. If the task cannot be performed by the package, a score of zero is assigned. If the task can be performed, but with some difficulty, a score of one is achieved. If the task can be performed with ease, that particular task scores a two. In de-

4. Data Administrator

Entity Definition

☐ **Create entity:** Define a table with at least one field per record.

☐ **Allocate Space for Entity:** Specify the initial data page allocation for the entity.

☐ **Define Entity Increments:** Specify the size of the data page to be allocated when entity space allocation is extended.

☐ **Limit Entity Size:** Specify the maximum amount of space that an entity can be allocated.

☐ **Define Entity Free Space:** Specify the amount of free space to be maintained on each data page of the editor.

☐ **Limit Index Size:** Specify the maximum amount of space that an index can be allocated.

☐ **Define Index Increments:** Specify the size of the data page to be allocated when index space allocation is extended.

Data Loading

☐ **Order:** Allow data to arrive in any order of record occurence.

☐ **Simultaneous Update:** Allow simultaneous update of the entity.

☐ **Loading Summary:** Provide a summary of data loading activities.

☐ **Multi-Media:** Allow data loading to be done from more than one medium (screen, tape, etc.).

Figure 2.   Sample tasks.

veloping the functionality list for database management systems, it became clear that some areas of functionality are similar for different application areas. For example:

The ability to exchange data with other packages, likely to be
always desirable.
The ability to customize the command language by the use of
synonyms and/or macros.
The inclusion of utility functions, like the ability to execute
operating system commands or to print working files.

Areas like extensibility and flexibility can be described in great
detail by enumerating the tasks or subtasks that facilitate those
goals. It is important to remember that the mere desirability of those
types of features does not guarantee inclusion in the functionality
list. For example, if a functionality list is being developed for an
application area, and none of the packages being examined offer
extensible features, tasks that facilitate extensibility will not appear
in the functionality list. This may be considered a disadvantage,
but, if a feature is not available from any commercial package, it
does not help users to tell them that it should be. The functionality
list is not static; as new products become available, with new
features, the functionality list is updated to reflect that. One consequence is that older products, over time, may begin to exhibit a
decline in their rating.

The total functionality score for an application package is simply
the sum of the individual 0-, 1-, or 2-point scores as depicted in
Figure 3. The guidelines for assigning those values are adapted from
Roberts and Moran (1983). To allow for meaningful between-product
comparisons, total scores for each package are statistically adjusted
to a common scale.

Usability

The usability of a software product relates to how easy or difficult
it is for the end user to access and implement functions provided
by the package to perform application tasks. Usability has historically
proven to be a difficult concept to measure (Eason, 1984), given the
diversity of end users and applications. Moreover, the characteristics
of what constitutes a "usable" system change constantly, usually in
response to developing user expertise, advances in hardware, and
so on.

Guidelines for the user interface design of application software
exist and are being enhanced and expanded with some regularity
(Smith & Mosier, 1984). However, the task of incorporating such
guidelines into the software development process is by no means
simple and straightforward (Eason, 1984). Ideally, controlled exper-

Tasks	Products		
	A	B	C
Data Manipulation			
Sort Operators			
Sort ascending	2	2	0
Sort descending	2	0	0
Sort on derived field	2	0	0
List Functions			
Create a list	2	1	1
Split a list	1	1	1
Search	1	2	2
Add to a list	2	2	2
Delete from a list	2	2	2
Set Functions			
Intersection	1	0	0
Union	2	1	1
Complement	1	1	0
Data Qualifiers			
Field to field	2	1	2
Field to constant	1	0	0
Group by	2	0	0
Field in range	0	0	0
Null value	0	1	1
	23	14	12

Figure 3. Functionality data collection sample.

imental studies would provide the most accurate data about the usability of software products. Both casual and expert users could be studied to determine variables like training time to a certain level of proficiency, task completion time, number of errors, etc. However, in a market-driven environment, there are constraints on such studies. The cost of such work is not the least of them. Our internal customers were simply unwilling to wait; scheduling lab time, finding subjects, running subjects, and analyzing the often voluminous data was rarely an option they were willing to consider. Other means of estimating usability had to be considered.

Learning how to use a system can be an important part of the usability dimension. Polson and Kieras (1985; Polson, Muncher, and Engelback, 1986) have developed a predictive model of learning time based upon the number of production rules a syntax has and the time required to learn the rules. This method can be applied to a core set of tasks as defined by Roberts and Moran (1983). Another alternative (Green, Payne, Gilmore, and Mepham, 1985) is to measure the ease of making "slips" in a command language, where a slip is an unintended action by the user (Reason, 1979). Two of the measures we used are discussed here.

The first measurement technique, the Keystroke Level Model (KLM), was developed by Card and Moran (1980). KLM is a performance-based measure of usability. The model predicts expert performance on a core set of tasks. The procedure does not necessarily require an "expert user," but the evaluator must be able to identify the correct keystroke sequences that an expert would use. Performance measures include task acquisition time, keystrokes, the time it takes to move the hands across the keyboard, and system response time. KLM yields a single numeric value that represents effort required by an expert to accomplish a predefined set of tasks. By performing the same core set of tasks with each of several software packages, one can readily make usability comparisons between the packages.

Sample KLM data scores are provided in Figure 4. (These raw scores are again "adjusted" to allow for between-product comparisons.) For example, a value of "M2K" indicates that some time was allocated to mental task acquisition (M), and that two keystrokes were required to perform the task (2K). There are additional variables that consider other user actions.

The above technique for measuring usability is objective, thorough, and quantitative. It is also very time consuming. An alternative evaluation methodology employs a Behaviorally Anchored Rating Scale (BARS) technique originally developed by Smith and Kendall (1963). This technique associates with each criteria a set of described behaviors that aid the reviewer in providing a consistent evaluation of the criteria. For our purposes, we developed a set of software evaluation criteria which are linked to several software design objectives. The software design objectives, in turn, are tied in to three overall design goals for developers of software systems: In the example, the design goal "Easy to Learn" is broken down into three design objectives. The three specific evaluation criteria are linked in turn to the "Consistent" objective.

In total, there are 28 usability evaluation criteria spread over nine design objectives which support the three software design goals. In the present methodology, a five-point rating scale anchored with statements of system behavior was constructed for each criterion along with a definition of that criterion. The usability review, both for the KLM method and the BARS method, was performed by the reviewer who completed the functionality review for the system. This generally required between 40 and 80 hours of system use, so

2.4 Paragraphs

Insert Paragraph	M494K	139.67
Copy Paragraph	M2KMKMK	5.17
Delete Paragraph	M2K	1.91
Replace Paragraph	M2KM489K	140.18
Move Paragraph	M2KMKMK	5.17
Split Paragraph	M2KM4K	4.38
Merge Paragraph	M2K	1.91

Figure 4.   Keystroke-Level Model data collection sample.

the reviewer was familiar with the command syntax and structure of the package. The evaluator reads each criterion definition and each of the BARS statements for that criterion. The evaluator decides which statement best fits the software package, and scores it accordingly. Space is provided for the evaluator to give detailed examples of system behavior which substantiate the rating.

A sample evaluation criterion date sheet is provided in Figure 5.

The total raw usability score is simply a sum of the 28 criterion scores.

Performance

Performance criteria have to be developed for each application area. Benigni (1984) considers it important that evaluations integrate both feature analysis (functionality) and performance analysis phases. There are several alternatives to making performance measurements, including cost models, simulation models, and benchmarking (Benigni, 1984). At the outset of the evaluation methodology development, a decision was made to treat cost separately, because there is not always a clear-cut relationship between the cost of a product

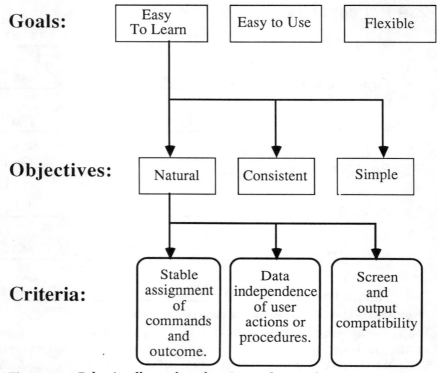

Figure 4a.   Behaviorally anchored rating scale sample.

and its quality. It is possible to develop a simulation model of the task load for an application area, but the cost of such a model can be very high.

Performance benchmarks can be developed easily from the core set of tasks taken from the functionality area. The performance of these tasks can be measured easily and at low cost by an operator using a manual stopwatch, or by utilizing timing routines that are already available as part of the operating system.

Benigni has identified three phases of a benchmark methodology:

Design—Establishing the environmental parameters of the test; system configuration, test data, system workload, and the fixed and free variables of each benchmark task.

Execution—Performing the benchmarks and collecting the performance data.

Goal: Easy to learn

Objective: Simple

Criterion: Ad hoc vocabulary requirements

Definition: Size of the ad hoc vocabulary required
to learn and use the system.

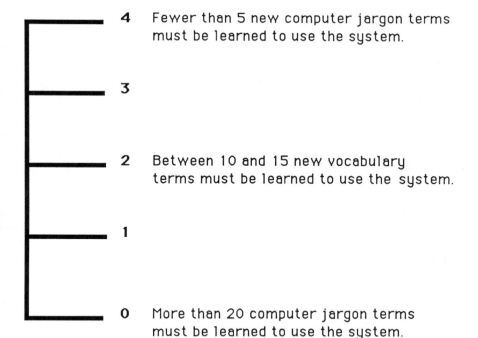

4   Fewer than 5 new computer jargon terms
must be learned to use the system.

3

2   Between 10 and 15 new vocabulary
terms must be learned to use the system.

1

0   More than 20 computer jargon terms
must be learned to use the system.

Criterion Score _____

Figure 5.   Usability sample.

Analysis—Analyzing the results and comparing performance across several systems.

The time required to complete a unit task is used as a metric. In the initial trial of the evaluation methodology, 12 different performance measurements were used. These included measurements like the time required to load the software, time required to load a sample data file, and various measurements aimed at measuring the efficiency with which the software manipulates the data. These metrics can be weighted by the user; some users may be willing to trade off long load time for fast performance, for example.

Each measurement is repeated five times. The average of the five scores is used as the final raw score. This smooths operator measurement errors and reduces minor variations in machine performance. Tests are conducted when no other users are logged on the system. An example of a data collection sheet used in one of the studies is provided in Figure 6.

Performance scores have to be considered very carefully. They are intended to provide a general guideline to the kind of performance that can be expected. Because the data is logged under conditions that the normal user rarely sees, the performance metric is more useful as a between-package comparison than as a predictor of real-world performance.

Support

This criterion gauges the willingness and ability of software manufacturers and distributors to support users. We developed four areas for consideration in the measurement process. A sample section of the data collection sheet used for support is provided in Figure 7. The information used in the evaluation is obtained from literature supplied by the vendor and by interviews with the vendor.
Availability of customer support.

Is there a hotline available for consultation? Is it a WATS line? What are the hours? Do the hours span normal working hours for both the East and West Coast?

Is there a dedicated support staff? What is the size of the staff? What is the experience of the staff? Are programmers and developers rotated periodically to support duties?

Is there a newsletter? How often is it released? What is the average length?

Is there a user group? Is it independent? Does the company provide any support?

Move from first page to last page of a 10K file

—   —   —   —   —   —

Search a 1K file

—   —   —   —   —   —

Search a 10K file

—   —   —   —   —   —

Search a 20K file

—   —   —   —   —   —

Make Global Changes to a 1K file

—   —   —   —   —   —

Figure 6. Data collection sheet sample.

Software control:

> Is the software copy-protected? If it is, does the company
> provide low-cost back-up diskettes?
> What is the frequency of software updates?
> How are software updates supplied?

1. Customer Support

Is there a hotline available for consultation? _____

Is the hotline a toll-free number? _____

Do the hotline hours span normal working
hours for the East and West Coast? _____

Is there a dedicated support staff? _____

Are programmers and developers rotated to
the support staff periodically? _____

Is there a newsletter? _____

Is the newsletter released at regular intervals? _____

Does the company support a user group? _____

Figure 7. Support criteria sample.

Are updates supplied free of charge? If there are fees, are they
reasonable?
If there a formal procedure for reporting and tracking software
bugs? Are all users informed of all known bugs?

Training quality:

Is there a dedicated training staff? What is their level of ex-
perience?
Are there dedicated training facilities at the company? Can
they deliver training at user sites?
Is there a training program for local dealers? Do local dealers
have dedicated training facilities?
Are there advanced courses available?
Are there self-paced tutorials (either on- or offline)?

Warranty provisions:

Are defective diskettes replaced free of charge?

Can you obtain a refund if the package does not perform as advertised?

Documentation

Documentation of a software product can be critical to the success or failure of the product (Galitz, 1984). Indeed, many software packages do fail in the marketplace because they are very poorly documented. *Documentation* here refers to users' manuals, tutorials, quick reference guides, job aids, and any other materials (hardcopy or online) that inform the user about how to access and exercise software functions and features.

We developed a list of evaluation criteria to measure documentation quality. The criteria fall into five categories, as follows:

Organization—Thoughtful organization greatly enhances the usefulness of software documentation. Every manual should have a table of contents, index, and tabs. Glossaries are extremely useful in defining new terms for the first time or casual user. Chapter headings and introduction and summary sections are more effective if they are presented in a task-oriented manner. For example, use "Saving a File" rather than "File Storage Procedures."

Typography and Legibility—Even the best of documentation efforts will fall short if presented improperly to the user. Printed materials should be carefully typeset, with attention given to font style, font size, layout, and use of highlighting characteristics (italics, bold, etc.).

Language—The style and level of written documentation can impact on how quickly and accurately information is read and understood. Readability is measured through a variety of indices and readability formulas which focus on the number of syllables in words, the number of words in sentences, commonality of words, and so on. Whether on not sentences are in the passive or active voice can also impact readability and comprehension. Sentences using the passive voice can often be more difficult to understand. These data were collected by randomly sampling five 150-word passages from the documentation, and using automated programs to determine the reading level and the ratio of active to passive sentences.

Graphics and Illustrations—Illustrations, half-tones, and other graphic images play a key role in documentation. They help to break up monotonous text and can, in some cases, actually provide a more effective vehicle for communicating ideas.

Physical Characteristics—One of the most obvious (but often overlooked) features of software documentation is its size and shape. Large, bulky documents are often perceived as uncomfortable or clumsy. Such documents can intimidate or annoy users and discourage effective use. Documentation materials should be easy to store and update, and should be made of durable materials.

A sample subset of evaluation criteria is provided in Figure 8.

3. Language

Is the readability at the 7th or 8th grade level? _____

Are technical terms used sparingly? _____

Are instructions clear and complete in thought? _____

Are paragraphs short (between 70-200 words)? _____

Is active voice used most of the time (> 70%)? _____

Is repetition of critical material used to
facilitate learning? _____

3.1 Reading Scores

Kincaid Score _____

Coleman-Liau Score _____

Flesch Score _____

Average _____

Figure 8. Documentation criteria sample.

Each criterion met by a given application package scores one point for that package. The total documentation raw score is simply a total of the scores.

SCORING

Each one of the five evaluation areas has its own set of criteria and scoring procedure. The raw point scores for each area are unrelated, so a statistical procedure is used to normalize all of the values. The procedure compares the unweighted performance score of each package to the unweighted performance score of all the other packages in the study, and maps an adjusted score onto a scale ranging between zero and four points. Figure 8a illustrates the range and meaning of the point scores.

As new products are evaluated in an application area (e.g., word processing), all scores are dynamically readjusted to reflect the new information available. Thus, a package is always evaluated relative to the current state of the market, with the score floating up or down as new products are released. This is much more useful than a static rating based on a checklist approach.

For example, a product released in the early stages of an application area may start out with a very high rating. As competitors begin to release alternative packages, the score may begin to drift downward, signaling developers that it is time to release upgrades and enhancements. If, on the other hand, the score remains high despite competitive products, the developers can comfortably allocate resources elsewhere. A sample summary chart is listed in Figure 8b.

The three products vary substantially in quality. Product A was rated highest, with a *Good* score, and products B and C followed, with ratings of *Fair* and *Poor*, respectively.

Very Poor	Poor	Fair	Good	Very Good
0.0--0.7	0.8--1.5	1.6 -- 2.3	2.4--3.1	3.2--4.0

Worst Rating   **Best Rating**

Figure 8a.   Point scores.

Criteria	Products		
	A	B	C
Functionality	3.1	0.6	1.5
Usability	2.7	1.3	0.4
Performance	2.7	2.2	2.2
Support	2.9	2.8	1.7
Documentation	3.2	3.0	1.1
Average Score	2.8 Good	2.0 Fair	1.4 Poor

Figure 8b.   Product summary chart.

WEIGHTING

As previously discussed, weighting is a critical part of the evaluation process. King (1967) has described three parts of a weighting structure.

1. Arbitrary numerical scales can be assigned, where the outcomes are measured relative to the best and worst products being evaluated.
2. A series of one-dimensional situations should be presented, rather than a single multidimensional one.
3. Individuals within the organization that will be using the product should be queried to develop weights.

Our system supports two weighting dimensions, and at more than one level for each dimension. Weighting can be applied to individual criteria within a criteria class, and/or between criteria classes. For example, without weighting, obscure or lightly used functionality criteria contribute as much to the final score as core tasks and other heavily used functions. This two level weighting scheme was also used by Pilitsis (1981). Assigning a higher weight to more important functions may provide a more accurate picture of their relative value. These weights are always developed in consultation with the user, who understands best the needs of the organization. As recommended by King (1967), an arbitrary weighting scale between 1 and 5 is used, where 1 is the lowest weight that can be applied to an individual feature or function, and 5 is the highest value.

Weighting can also be applied according to user type. Using functionality as an example again, different user groups may each have a different set of "important" functions. By assigning different weights to functions according to user type, a single package can be evaluated with respect to the needs of several different user groups, or multiple packages can be evaluated across different user groups.

Figure 8c is similar to that in the previous section, but two sets of weights have been added, illustrating how the ratings may change, based on a set of weighting criteria developed for two different users types. For each user type, 100 points have been allocated among the five evaluation areas. The higher the weight, the more important the area. User type A places more emphasis on functionality and performance, while user type B weights support and documentation more heavily. These two classifications could correspond to the expert and novice users, respectively.

Note that the rating for product B changed from *Fair* to *Poor* when weighted for user type 1. The rating for product C also changed the same way for user type 1. This illustrates how the weighting can be used on the highest level. The individual criteria that make up an evaluation area can also be weighted in a similar fashion. Figure 9 shows the points in the evaluation process at which weighting can be applied.

EVALUATION IN THE SOFTWARE DEVELOPMENT LIFE CYCLE

Many system theorists and system developers have proposed conceptual and pragmatic approaches to systems development. Typically, there are five key phases of system development (DeGreen, 1970; Meister, 1985):

Concept Phase
Design Phase
Development Phase

Criteria	User Figure 1	User Figure 2	Products A	B	C
Functionality	30	10	3.8	0.6	1.5
Usability	15	30	2.7	1.3	1.3
Performance	30	10	2.7	1.9	1.3
Support	10	25	2.3	2.8	2.5
Documentation	10	25	2.1	3.0	2.6
Unweighted Average			2.7 Good	1.9 Fair	1.8 Fair
User Type A Weighted Average			2.8 Good	1.5 Poor	1.5 Poor
User Type B Weighted Average			2.6 Good	2.1 Fair	1.9 Fair

Figure 8c.   Weighted product scores.

Test and Evaluation Phase
Installation/Maintenance Phase

Software systems can readily be viewed within this framework. Metzger (1981), in fact, has proposed an adaptation of such systems development work to the software development area. Metzger proposes the following six phases in the software development cycle:

> *Definition Phase*—A plan for the software project is developed. The customer's problem is reviewed, analyzed, and fed back to the customer for confirmation. Market requirements are gathered and defined. General research and development activities are conducted.
> *Design Phase*—A detailed functional design specification is developed. The design specification spells out what the software product will do and how it will do it. If the product is being designed for a specific customer, the product specification must be checked to see that it meets customer requirements articulated in the definition phase. Care should be taken in the design phase that software programs are designed to be modular, for ease of programming, debugging, and future enhancements.

Weighting Scheme

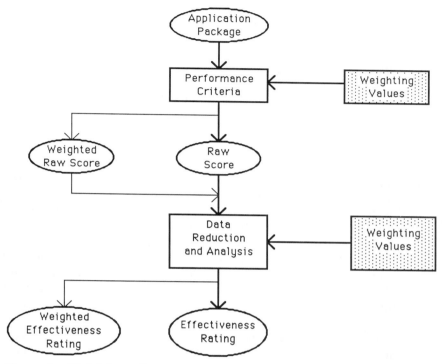

Figure 9.   Weighting scheme.

Programming Phase—The software product is developed here. Compliance with applicable software standards should be adhered to whenever possible. Essential to this phase is the proper documentation of software programs.

System Test Phase—*System test* means different things to different people. Generally, once a software product is completed, it is first tested against the specification from which it was developed. This is a means of verifying that the product does what it was designed to do. Further tests are conducted to "exercise" the product using real world tasks and data. Often a customer test bed is also selected, and the product is tested in an actual work environment. Systematic procedures need to be in place for identifying, reporting, and correcting system software problems at each level of testing.

Acceptance Phase—When working with a specific customer,

this phase is critical. System software and system and user documentation, as well as software training programs and materials, must be accepted by the customer as having met contractual requirements. In an "open market" situation where a software product was not defined for a specific customer, acceptance takes on a simpler meaning: sales.

Installation and Operation Phase—The software product is installed at end-user sites. Training is conducted where appropriate or required. Customer service groups must be easily accessible and responsive to customer questions and problems. Visits to customer sites are often required.

Carroll and Rosson (1985) have suggested an iterative design process that includes exploratory testing of both functional specifications and usability specifications. Unfortunately, business constraints often minimize or eliminate such activities. Iterative development is not part of Metzger's paradigm; in the typical software life cycle, most evaluation (when it takes place) occurs toward the end of the cycle. This is unfortunate, because product changes are not only harder to make as the development process continues, they are more costly as well. Figure 10 illustrates the kind of effect that one might see on cost as changes are made during the development process.

By focusing more attention on earlier phases of the software development process, software developers can produce better-quality products and can reduce the need to make frequent and costly product changes. The same criteria that are used to evaluate systems

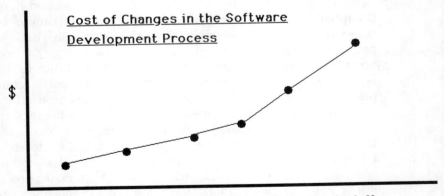

Cost of Changes in the Software Development Process

Definition   Design   Program   Test   Accept   Install

Figure 10.   Effects of change on cost of development.

should be used, up front, to design them. The evaluation criteria that we have developed can be used in various stages of the software life cycle to provide feedback to developers on the utility of the system. Figure 11 illustrates this.

One of the results of evaluating software in an application area is the gradual creation of a database that can be manipulated as needed to provide information about software products. As new products are evaluated, the information is added to the database, and the scores of all the previous products are automatically re-computed to reflect the new data.

The task and user weighting models can also be stored in a database so that the data can be used by different analysis systems. With respect to the software development life cycle, this information can be used as part of an analytical tool that will predict the economic impact of adding or deleting features from a system under development.

One additional set of data is required. Time and cost estimates are needed for each feature on the functionality list. Figure 12 illustrates the components that such a system might have.

The basis of the analytical tool is the functionality list, containing the complete set of features available in all packages for a given application area. Also contained in the tool is a set of rules that describes how to combine and manipulate data from the three databases: competitive product evaluations, task/user weighting models, and time/cost data for each feature in the functionality list. The manager of a software development project can now build "what-if" scenarios based upon some or all of the data available to the tool.

By combining weighting models with time and cost data, the tool can predict the cost of developing a piece of software. The important difference between this tool and other project management tools available is that this process, in addition to time and cost estimates,

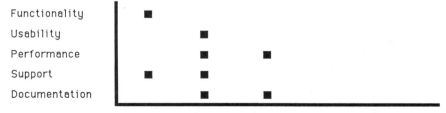

Definition Design Program Test   Accept   Install
Figure 11.   Applying evaluation criteria to development.

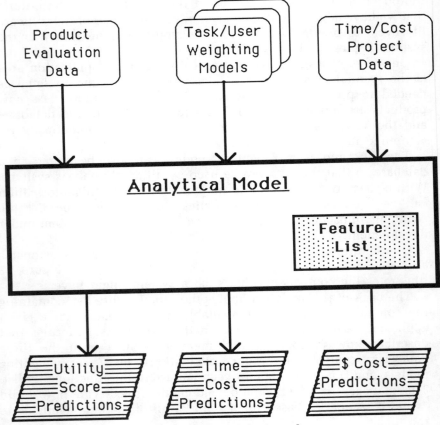

Figure 12.   Comprehensive software analysis tool.

also provides an objective, quantitative measure of the completeness of the final product (the functionality effectiveness score). This measure of completeness can be compared instantly to competing products that are stored in the competitive product database. The tool could predict other situations also.

The cost of the project can be predicted on a feature-by-feature basis. By applying the weighting models at this point, features can be added or dropped on the basis of cost and impact on the effectiveness score. It may be that some low-weight features have a very high cost associated with them, so that the cost of the project could be reduced without significantly affecting the effectiveness score of the product.

The time and cost data could be broken down into subunits (by feature) for each of the six development life cycle phases. This would give a finer level of detail about where costs lie, and about the impact of adding or dropping features as the project moves through each phase.

Features may very well become milestones for planning and tracking purposes, and the effect of late milestones on the effectiveness score of the product can be measured with the tool.

The concept of a comprehensive, automated analysis system gives human factors engineers a tool to link the traditional task analysis studies (represented here as task/user weighting models) with the software development life cycle. Previously, it has been difficult to show quantitatively the effect of adding or deleting features from a piece of software. The effect can be represented in three dimensions: time, dollar cost, and impact on the effectiveness score.

Developers who insist on adding features that have not been recommended by human factors engineers can be shown in an objective way that the feature may contribute little to the effectiveness score of the product.

SUMMARY

As the computer industry has matured, methods for measuring the manufactured quality of software have been developed. Many of these procedures have been automated, so that it is now relatively easy to acquire and use this information in the software development life cycle, with the aim of producing better software. But these measurements address only the needs of the developer of the software. They do not address those of the end user of the same package.

Users of software face a formidable task in choosing software, complicated by the fact that relentless innovation in hardware is driving development in software. Each time a new, more sophisticated piece of hardware is introduced, new, more sophisticated software follows shortly. This would not be a serious problem if software developers continued to support older software, but that is not always the case. Users must choose carefully, to ensure that the software they purchase will meet not only their functional and performance needs, but also their requirements for documentation and support.

A shortcoming of the methodology presented in this chapter is that it has not been validated experimentally. Further work is needed to isolate any validity or reliability problems. It is also possible that the robustness of the system could be enhanced by additional criteria classes; cost, although deliberately left out, could be added in easily for a more complete model of the process of selecting and purchasing software. New techniques for measuring usability are constantly being developed, and these too could be incorporated into the model.

The goal in this work has been to facilitate the measurement of utility in software, incorporating several important concepts.

The methodology is an attempt to quantify human judgement. A framework has been developed to collect data that does not rely on individual skills.

The hierarchical structure of the system makes it easy to understand. At the top level, a single score represents the utility value for each package, but this single score can be dissected progressively to provide more detail as needed.

The flexibility of the weighting system enables users to tailor the data analysis to meet their needs. Organizations with more than one type of user, or with multiple task environments, can manipulate a single set of raw data with multiple weighting models to provide utility measures for every situation.

The system is versatile. A single framework can accommodate many different kinds of applications, by developing new sets of criteria for functionality, usability, and performance. Regardless of the kind or type of criteria, though, the final scores are always presented in the same way, so that users do not have to learn the meaning of new measurements.

The system is product oriented. Evaluation criteria are developed by surveying products to which users already have access. This insures that the results will be meaningful. The system will not recommend features that cannot be obtained.

Evaluation scores are dynamic. As new products come on the market, they can be tested easily against all products that have already been evaluated, and both the new and old products receive a new rating. This continuous updating of data insures that the user always receives current and pertinent information about the software.

Applying the methodology and the data generated by it to the software development life cycle has great potential for integrating quantitative information about the user early in the design and development of software. Some of the advantages of this approach include shorter development times, lower development costs, and higher quality software. The net result is increased user satisfaction.

A single tool may incorporate methods for the measurement of both manufactured quality and utility, along with the classical project management tools. This would give software developers a powerful, multidimensional modeling and control environment that would remove much of the uncertainty now found in the development and evaluation of software.

REFERENCES

Basili, V.R., & Reiter, R.W., Jr. (1979, October). Evaluating automatable measures of software development. *IEEE Proceedings, Workshop on Quantitative Software Models,* (pp. 107–116). New York: IEEE.

Benigni, D.R. (1984). *A guide to performance evaluation of database systems.* National Bureau of Standards Report 500–118. Washington, DC: U.S. Dept. of Commerce.

Boehm, B.W., Brown, J.R., & Lipow, M. (1976). Quantitative evaluation of software quality. *Proceedings of the IEEE, Second International Conference on Software Engineering,* (pp. 592–605). New York: IEEE.

Borenstein, N.S. (1985). The evaluation of test editors: A critical review of the Roberts and Moran methodology based on new experiments. *Proceedings of CHI '85 Human Factors in Computing Systems,* (pp. 99–105). New York: ACM.

Brems, H. (1968). *Quantitative economic theory.* New York: John Wiley and Sons.

Card, S.K., & Moran, T.P. (1980). The Keystroke-Level Model for user performance time with interactive systems. *Communications of the ACM, 23*(7), 396–410.

Carroll, J.M., & Rosson, M.B. (1985). Usability specifications as a tool in interative development. In H.R. Hartson (Ed.), *Advances in Human-Computer Interaction.* (Vol. 1). Norwood, NJ: Ablex Publishing Corp.

DeGreen, K.B. (1970). *Systems psychology.* New York: McGraw-Hill.

Eason, K.D. (1984). Towards the experimental study of usability. *Behaviour and Information Technology, 3*(2), 133–145.

Galitz, W.O. (1984). *Humanizing office automation.* Wellesley, MA: QED Information Systems.

Green, T.R.G., Payne, S.J., Gilmore, D.J., & Mepham, M. (1985). Predicting expert slips. In B. Shackel (Ed.), *Human-computer interaction—INTERACT '84.* North Holland, Netherlands: Elsevier Science.

King, W.R. (1967). *Quantitative analysis for marketing management.* New York: McGraw-Hill.

Kotler, P. (1980). *Marketing management.* Englewood Cliffs, NJ: Prentice-Hall.

McCabe, T.J. (1976, December). A complexity measure. *IEEE Transactions on Software Engineering,* (pp. 308–320). New York: IEEE.

Meister, D. (1985). *Behavioral analysis and measurement methods.* New York: John Wiley and Sons.

Metzger, P.W. (1981). *Managing a programming project.* Englewood Cliffs, NJ: Prentice-Hall.

Mills, H.D. (1976, December). Software development. *IEEE Transactions on Software Engineering,* (pp. 265–273). New York: IEEE.

Pilitsis, J.V. (1981). *A methodology for estimating span of control supervision* [internal report]. Morristown, NJ: AT&T Human Resources Dept.

Polson, P.G. & Kieras, D.E. (1985). A quantitative model of the learning and performance of text editing knowledge. *Proceedings of CHI '85 Human Factors in Computing Systems.* New York: ACM.

Polson, P.G., Muncher, E., & Engelback, G. (1986). A test of common elements transfer. *Proceedings of CHI '86 Human Factors in Computing Systems.* New York: ACM.

Reason, J. (1979). Actions not as planned: The price of automatization. In G. Underwood & R. Stevens (Eds.), *Aspects of Consciousness* (Vol 1). London: Academic Press.

Roberts, T.L. & Moran, T.P. (1983). The evaluation of text editors: Methodology and empirical results. *Communications of the ACM, 26*(4) 265–283.

Smith, P.C. & Kendall, L.M. (1963). Retranslation of expectations: An approach to the construction of unambiguous anchors for rating scales. *Journal of Applied Psychology, 47,* 149–155.

Smith, S.L. & Mosier, J.N. (1984). *Design guidelines for user-system interface software,* (Report MTR-9420). Bedford, MA: Mitre Corporation.

CHAPTER 5

The Gift of Good Design Tools

Tom Carey

*Department of Computing
and Information Science,
University of Guelph. Guelph, Canada*

INTRODUCTION

I teach at a university which started out as an agricultural college. When I am introduced to professional audiences as a speaker on user interface design, sometimes they expect my presentation to have a rural flavor to it. So I often use the following quote to show that we haven't deserted our agricultural roots:

> The most necessary thing in user interface design, for instance, is not to invent new technologies or methods, not to achieve 'breakthroughs,' but to determine what tools and methods are appropriate to specific people, places, and needs, and to apply them correctly. Application . . . is the crux, because no two organizations or users are alike. Just the changing of tasks, organizational structure, reward systems, people and the organizational environment makes for differences of the most formidable kind. Abstractions never cross these boundaries without either ceasing to be abstractions or doing damage. And prefabricated industrial methods and technologies *are* abstractions.

I have adapted this quote from an essay by Wendell Berry (1981, p. 280). Berry is both a farmer and a philosopher of farming. The original reads, "The most necessary thing in farming technology. . . . No two farms are alike. . . . Just the changing lay of the land on each farm makes for differences," and so on. Berry is writing about the way modern agricultural tools and techniques can be applied inappropriately to people-scale smaller farms, ignoring the local conditions which are unique to each situation.

You can substitute almost any obtrusive technology into this all-purpose quotation. Readers of this book would probably be the first to agree that computer systems can be a heroic-scale technology, and that they can overwhelm the people who use them unless they are designed for specific people, places, and needs.

The user interface to the computer system shows how well we have done at determining appropriate tools and methods.

It used to be the case that user interface designers built interactive systems with human/computer dialogues which might be well suited to programmers, but were not "fitting" for those who actually worked with the system. Now, knowledgeable user interface designers exercise considerable care to determine who will use the system and what services are really needed.

I wonder sometimes, though, if we haven't turned the tables on ourselves: In our enthusiasm for thorough study of groups with vastly differing characteristics, we may be neglecting an important group of users in our own backyard. My current research activity is focused on tools for user interface designers to employ in building interactive software. Berry's quote applies just as much to them as it does to their clients. User interface designers are also specific people, in specific places, with specific needs.

The point I want to make in this chapter is that all our techniques and tools for human–computer interaction are "prefabricated industrial methods." As these methods become more sophisticated, we need to study all the more those people and organizational environments forming the context for their use. The next section outlines how one popular dialogue design tool was used in practice by large data processing organizations. This is followed by a section on the diversity of contexts in which user interface design occurs, relating some experiences from commercial environments producing interactive software. The last section discusses how the lessons learned from these experiences are influencing the goals currently being developed in our research lab.

DIALOGUE DESIGN WITH ACT/1

Along with my colleague Dick Mason, I was involved in a major study of a commercial product used for designing interactive dialogues. The details of the product and results of our study are recorded elsewhere (Carey & Mason, 1983; Mason & Carey, 1981, 1983); in this chapter, I want to relate its development and how it was actually used. ACT/1 was the result of work by Art Benjamin, directed toward improving the quality of interaction for mainframe software in IBM operating system environments of the early 1980s (TSO, CMS, CICS). Art and his associates developed ACT/1 as a product which implemented their ideas about both the process and the content of dialogue design.

ACT/1 supported the process of prototyping interactive information systems. This process focused on scenarios and demonstrations of the user interface as a method for refining the requirements of an interactive system. In the late 1970s, this notion ran counter to the prevailing attitude that rigorous written specifications of system functions should be a prerequisite to any software development. (That attitude, of course, was itself a solution to the problems of a decade earlier.) The prototyping approach was frequently perceived as an expensive method for defining requirements, even among those who recognized the quality improvements it could bring. The ACT/1 team developed software which allowed efficient production of prototypes.

The applications environment centered on transaction-oriented interactions which were presented to the user as full screen displays on IBM 3270-class terminals. ACT/1 provided a tool for quickly generating the screen panels, including the ability to use standard templates and to manipulate sections of the screen as single units. The screens were linked together in a scenario by specifying a flow table. The flow between screens was described by example: the developer entered typical values into a transaction screen, and ACT/1 then asked which screen was to be shown in response. In addition to displaying screen sequences, developers could build scenarios with nested sequences of interactions or calls to procedural code written in PL/I or Cobol which manipulated data values.

The ACT/1 team used the product themselves on development of future releases—each product version was prototyped for internal review, in much the same way ACT/1 was itself to be used externally. This process refined the product into a finely tuned professional tool. The organizational context involved a community of highly motivated developers with supportive management, very sensitive to user interface quality.

What happened to the product in the field, where some elements of that organizational context might be missing or transient? The product attracted a committed set of users, and was installed in over 100 commercial sites when we studied its use. Despite the acknowledged quality of the product, we found organizational factors to be the key determinant of how much the product was actually used after purchase.

Among the situations we examined, there was certainly usage as the developers had envisioned—as a standard tool to support prototyping of interactive information systems for iterative refinement. But other situations were also frequent. For example, ACT/1 provided superior screen generation facilities. Developers could use the tool to define transaction screens and generate print images of them to include in requirements documents, independent of any prototyping. For such users, the tool improved the efficiency of requirements definition without affecting the contents of the requirements.

In other cases, interest in the prototyping methodology often centered on key individuals or specific projects. When the individual moved to other tasks or the target project was completed, the tool could cease to be used unless there had been strong management commitment. The reverse case also occurred: management commitment to the tool or the development method did not guarantee usage. The development staff could bypass the tool when short term deadlines dominated their schedule, or when training for the tool was not adequately supported.

Another organizational factor which affected tool use was the way roles were divided between analysts and programmers. When analysts were responsible for functional requirements and the programmers designed the screen formats, ACT/1 could be lost in the gap between the two groups. In some other cases, the analysts did not have the same quality of computer access as the programmers, and could not access the tool as easily. Use of ACT/1 by analysts could also be considered as an infringement on the programmers' responsibilities.

These organizational dimensions did not surface during the prototyping of the product, since the development environment did not match the target situations. The designers had also not anticipated the impact of the tool on job satisfaction. Any tool perceived as eliminating a complex skill can only survive if the organizational climate shifts its reward system to avoid "deskilling." Designing screens and program skeletons was indeed a complex task—inordinately complex, as ACT/1 showed. But that complexity formed an important part of some developers' job security. And staff could be put off by a missionary zeal from the tool's local promoters, whose enthusiasm for better interfaces could easily come across as belittling traditional practices.

Despite all these organizational variations, the product did gain an enthusiastic following. Quite apart from benefits in the efficiency and quality of their work, many developers valued the increased rapport with the clients for their system. This was an effect of the prototyping process which ACT/1 facilitated: The developers would show the clients visible progress at short intervals, rather than disappearing for a long period to generate a written specification.

A second product was subsequently developed to allow an application prototyped with ACT/1 to evolve into a full production version. In the original design tool, the prototype was regarded as part of the requirements definition; it was documented and maintained throughout the system's life, but the screen designs and flow logic were reprogrammed for production release. The second product, the ACT/I production tool, allowed the screen designs, flow logic, and accompanying procedural code to be incorporated into production software. It was assumed that this software would probably be less efficient to run than programs written in a conventional language. However, there were clear gains in development and maintenance productivity, both in elapsed time and in cost. The production tool appeared to be an attractive route for applications which were not heavily used (some of which were known to consume more computing resources during development than during their entire lifetime of use).

The production tool did not gain the same measure of acceptance that the design tool had. One of the factors in some organizations was the role conflict between analysts and programmers, as outlined alone. But another important factor was the division of responsibilities at a group level, between development departments and operations departments. Use of the ACT/1 production tool often required approval from operations staff. The operations people received no direct benefit from the tool, and in turn would bear the costs associated with increased machine resource requirements. Unless a higher level of management could be convinced that there was overall benefit to the use of the production tool, the product would be used experimentally and then quietly abandoned.

As a result of an observation of ACT/1 in commercial settings, we summarized the experience in three marketing axioms for dialogue tools:

1. "The tool solves a problem which is among the top three work-related concerns for at least one third of potential users." The numbers in this axiom could vary from one situation to another. The point of the axiom is twofold. First, the tool should relieve some frustrating aspect of the job—the tedium of screen design in the case of ACT/1—in addition to any more positive impacts. This provides an immediate gain for the users. Second, some critical mass of users needs to be won over in order to maintain the momentum behind adoption of the tool.

2. "The tool provides both efficiency and quality benefits." Having benefits of both kinds broadens the tool's appeal to different kinds of people.
3. "The tool is priced within the budget of the users' manager and the tool's impact on work patterns does not fall outside that manager's responsibilities." As the price or impact of the tool placed the purchase decision farther away from the users, their enthusiasm became less and less important.

SOME CONTEXTS FOR USER INTERFACE DESIGN

The previous section dealt with a particular development environment: transaction-oriented mainframe applications built for use within an organization. If we broaden our scope to include software products developed by both small and large companies, the organizational context of dialogue design becomes even more varied. Joseph Fox (1982) has made a useful summary of these differences between a "product" environment and a "project" environment. The key differences are the competitive pressures on product developers and the open-endedness of many product specifications.

I have observed at close range the context of user interface design in a number of software companies, often together with my colleague Sabine Rohlfs of IF Interface Consulting in Ottawa. Like Berry's individual farms, each company has unique needs for dialogue tools. Dialogue tools solving problems in one organization might well create them in another.

Some capsule summaries will illustrate the range of environments in which dialogue design occurs:

1. A senior manager in a small computer company asked for help in establishing user interface standards for the company's personal computer applications. He was concerned that their software was being built by autonomous individuals, without overall consistency.

    We soon discovered that the software development was dependent on a few "whiz kids," most of whom did not look old enough to get a driver's license. They revelled in cryptic assembly language routines to increase the performance of their video graphics. Specifications were treated as a necessary evil on the way to dazzling code. There wasn't much enthusiasm for tools or standards which would confine their interfaces in the interests of consistency. Eventually, we achieved agreement on minimal dialogue standards, but the standards very quickly withered away in practice. (So did the company.)

2. In a small company producing business software for microcomputers, user interface design was the responsibility of the company's founder. He had nurtured the product through a long gestation, had now assembled a programming staff to complete development and provide product support, and requested an external review of the product's factors.

We recommend controlled testing of the software to assess the effectiveness of the user interface. The founder took the recommendation as a personal insult. He had confidence in his own ability to design appropriate dialogues. However, he would have been eager to see dialogue language tools which could have improved his programmers' productivity in implementing designs. The product nearly bogged down completely in the long delay from design to working code.

3. Another company producing microcomputer software engaged a team of outside consultants to perform extensive human factors studies on their designs. A second external group, hired to write user manuals, produced documentation of exceptional quality.

However, the company had made a marketing decision to release its product for a minimal memory configuration on the microcomputer, which would position it below its competitors in required memory. This decision forced the programmers to produce numerous code overlays. Some menus were rearranged based on the size of the resulting overlays—shorter code meant the function could be on the primary menu! The program structure led to delays when the software was being used, as well as to an unwieldy pattern of diskette swapping during initial loading.

4. We have observed several companies producing office systems software by prototyping key functions until the user interface has a satisfactory style. This often includes testing scenario prototypes with typical users. Commendable as this may be, as a design method it can have drawbacks of its own.

For example, when all the other functions are added for a production release, the feel of the interface can change dramatically. Sometimes, this is caused by a growth in the overall complexity faced by the users. At other times, the system performance degrades so that the early interface testing results are invalidated.

In the prototype stage, an emphasis on appearance and style can often mask gaps in functional definitions. One design team had settled on what they regarded as a "desktop metaphor" for their system, a user workstation integrating facilities on a network of computers. Users would access remote facilities or bring data to their desktop (personal computer) for processing. However, the nature of the desktop remained ambiguous. A typical item on the desktop was a list of objects like mail messages. But was the list updated when mail arrived, or only at user's request? (The implementors eventually chose the second option.) Why were objects brought onto the desktop at all? The answer couldn't involve efficiency of processing, since one assumption of the design was that the user didn't need to know where functions were actually carried out. In this particular system, users' desktops were to be available to them from any network access point, including simple terminals.

The product design went through numerous revisions as the ambiguities were ironed out during implementation. The designers recognized the need to systematize their design approach, so that the appearance of prototype screens followed other design decisions, rather than driving them.

5. As part of the Canadian Government's Office Communications Systems program, I produced a series of reports outlining a top-down method of user interface design (Carey, 1982) derived from work of Jim Foley and his colleagues (Foley & Wenner, 1981). The method began with a task analysis and a conceptual system model for users, then developed more concrete levels of dialogue style, interaction language, and physical representations. The method was intended to encourage a top-down design approach, in which decisions with the most impact were made early on.

We found methods like these worked well on designs that began with a "clean slate," i.e., no preconceptions about what the final interface should be. This was particularly effective at delaying decisions to incorporate flashy features which had caught a developer's eye in some other product, but served no well-defined purpose in the interface under construction. The top down method forced a definition of information flows before designing display screens to implement them.

In other instances, the top-down approach did not work. One design team tried to apply the method to another product design, a word processor on a shared departmental office system. Based on marketing considerations, the company had decided their word processor should feel familiar to users of a particular microcomputer package. The micro package was efficient to use but difficult to learn. However, they wanted to access the system from terminals with minimal capability, so the team couldn't assume there would be function keys as in the original package.

The top-down design methods were of little help in this case, because the existing micro package could not be retrofitted into a consistent top-down framework. Eventually, the team engineered a two layer user interface which they judged to be compatible for existing users of the micro package, but easier for new users to learn. Novices could use a basic command set from the micro package, with a few command extenders which increased the scope of any function (line to paragraph to section, for example). This compensated for the potential lack of function keys. When function keys were present, the full command set of the micro package could also be used. This solution, the creation of one inventive designer, was commended in the external review and included in the final office system. However, the command extenders were not integrated into other components of the office system, leaving some inconsistencies in the interface.

6. A large multinational vendor had addressed these last two problems, incomplete specifications and integrated interfaces. Each product required a rigorous user interface specification, which passed through formal testing and extensive approvals. A major concern during the approval process was consistency across a varied product line.

    But the size of the formal specifications (hundreds of pages) and the elapsed time for approvals often made the design process cumbersome. The implementers found the specification difficult to comprehend, and made their own decisions when faced with ambiguities close to deadline. The separation of design and implementation teams was both a strength and a weakness of the organizational context. (They were in autonomous divisions in different countries.) Products were late to market and incomplete. The company has instituted a major development project to produce design tools which will meet some of these needs.

DESIGNING DIALOGUE TOOLS

The last section presented capsule views of dialogue design in real product settings, outside the research labs where we build our new dialogue design tools. How can we incorporate the needs of these specific people and places into our next generation of tools?

In this section I will illustrate how what we have learned is influencing our research group in developing new tools for user interfaces. We are targeting our tools to meet the problems we observed in several companies, such as those in cases (4) and (6) of the previous section. These companies use available tools to efficiently produce dialogue objects, like menus, and to handle the syntax of user interactions. Their pressing need is for tools which will allow them to manage the complexity of their user interface specifications, to ensure that their efficient implementations produce what was intended.

We have been developing a toolkit which provides a specification method for user interfaces, and links to an interpreter which runs the specification as a prototype. The features of the toolkit are motivated by specific needs we observed in our target clients. For example:

1. Interface consistency across a product line is an important issue for our target clients. John Bennett (1984) has labelled this issue the "architecture problem." Management needs to be assured that there is a clear boundary between the product line standard and the application dependent features.
2. While the managers want to see prototypes which give the flavour of the product, they do not want to personally see specifications which show how to generalize from the prototype to the full product. The designers need to generate, and the programmers need to use, this kind of specification. But it must be rigorous without being voluminous. So the toolkit must provide a formal, concise, and interpretable specification language.
3. One potential issue, automatic generation of program code, is not a key concern for these users. They do not identify programming as a bottleneck, if specifications are clear and standard interface facilities are available. Moreover, an attempt to work on this area would run into the organizational conflicts outlined in section two with the ACT/1 production tool.
4. If the specification can be interpreted to produce a rapid prototype, the designers should experience productivity gains (they currently program scenario prototypes themselves, sometimes with programmers as assistants). To provide quality gains for them, the toolkit can allow them to express parts of their design task which were not previously supported. For example, the dialogue styles being developed depend on intensive interaction with the people who use them. The simple transaction-oriented screens of ACT/1 are no longer sufficient—the toolkit must support specification for direct manipulation of screen objects.

The specification must include both appearance and the semantics underlying the appearance.

We found in observing ACT/1 that designers invariably drew on paper an overall view of their screen sequence. This activity structure should have been built into the ACT/1 product. Our toolkit is intended to provide an efficient, maintainable, high level perspective on the possible dialogue states.

5. If the toolkit meets organizational needs and provides both effectiveness and efficiency gains for designers, the tool may still not be welcomed. Job satisfaction has to remain at least as high as it was without the toolkit. The designers do not regard formal specification as a very rewarding job component. Once they have created an interface and seen it work as a prototype, documenting the details for someone else is perceived as a much less creative activity. A specification toolkit doesn't necessarily increase the effort devoted to this formalization—it should reduce it—but it does force it earlier in the design task, where it is more noticeable. Is there a way to compensate designers so that the formalism is not so intrusive?

    One aspect of system development which seems to be universally disliked is creation of error and help messages covering all the situations which a user might encounter. We are experimenting with using the specification to generate these messages, since it contains considerable semantic information. Our motivation for doing so is to provide an incentive for use of the toolkit. If we can produce a prototype without requiring designers to exhaustively generate error messages, we believe the toolkit will be more attractive to them (not just to management).

6. The toolkit also must accommodate individual differences. Testing has shown us that our original toolkit design reflected our own cognitive styles. We originally imposed the top down framework outlined in one of the cases in the last section. But we found our test users were frequently designing bottom up, from screen image to a description of meaning.

    Future versions of the toolkit will work from screen mockups back to the specification of application data objects.

The details of our prototype toolkit are described elsewhere (Carey, 1986; Carey & Graham, 1987). The appendix to this chapter sketches in a few features which show how some of the needs described above can be addressed. The toolkit is still in its preliminary stages, and we are by no means sure that we have the answers right. But we do feel confident that we are asking the right questions—that we understand the potential users of the toolkit, and the contexts in which they work.

THE GIFT OF GOOD DIALOGUE DESIGN

The essay by Wendell Berry that I quoted earlier is entitled "The Gift of Good Land." To large-scale agricultural methods, a specific piece of land can appear as an idiosyncratic nuisance, to be levelled into uniformity with the model farm around which the method has been built. To the people-scale farmer, the land is a gift. Every hill and gully is to be nurtured in a way specific to its gift, to produce the singular harvest for which it is appropriate.

Software designers have to be regarded in the same light. The peculiarities of each specific design situation are gifts, which lend themselves to certain methods and result in unique products. We have to avoid tools which ignore the gifts and specific needs of each design context.

Berry uses the term *heroic technology* to describe these technological solutions to nonproblems. I'm afraid some of the existing tools and techniques for user interface design are like that, answers in search of a question. They will never make the contribution we hope unless we design them to address the real needs and specific context where user interfaces are produced. The earlier quote on large scale technologies concludes with these words:

> The bigger and more expensive, the more heroic they are, the harder they are to apply considerately and conservingly. (Berry, 1981, p. 280).

APPENDIX—THE SPIRAL TOOLKIT

This appendix provides a skeletal description of the toolkit being developed in our research lab to address the needs outlined in section four of the chapter. This discussion is more technical than the chapter itself, and will be of interest to others building tools of a similar nature. This overview will sketch how the objectives of the toolkit have shaped its design. The references provided with the chapter contain fuller details.

We have been developing the Spiral toolkit for specifying interactive dialogues, using a model of user interfaces which contains two kinds of information. As with most user interface specifications, we use extended finite state diagrams to picture the states which the dialogue goes through in response to user actions.

In addition, we use semantic nets to explicitly represent the objects involved in the dialogue:

- the spreadsheets, documents, etc., manipulated in the user's task
- the windows, menus, command streams, etc., involved in the interaction itself
- the physical objects, such as function keys and screen displays.

The interface is represented by object descriptions and state diagrams (with actions) in these three components: task, interaction, and media. The three levels of action correspond, for input, to

- individual user movements, like keystrokes
- interpreted units of actions, like menu selection or command entry
- a functional unit, manipulating the task data in some way.

These three components, taken together, correspond to the elements in the conceptual model which the designer wants the user to develop for the interface. None of the concepts we use are particularly novel; we have adapted existing techniques in conceptual modelling to the special case of user interfaces.

How Are Standard Product Interfaces Defined?

Suppose we want to include in our standard product interface a requirement for "command menus always available at the bottom of a screen." This represents an information flow to the user, separate from windows showing data objects. In the interaction component of the model, this is defined as an information pathway object— common to all states of the dialogue.

Its specification includes a formal definition of its contents. The definition uses the vocabulary of the extended finite state diagrams to construct a relation formalizing the informal notion of "available commands." The relation can be applied to any such state diagram, so that any specification which includes it will have the desired menu.

The full specification of this feature includes a pathway definition in the interaction component, and a definition in the media component which determines its location at the bottom of the screen. This specification can be retained in a component library, to be retrieved by designers in constructing their designs. The three components of the model provide a unique advantage for this kind of standard: most specification models separate the details of physical appearance from the syntax and semantics, but, to define a feature such as the above menus, the model must allow definitions which cross these levels.

How Do You Keep the Specification Concise?

In the designer's mind, the interface design usually has a conceptual simplicity, even when it is a little fuzzy around the edges. The specification becomes cumbersome when the specification method doesn't fit with the designer's natural structuring of the design. For example, the requirement to display an action menu at all times must be stated once in the specification rather than with all possible states.

Appropriate abstractions allow us to capture these aspects. In the Spiral toolkit, there is a built-in "kind of" abstraction, which allows the designer to form natural classes sharing properties. In the case of the omnipresent menu, the designer defines a class of dialogue states having that menu, and then specifies that all states belong to that class.

Could You Generate User Interface Code From a Specification?

The separation of information in the model doesn't appear to lend itself to generation of code to follow the model's components. That is, the three components are restricted in the information they contain about each other. This appears to be an effective mechanism for specification, but not for implementation.

How Does the Designer Record Semantics?

Each action available to the user is specified with preconditions which must hold for that action to be valid, and postconditions which will hold if the action is taken. These conditions can be used by an interpreter to simulate use of the interface.

The designer shows the overall task structure by constructing a state diagram which is independent of the particular interaction style being used. Just as a given standard style can be applied to different applications, a given application can be combined with different interaction styles.

How Might You Generate Error Messages?

While we have not yet implemented any error messages to the user of a simulated interface, the necessary information is present in the specification. The preconditions indicate when actions are valid, and the designer can define an information pathway to the user showing valid conditions and/or invalid conditions. This allows a specification of a window showing error messages (the actual message shown to the user would have to be translated into something closer to natural language format).

Similarly, some of the information necessary to produce navigational assistance is also present in the specification. Since the postconditions of each action are defined, we can consider answering questions like "how do I get there from here?"

How Do You Accommodate Individual Differences Among Designers?

The toolkit provides a graphic style of interaction with the model. Initially, designers had to work top down, from the task description through the interaction and media components. We are currently working on a version which allows the designer to begin with a screen mockup and work backwards to specification of function. This involves asking the designer for the appropriate generalizations of the objects on the display screen.

What is the Current Status of the Toolkit?

Initial versions of the Spiral toolkit have been built over the last 2 years. The latest version runs on a Sun workstation, with implementation in C and Sunviews. The interpreter work has been done in Prolog. The method has been used to describe a spreadsheet package, a computer conferencing system, and a screen paint program. It has been used by staff of the research project, and reviewed by user interface designers from the target industry groups.

Development of the toolkit has been supported by strategic grants from the Natural Sciences and Engineering Research Council of Canada.

REFERENCES

Bennett, J.L. (1984). The concept of architecture applied to user interfaces in interactive computer systems. In B. Shackel (Ed.), *Human Computer Interaction—Interact '84* (pp. 127–131). Amsterdam: North-Holland.

Berry, W. (1981). *The gift of good technology.* San Francisco, CA: North Point Press.

Carey, T.T. (1982). *User interfaces for office communications systems. Part I: Components. Part II: Designing. Part III: Tools.* Ottawa, Canada: Government of Canada, Department of Communications.

Carey, T.T. (1986). Evaluating formal specifications for user interfaces. *Proceedings, Fourth Symposium on Empirical Foundations of Information and Systems Sciences: Evaluating User Interfaces. Atlanta, GA: Georgia Institute of Technology.*

Carey, T.T., & Graham, H. (1987). *Modular specification of user interfaces: Two case studies. In H.J. Bullinger (Ed.), Human Computer Interaction—Interact '87.* Amsterdam: North-Holland.

Carey, T.T., & Mason, R.E.A. (1983). Information systems prototyping techniques, tools and methodologies. *Infor: Canadian Journal of Operational Research and Information Processing, 21*(3), 177–191.

Foley, J., & Wenner, P. (1982). The George Washington University core system implementation. *Computer Graphics, 15*(3), 123–131.

Fox, J. (1982). *Software and its development.* Englewood Cliffs, NJ: Prentice-Hall.

Mason, R.E.A., & Carey, T.T. (1981). Productivity experiences with a scenario tool. *Proceedings IEEE Compcon. Fall 81.* Washington, DC: IEEE.

Mason, R.E.A., & Carey, T.T. (1983). Prototyping interactive information systems. *CACM, 26*(5), 347–354.

CHAPTER 6

Design and Implementation of an Object-oriented User Interface Management System

John L. Sibert
William D. Hurley
Teresa W. Bleser

*Department of Electrical Engineering and
Computer Science
School of Engineering and Applied Science
The George Washington University*

INTRODUCTION

Although the first published paper to use the term *user interface management system* (UIMS) was probably Kasik (1982), many of the basic principles date back at least to Newman's *reaction handler* (Newman, 1968). The term was popularized by a workshop (GIIT; Thomas & Griffith, 1983) which met in June 1982 to consider issues of graphical interaction. Essentially, a UIMS mediates the interaction between the end user of an application and the application code itself (Figure 1). This results in a separation of responsibility between the UIMS and the application, with the application being responsible for carrying out the "work" while the UIMS handles all details of communicating with the end user. This separation can lead to a number of advantages, summarized from Olsen, Buxton, Ehrich, Kasik, Rhyne, and Sibert (1984):

- The correct roles of individuals involved in interface development are supported and represented.
- Application programmers are not required to devote attention to human–computer interaction.

- The interface can be designed by specialists such as human factors experts.
- There can be more consistent interfaces within and across applications.
- Applications can be reused and organized in different ways to suit institutional needs.
- An interface can be quickly modified without changes to the application code; this means more rapid prototyping.
- Applications can be modified more quickly and maintained more easily.
- Different interfaces to the same application can be tailored for type or individual differences among end-users.
- Application programs become highly portable between different installations; the differences are accounted for by the user interfaces.
- Assuming sufficient information about the application program, interfaces can be developed independently from the development of application code.

Researchers have developed a variety of different UIMSs in hopes of achieving some or all of these advantages. Our highest priority has been to develop a useful tool for ourselves and others engaged in user interface development. Because of this emphasis, the George Washington user interface management system (GWUIMS) has developed as a tool for rapidly prototyping interactive user interfaces more than as a full capability UIMS. However, we feel comfortable calling it a UIMS because the design does allow for its use with "real" applications, although they must be packaged appropriately.

Throughout the design and implementation of the GWUIMS, we have had a variety of goals in mind. We wish to design interfaces using interaction techniques which closely resemble those used in the end product. Because many systems are now featuring some form of direct manipulation of objects, such as icons or menus, we

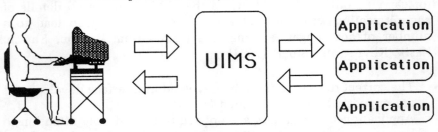

Figure 1. A UIMS mediates human-computer interaction.

feel that it is natural to design such interfaces by direct manipulation as well. Furthermore, we believe that, at any time in the design process, it is important to be able to "try out" a portion of the design with a realistic simulation of the system's behavior. These and other considerations led us to an object-oriented model for our UIMS design.

In addition to the development of a natural and easy to use rapid prototyping system, we are using the GWUIMS to examine alternative conceptual models for user interfaces. A major theme of this chapter is how the GWUIMS provides a framework for investigating these different models and overcoming their deficiencies.

A final motivation of our work has been to develop a system to serve as a test bed for developing knowledge-based systems to aid in designing certain aspects of the user interface. This is a longer-range goal, but the GWUIMS represents a large step in that direction. In the following pages, we will present a detailed overview of the GWUIMS design, along with a scenario of the system in use. But first, we provide a sampling of other UIMS developments.

A SAMPLING OF SELECTED UIMS DEVELOPMENTS

The current interest in UIMSs was given direction and initial impetus by a workshop held in Seattle Washington in 1982. The workshop consisted of 24 invited professionals from industry and academia. The primary results, summarized from Thomas and Griffith (1983), were:

- Clarification of the role and advantages of a UIMS.
- Definition of three dimensions for classifying a UIMS: single vs. multiple threads of control, external vs. internal control of the application, and simple vs. hierarchial dialogues.
- Definition of logical UIMS models.
- Agreement on the following points:
  - The design of user interfaces requires better tools to free the designer from implementation details and allow concentration on the human factors of the interface.
  - A coordinated effort by several interdisciplinary specialists is required to build quality user interfaces.
  - The UIMS can be separate from the application program and the graphics output package.
  - There is a need for user-driven, versus application-driven, dialogues.

- Application programmers should separate application functions from user interface functions now, in order to allow the use of UIMS tools in future implementations.
- The following research issues were raised:
  - A methodology for dealing with physical device pragmatics is needed in order to incorporate "natural" interaction techniques into the user interface.
  - A conceptual model is needed for the connections among a UIMS, graphics package, and the application.
  - A model and language for specifying user interactions are needed which are based on experience with real-world applications.
  - Precise definitions are needed of both user input style and style-independent interface.

Since that conference, three issues appear to have emerged as fundamental to the understanding and future successful development of UIMSs. The first issue is the separation of three components: application program, dialogue specification, and graphics software. The second issue is the form of the dialogue specification itself. Much work has been done using formal languages to specify and analyze user interfaces (Reisner, 1981; Bleser & Foley, 1982; Jacob, 1983). Most recently, the accessibility of artificial intelligence tools and techniques has been a catalyst for the notion of using knowledge-based subsystems (Roach, Pitman, Reilly, & Savarese, 1982; Cochran & Stocker, 1985; Myers & Buxton, 1986; Mackinlay, 1986; Mark, 1986).

The remainder of this section provides a sampling of UIMS developments. The purpose is three-fold: first, to provide an overview of the various UIMS research and development efforts; second, to highlight what has and has not been accomplished related to the three fundamental issues mentioned above; and, finally, to indicate what we see as a trend towards a more object-oriented approach.

The systems feature conceptual models of the user interface falling into two broad categories. The more frequently used of these contains the *linguistic* models (Foley & van Dam, 1982; Moran, 1981), which view the interaction between human and computer as a dialogue, analogous to a conversation between two persons. The user interface, including interactive inputs, all output, and the synchronization of input and output, can be viewed as effectively defining the "language" in which this dialogue takes place. Following this model, we can think of the user interface language as having lexemes, syntax, and semantics just as any other language does. In this case, the lexemes are sequences of events with physical devices, such as typing on a keyboard, for input, and displaying primitives, words, lines, icons, etc., for output. The syntax is the structure of the input language or the display screen layout. The semantics are embodied in the units of work to be done by the application behind the user interface.

The second category of user interface models are the *spatial* models, which include interactive graphic or direct manipulation models. The object-oriented paradigm is another inherently spatial model.

Among the UIMS developments described below, the *abstract interaction handler* (AIH; Feldman & Rogers, 1982) represents an extreme application of the linguistic model. We can take the AIH as the starting place in the evolution towards object-oriented models. EZWin (Lieberman, 1985), at the other extreme, has a very strong object orientation.

The number of UIMS researchers is increasing ever more rapidly; space and time do not permit description here of all their fine efforts. The following, regrettably, must be merely a sampling. Furthermore, we have chosen our sampling to reflect systems oriented towards interactive computer graphics, partly because this is our own emphasis, and partly because we feel that graphic interfaces offer a wider range of problems to the user interface designer.

Abstract Interaction Handler

Rosenthal (1981) and Feldman and Rogers (1982) suggested the physical separation of application modules and interactive sequences. Feldman and Rogers (1982) went a step further, by proposing a language which enforces logical separation. They proposed the separation of application semantics from information which is specific to user interaction style. Interaction style was defined as the user's perception of a dialogue with a computer, i.e., the totality of interaction techniques, combined with syntax of the input language, display layout, etc. The abstract interaction handler (AIH) is the vehicle for implementing this separation. It is responsible for exchanging style-independent information with the application modules, and communicating with style modules which contain details of specific interaction styles.

The AIH has two principle components. The *intermediate language* (IL) enforces the logical separation between interactive dialogue and application programs. It describes the structure of a dialogue, the sequence of application module invocations, and the style-independent part of the interactive system. The IL is a directed graph (equivalent to a finite state transition network) whose nodes contain interactive operations, and prompt and help text, and whose arc labels specify application modules.

The second AIH component is an *interaction handler* (IH) which interprets the IL code, resulting in calls to style modules to get user input and to invoke application modules. Binding between interactions and specific devices in the AIH was designed to be handled by a standard graphics package, in this case SIGGRAPH/CORE.

In practice, use of the AIH proved difficult (Kamran, 1985; Sibert, Belliardi, & Kamran, 1985). Nontrivial interactive dialogues, especially those making heavy use of interactive graphics, were cumbersome to specify. Lack of concurrency in the language definition made it difficult to include universal availability for such functions as "help" and "undo last action." The strict separation between the syntactic and semantic levels of the dialogue made semantic error handling and application-determined flow of control impossible in some cases.

The AIH in one sense represents the extreme application of the linguistic model. This was intentional, as a major motivation was to determine the limits of a finite state grammar as a dialogue specification.

TIGER UIMS

Kasik's (1982) paper "A user interface management system," describes the TIGER UIMS, which was designed to remove from the system designer the burden of specifying physical interaction handling. This is accomplished by decoupling physical interaction handling from logical function performance. The TIGER UIMS uses a technique of logical and physical separation of the interactive dialogue sequences from graphics devices. The technique is analogous to that of graphics systems like SIGGRAPH/CORE, in which a standard set of operations for a logical device is automatically mapped to different physical devices.

An application-independent dialogue specification language is similar to a schema definition language in a data base management system. The dialogue specification language indicates a function name and interaction technique; the application program specifies the semantic feedback. A preprocessor compiles the dialogue specifications into a tree-structured menu file which is read by an interpreter at run-time.

The interpreter provides external control of the application by reading the menu file, handling the end-user's physical interactions, and invoking application procedures in response to the end-user's inputs. The behavior of the interpreter can be described as follows. The interpreter collects and processes interrupts. This may cause invocation of an application procedure, or may define input parameters to a function. If an application function is invoked by the end-user, the interpreter first invokes functions which impose application-defined constraints on dynamically entered user inputs. When the constraints are met, the interpreter invokes the application procedures, passing them information via parameter lists that are specifically tailored to a particular input. In the event of an error, the application procedure returns an error code which is also part of the parameter list. The interpreter contains all the form, positioning, and style specifications of the display; the application program determines the form of the presentation of application output.

The design of this system focuses on the input language specification. The system has a limited set (pick is the only one mentioned) of virtual devices whose feedback is hardcoded into them. The UIMS provides a predefined external presentation of the interactive dialogue (menu system) which is not significantly modifiable.

Note that, while the AIH of Feldman and Rogers (1982) relied on a graphics package for input and output, the TIGER UIMS uses a graphics package for output only; input is handled by the UIMS, but uses a virtual device concept similar to that of SIGGRAPH/ CORE, with similar device independence.

SYNGRAPH

The Syngraph UIMS (Olsen & Dempsey, 1983) generates interactive Pascal programs from a description of the input language grammar. The input language is specified in an extended BNF which includes logical input token names, application actions, and the syntactic specification of the interface. The specification language closely resembles that of Bleser and Foley (1982), but is used for implementation of the dialogue as well as specification. The input techniques and devices are bound to "logical" token names. The application actions are Pascal procedures. The syntactic specification defines valid sequences of input tokens, prompts, and echos.

A parser automaton is generated from the grammar; it contains complete syntactic information about the interface. The user interface is divided into and specified by levels of interaction (subdialogues). This results in the removal from the application program of all control and management of interactive devices.

Syngraph is limited to a menu-driven interface in which the allocation and organization of menus and virtual devices are performed automatically and are fixed at design time. It uses built-in feedback techniques; the simulated valuators have feedback techniques hard-coded. Output specification is in the application actions.

GRINS

The Graphical Interaction System (GRINS) is a UIMS which consists of an automaton-based dialogue controller and a dynamic display model. Olsen, Dempsey, and Rogge (1985) described GRINS, focusing the description on the linkage between a logical device interface and the graphical presentation of virtual devices, specifically between input language parsing and graphical feedback.

GRINS parses a description of an interactive interface which is described in a *dialog design language.* The output of the parser is an *interactive push-down automaton* (IPDA) and a *display object definitions file.* The dialog design language and the IPDA correspond to the user interface specification language and executable IPDA discussed in Olsen's earlier work (Olsen, 1983b). The display objects definitions file describes to some degree the structure of the application. In the concept of display objects, we find a movement towards an object-oriented view of the UIMS-application interface. We will return to a description of display objects later; first, an overview of the GRINS system.

A *dialog manager* interprets IPDA and controls the interaction; it receives inputs from logical and physical device handlers, and makes calls on both the application and a *constraint interpreter.* Two virtual devices are supported: picks and menu items. Physical devices can of course be bound to multiple logical devices.

The IPDA partitions a dialogue into subdialogs (called *modes*). Each subdialog is characterized by a set of logical devices accessible to that mode. Acceptable inputs are defined by the current state of the dialogue; devices are enabled and disabled by the dialog manager upon each change of state. When the dialog manager accepts an input, it is considered acknowledged. Inputs stay in an acknowledged state until a condition called closure (syntactic) is reached as determined by the dialog manager.

A layout editor is provided for designing screens, menus, space for feedback and prompts, etc. The editor constructs a layout for each mode of the IPDA. Each menu item represents a logical input device, and the designer indicates the state of the device (enabled/disabled, acknowledged/unacknowledged) for each mode. The layout editor is used to color code menu item icons for these four states. The GRINS logical input device handler modifies attributes during runtime as states change.

Now we return to a discussion of display objects. The authors found that graphic data structures, such as the display files provided by SIGGRAPH/CORE and GKS, and their own structure for describing screen layouts, are not sufficient for providing feedback involving input techniques more dynamic than menu icons. A computational linkage between input values and output parameters is required. The display objects were developed to provide this linkage based on three principles:

• Simple value substitution is not sufficient to link inputs to outputs.
• I/O linkage is frequently application specific.
• An image represents an application data object whose presentation is being defined.

In GRINS, display objects are intended to reflect the structure (to some degree) of the application program. The display object definitions contain the computationally constrained portion of the output definition. Display objects are defined at dialogue design time using an object description language for modeling application specific display objects. The definition includes graphical primitives and their arguments (constants, control values, object parameters). From this definition, a template is created in the display manager. If a control value is changed, assertions in the display object are checked; if an assertion fails, the image remains unchanged. Thus, the design is such that any mechanism which allows the UIMS to change the form of a displayed image has a provision for the application to veto the change. This is possible because the functions which compute assertions and implied values can be application-specific functions.

A display object can be used as a component of another object. The propagation of values between an object and its component object is functionally identical to an attribute grammar. An incremental attribute flow algorithm is used to determine which values (attributes) must be recomputed after a change is made.

The separation between application and UIMS is evidenced in that the application sees only certain arguments in its own units, and the dialog manager sees only control variables (and knows their unit systems).

GRINS represents an evolutionary change of SYNGRAPH in that it substitutes the more powerful IPDA for the BNF specification of the earlier system. Despite the introduction of display objects, GRINS is still in the mainstream of the linguistic model approach. But it represents the end of a trend towards increasingly powerful syntactic specifications of human–computer dialogues which began with the AIH.

EZWin

During the latter part of the period covered by the developments summarized above, systems based on the spatial type of model began to appear. One example, the EZWin system (Lieberman, 1985), is a graphical interface kit for building menu-driven interfaces and applications which manipulate graphical objects. EZWin is an object-oriented interpreter (analogous to a programming language interpreter) used to build interfaces to a restricted class of applications: those which edit sets of graphical objects. The functionality is thus restricted to manipulating and modifying graphical objects, or components of graphical objects. This restriction precludes classifying EZWin as a general purpose UIMS. This restriction is, at least conceptually, quite artificial; there is no inherent reason why application functionality could not be extended.

EZWin allows prefix, postfix, or infix syntax for command entry. It assembles a call to a command object and sends it a DO-IT message when all the arguments are chosen. For prefix, the EZWin object ensures that, at all times, only objects currently acceptable as arguments are mouse sensitive. For postfix, after each argument is selected, the set of commands is filtered by asking each command object whether or not the current list of arguments is acceptable; mouse sensitivity for that command is on only if the current list of arguments is acceptable.

Error prevention is implemented by controlling the mouse sensitivity of objects so that only "legal" objects are sensitive, and by using pop-up command menus which display only valid commands based on the current set of arguments. A limited form of undo is implemented with standard command objects, called delete and undelete, which share a delete-history list of deleted objects. A menu of deleted objects is also available.

In addition to the restricted functionality of application programs, we note that EZWin objects restrict the user dialogue to a fixed top-level command loop for menu-driven systems. As mentioned above, EZWin is not a true general purpose UIMS, but we did include it in this abbreviated survey because of its strong object orientation and use of graphic interaction.

Summary

We have seen from these samples that both the purely linguistic and the purely spatial models have been successfully used to build UIMSs. However, both types of models have disadvantages. Although the linguistic models provide a useful framework for focusing on issues that occur within the semantic, syntactic, and lexical levels of a dialogue, these models encourage the designer to view each of these levels in isolation. In addition, they have limitations when used to specify interactive graphics or direct manipulation interfaces. Spatial models, on the other hand, lack straightforward syntactic mechanisms for sequencing events such as those provided by linguistic models. Furthermore, linguistic models provide a means of formal specification of interactive dialogues (Reisner, 1981; Bleser & Foley, 1982; Jacob, 1983). Such formal specifications allow rigorous analysis of interactive dialogues prior to implementation.

We have experience in designing UIMSs within the context of both classes of model. The current version of the GWUIMS is the most recent in a series of UIMSs developed at The George Washington University. Its immediate predecessor (Sibert & Hurley, 1984) was a system based on an augmented transition network (ATN), the equivalent of a context sensitive grammar. Based on our experiences, we have become increasingly dissatisfied with the linguistic model as a holistic model of user–computer interface (Sibert, Belliardi, & Kamran, 1985). This is particularly true concerning interfaces which make heavy or innovative use of interactive graphic techniques. As an alternative, we have turned to an object-oriented model. We believe the GWUIMS to be the first full scale object-oriented UIMS to be designed as such, although several recent efforts (in particular, Green, 1985) include a strong degree of object orientation.

In the following sections we discuss the theoretical underpinnings of the GWUIMS, its design and implementation, and how GWUIMS provides a framework for investigating different user interface models and overcoming their deficiencies.

DESIGN PHILOSOPHY OF THE GWUIMS

We feel that current examples of good user interfaces normally incorporate aspects of both linguistic and spatial models. Though we chose to adopt an inherently spatial object-oriented paradigm, we include some aspects of the linguistic model by defining the boundaries of the lexical, syntactic, and semantic levels of the interface language within objects. Each boundary between two levels is embodied in a specialized object class with sufficient knowledge about adjacent linguistic levels for it to accomplish its function.

Our design philosophy has been influenced by the development of object-oriented programming, dating from the Simula language (Dahl & Nygaard, 1966) and popularly known in Smalltalk (Goldberg, 1984). Object-oriented programming has been intimately related to graphics for some time; concepts can be recognized in Anson's device model (Anson, 1982), as well as in other recent interactive graphics applications (Foley & McMath, 1986; Beach, Beatty, Booth, Plebon, & Fiume, 1982; and Lipkie, Evans, Newlin, & Weissman, 1982, to name a few).

We gain several advantages from this object paradigm. First, it provides a natural mechanism for representing our system at several levels of abstraction, since an object may be anything from a very high level concept, such as an icon construction tool, to a very low level concept, such as an input device driver. The designer of a user interface may wish to work at very different levels of abstraction, depending on whether a new interaction technique is being developed or an interface to an application such as a CAD system is being designed. A second advantage is the ease with which simple objects can be combined into more complex objects, making it possible for us to define new components of a system interactively by building them from existing objects. A third advantage is the inherent flexibility of systems defined in terms of message-passing protocols. It is easy for us to add new capabilities to the system without extensive recoding. Finally, the object paradigm allows us to relegate design constraints (for our UIMS implementation, not for user interfaces designed using it) imposed by hardware and operating systems, to low levels of the implementation.

THE GWUIMS SYSTEM DESIGN

In this section, we provide an overview of our object-oriented UIMS design, after defining our use of terms related to object-oriented programming.

Objects in the GWUIMS

There are numerous versions of the object-oriented abstraction and probably as many different sets of terminology; for example, see

Stefik and Bobrow (1986). This section defines our use of the terminology.

We define an *object* as an entity with *attributes* and *relationships*
with other objects (e.g., an object for a temperature gauge might
include attributes describing its temperature range, size, color, danger level, etc., while the value of a relationship could be the identity
of an alarm object). The behavior of an object is embodied in *methods*
which are procedures for performing activities (these would include
graphics routines to display the temperature dial). All activity in
an object-oriented system is caused by communication between
objects. Objects communicate by sending *messages* to other objects
requesting information from them, or requesting them to exhibit
some form of behavior (e.g., another object in the system can send
a message to the temperature gauge, requesting it to display itself).

We define different *classes* of objects, and each object is an
instance of one class. Each instance of a class has the same methods
as all other instances of that class; it differs from other instances
only in the values of its attributes and relationships. For example,
the temperature gauge described above is an instance of the class
graphic object. The following pseudo code defines the class:

> *Class:* graphic_object;
> *Attributes:* color, font, linestyle, position, visibility,
>   hot_spot_extent, pickability, vector_list, text_list, pix_rect_list;
> *Relationships:* graphic_object_list;
> *Methods:* display, make_invisible, change_position;
> *Messages:* none;

The only relationship defined is a list of graphic objects making
it possible to build object hierarchies. The graphic object originates
no messages; it only responds to messages to perform its methods,
and forwards messages to the objects on its graphic object list. In
addition to the methods listed above, graphic objects share with all
objects certain common behaviors such as adding, setting, and retrieving attribute values.

Overview

Our system architecture is partly a reaction to earlier work at GW
(Feldman & Rogers, 1982; Kamran & Feldman, 1983) which maintained a strict logical separation between the lexical, syntactic, and
semantic levels of the user computer interface. We are convinced
that it is not possible to build systems which handle semantic errors

and feedback intelligently if we maintain a strict separation between the lexical/syntactic domain in the UIMS on the one hand, and the semantic domain of the application on the other (Sibert, Belliardi, & Kamran, 1985). Our current design embodies these boundaries between linguistic levels within objects, so that an object's behavior can depend on information about more than one level.

Figure 2 is an upper level view of our system. The box labeled *USER INTERFACE* represents a collection of objects which will be described later; at this point, it is taken as a black box. In addition to the *USER INTERFACE,* the system consists of *representation objects* (R_objects), *interaction objects* (I_objects), and *application objects* (A_objects). The arrows in Figures 2–4 indicate allowed message paths. For example, a representation object may only send messages to an interaction object or to objects within the USER INTERFACE, and it receives messages only from the same set of objects. This design restriction on message paths is a means of enforcing a logical separation between different linguistic levels within the UIMS. Messages are forced to pass through objects which incorporate boundaries between levels.

The A_objects on the right in Figure 2 embody the semantics of the application. For prototyping user interfaces, the A_objects are simulators which are parameterized to simulate aspects of an application's behavior which could affect the user interface. To use our system with a real application, the procedural code and data structures of the actual application must be packaged into A_objects. The difficulty of doing this with an existing application clearly varies with the structure of the application code.

The A_objects may send messages to, and receive messages from, the interaction objects (I_objects), which encapsulate the syntactic/semantic boundary. I_objects have some general knowledge of the application semantics, but the implementation of these semantics is completely within the A_objects. Typically, an I_object sends a message to an A_object, requesting that it perform its function and supplying it with any data or parameters it might need. There is information within the application domain which the UIMS must understand if it is to properly handle error recovery, application control flow, and presentation of results. Examples include the nature of semantic errors, the results of intermediate calculations, and results for presentation to the end user. The A_object supplies this information by sending messages to an appropriate I_object.

The representation object (R_object) is responsible for determining how information is to be displayed to the end user and for partially verifying the syntax of any input from the end user before passing it on to the interaction object (see the section on input parsing for

Lexical   Syntactic   Semantic

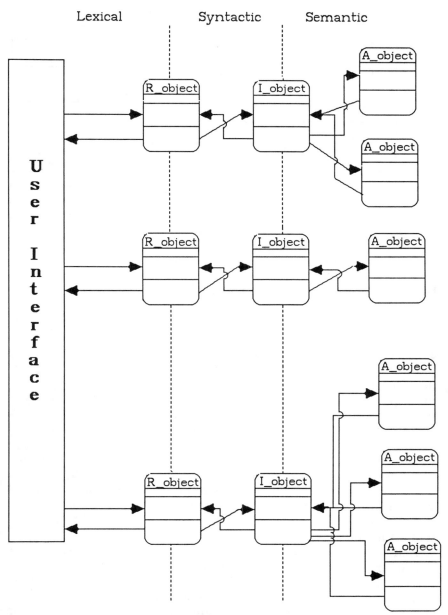

Figure 2.   Overview of the GWUIMS.

more details of the R_object's role). R_objects embody the boundary between the lexical and syntactic levels of the UIMS.

Now let us take a more detailed look at how information is

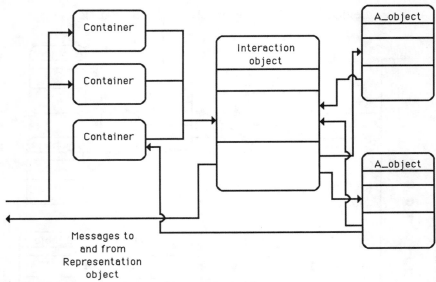

Figure 3.   An interaction object and containers.

handled within the interaction object. Figure 3 gives a detailed view
of the structure of an interaction object. Among its relationships is
a list of *containers.* The purpose of these containers is to hold
information for transmission in both directions between the user
interface and the application. We use the term *container* collectively
to refer to six classes of objects: *items, slots,* and *results,* each of
which are either *active* or *passive.* The distinction among items,
slots, and results is based on the observation that the tasks of
selecting, entering information, and reporting results are conceptually different to the interface designer. The contents of an item
are determined at design time and cannot be altered by the end
user at run time. This is analogous to menu items or button values
which can be selected but not changed by the end user. In contrast,
the contents of a slot may be modified at run time by the user,
while the contents of a result may be altered by the application.

Active containers are subclasses of passive containers. A passive
container can be selected or filled, but does nothing to cause a
message to be sent to the application. In contrast, an active container,
when selected or filled, causes a message to be sent to a pre-specified
A_object asking it to perform its function. It is therefore selection
of an active item or filling of an active slot which causes something
to happen in the application domain. In this respect, our UIMS is
similar to COUSIN (Hayes, Szekely, & Lerner, 1985).

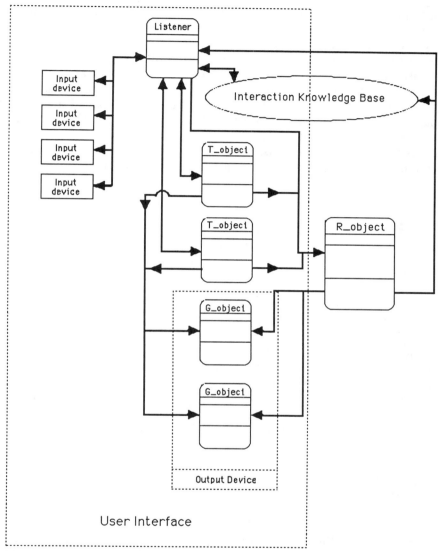

Figure 4.   The user interface in detail.

Containers can be filled or selected as a result of messages sent by either application or representation objects (the latter as a result of end user actions). By filling or selecting an active results container, the application can influence flow of control. Results contents can also be sent to an R_object for ultimate display to the end user.

When an active container is accessed, it sends a message to an

I_object both identifying the A_object which is to perform its function and providing a list of containers where information needed by the A_object and/or the I_object has been stored. The I_object in turn sends a message to the appropriate A_object, including information needed by the A_object to carry out its action. This message path allows the I_object to extract the necessary information from the container list. At the same time, the I_object provides partial semantic error checking by making sure that the message to the A_object is complete and semantically correct.

As an example of the class inheritance between active and passive containers consider the following item class definitions:

> *Class:* active_item;
> *Attributes:* none;
> *Relationships:* Application_object_id, Interaction_object_id, parameter_container_list;
> *Methods:* change_flag;
> *Messages:* send
> [interaction_object_id invoke_action
> (application_object_id parameter_container_list)];
> *Component_objects:* passive_item;

Notice that the active item has a component object from which it inherits attributes, relationships and methods. The component object, a passive item, is defined as:

> *Class:* passive_item;
> *Attributes:* status, value, select_flag;
> *Relationships;* representation object_id;
> *Methods:* change_value, augment_value, change_status, change_flag;
> *Messages:* none;

An active item inherits all methods of a passive item. Note the redefinition of the change_flag method (which is responsible for selecting and deselecting items) for the active_item class. The active item must recognize that its select flag has been set in order to send its message; therefore it requires a different method. The active item has a message which it can send to an I_object. We represent messages in our system in the following format:

> *send*
> *[destination_object_id, method_name,*
> *(argument_list)].*

In the preceding example, the only message an active item can send is to an interaction object requesting it to exercise its "invoke_action" method. The message provides it with the name of the A_object which can carry out the specified semantic action, and a list of containers which hold the parameters the A_object requires.

Encapsulating the semantic/syntactic boundary allows an I_object to have some intelligence concerning the way in which the syntax and semantics interact. For example, an I_object could have access to rules enabling it to infer a reasonable action to take based on a semantic error message from the application. The error may require the respecification of a series of parameters by the end user. In this case, the I_object would empty the appropriate containers and send a message to a specified R_object, requesting it to provide an appropriate communication to the end user.

Figure 4 opens the user interface black box seen in Figure 2, illustrating the relationships between an R_object and the components of the user interface. The R_object controls the visual form of the end user's display by sending messages to *graphic objects* (G_objects). Everything that can be displayed is a G_object. A G_object receives messages which control attributes such as visibility, color, position, etc. G_objects may also send messages to other G_objects allowing us to establish object hierarchies.

Each R_object receives messages from one or more *technique objects* (or T_objects). T_objects represent the lexical level of input and feedback for a given user interface design. They are coordinated by an object called the *listener.* There is only one instance of a listener object. Its role is to interpret input from the currently enabled set of physical input devices and pass the input on to the appropriate T_object. The listener carries out this task by parsing the input based on a representation of the current interface, as described in the next section. This representation is maintained in the interaction knowledge base, so named because it contains rules, constraints, and state specifications which various objects can use to modify their behavior. (Currently, the contents of the knowledge base are minimal; one of our major goals for the future is to expand the knowledge base.) Each object is responsible for keeping this knowledge base current. For example, whenever an R_object is "activated" (made available for interaction) or "deactivated," it updates the knowledge base.

Input Parsing in the GWUIMS

An important responsibility of the UIMS is understanding and verifying input from the end user. The domain of this input parsing ranges from recognizing and providing dynamic feedback for mouse movements, to validating sentences for correct syntax and semantics. In the GWUIMS, this parsing is distributed among the following objects: the listener, T_objects, R_objects, and I_objects.

At the lowest level, parsing responsibility is shared by the listener and the T_objects. The listener, using both the identity of the source physical device and the type and value(s) of the input, determines for which R_object the input is intended and which T_object should control further parsing. It does this using a generalized extent test applied to the input and a data structure contained in the knowledge base. This data structure includes extent definitions and physical device associations for all currently active R_objects, as well as all of their associated G_objects, and is similar to those found in window managers.

The listener hands both control and the input over to the appropriate T_object, which completes this low level of parsing by identifying the G_object whose sensitivity extent includes the input. At this point, the T_object receives input directly from the device driver level and provides lexical feedback until either the context of the input changes and control is passed back to the listener, or an event occurs causing the T_object to send a message to the listener. The message identifies the current G_object and includes any accumulated input information, such as a text string or numeric input from a keyboard, which the T_object has gathered. The listener forwards the message to the previously identified R_object. At this point, the "lexical analysis" phase of the parse is complete.

The next phase of parsing is handled by the R_object and consists of checking a set of parameterized rules in the knowledge base against a set of parameter values which the I_object owns. An example of this sort of rule is:

only k *of* n *entities may be concurrently selected;*

The parameters *n* and *k* are attributes of the R_object which have been set previously, probably at interface design time. A common example is the popularly known "radio button," where selection of one button causes a previously selected button to be automatically deselected.

Once the R_object has satisfied its constraints, it sends a message to one or more containers, filling, selecting, or deselecting them. The destination is known to the R_object because of a correspondence, established at design time, between each selectable G_object and a fillable/selectable container. At this point, further parsing becomes the responsibility of the I_object which receives a message from the container.

The I_object completes the syntactic level parsing begun by the R_object. Recall from the preceding section that containers gather information by being filled/selected until an active container requests the I_object to invoke a semantic action. The I_object then verifies the completeness of the parameter list for the A_object which actually performs that action, and sends a message to the A_object.

This overview has introduced the major object types in our UIMS, and described the general nature of their relationships to each other, as well as describing the sequence of events in input parsing. In the next section, we present a more detailed example of the system in use to help clarify these relationships.

DIRECT MANIPULATION USING GWUIMS

Remember that one of our stated motivations is to develop tools for design and rapid prototyping of user interfaces. In this section, we describe the use of one such tool during the design process. It is significant that the tool is itself an application of the UIMS.

For each of the three stages in the following scenario, we will first present the actions of the system from the perspective of the user/designer, followed by a description of the internal actions of the UIMS which are responsible for the observed behavior. The scenario follows the steps necessary to customize a bank of "soft" (virtual) buttons starting from a default template. Soft buttons are entities which behave like special purpose keys on a keyboard, but appear on a display screen and are "pushed" by moving a screen cursor over them and depressing a button on either the keyboard or some other physical device. The scenario presented here is only one of many possible approaches to this activity which are supported by our system. It is intended to reveal some of the capabilities of the GWUIMS, but is by no means representative of the *only* style of design it supports. For example, we assume the use of a mouse and a style based primarily upon pointing. However, the same set of tasks could be carried out with an approach primarily using keyboard selection or a command language.

Startup: The Designer's View

When the system is initiated, the menu shown (Figure 5) is the first thing the designer sees. It is an "appearing" menu, which means that it is not always visible. If we wish it to disappear, we may position the screen cursor in the small box in the upper border of the menu and click (depress and immediately release) the mouse button. Since this is the main menu, there must be a simple way to make it visible again. For this reason, the menu is replaced by a small icon, and can be made to reappear by clicking on the icon. We can position the menu (or its icon) wherever we choose, but it must have a default starting position, and this has been defined as the upper right corner of the display. Once we have repositioned the menu, its current position becomes its default position, and it will always reappear in the position it most recently occupied.

The menu gives us a set of choices for design activities. In this example, we may either customize one of three different objects from predefined templates (menu, button bank, form), or create a new object (either a static or dynamic icon). We decide to customize a button bank and so move the cursor over *Button Bank* on the menu. Each item in the menu is "highlighted" as the cursor moves it, in this case by enclosing the item within a box. Wen we click on *Button Bank,* a second menu appears, as in Figure 6. This special type of menu, sometimes called a property sheet, allows several items to be selected simultaneously. Each item has a small box in front of it and the items whose boxes are black are currently set. There are three groups of items, and only one selection from each of the groups makes sense at any time (e.g., one would not be able to choose both *Vertical* and *Horizontal* simultaneously). Accordingly, when we make a new selection within one group, the current

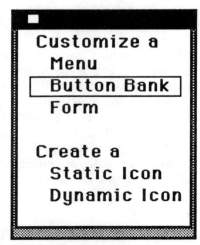

Figure 5. The top-level designer's menu.

selection in that group is automatically deselected. A corollary is that each group must contain at least one selected item. This restriction is easily imposed because there is no way to directly deselect an item.

When we have set this property sheet to our satisfaction, we click anywhere within the box containing *OK,* at the bottom of the sheet, and an instance of a button bank (Figure 7) appears on the screen. It appears attached to the cursor; we can drag it to the position where we wish it to remain and leave it there by clicking. We are now ready to begin customizing.

Startup: What the System Does

As an aid in understanding the discussion of system actions, we identify the specific objects used in this stage of the scenario, and provide the following pseudo code (on page 199) which shows the messages that are sent.

While reading this section, the reader may also wish to refer to Figures 8 and 9 which illustrate generic message paths among generic objects. Figure 8 illustrates the standard messages among objects for handling input from the user (designer in this scenario), and Figure 9 illustrates a set of standard messages which result from invoking an A_object.

The top level menu is an example of the *physical appearance* of

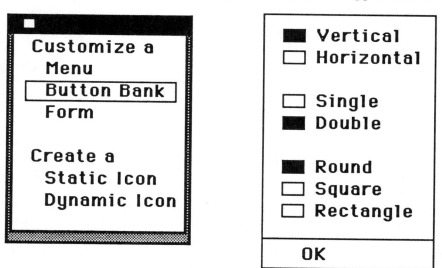

Figure 6.   A property sheet for customizing buttons.

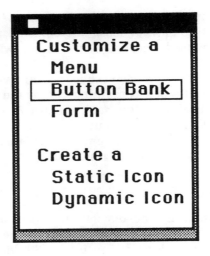

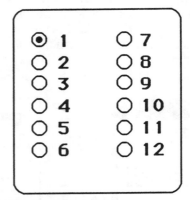

Figure 7. A button bank ready for customizing.

an R_object. The menu consists of a set of G_objects, a "master"
G_object which includes the border and the labels *Customize a* and
Create a, and one G_object for each selectable "item" on the menu
(i.e., *Menu, Button Bank,* etc.). In this example, each G_object representing a selectable menu item has a "hot spot" in the form of
a rectangle enclosing it. The T_object uses these hot spots to determine which G_object the cursor is currently over, for highlighting
and selection. As the cursor passes over each selectable item, the
T_object sends messages directly to the G_objects, telling them to
highlight and dehighlight for feedback to the end user (Figure 8).

{*specific objects used in this example are*}
T_object_one   {menu selection using mouse}
R_object_one   {top level menu}
R_object_two   {property sheet}
R_object_three   {button bank}
A_item_one   {Button Bank on top level menu}
A_item_two   {OK rectangle on property sheet}
I_object_one   {top level menu}
I_object_two   {property sheet}
I_object_three   {button bank}
G_object_one   {Button Bank on menu}
G_object_two   {master for property sheet}
G_object_three   {OK rectangle on property sheet}
G_object_four   {master for button bank}
G_object_id   {arbitrary graphic object}

send{*from T_object_one*}
  [listener, selected,
    (G_object_one)]

send {*from listener*}
  [R_object_one, selected,
    (G_object_one)]

send {*from R_object_one*}
  [A_item_one, change_flag,
    (selected)]

send {*from A_item_one*}
  [I_object_one, invoke_action,
    (A_object_one, I_object_two)]

send {*from I_object_one*}
  [A_object_one, invoke_action,
    (I_object_two)]

send {*from A_object_one*}
  [I_object_two, change_sleep_state]

send {*from I_object_two*}
  [R_object_two, change_sleep_state]

send {*from R_object_two*}
  [G_object_two, display]

send {*from G_object_two*}
  [G_object_id, display]

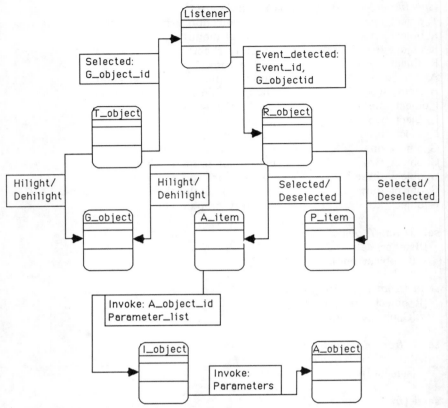

Figure 8.   Message paths for handling user input.

When the designer clicks on *Button Bank,* the T_object sends a message to the listener indicating which G_object has been selected. The listener repeats its message to the R_object that is associated with the selected G_object. The R_object then sends a message to the appropriate container, telling it that it was selected. In this case, the container is an active item (it corresponds to *Button Bank*). The active item sends a message to its I_object requesting it to invoke an A_object. Generally, this message specifies the identity of the A_object and includes a list of parameters for the A_object. The I_object receiving the message from the active item then verifies that the parameters to the A_object are semantically correct, and sends these parameters to the A_object in a message which requests the A_object to perform its semantic function. In this case, the A_object is actually part of an application for designing user interfaces. (Recall that the designer's interface is implemented as an

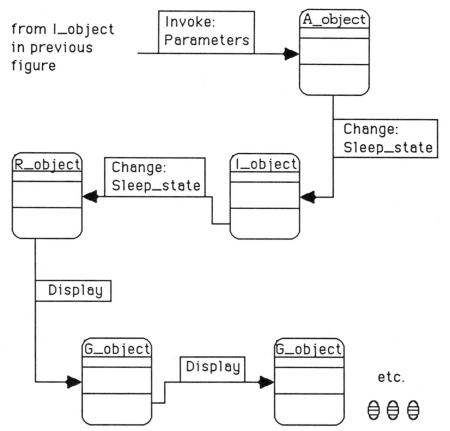

Figure 9.   Message paths for handling application output.

application of the UIMS.) This A_object's function is to toggle the sleep state (between awake and asleep) of each object on the message parameter list. In this case, the parameter's value is the identity of the I_object associated with the property sheet. So the A_object sends a "change sleep state" message to the I_object for the property sheet (Figure 9). The I_object sends a similar message to the R_object for the property sheet. It awakens and notifies the knowledge base that it and its associated G_objects are selectable. The R_object then tells its master G_object to display. The master G_object responds by making itself visible on the display, and repeating the display message to all of its associated G_objects. This results in the property sheet appearing on the display as in Figure 6.

At this point, the screen includes both menus (see Figure 6). The

G_objects on the second menu represent *passive* items, with the exception of the *OK* object. This is in contrast with the first menu, where all of the items were *active*. When a selection is made within the main body of this menu, the feedback is not handled solely by the T_object, as it was in the first menu. In this case, choosing an alternative like *Horizontal* will cause another alternative, in this case *Vertical*, to be deselected. The R_object knows about this constraint, since it has a set of rules defining all of the constraints mentioned in the preceding section, so that, when it receives a message that the *Horizontal* G_object has been selected, it sends three messages (see Figure 8): "deselect" to the passive item for *Vertical*, "dehighlight" to the G_object for *Vertical*, and "select" to the passive item for *Horizontal*. This is an example of *syntactic* feedback since it occurs in response to rules concerning the syntax, or structure, of the interactive dialogue. Nothing further occurs because the items involved are all passive.

As an aid in understanding the discussion of system actions when

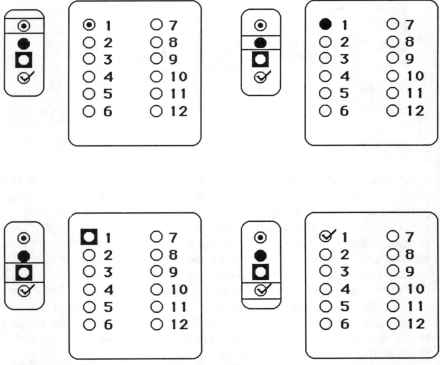

Figure 10. Changing the feedback specification.

the designer clicks on the *OK* rectangle, we refer the reader to the list of specific objects provided earlier, and present the following pseudo code which shows the messages that are sent.

```
send {from T_object_one}
  [G_object_three, highlight]
  [listener, selected,
    (G_object_three)]

send {from listener}
  [R_object_two, selected,
    (G_object_three)]

send {from R_object_two}
  [A_item_two, change_flag,
    (selected)]

send {from A_item_two}
  [I_object_two, invoke_action,
    (A_object_one, (I_object_two I_object_three))]

send {from I_object_two}
  [A_object_one, invoke_action,
    (I_object_two I_object_three)]

send {from A_object_one}
  [I_object_two, change_sleep_state]
  [I_object_three, change_sleep_state]

send {from I_object_two}
  [R_object_two, change_sleep_state]

send {from R_object_two}
  [G_object_two, undisplay]

send {from G_object_two}
  [G_object_id, undisplay]

send {from I_object_three}
  [R_object_three, change_sleep_state]

send {from R_object_three}
  [G_object_four, display]

send {from G_object_four}
  [G_object_id, display]
```

As listed above, when the designer clicks on the *OK* rectangle, the following messages are sent: from the T_object to a G_object to highlight (lexical feedback); from the same T_object to the listener; from the listener to the R_object for the property sheet; from this R_object to the active item which corresponds to *OK;* from the active item to the I_object for the property sheet; and from the I_object to an A_object. The message from the I_object to this A_object contains the identities of the I_objects for both the property sheet and the button bank. Following the message paths in Figure 9, the I_object and R_object for the property sheet go to sleep, the property sheet disappears from the screen, the I_object and R_object for the button bank are awakened, and the button bank appears as in Figure 7. We now are ready to return to the designer's role.

Customizing An Object: The Designer's View

As a designer, we now have a number of options available. We may directly change the button bank by moving or resizing it. To move it, we simply position the cursor anywhere on the top edge, press and hold the mouse button while we move the mouse, and release it when we wish to "drop" the button bank in a new position. While the bank is being moved, a rectangle (drag box) of the same size and shape is "dragged" by the cursor. When the button is released, the bank disappears and is redrawn in its new position, thus giving the designer dynamic feedback in placing the button bank with respect to other objects on the screen.

We may also modify the contents of the button bank. The numbers in Figure 7 are labels for the buttons. By clicking on a number, we indicate that we wish to change that label. The old label disappears, and we may now enter the new label by typing it at the keyboard. We terminate entry of a new label by simply moving the cursor elsewhere and beginning a new action. Some modifications require a further selection. If the mouse button is pressed and held while the cursor is over the currently selected button, a menu appears that has alternative feedback specifications for button selection (Figure 10). While continuing to hold the button down, we move the cursor vertically over the feedback menu, causing different feedback options to be temporarily displayed at the button labelled *1* (the currently selected button), showing us how the newly selected feedback will look on the button bank itself. When we release the mouse button, the currently displayed option becomes the new selection feedback technique. For this example, we decide to change the feedback (for the currently selected button) from a dot in the center of the button (the default) to a completely filled in button. The result appears in Figure 11.

Customizing An Object: What the System Does

In the preceding section, three specific actions were discussed: moving the button bank; changing labels; and changing the feedback specification. Each of these is handled somewhat differently by the system. Moving the button bank is handled primarily within a T_object. The listener recognizes that the mouse button is depressed while the cursor is over the button bank and hands control over to the T_object responsible for managing, shaping, and moving menu objects. The T_object remains in control as long as the button is held down. The T_object recognizes that the cursor is located over the top edge of the button bank and so it creates a "drag box" for feedback. Every time the T_object receives an updated cursor position, it moves the drag box using a common technique known as double exclusive-or replacement (this technique is explained in any computer graphics text book), thus providing dynamic feedback for the current location of the bank. When the button is released, the T_object sends a message (via the listener) to the R_object for the button bank, informing it of the position change. The R_object sends messages to its G_objects, telling them to disappear and reappear

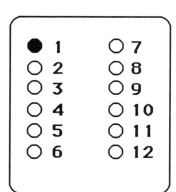
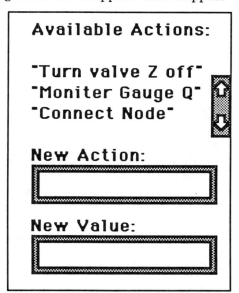

Figure 11. Specifying a semantic action binding.

in their new locations. The I_object is not involved, since this is a purely syntactic change.

The button label change is similar to the position change, except that it is handled entirely by the T_object since it is solely a lexical change. The T_object recognizes that one click over a label means that the label is to be replaced (a double click has a different meaning, as we will see in the next section), and manages the details of causing the portion of the G_object representing the label to disappear. It also accepts the keyboard input for the replacement label and causes it to be displayed. The T_object communicates directly with the G_object to change the contents of the text string for the label.

The button feedback is at the lexical level in the context of the button bank, but changing it is part of the semantics of the designer's interface. The change cannot be handled by a T_object alone, since it requires the use of the appearing menu, which in turn implies that an additional I_object and an R_object, the ones associated with the appearing menu, are required. When the mouse button is pressed and held with the cursor over the currently highlighted button, messages are sent from T_object to listener; from listener to the R_object for the button bank; from this R_object to the active item for the button bank; from the active item to the I_object for the button bank; and from the I_object to an A_object. This time, the I_object and R_object associated with the appearing menu of feedback options are awakened, and the menu is displayed (see Figure 10). The T_object then manages the rest of the interaction, changing the feedback in the button bank, as described in the preceding section, by interacting directly with the G_objects. When the button is released, the T_object sends a message via the listener to the R_object for the appearing menu, indicating which object on the appearing menu was selected. A "selected" message is then sent by the R_object to the active item corresponding to the new feedback specification. The active item sends a message to the I_object for the appearing menu to invoke a specific A_object. This A_object (which does not appear in the figures) sends a message to the R_object for the button bank, and the R_object sends messages to its G_objects, giving them the new feedback specification.

It is clear that this example includes many redundant messages. We do this purposely to force a complete specification of the interaction technique. For use at run time, the redundant messages may be removed to improve performance.

Actions and Values: The Designer's View

We now return to our scenario for the final time. At this point, we have a button bank for which we have specified a location, new labels, and a new selection feedback. However, we have not yet associated any meaning (semantics) with the buttons. There are two types of meanings we can associate with "pressing" a button. One is to cause some action to occur, while the other is to cause some value to be set. When the designer positions the cursor over a button and "double clicks" (clicking twice in rapid succession), the menu shown in Figure 11 appears. This menu has three parts. The first is a list of all actions currently known to the system. In the event that there are too many actions to fit conveniently on the menu, it may be paged using the bar on the right. Selection of one of these available actions will cause that action to be bound immediately to the soft button that was double clicked. No compilation is necessary; the button bank is live and may be tested throughout the design process. The designer can now single click on that soft button. If an A_object embodying the semantics for the action exists, and all necessary parameters for the action are specified, the action will occur. If the action does not exist (i.e., it has been named, but the application object necessary to carry it out has not yet been created), or there are missing parameters, the system will issue a warning message to the designer.

The second part of the menu is a box within which the designer can enter a new action name, while the third is a similar box for specifying a value. In this example, we position the cursor over the value box, click once, and type in a value, terminating by pressing the "return" key. The appearing menu disappears, and we are free to continue customizing the button bank.

Actions and Values: What the System Does

The double click on the soft button causes the T_object to send a message which results in awakening the R_object for the appearing menu in Figure 11. The system behaves in much the same way as it did when specifying a new selection feedback. When an action is selected from the list or entered in the new action field, a message is sent through the R_object and I_object associated with the appearing menu to an A_object which sends a message to the I_object for the button bank, instructing it to bind the specified action to the selected item and make it an active item. If a value is specified, a message is sent over the same route, instructing the I_object to bind the value to the selected item and make it passive.

Summary

This scenario illustrates some of the power of our system. The example of interactive feedback specification illustrates a composite interaction technique built from primitive objects. The technique is built by specifying attribute and relationship values for the objects involved. Another feature of the system is the run-time binding of actions to buttons or menu items, and their immediate availability. This makes possible dynamic, incremental testing of pieces of the user interface as they are being built, and facilitates rapid interface prototyping.

IMPLEMENTATION OF THE GWUIMS

The implementation of our system is described in detail in Sibert, Hurley, and Bleser (1986a), which includes complete specification of the semantics and syntax of all objects in the system; and in Hurley (1985), which describes our object-oriented programming environment. Briefly, the GWUIMS is implemented on a Sun microsystems workstation using a locally-developed programming environment built on top of Franz LISP with Flavors. The graphics routines are written in the "C" programming language. The locally-developed programming environment, which we call the *metasystem* because of the knowledge it has about systems developed with it, includes a number of extensions to Flavors which we found necessary for implementation of our UIMS. These extensions include the following:

- It is possible to save the current state of a system and all of its components to secondary storage. This is clearly critical for incremental development and customizing of user interface designs as described above.
- When a class is redefined, the metasystem can immediately and automatically modify all existing instances of that class. This enables us to make changes to the definition of a class of object in our system (such as an I_object) and automatically propagate those changes throughout all instances of that class. This is essential to the system's ability to expand over time with a minimum of additional programming.

- The metasystem can answer queries about class definitions, method definitions, values of instance variables, etc.
- The system automatically generates unique identifiers for all instances. This feature is necessary to avoid ambiguity internally, but does not prevent the user/designer of the GWUIMS from assigning arbitrary names.

In addition to these capabilities which are required for the current implementation of the GWUIMS, the metasystem provides us with a good framework for knowledge acquisition, exploratory development, and iterative growth. This framework is crucial to our plans for adding design knowledge and reasoning to the system.

CONCLUSIONS AND FUTURE EVOLUTION

When we set out to build this system, we had several goals in mind. First and foremost was developing a capability for realistic prototyping of highly interactive graphic user interfaces. We are currently using our system in this manner, and plan to build increasingly more sophisticated prototypes as our experience with the system grows and as we add more interaction techniques. We have been concentrating on mouse- and keyboard-oriented techniques, but hope to add techniques using touch screens, several different graphic tablets, and both voice and character recognition.

Another goal of our work has been to investigate the applicability of the linguistic model of the user interface. We have for some time felt that this model is limited in its ability to describe the natural use of interactive graphics in user interfaces. In this work, we focused on defining the boundaries of the lexical, syntactic, and semantic levels of the interface "language" in terms of objects, rather than as strictly defined interfaces. Each interface between two levels is embodied in an object with sufficient knowledge about both levels to handle their interface intelligently. For example, embodying the syntactic/semantic boundary in the I_object allows many situations requiring knowledge of both syntax and semantics, such as semantic error handling and semantic feedback, to be handled within the UIMS in a manner specified by the dialogue designer rather than the application programmer.

Localization of these boundaries within objects is also important, for our approach, to our longer term goal of developing knowledge-based "assistants" to aid the designer of user interfaces. We intend to develop assistants first in two specific areas: semantic error handling and selection of natural interaction techniques for given application tasks. (For a detailed discussion of interaction tasks and techniques, see Foley, Wallace, & Chan, 1984.) Within our current model, the first of these assistants fits at the same level of abstraction as an I_object, and the second at the level of an R_object.

We are currently exploring knowledge representations and knowledge acquisition techniques to enable us to add these assistants to our system. The reader familiar with knowledge representation may have noticed the similarity between our objects (most apparent in the I_object) and frames with procedural attachment. This similarity is not coincidental, since we have consciously designed our system to include an expansion of our current simple knowledge base. We are still in the early stages of this enhancement, and cannot predict with certainty where it will lead. Ultimately, we intend for the GWUIMS to develop into a true partner for the user interface designer; at present, we are working on understanding it as a tool.

ACKNOWLEDGEMENTS

The work reported in this chapter was supported in part by the National Aeronautics and Space Administration under contract NAS5-27585. We also wish to acknowledge the thoughtful comments of the reviewers and the editors. Portions of this chapter are expanded from a paper presented at the SIGGRAPH-86 conference (Sibert, Hurley, & Bleser, 1986b).

REFERENCES

Anson, E. (1982). The device model of interactive computer graphics. *Computer Graphics, 16*(3), 107–114.

Beach, R., Beatty, J., Booth, K., Plebon, D., & Fiume, E. (1982). The message is the medium: multiprocess structuring of an interactive paint program. *SIGGRAPH '82 Conference Proceedings, 16*(3), 277–287.

Bleser, T., & Foley, J. (1982). Towards specifying and evaluating the human factors of user-computer interfaces. *Proceedings, Human Factors in Computer Systems* (pp. 309–314). Gaithersburg, MD.

Cochran, D.R., & Stocker, F.R. (1985, October). RIPL: an environment for rapid prototyping with intelligent support. *SIGCHI Bulletin, 17*(2), pp. 29–36.

Coutaz, J. (1985). Abstractions for user interface design. *Computer, 18*(9), 21–34.

Dahl, O.J., & Nygaard, K. (1966). SIMULA—An Algol-based simulation language. *Communications of the ACM, 9*, 671–678.

Feldman, M.B., & Rogers, G.T. (1982). Toward the design and development of style-independent interactive systems. *Proceedings, Human Factors in Computer Systems* (pp. 111–116). Gaithersburg, MD.

Foley, J.D., & McMath, C.F. (1986). Dynamic process visualization. *IEEE Computer Graphics and Applications, 6*(3), 16–25.

Foley, J.D., & van Dam, A. (1982). *Fundamentals of interactive computer graphics*. Reading, MA: Addison-Wesley.

Foley, J.D., Wallace, V.L., & Chan, P. (1984). The human factors of computer graphics interaction techniques. *IEEE Computer Graphics and Applications, 4*(11), 13–48.

Goldberg, A. (1984). *Smalltalk-80: The interactive programming environment*. Reading, MA: Addison-Wesley.

Green, M. (1985). The University of Alberta user interface management system. *Computer Graphics, 19*(3), 213.

Hanau, P.R., & Lenorovitz, D.R. (1980). Prototyping and simulation tools for user/computer dialogue design. *Computer Graphics, 14*(3), 271–278.

Hayes, P., Szekely, P., & Lerner, R. (1985). Design alternatives for user interface management systems based on experience with COUSIN. *Human Factors in Computing Systems, CHI '85 Proceedings* (pp. 169–175). NY: Association for Computing Machinery.

Hurley, W.D. (1985). *Human-computer interface prototyping environment, design and development of an external to internal dialog translator* (GWU-IIST-85-09). Washington, DC: George Washington University Institute for Information Science and Technology.

Hurley, W.D., Sibert, J., & Bleser, T. (1985). *Use of a user interface management system in a command and control environment* (GWU-IIST-85-10). Washington, DC: George Washington University Institute for Information Science and Technology.

Jacob, R.J.K. (1983). Using formal specifications in the design of a human–computer interface. *Communications of the ACM, 26*(4), 259–264.

Jacob, R.J.K. (1985). A state transition diagram language for visual programming. *IEEE Computer, 18*(8), 51–59.

Kamran, A. (1985). Issues pertaining to the design of a user interface management system. In G.E. Pfaff (Ed.), *User interface management systems* (pp. 43–48). New York: Springer-Verlag.

Kamran, A. & Feldman, M.B. (1983). Graphics programming independent of interaction techniques and styles. *Computer Graphics, 17*(1), 58–66.

Kasik, D.J. (1982). A user interface management system. *Computer Graphics, 16*(3), 99–106.

Lieberman, H. (1985). There's more to menu systems than meets the screen. *Computer Graphics, 19*(3), 181–189.

Lipke, D., Evans, S., Newlin, J., & Weissman, R. (1982, July). Star graphics: an object-oriented implementation. *SIGGRAPH '82 Conference Proceedings, 16*(3), 115–124.

Mark, W. (1986). Knowledge-based interface design. In D. Norman & S. Draper, *User-centered system design* (pp. 219–238). Hillsdale, NJ: Erlbaum.

Mackinlay, J. (1986, April). Automating the design of graphical presentations. *Transactions on Graphics Special Issue on User Interface Software,* 5(2), 110–141.

Moran, T.P. (1981). The Command Language Grammar: a representation for the user interface of interactive computer systems. *International Journal of Man-Machine Studies, 15,* 3–50.

Myers, B., & Buxton, W. (1986). Creating highly-interactive and graphical user interfaces by demonstration. *SIGGRAPH '86 Conference Proceedings, 20*(4), 249–258.

Newman, W. (1968). A system for interactive graphical programming. *SJCC 1968* (pp. 47–54). Washington, DC: Thompson Books.

Olsen, D.R., Jr. (1983a). Automatic generation of interactive systems. *Computer Graphics, 17*(1), 53–57.

Olsen, D.R., Jr. (1983b). Push-down automata for user interface management. *ACM Transactions on Graphics, 3*(3), 177–203.

Olsen, D.R., Jr., Buxton, W., Ehrich, R., Kasik, D., Rhyne, J., & Sibert, J. (1984). A context for user interface management. *IEEE Computer Graphics and Applications, 4*(12), 33–42.

Olsen, D.R., Jr., & Dempsey, E.P. (1983). SYNGRAPH: A graphical user interface generator. *Computer Graphics, 17*(3), 43–50.

Olsen, D.R., Jr., Dempsey, E.P., & Rogge, R. (1985). Input/output linkage in a user interface management system. *Computer Graphics, 19*(3), 191–197.

Pfaff, G.E. (Ed.). (1985). *User interface management systems.* New York: Springer-Verlag.

Reisner, P. (1981). Formal grammar and human factors design of an interactive graphics system. *IEEE Transactions on Software Engineering, SE-7*(2), 229–240.

Roach, J., Pittman, J., Reilly, S., & Savarese, J. (1982). A visual design consultant. *Proceedings of the IEEE Systems, Man and Cybernetics Conference.* Washington, DC: IEEE Computer Society Press.

Rosenthal, D.S. (1981). Methodology in computer graphics reexamined. *Computer Graphics, 15*(2), 152–162.

Sibert, J., Belliardi, R., & Kamran, A. (1985). Some thoughts on the interface between user interface management systems and application software. In G. Pfaff (Ed.), *User interface management systems* (pp. 183–192). New York: Springer-Verlag.

Sibert, J.L., & Hurley, W.D. (1984). *A prototype for a general user interface management system* (GWU-IIST Report 84–47). Washington, DC: George Washington University.

Sibert, J.L., Hurley, W.D., & Bleser, T.W. (1985). An environment for prototyping human computer interfaces. *Proceedings of the International Symposium on New Directions in Computing.* Washington, DC: IEEE Computer Society Press.

Sibert, J.L., Hurley, W.D., & Bleser, T.W. (1986a). *User interface prototyping system design document* (GWU-IIST Report 86-01). Washington, DC: IEEE Computer Society Press.

Sibert, J.L., Hurley, W.D., & Bleser, T.W. (1986b). An object-oriented user interface management system. *Computer Graphics, 20*(3), 259–67.

Stefik, M., & Bobrow, D. (1986). Object-oriented programming: themes and variations. *The AI Magazine, 6*(4), 40–62.

Thomas, J.J., & Hamlin, G. (1983). Graphical input interaction technique workshop summary. *Computer Graphics, 17*(1), 5–30.

Wong, P., & Reid, E.R. (1982). Flair—user interface dialog design tool. *Computer Graphics, 16*(3), 87–98.

CHAPTER 7

A System for Evaluating Screen
Formats: Research and Application[1]

Thomas S. Tullis

*McDonnell Douglas Astronautics Company
Huntington Beach, California*

INTRODUCTION

Most direct interaction between a human and a computer occurs at some type of visual display terminal. What information is presented on the terminal's screen, and how it is presented, can have a substantial impact on both the users' acceptance of the system and their ability to process the information. For example, Tullis (1981) found that a redesign of the main display from a system for testing telephone lines resulted in a 40% reduction in the time required by the users to interpret the display.

Given the critical role that screen design plays in human–computer interaction, it is important to understand what characteristics of screens influence user acceptance and performance. The purpose of this chapter is to present a set of screen characteristics that appear to be important determinants of acceptance and performance, to describe a computer program for measuring those characteristics, and to present the results of two experiments used to develop and validate a system for predicting user acceptance and performance based on the screen characteristics.

Through a review of the literature related to monochromatic, alphanumeric screens, Tullis (1983) derived a series of objectively defined characteristics for describing screen formats. This particular class of screens was chosen because of their widespread use in traditional office and data processing settings. While display devices

---

[1] Much of this chapter is based upon the author's doctoral dissertation in engineering psychology for Rice University (Tullis, 1984a). Experiments 1 and 2 were conducted at AT&T Bell Laboratories.

with bit-mapped graphics and color are becoming increasingly common, there is still a vast installed base of traditional monochromatic, alphanumeric terminals. Understanding the relevant characteristics of even these rather simple displays is no easy task, and is an important first step toward understanding the full range of screen design techniques.

In deriving the screen format characteristics, Tullis (1983) reviewed and synthesized two major classes of literature related to screen design: guidelines (e.g., Engel & Granda, 1975; Smith & Aucella, 1983) and empirical studies (e.g., Ringel & Hammer, 1964; Dodson & Shields, 1978). The goal in reviewing these two classes of literature was to identify the underlying characteristics of screen formats that either the guidelines or empirical studies suggested as important determinants of user acceptance or performance. The result was the derivation of six measures that can be used to describe the *spatial array* of characters on any alphanumeric display:

Overall density—the number of characters on the screen, expressed as a percentage of the number of character spaces available.

Local density—the number of characters within a 5-deg visual angle of each character, expressed as a percentage of the number of spaces within that area. This is essentially a measure of how tightly packed the screen is.

Number of groups—the number of distinct groups of characters detected using a proximity clustering technique. For most cases, a group generally consists of characters that are separated by no more than one intervening space horizontally, and that fall on adjacent lines.

Size of groups—the average visual angle subtended by the groups of characters, where each group's size is weighted by the number of characters in the group.

Number of items—the number of distinct labels or data values on the screen.

Layout Complexity—the amount of information, in bits, conveyed by the horizontal and vertical positions of the display items. This is essentially a measure of how poorly aligned the screen elements are with each other: aligning the labels and data values vertically and horizontally reduces layout complexity.

As pointed out by Tullis (1983, p. 662), these display characteristics are not necessarily independent of each other. For example, as will be shown in Experiment 1 (to be described shortly), screens typically exhibit a positive correlation between overall density and local density. Likewise, increasing the number of groups tends to decrease the average size of those groups, thus resulting in a negative correlation. These kinds of correlations are quite natural. No attempt was made to identify screen characteristics that are completely orthogonal to each other. However, for the displays that these characteristics have been applied to, none of the correlations have been perfect, reflecting the fact that each measure contributes some unique information to the characterization of the screen's format.

It is important to note that these six measures only describe screen *formats*. They do not take into account the *semantics* of the screen. This was intentional, because the goal of defining these characteristics was to develop a computer program that could measure them. Trying to include semantics in such a program would have made the task almost impossible due to the tremendous amount of semantic information that the program would have to be "taught." By developing a program that can assess these *format* characteristics for any alphanumeric display, however, it is possible to aid a screen designer in making decisions about the visual representation of the *semantic* characteristics. For example, by having a program that can predict the visual groups of characters a user would perceive, the screen designer can ensure that those visual groupings are compatible with the semantics (e.g., that each group contains logically related items).

A program for measuring these six screen format characteristics was written in the C programming language. The inputs to the program are as follows:

- A literal example of the display to be analyzed, stored in an ASCII file.
- Characteristics of the display device on which the display will be shown:
  - Maximum number of screen lines (default = 24)
  - Maximum number of characters per line (default = 80)
- Distance between character centers vertically (default = 0.2 in)
  - Distance between character centers horizontally (default = 0.1 in)
- Viewing distance of the display from the user, for calculating visual angles (default = 19 in).

A sample output from the program is shown in Figure 1. The output contains the following:

- The original screen as it was input to the program.
- The groups of characters on the screen detected by the grouping algorithm. Each group is represented by a different symbol. For example, in Figure 1, 16 different groups are represented.
- Results of the six measurements (overall density, local density, number of groups, average visual angle of the groups, number of items, and layout complexity).

Having developed a program for measuring these characteristics of screen formats, the next task was to determine how these char-

```
File air1:
------------------------------------------------------------------------
To: Atlanta, GA

    Departs     Arrives      Flight

Ashville, NC             First: $92.57    Coach: $66.85
    7:20a       8:05a       PI 299
   10:10a      10:55a       PI 203
    4:20p       5:00p       PI 259

Austin, TX               First: $263.00   Coach: $221.00
    8:15a      11:15a       EA 530
    8:40a      11:39a       DL 212
    2:00p       5:00p       DL 348
    7:15p      11:26p       DL 1654

Baltimore, MD            First: $209.00   Coach: $167.00
    7:00a       8:35a       DL 1767
    7:50a       9:32a       EA 631
    8:45a      10:20a       DL 1610
   11:15a      12:35p       EA 147
    1:35p       3:10p       DL 1731
    2:35p       4:16p       EA 141
------------------------------------------------------------------------
111 11111111 11

   2222222   3333333    444444

5555555555 55          666666 666666   777777 777777
    55555      88888        66 666
   555555     888888        66 666
    55555      88888        66 666

9999999 99          ::::::: :::::::   ;;;;;; ;;;;;;
   99999     <<<<<<     ::  :::
   99999     <<<<<<     ::  :::
   99999     <<<<<       ::  :::
   99999     <<<<<<     ::  ::::

========== ==        >>>>>> >>>>>>>   ?????? ??????
    =====       00000     >> >>>>
    =====       00000     >> >>>
    =====      000000     >> >>>>
    =====      000000     >> >>>
    =====       00000     >> >>>>
    =====       00000     >> >>>
------------------------------------------------------------------------
          Overall   Local             Av. Visual              Layout
Filename  Density   Density  #Grps  Angle of Grps  #Items  Complexity
air1       18.2%     41.7%     16       4.2 deg       72       7.33
```

Figure 1. Experiment 1: Output from the analysis program for 1 of the 26 display formats for presenting lists of airline flights.

acteristics actually relate to the usability of a display. That was the purpose of Experiment 1.

EXPERIMENT 1: DEVELOPMENT OF THE PREDICTION SYSTEM[2]

The general approach to determining the relationship between these display measures and usability was to develop a wide variety of display formats differing on these measures, and then use multiple regressions to fit search times and subjective ratings of the displays using the measures.

Method

Displays. Displays for presenting two types of information were developed: lists of data about airline flights and lists of data about motels and hotels. These topics were chosen simply because most people are familiar with them. Specifically, 26 different formats for presenting airline listings and 26 different formats for presenting motel listings were developed. These numbers of formats were felt to be the minimum that would result in a reasonable distribution of values for the six display measures.

Each airline display contained information on flights to a particular city. For all formats, the flights' originating cities were listed in alphabetical order, and within each city the flights were listed by departure time. Other information included the first class and coach fares, arrival times, and flight numbers. An example of one of the airline displays used is shown in Figure 1, along with the output from the program.

Each motel display contained listings of motels and hotels for a particular state. For all formats, cities were listed alphabetically, and within each city the motels were listed alphabetically by name. Other information included the area code, telephone number, single room rate, and double room rate. An example of one of the motel displays used is shown in Figure 2, along with the output from the program.

For each of the 52 display formats, 10 examples containing different data were developed. Since search times and subjective ratings are to be collected for each format, it was felt that 10 examples

---

[2] Experiment 1 was summarized in a paper presented at the INTERACT '84 Conference on Human-Computer Interaction (Tullis, 1984b).

```
File motel3:
-----------------------------------------------------------------------------------
South Carolina

                                 Area               Rates
City         Motel/Hotel         Code   Phone    Single  Double
Charleston   Best Western        803    747-0961   $26     $30
Charleston   Days Inn            803    881-1800   $18     $24
Charleston   Holiday Inn N       803    744-1621   $36     $46
Charleston   Holiday Inn SW      803    556-7100   $33     $47
Charleston   Howard Johnsons     803    524-4140   $31     $36
Charleston   Ramada Inn          803    774-8281   $33     $40
Charleston   Sheraton Inn        803    744-2401   $34     $42
Columbia     Best Western        803    796-9400   $29     $34
Columbia     Carolina Inn        803    799-8200   $42     $48
Columbia     Days Inn            803    736-0000   $23     $27
Columbia     Holiday Inn NW      803    794-9440   $32     $39
Columbia     Howard Johnsons     803    772-7200   $25     $27
Columbia     Quality Inn         803    772-0270   $34     $41
Columbia     Ramada Inn          803    796-2700   $36     $44
Columbia     Vagabond Inn        803    796-6240   $27     $30
Dillon       Days Inn            803    774-6041   $18     $22
Dillon       Holiday Inn         803    774-4161   $28     $37
Dillon       Howard Johnsons     803    774-5111   $31     $40
-----------------------------------------------------------------------------------
11111 11111111
                         2222                 33333
4444       5555555555    2222   66666     333333   333333
4444444444 5555 5555555  222    66666666  333      333
4444444444 5555 555      222    66666666  333      333
4444444444 5555555 555 5 222    66666666  333      333
4444444444 5555555 555 55 222   66666666  333      333
4444444444 555555 55555555 222  66666666  333      333
4444444444 555555 555     222   66666666  333      333
4444444444 55555555 555   222   66666666  333      333
44444444   5555 5555555   222   66666666  333      333
44444444   55555555 555   222   66666666  333      333
44444444   5555 555       222   66666666  333      333
44444444   5555555 555 55 222   66666666  333      333
44444444   555555 55555555 222  66666666  333      333
44444444   555555 555     222   66666666  333      333
44444444   555555 555     222   66666666  333      333
44444444   55555555 555   222   66666666  333      333
444444     5555 555       222   66666666  333      333
444444     5555555 555    222   66666666  333      333
444444     555555 55555555 222  66666666  333      333
-----------------------------------------------------------------------------------
           Overall  Local          Av. Visual          Layout
Filename   Density  Density #Grps  Angle of Grps #Items Complexity
motel3      36.8%    59.5%    6       11.4 deg     117     7.14
```

Figure 2.   Experiment 1: Output from the analysis program for 1 of the 26 display formats for presenting lists of motels and hotels.

(i.e., 10 trials) would be sufficient to yield stable performance and acceptance data. Thus, a total of 520 displays were used in the experiment. In order to illustrate the resulting values for the six display measures, Table 1 shows their means, standard deviations, and ranges.

No attempt was made to develop displays that would provide orthogonal combinations of the six display measures. That would have been virtually impossible due to the interrelated nature of the measures. Instead, the displays were designed to keep the correlations among the six measures to a minimum. Table 2 shows the correlations among the six measures for the 520 displays.

Table 1.   Means, Standard Deviations, and Ranges of Six Display Measures for 520 Displays Used in Experiment 1

	Mean	Standard Deviation	Range Minimum	Maximum
Overall Density	27.9%	12.0%	8.4%	62.1%
Local Density	50.2%	11.7%	29.2%	71.9%
Number of Groups	21.3	22.2	1	107
Size of Groups	7.7 deg	5.2 deg	2.0 deg	26.0 deg
Number of Items	86.1	37.0	30	202
Layout Complexity	7.2 bits	0.8 bits	5.9 bits	9.8 bits

Table 2.   Correlations among Six Display Measures for 520 Displays Used in Experiment 1

	Overall Dens.	Local Dens.	# Grps.	Size Grps.	# Items	Layout Complex.
Overall Density	--	.65	-.04	.51	.97	.70
Local Density		--	-.64	.73	.58	.46
Number of Groups			--	-.59	.04	-.05
Size of Groups				--	.45	.54
Number of Items					--	.73
Layout Complexity						--

As Table 2 shows, the highest correlation was between overall density and number of items ($r = .97$). This is quite natural, and no attempt was made to reduce it. This is analogous to a correlation between number of characters per page and number of words per page in a book. None of the other correlations had an absolute value greater than .73. In general, the correlations make sense. For example, higher local density is associated with larger size groups ($r = .73$), because there are fewer blank spaces on the screen to segregate the characters into smaller groups.

Apparatus. The entire study was controlled by an IBM Personal Computer. The displays were shown on an Amdek Model 300 green-phosphor monochrome monitor that displayed 24 lines of 80 characters each. The monitor was driven by the standard IBM Color Graphics Adaptor. The monitor was adjusted so that the width of the display area was 200 mm and the height was 120 mm. The distance between character centers was 2.5 mm horizontally and 5.0 mm vertically.

Subjects. Ten employees of AT&T Bell Laboratories participated in the study, for about 4 hours each. Each subject participated individually in a single session, although they were allowed to take short breaks whenever desired. Eight of the subjects were clerical employees, and the other two were technical and assistant technical. Nine of the subjects were female, and nine used corrective lenses.

The subjects ranged in age from 24 to 58 years, with a mean of 34. Their experfence with the Bell System ranged from 1 month to 34 years, with a mean of 4.5 years. Their amount of experience in working with computer systems ranged from 0 to 2 years, with a mean of 7 months. None of the subjects had any programming experience.

The main reason for using a relatively small number of subjects was that the primary purpose of the experiment was to determine the effects of differences in displays, not differences in subjects. Thus, the philosophy of the experiment was to collect a great deal of data from each subject, rather than a smaller amount of data from more subjects.

Procedure. Each subject saw 10 different examples of all 52 display formats and answered a question using each example. Thus, each subject saw 520 displays and answered as many questions. The same basic kinds of questions were used for each set of 10 displays in one format. The questions used are illustrated in Table 3.

The subjects saw the airline displays in one block and the motel displays in another. Half of the subjects saw the airline displays first, and half saw the motel displays first. At the beginning of each block (airline or motel), the subjects were first shown 10 examples of a "practice" format whose data were not used in the analysis. The 26 formats for that block (airline or motel) were then shown in an order that was randomly determined for each subject.

For each format, the subject was first shown an example to study. That was followed by 10 trials (each with different data on the

Table 3. **Examples of Questions Asked for Airline and Motel Displays in Experiment 1**

Type of Display	Example of Question	Number Asked per Format
Airline	What is the coach fare from Baltimore?	2
	What is the first class fare from Nashville?	2
	What is the arrival time of the 6:50pm flight from Cincinatti?	3
	What is the flight number of the 3:10pm flight from Houston?	3
Motel	What is the area code for Ashland?	2
	What is the phone number (first 3 digits) of the Holiday Inn in Concord?	2
	How much is a single room at the Ramada Inn in Charleston?	3
	How much is a double room at the Howard Johnsons in Newark?	3

screen) in which the subject had to search the display to find the answer to a question. The sequence of events for one trial is illustrated in Figure 3. The question was always shown first, by itself. Then, when the subject pressed the space bar on the keyboard, the question disappeared and the display immediately appeared. (The display appeared almost immediately because it had been written to a nondisplayed "page" of the PC's memory while the subject was reading the question.) The subject searched the display for the answer to the question and then pressed the space bar again when it was found. That caused the display to disappear. Search time was measured from the appearance of the display until the subject pressed the space bar, making the display disappear. Although the subjects were not told that this search time was being measured, they were instructed to proceed through the trials as quickly as possible while still always finding the answers.

After the display disappeared, the question was shown again, along with three multiple-choice answers: the correct answer, an incorrect answer, and "Don't Know." The subject then chose one of those answers. Since the subjects were encouraged to always find the answer to the question while the display was on the screen, this approach seemed adequate to test whether the subject had found the answer. The subjects were told, however, that it would be better to choose "Don't Know" than to guess. (In fact, as will be described shortly, the resulting accuracy levels were nearly perfect— well above the 50% chance level.) The subject was not allowed to go back to the display after getting to the multiple-choice question.

After the 10 trials for one format, the subjects were asked to rate how easy it was to use that format on a scale of 1 to 5, with 1 being "Very Easy to Use" and 5 "Very Difficult to Use." After the subjects had used all 26 formats in a block (airline or motel), they were given paper copies of one example from each format (in a random order) and asked to sort the copies into five stacks, depending upon ease of use. This was simply an additional rating, like the one that was done immediately after presentation of that format on the computer, but the paper copies allowed comparisons between the formats.

Results

The results for the two main dependent measures, search time and subjective ratings, will be discussed separately.

Search time. Overall, the subjects answered 97.7% of the questions about the displays correctly, indicating that they followed the in-

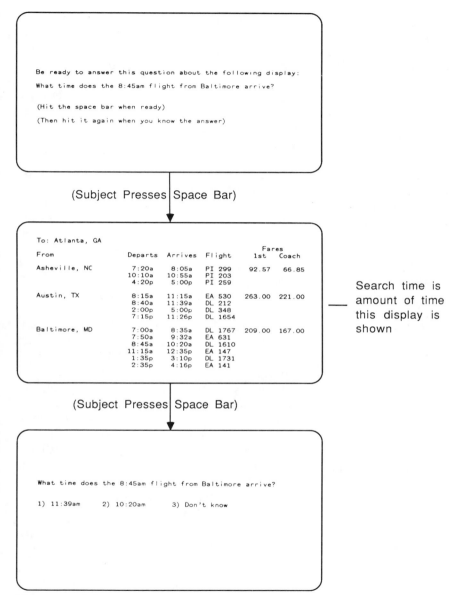

Figure 3. Schematic representation of sequence of events for one trial.

struction to be very accurate. A mean search time was calculated across subjects for each format, based on the correct trials only. (Error trials were not included, because one cannot determine what the subjects actually searched for on those trials, if anything.) All subsequent analyses were performed on these mean search times. The mean search times for the 52 formats ranged from 2.60 to 5.63 s, with a mean of 3.68 s and standard deviation of 0.59 s.

The simple correlations of the six display measures with mean search times are shown in Table 4. The average size of the groups was the measure that had the highest simple correlation with search time ($r = .56$). Thus, as the average size of the groups of characters increased, search time tended to increase.

The lowest simple correlation was for number of groups ($r = -.06$). The reason for this is that the function using number of groups to predict search time appears to be nonlinear. Specifically, the function is approximately U-shaped, with the lowest search time falling between 20 and 40 groups. However, an analysis of the number of groups in conjunction with the size of those groups indicated that the displays with small numbers of groups tended to have larger sized groups. Thus, the higher search times for displays with small numbers of groups seems to be due to the size of those groups rather than their number. See Tullis (1986b) for a complete discussion of this relationship.

Multiple regressions using various subsets of the six display measures to predict search time were also conducted. Figure 4 plots R^2 for several multiple regressions as a function of the number of variables in the regression equation. These regressions used a technique known as "regressions by leaps and bounds" (Furnival & Wilson, 1974) to find the best-fitting regression equation at each number of predictor variables. As Figure 4 shows, the largest increase in R^2 occurred between one and two predictor variables: the addition of the "number of groups" predictor to the "size of groups" predictor resulted in an increase of R^2 from .31 to .42. All of the subsequent regressions found that the best fit always included these two predictor variables. Table 5 shows the regression equations for the best fit at each number of predictor variables from two to six.

Table 4. Experiment 1: Simple Correlations of Six Display Measures with Search Time and Subjective Rating

	Search Time	Subjective Rating
Overall Density	.33	.63
Local Density	.39	.65
Number of Groups	-.06	-.16
Size of Groups	.56	.67
Number of Items	.34	.66
Layout Complexity	.42	.75

As Table 5 shows, the multiple regression using all six predictors resulted in a multiple R^2 of .508, meaning that the regression accounted for 50.8% of the variance in search time. Interestingly, the regression using the five predictors besides layout complexity also resulted in an R^2 of .508, meaning that layout complexity did not contribute to the prediction. Individual t tests on the coefficients from this regression showed that the coefficients for overall density, local density, number of groups, and size of groups were all significant, while the coefficient for number of items was not.

The best-fitting regression using four predictors (overall density, local density, number of groups, size of groups) resulted in a multiple

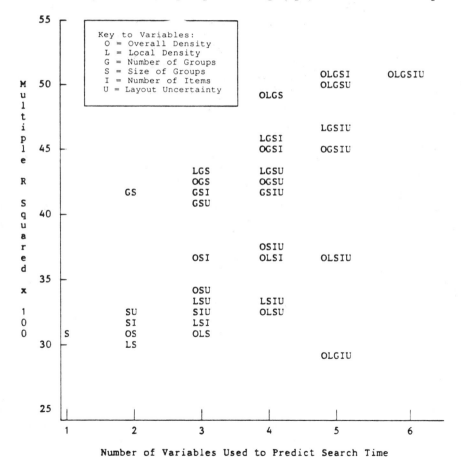

Figure 4.   Experiment 1: Plot of R^2 for multiple regressions using different numbers of display measures to predict search time.

R^2 of .488, while the best-fitting regression using three predictors (local density, number of groups, size of groups) resulted in a multiple R^2 of .432. For that three-predictor equation, only the coefficients for number of groups and size of groups were significant. Overall, the results indicate that the two display measures related to grouping are the most important predictors of search time.

A reasonable approach to choosing the best model for predicting search time would be to select the regression equation with the smallest number of predictor variables for which no other equation has a significantly higher R^2. That would be the four-predictor model shown in Table 5, since the increase in R^2 from .488 to .508 is not significant, t (45) = 1.13. The results of the regression using these four predictors are graphically depicted in Figure 5.

Table 5.   Experiment 1: Best-fitting Multiple Regressions Predicting Search Time at Each Number of Predictor Variables from Two to Six

	Coefficient		t	
Search Time =	2.7313		14.91	**
	+ .0107	× Number of Groups	3.03	**
	+ .0896	× Size of Groups	5.90	**
R^2 = .418				
Search Time =	2.3171		5.49	**
	+ .0093	× Local Density	1.09	
	+ .0123	× Number of Groups	3.23	**
	+ .0784	× Size of Groups	4.28	**
R^2 = .432				
Search Time =	1.6696		3.38	**
	− .0209	× Overall Density	−2.28	*
	+ .0286	× Local Density	2.43	*
	+ .0201	× Number of Groups	4.01	**
	+ .0914	× Size of Groups	4.95	**
R^2 = .488				
Search Time =	1.7020		3.47	**
	− .0529	× Overall Density	−2.09	*
	+ .0282	× Local Density	2.41	*
	+ .0184	× Number of Groups	3.61	**
	+ .0917	× Size of Groups	5.01	**
	+ .0106	× Number of Items	1.35	
R^2 = .508				
Search Time =	1.5106		1.72	
	− .0515	× Overall Density	−1.97	
	+ .0284	× Local Density	2.40	*
	+ .0184	× Number of Groups	3.56	**
	+ .0895	× Size of Groups	4.44	**
	+ .0097	× Number of Items	1.13	
	+ .0318	× Layout Complexity	0.26	
R^2 = .508				

** $p < .01$ (Two-tailed)
* $p < .05$ (Two-tailed)

Subjective ratings. A mean subjective rating on the 1 to 5 scale (1 = Very Easy to Use, 5 = Very Difficult to Use) was calculated for each format, based on the two ratings that each of the 10 subjects provided. The mean subjective ratings ranged from 1.45 to 4.60, with a mean of 2.83 and standard deviation of 0.87. Subjective ratings tended to be positively correlated with search times (r = .68), as one would expect. Higher (worse) subjective ratings were associated with longer search times.

The simple correlations of the six display measures with the mean subjective ratings are shown in Table 4. Most of the correlations were rather high, except for the correlation with number of groups. The correlation with number of groups (r = −.16) was low, due to the same kind of nonlinearity described earlier for the search times. Interestingly, unlike the search time data, the measure that

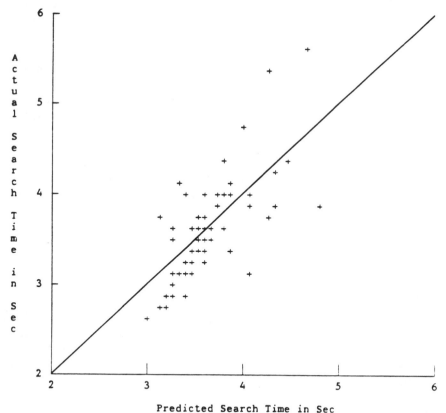

Predicted Search Time in Sec

Figure 5. Experiment 1: Plot of actual search times versus search times predicted from a multiple regression, using overall density, local density, number of groups, and size of groups.

had the highest simple correlation with subjective rating was layout complexity ($r = .75$).

The results of a set of multiple regressions using the "leaps and bounds" technique are shown in Figure 6, which plots R^2 as a function of the number of predictors used. The largest increase in R^2 occurred between one and two predictors: the addition of "local density" to "layout complexity" resulted in an increase of R^2 from .563 to .682. All of the subsequent regressions found that the best fit always included these two predictors. Table 6 shows the regression equations for the best fit at each number of predictor variables from two to six.

As Table 6 shows, the regression using all six predictors resulted in a multiple R^2 of .805, meaning that these six display measures accounted for 80.5% of the variance in rated ease of use. This degree of fit is quite impressive, and indicates that the display measures are better at predicting subjective ratings than search times (R^2 of .805 vs. .508). In addition, individual t tests on the regression coefficients showed that all of the coefficients were significant, unlike the results for search time. This indicates that all six measures play a role in predicting subjective ratings. It appears, however, that the two most important predictors of subjective rating are layout complexity and local density, since those two predictors alone accounted for 68.2% of the variance in subjective ratings.

As before, a reasonable approach to choosing the best model for prediction would be to choose the equation with the smallest number of predictor variables for which no other equation has a significantly higher R^2. That would be the complete six-variable model shown in Table 6, since the increase from the five-variable model (.781) to the six-variable model (.805) is significant, $t(45) = 2.35$, $p < .05$. The results of this regression using all six variables are graphically depicted in Figure 7.

Discussion

Overall, the results of Experiment 1 were quite encouraging. The fact that the regressions accounted for 49% of the variance in search times and 80% of the variance in subjective ratings indicates that it may be possible to use these display measures to predict the usability of a display format.

One of the interesting findings of Experiment 1 was that the display measures were better at predicting subjective ratings than search times. This is not really very surprising when one considers the source of the display measures assessed by the analysis program.

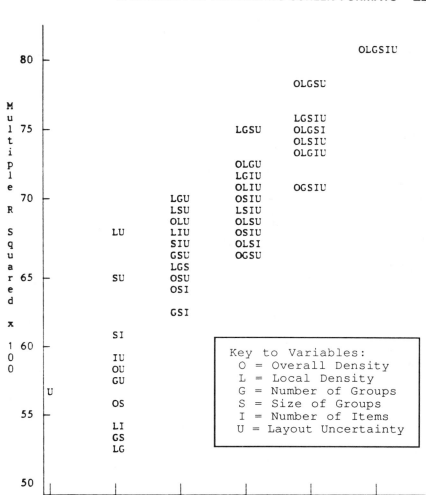

Figure 6. Experiment 1: Plot of R^2 for multiple regressions, using different numbers of display measures to predict subjective rating.

As described by Tullis (1983), those measures were designed to assess characteristics of displays that published guidelines (and, to a lesser extent, empirical data) claimed are important. For the most part, those guidelines are simply their authors' ideas about what makes a "good" display. The fact that 80% of the variance in subjective ratings could be accounted for using these measures

Table 6. Experiment 1: Best-fitting Multiple Regressions Predicting Subjective Rating at Each Number of Predictor Variables from Two to Six

	Coefficient		t	
Rating =	−3.0593		−4.87	**
	+ .0292	× Local Density	4.27	**
	+ .6102	× Layout Complexity	6.29	**
R^2 = .682				
Rating =	−3.3520		−5.34	**
	+ .0420	× Local Density	4.52	**
	+ .0085	× Number of Groups	1.96	
	+ .5374	× Layout Complexity	5.31	**
R^2 = .706				
Rating =	−2.4748		−3.76	**
	+ .0334	× Local Density	3.66	**
	+ .0137	× Number of Groups	3.10	**
	+ .0604	× Size of Groups	2.90	**
	+ .3962	× Layout Complexity	3.73	**
R^2 = .750				
Rating =	−3.8402		−4.67	**
	− .0258	× Overall Density	−2.54	*
	+ .0538	× Local Density	4.56	**
	+ .0208	× Number of Groups	4.14	**
	+ .0655	× Size of Groups	3.30	**
	+ .5163	× Layout Complexity	4.65	**
R^2 = .781				
Rating =	−3.1627		−3.79	**
	− .0801	× Overall Density	−3.23	**
	+ .0522	× Local Density	4.64	**
	+ .0184	× Number of Groups	3.75	**
	+ .0729	× Size of Groups	3.80	**
	+ .0194	× Number of Items	2.37	*
	+ .4121	× Layout Complexity	3.60	**
R^2 = .805				

** $p < .01$ (Two-tailed)
 * $p < .05$ (Two-tailed)

means two things, then: (1) The display measures as implemented in the C program successfully captured the characteristics of displays that the authors of the guidelines said are important; and (2) those authors' subjective reactions to displays are similar to those of the subjects in this experiment.

A key finding of this experiment was that different display variables are important in predicting search times vs. subjective ratings. This is apparent from a comparison of Figures 4 and 6. The single best predictor of search times was the average size of the groups on the display ($r = .56$); the single best predictor of subjective ratings was the average complexity of the layout of items on the display ($r = .75$). Interestingly, this layout complexity measure was not

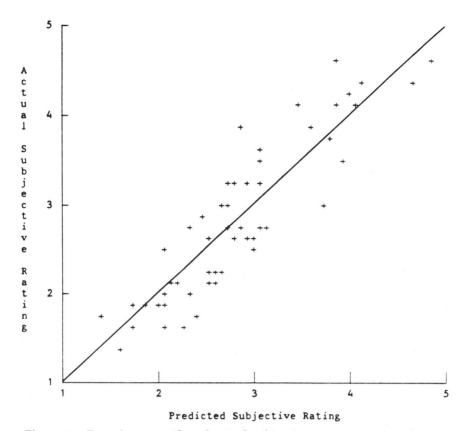

Figure 7. Experiment 1: Plot of actual subjective ratings versus subjective ratings predicted from a multiple regression, using overall density, local density, number of groups, size of groups, number of items, and layout complexity.

important in predicting search time, since adding it to the regression containing the other five variables did not change R^2. The two best predictors of search time were number of groups and size of groups ($R = .65$); the two best predictors of subjective rating were local density and layout complexity ($R = .83$).

In summary, search times are most closely related to the way characters are grouped on the screen, while subjective ratings are most closely related to how tightly the screen is packed (local density) and how well the labels and data values are aligned (layout complexity).

EXPERIMENT 2: VALIDATION OF THE PREDICTION SYSTEM

The results of Experiment 1 indicated that it may be possible to predict search times and subjective ratings of displays based on regression equations that use certain display measures. The major question that remains is how well these regression equations will generalize to other displays and other subjects. Experiment 2 addressed that question by using the regression equations developed in Experiment 1 to predict, a priori, the search times and subjective ratings for a completely new set of displays and new group of subjects.

Method

Displays. Fifteen different formats for presenting listings of data about books were developed. On each display, authors were listed alphabetically by last name, and, for each author, books were listed alphabetically by title. Additional information included an arbitrary author number, the price of the book, publisher, and number of pages. One of the book displays used is shown in Figure 8, along with the output from the analysis program.

To reduce any tendency for these book displays to be similar in format to the airline and motel displays, over half of the book formats (eight) were designed by people not familiar with the displays used in Experiment 1. These eight formats were designed by four acquaintances of the author who had no prior experience in computer system design or user interface design. Each of them was asked to design (on coding forms) two ways of presenting the specified book data. The only other information provided was the maximum length of each of the data items (e.g., author, title, etc.). The original intention was to have all of the displays in Experiment 2 designed by people other than the author, but the display formats designed by other people tended to be similar to each other. Consequently, the author designed the remaining seven formats in order to introduce more variation and provide a better test of the prediction system.

For each of the 15 display formats, 10 examples containing different data were developed. Thus, a total of 150 displays were used in the experiment. To illustrate the resulting values for the six display measures, Table 7 shows their means, standard deviations, and ranges. A comparison of this table to Table 1, which gives similar data for Experiment 1, shows that, overall, the displays used

```
File book5:
----------------------------------------------------------------------------------
Books

Author:      Aird, C
Author#:     33
Title:       Henrietta Who?
Price:       $5
Publisher:   Macmillan
#Pages:      253

Author:      Aird, C
Author#:     33
Title:       His Burial Too
Price:       $4
Publisher:   Macmillan
#Pages:      287

Author:      Aird, C
Author#:     33
Title:       Late Phoenix
Price:       $8
Publisher:   McGraw
#Pages:      362
----------------------------------------------------------------------------------
11111

2222222      33333 3
22222222     33
222222       333333333 3333
222222       33
2222222222   333333333
2222222      333

4444444      55555 5
44444444     55
444444       555 555555 555
444444       55
4444444444   555555555
4444444      555

6666666      77777 7
66666666     77
666666       7777 7777777
666666       77
6666666666   777777
6666666      777
----------------------------------------------------------------------------------
           Overall   Local                  Av. Visual              Layout
Filename   Density   Density  #Grps  Angle of Grps  #Items  Complexity
book5       12.3%     46.8%      7       4.9 deg       37      5.84
```

Figure 8.   **Experiment 2: Output from the analysis program for 1 of the 15 display formats for presenting data about books.**

in the two experiments did not differ dramatically on most of the measures. The largest difference was in mean number of items (86.1 in Experiment 1 vs. 58.6 in Experiment 2).

Predictions. For each of the 15 display formats, search times and subjective ratings were predicted using the most appropriate models from Experiment 1. For search times, that was the four-predictor model shown in Table 5. For subjective ratings, it was the full six-predictor model shown in Table 6. The mean of the predicted search times was 3.69 s, and the range was 3.03 to 4.64 s. The mean of the predicted subjective ratings was 2.46, and the range was 0.82 to 4.78. The minimum value of that range for the subjective ratings

Table 7. Means, Standard Deviations, and Ranges of Six Display Measures for 150 Displays Used in Experiment 2

	Mean	Standard Deviation	Range Minimum	Maximum
Overall Density	20.3%	11.9%	4.5%	56.7%
Local Density	46.8%	11.7%	27.5%	67.5%
Number of Groups	19.1	19.5	1	67
Size of Groups	7.9 deg	5.3 deg	2.3 deg	25.5 deg
Number of Items	58.6	36.4	13	169
Layout Complexity	6.7 bits	1.4 bits	4.2 bits	9.3 bits

(0.82) points out an interesting aspect of the predictions: Three of the book display formats yielded predicted ratings under 1. The rating scale used by the subjects, however, has a possible range of only 1 to 5. Thus, the predictions under 1 will by definition be wrong.

The fact that the predicted subjective ratings can be less than 1, and even less than 0, is apparent from Table 6, which shows that the six-predictor model has a negative intercept value (-3.1627). Thus, as the values of the six display measures get very small, the predicted subjective rating will approach a lower limit of -3.1627. (Note that it is impossible for any display to ever reach this limit, since that display would have to be totally empty.)

This points out a basic difference between the search times and subjective ratings. The subjective ratings assigned by the subjects are really *relative* comparisons of the displays in some set to each other; thus, the rating given to one display depends upon the characteristics of the other displays in the set. The search times, on the other hand, may be considered more stable measures, in that they are not dependent on the characteristics of the entire set of displays.

Apparatus. The apparatus was the same as in Experiment 1, and the monitor was adjusted to the same parameters.

Subjects. Fourteen AT&T Bell Laboratories employees participated in the study for about 1 hour each. All of the subjects were either assistant technical or senior assistant technical. Five of the subjects were female, and eight used corrective lenses. The subjects ranged in age from 23 to 45 years, with a mean of 30 years. Their experience with the Bell System ranged from 2 to 23 years, with a mean of 7.3 years. Their experience in working with computer systems ranged from 1 to 15 years, with a mean of 5.3 years. Eight of the subjects had programming experience.

In general, the subjects in Experiment 2 were much more experienced in working with computers than were those in Experiment

1 (5.3 years for Experiment 2 vs. 7 months for Experiment 1). This was not really intentional, but rather a function of what subjects were available when the two experiments were run. This provided a test of how well the regression equations from Experiment 1 would generalize to a different subject population.

Procedure. Each subject saw 10 different examples of each display format and answered a question using each example. Thus, each subject saw 150 displays and answered as many questions. The same basic set of questions was used for each set of 10 displays in one format. The questions used are illustrated in Table 8.

The rest of the procedure was basically the same as in Experiment 1, except that only 15 different formats were used and they were presented in one block. As in Experiment 1, search times were recorded on each trial. Subjective ratings were obtained at the end of each format and again at the end of the experiment.

Results

Search time. Overall, the subjects answered 98.8% of the questions about the displays correctly, reflecting a high level of accuracy similar to that in Experiment 1. A mean search time was calculated across subjects for each format, based on the correct trials only. Those mean search times ranged from 2.10 to 4.75 s, with a mean of 3.28 s and standard deviation of 0.65 s.

The result of most interest is the simple correlation between these actual mean search times and the search times predicted using the four-predictor regression equation from Experiment 1 (Table 5). The four-variable model predicted search times quite well: $r = .800$. The scatterplot of actual search times and search times predicted using this model is shown in Figure 9.

Figure 9 also shows the regression line that provides the best fit between predicted and actual search times. If this were a perfect prediction system, the intercept of that line would be 0 and the slope would be 1. The actual intercept of −0.62 and slope of 1.06 are surprisingly close to those "perfect" values. As the standard

Table 8. Examples of Questions Asked for Book Displays in Experiment 2

Example of Question	Number Asked per Format
How many pages is Under the Lilacs by Alcott, L M?	2
What is the author number for Silverberg, R?	3
Who is the publisher of Murderess Ink by Winn, D?	2
What is the price of Genesis Machine by Hogan, J P?	3

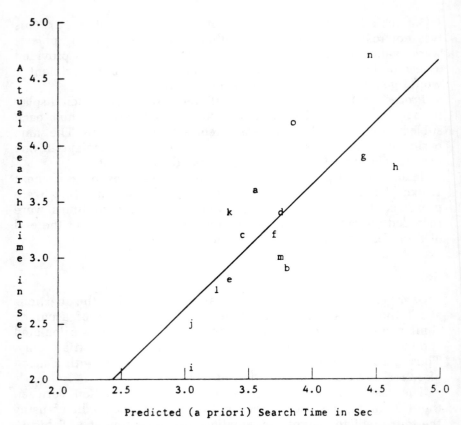

Figure 9. Experiment 2: Scatterplot of actual search times and search times predicted from a model developed in Experiment 1 that uses overall density, local density, number of groups, and size of groups. Letters indicate different displays.

errors of the intercept (0.82) and slope (0.22) reflect, the actual values do not differ significantly from 0 and 1, respectively.

The most surprising finding was the high value of r^2 (.64). The original regression equation from Experiment 1 that used overall density, local density, number of groups, and size of groups had an R^2 of .49. (See Table 5.) One would expect, in a validation study such as Experiment 2, that r^2 would be no greater than the corresponding R^2 found in the original experiment. However, apparently all the displays used in Experiment 2 fit into the original model quite well, resulting in a higher r^2 (i.e., there were no significant outlyers).

As additional confirmation of the predictive validity of the various display measures, Table 9 shows the simple correlations between the actual search times and the search times predicted by *all* of the models listed in Table 5. As expected from Experiment 1, the predictions from the four-variable model had the highest correlation with actual search times. More important, however, is that *all* of the correlations were quite high (.713 to .800).

Subjective ratings. A mean subjective rating on the 1 to 5 scale (1 = Very Easy to Use, 5 = Very Difficult to Use) was calculated for each format, based on the two ratings that each of the 14 subjects provided. Those mean subjective ratings ranged from 1.36 to 3.46, with a mean of 2.31 and standard deviation of 0.58. As in Experiment 1, the subjective ratings were positively correlated with search times ($r = .80$).

The simple correlation between actual subjective ratings and subjective ratings predicted using the six-variable model from Experiment 1 (Table 6) was quite high: $r = .799$. The scatterplot of actual subjective ratings and subjective ratings predicted using this model is shown in Figure 10.

Figure 10 also shows the regression line that provides the best fit between the predicted and actual subjective ratings. As with the search times, perfect prediction would yield an intercept of 0 and slope of 1. The actual intercept of 1.32 and slope of 0.40 diverge from those perfect values. The standard errors of the intercept (0.23) and slope (0.08) indicate that the values differ significantly from 0 and 1, respectively.

The reason for the difference in slope and intercept values appears

Table 9. Simple Correlations Between Actual Search Times from Experiment 2 and Predicted Search Times Based on Five Different Regression Equations from Experiment 1

Display Variables Used in Regression	Correlation (r) of Actual and Predicted Search Times
Number of Groups, Size of Groups	.713
Local Density, Number of Groups, Size of Groups	.759
Overall Density, Local Density, Number of Groups, Size of Groups	.800
Overall Density, Local Density, Number of Groups, Size of Groups, Number of Items	.795
Overall Density, Local Density, Number of Groups, Size of Groups, Number of Items, Layout Complexity	.796

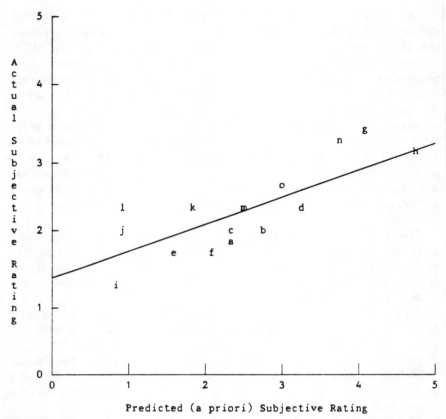

Figure 10. Experiment 2: Scatterplot of actual subjective ratings and subjective ratings predicted from a regression equation developed in Experiment
1 that uses overall density, local density, number of groups, size of groups,
number of items, and layout complexity. Letters indicate different displays.

to lie in a difference between the ranges of the predicted and actual
values, rather than a difference between the means (2.31 for actual
vs. 2.46 for predicted). The range for the actual subjective ratings
(1.36 to 3.46) is more restricted than the range for the predicted
subjective ratings (0.82 to 4.78). The most likely explanation for this
difference in ranges appears to be the different populations of subjects represented in Experiment 2 compared to Experiment 1. The
subjects in Experiment 2 had far more experience with computer
systems, both as users and programmers, than did the subjects in
Experiment 1. Perhaps their wider experience with computer systems and CRT displays, both good and bad, led the subjects in

Experiment 2 to view these displays as covering a relatively small part of the "good-to-bad" continuum.

Unlike the results for search time, r^2 for subjective ratings decreased in Experiment 2 (.638) relative to the corresponding R^2 in Experiment 1 (.805). This shrinkage in R^2 is larger than would have been expected based upon Experiment 1. The so-called "shrunken R^2" can be derived from Experiment 1 to provide an unbiased estimate of the population R^2. (See, for example, Cohen & Cohen, 1975, p. 106.) That shrunken R^2 estimated from Experiment 1 is .779, which is still larger than r^2 from Experiment 2. This is, perhaps, additional evidence for the effect of different subject populations in Experiments 1 and 2.

Further confirmation of the predictive validity of the display measures is provided by Table 10, which shows the simple correlations with subjective rating for all of the models listed in Table 6. As expected from Experiment 1, the predictions from the six-variable model had the highest correlation with actual subjective ratings. However, as with search times, *all* of the correlations were high (.723 to .799).

Discussion

The results of Experiment 2 showed that the prediction system developed in Experiment 1 generalizes quite well to a different set of displays and different subject population. In particular, the high correlations between predicted and actual search times ($r = .800$) and subjective ratings ($r = .799$) were most encouraging.

Table 10. Simple Correlations Between Actual Subjective Ratings from Experiment 2 and Predicted Subjective Ratings Based on Five Different Regression Equations from Experiment 1

Display Variables Used in Regression	Correlation (r) of Actual and Predicted Subjective Ratings
Local Density, Layout Complexity	.734
Local Density, Number of Groups, Layout Complexity	.723
Local Density, Number of Groups, Size of Groups, Layout Complexity	.756
Overall Density, Local Density, Number of Groups, Size of Groups, Layout Complexity	.772
Overall Density, Local Density, Number of Groups, Size of Groups, Number of Items, Layout Complexity	.799

Another way of looking at the accuracy of the prediction system is to consider how it would be used in a real application. Typically, a system designer's task is to choose which of several alternative display formats is *best*. What is meant by "best" depends on the circumstances. If the system is to be used in a situation where speed is important (e.g., power plant control), then search time would probably be emphasized. If the system is to be marketed to the general public (e.g., home information retrieval), then subjective ratings might be emphasized. In many cases, however, the system designer would probably want to give equal weights to search time and subjective rating. One way of doing that would be to convert the search times and subjective ratings to z scores, and then simply add them together. A scatterplot of the predicted and actual scores transformed in this manner is shown in Figure 11.

Since a system designer may not have empirical data on the usability of alternative formats, he or she could only rely on predicted scores to guide the display selection. Based on Figure 11, the system designer faced with choosing the best format for these book displays would choose format "i" since it yielded the lowest predicted score (-2.66). (This is also relatively obvious from Figures 9 and 10.) Inspection of the actual scores shows that format "i" is indeed the best choice, since it yielded the lowest actual score as well.

Another reasonable choice based on the predicted scores would have been format "j," since its predicted score (-2.64) was quite close to the lowest one. It too would have been a reasonably good choice since its actual score was one of the three lowest. In short, the prediction system seems to perform well when used in the manner that it might be in a real system design application.

APPLYING THE SYSTEM TO OTHER DISPLAYS

Modifications to the Program

As a result of the findings from Experiments 1 and 2, the program for analyzing displays was enhanced to do more than just measure the six display characteristics. The intent behind the enhancements was to make the program more useful as a design tool. This was done by trying to give the designer more information about *why* the results came out the way they did. In some senses, these enhancements add an expert-system "flavor" to the program. The specific enhancements included the following:

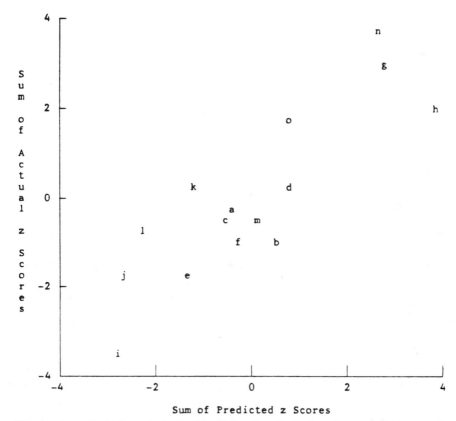

Figure 11. Experiment 2: Scatterplot of actual transformed scores and predicted transformed scores based on regression equations developed in Experiment 1. Transformed scores are the sum of z-score transformations for search times and subjective ratings. Letters indicate different displays.

- The four-predictor regression equation from Table 5 was incorporated into the program to predict search times, and the six-predictor regression equation from Table 6 was incorporated to predict subjective ratings.
- Several thresholds were added to cause messages to be printed if the values of any of the display measures are higher than normal. Most of these thresholds were based upon the means and standard deviations of the display measures from the 520 displays studied in Experiment 1 (Table 1). In each case, the threshold is approximately the mean plus one standard deviation. Each of the messages states that the particular value is unusually high (e.g., "Layout complexity is high"), gives some additional

descriptive information (e.g., "This means that the display items are not well aligned with each other") and then makes suggestions about how the problem might be alleviated (e.g., "Numeric items should be vertically aligned on their decimal point and character items should be vertically aligned by their starting characters").

- In addition to the "group map" already being printed by the program, a "local density map" was added to show the local density at each character position, and a "layout map" was added to show the starting positions of each data item and label. These were added to give the designer additional information for use in deciding what changes should be made to the display.

Examples of the output from the enhanced program are shown in Figures 12 and 13 for two hypothetical displays of employee information. Figure 12 shows the analysis of an obviously rather bad display, while Figure 13 shows the analysis of a redesigned version. Notice that many of the messages suggesting techniques for reformatting the display were printed in Figure 12, since the thresholds for local density, group size, and layout complexity were exceeded. The display shown in Figure 13 was then designed by following the suggested revisions (e.g., distributing the information more evenly across the screen, breaking the display into smaller groups, aligning data items). Notice that the redesigns resulted in a 42% improvement in predicted search time (4.75 s vs. 3.21 s) and a 57% improvement in predicted subjective rating (3.89 vs. 1.66).

This enhanced version of the program, now called the Display Analysis Program (Version 4.0), is available from The Report Store to run on the IBM PC and PC-compatible computers (Tullis, 1986a). Additional details about the enhancements to the program are presented in Tullis (1986c).

Application to Other Displays with Known Search Times

While the analyses shown in Figures 12 and 13 illustrate the potential usefulness of the Display Analysis Program, the validity of the usability predictions for these examples cannot be assessed, since no empirical usability data exist for these particular displays. There have, however, been several studies of alphanumeric displays that have manipulated display format and measured the effects on user search time. A good test of the Display Analysis Program would be to apply it to the displays used in these other studies and see how its predictions correspond to the actual findings.

Table 11 summarizes the findings from seven studies that pre-

```
Display Analysis Program, Version 4.0
       Copyright (c) 1986
  by Thomas S. Tullis, Ph.D.

File employ1:
---------+---------+---------+---------+---------+---------+---------+---------+---------+---------+
                   EMPLOYEE INFORMATION
EMPLOYEE NAME: MARGARET A. EDWARDS  DATE OF HIRE: 10/14/83
PAYROLL NUMBER: 15131  BIRTHDATE: 11/16/52
JOB TITLE: PROGRAMMER/ANALYST  SEX: F
SOCIAL SECURITY #: 413-77-2856  MARRIED? Y
HOME ADDRESS: 27786 ARBOLITOS  APARTMENT #:
CITY: MISSION VIEJO  STATE: CA  ZIP CODE: 92692
HOME PHONE: 714-555-9034
DEPARTMENT: DATA PROCESSING  SUPERVISOR: T. A. HART
SECTION: SYSTEM SERVICES  COST CENTER: 6720
ROOM NUMBER: 1020  EXTENSION: 3307
SPOUSE'S NAME: STUART T. EDWARDS  EMPLOYER: BURROUGHS CORP
WORK PHONE: 714-380-2875  CITY: IRVINE
HEALTH CARE PLAN: 1  (1. HMO    2. HOSPITALIZATION)
LIFE INSURANCE: 2 (1. EMPLOYEE ONLY  2. ENTIRE FAMILY)
---------+---------+---------+---------+---------+---------+---------+---------+---------+---------+
                     Number     %
Upper-case letters     422     77.0
Lower-case letters       0      0.0
Digits                  74     13.5
Other characters        52      9.5
Total                  548

Overall Density =  28.5%

The percentage of upper-case letters is high.
   Consider using more lower-case letters, since text printed in normal upper-
   and lower-case letters is read about 13% faster than text in all upper-case.
   Reserve all-upper-case for items that need to attract attention.

Local Density Analysis:    Key:  0%  . ' " : = * % $ # @   100%
---------+---------+---------+---------+---------+---------+---------+---------+---------+---------+
                ==******* ********===
:===**** ****% %%%%$$%% %$ $$%%%%% **== :: """""" """"""""::
=**%%$$ $$$$$$$ $$$$$ $#####$$$$ $%%%**=:
=*% $$#### ################### $$$$ %
*%%$$# ######## ## ##########$$$ $$$$$$%* =
*%%$ ######## ##### #####$$$$ %%%$%$%%* =:
*%%$$ ####### ##### ###$$$% %* %%% %%%%* ==::"
*%$$ ###### ##########$$ 
*%$$########## #### ########$$$ %%%%%%%%%%** *= =: :"""
*%$$#### ###### #######$ $%%% %%%%% *===
*%$$ ####### #### #####$$$$$ $$%% 
*%$$$### ##### ##$##$ ## $$$$$$$ $$%%%%*** *======:: ""''
=*%$ $$#$## $#$$$$$$$$$$ $$$$% $%%%%
=**%%% $$$$ %%%%% % *%% *%% ** $**%%********%===
::== ********** * === **=**%== ==== == ===== ===::"""
---------+---------+---------+---------+---------+---------+---------+---------+---------+---------+
Maximum local density = 89.9% at row 9, column 8
Average local density = 67.0%

Average local density over most of the screen is high.
   The area with the highest local density is identified above, but other
   areas with high density can be identified from the density map.  In general,
   you should strive for a density map that has very few symbols higher than
   "%" (as shown in the key).  You can reduce local density by distributing
   the characters as evenly as is feasible over the entire screen.
Grouping Analysis:
---------+---------+---------+---------+---------+---------+---------+---------+---------+---------+
                11111111 11111111111
11111111 11111 11111111 11 1111111  1111 1~ 22222 22222222
1111111 1111111 11111  1111111111 11111111
111 111111 1111111111111111111  1111 1
111111 11111111 11 11111111111  11111111 1
1111 11111111 11111 111111111  111111111 11
11111 1111111 11111  111111 11  111 11111 11111
1111 111111 11111111111
11111111111 1111 111111111  11111111111 11 11 1111
11111111 111111 11111111  1111 1111111 1111
1111 1111111 1111  1111111111 1111
11111111 11111 111111 11 1111111  111111111 111111111 1111
1111 111111 111111111111  11111 111111
111111 11111 11111 1  111 111   11 1111111111111111111
1111 1111111111 1 111 11111111 1111  11 111111 1111111
---------+---------+---------+---------+---------+---------+---------+---------+---------+---------+
(The character '~' in the grouping output stands for a 'bridge' between groups)
```

```
Group   # Characters  Visual Angle
1            534            19.2 *
2             13             4.2

Number of groups =   2

Maximum size   =  19.2 degrees (Group 1)
Average size   =  18.8 degrees (weighted by # of characters in group)
```

The display contains large groups.
   The largest groups are marked with an asterisk (*) in the list above.
   Consider breaking these groups into their logical components. In general,
   each of these components can then be identified as a group by separating
   it from other characters by at least one blank line vertically and two
   blank spaces horizontally. The best compromise between the number of groups
   and their average size appears to be a maximum of about 35 groups with an
   average size no larger than about 4.2 degrees (for a 24 x 80 screen).
Layout Analysis:

Starting position of character items (C) or decimal point of numeric items (N):

```
---------+---------+---------+---------+---------+---------+---------+---------+
          C
          C                              C                   N
C                   N C              N
C         C                      C   C
C              N              C
C             ·NC             C
C     C         C      C   C              N
C         N
C         C              C          C
C      C              C          N
C             N C            N
C         C              C
C     N         C   C
C             N C         N C
C         NC                   N C
---------+---------+---------+---------+---------+---------+---------+---------+
```
Total number of items = 58

```
Number of different rows used    =  15    Vertical complexity   = 3.83 bits
Number of different columns used =  27    Horizontal complexity = 4.19 bits

Total Layout Complexity =  8.02 bits
```

Layout complexity is high.
   This means that the display items (labels and data) are not well-aligned
   with each other. Vertical complexity can be reduced by using fewer lines
   on the screen-- which may not be practical. Horizontal complexity can be
   reduced by starting items in fewer different columns on the screen (that
   is, by aligning them vertically). In general, numeric items (indicated by
   "N's" above) should be vertically aligned on their decimal point (or right-
   justified if they don't have one). Character items (indicated by "C's"
   above) should be vertically aligned by their starting characters (i.e.,
   left-justified).

SUMMARY:

Filename	Overall Density	Local Density	#Grps	Av. Visual Angle of Grps	#Items	Layout Complexity
employ1	28.5%	67.0%	2	18.8 deg	58	8.02

```
Predicted Search Time =          4.75 sec
Predicted Subjective Rating = 3.89 ( <2 is good; >4 is poor )
```

The percentage of upper-case letters is high.
   Consider using more lower-case letters.
Average local density is high.
   Try redesigning the display so it is less tightly packed.
The display contains large groups.
   Consider breaking the data into smaller groups.
Layout complexity is high.
   Try to align data elements vertically and horizontally.
Display Analysis Program, Version 4.0
      Copyright (c) 1986
    by Thomas S. Tullis, Ph.D.

Figure 12. Output from Display Analysis Program (Version 4.0) for a hypothetical employee information display.

```
File employ3:
---------+---------+---------+---------+---------+---------+--------+---------+
                        EMPLOYEE INFORMATION

Employee Name:   MARGARET A. EDWARDS         Date of Hire:  10/14/83
Payroll Number:  15131                       Birthdate:     11/16/52
Job Title:       PROGRAMMER/ANALYST          Sex:           F
Social Sec. #:   413-77-2856                 Married?       Y

Home Address:    27786 ARBOLITOS             Apartment #:
City:            MISSION VIEJO               State: CA Zip Code: 92692
Home Phone:      714-555-9034

Department:      DATA PROCESSING             Supervisor:    T. A. HART
Section:         SYSTEM SERVICES             Cost Center:   6720
Room Number:     1020                        Extension:     3307

Spouse's Name:   STUART T. EDWARDS           Employer:      BURROUGHS CORP
Work Phone:      714-380-2875                City:          IRVINE

Health Care Plan: 1                          Life Ins:      2
                 (1. HMO)                                   (1. Employee)
                 (2. Hospitalization)                       (2. Family)
---------+---------+---------+---------+---------+---------+--------+---------+
                        Number     %
Upper-case letters        191    35.9
Lower-case letters        210    39.5
Digits                     74    13.9
Other characters           57    10.7
Total                     532

Overall Density = 27.7%

Local Density Analysis:     Key:   0%   . ' " : = * % $ # @   100%
---------+---------+---------+---------+---------+---------+--------+---------+
                     "":::::: :::::::"""""

:===**** *====   ===*****  ** ====:::    :::== == :::::  :::::::::"
==**%%% %****==   *****                  ==*****==:       :::::::::"
=** %%%%%*        **%%%%%%%**===::"       :==*              "
=**%%% %*** ==    **%%%%%%%**             ==***==           "

:==* ****==::     =**%% %%%%**=::         :===**==:  ""
:====            =**%%%% %%*==           ::==== =:  :"""  """:" """""'
:=** ***=::      =**%%%%%%**                                
                                                            
==*%%%%*==:      ==** %*%%***=::          :==****===   :: ::  """"'
==***%**         ==**** ****==::          :=** %***==:  ::::
==** %%%*==:     :===                     ==*%%%%**=   ::::
                                                        
:=***%** *==::   ====== == ==:;""'        :==**===:   ::====:::: """'
::== ***===      ========:::             :::=:        ::::::
                                                        
"":::: :::: :::::: =                      """; """""      "
                 ::: =:::                                ":: =====:;""
                 "::  :::::::::::;""""'                   "":  :==:::"
---------+---------+---------+---------+---------+---------+--------+---------+
Maximum local density = 69.3% at row 8, column 24
Average local density = 44.7%

Grouping Analysis:
---------+---------+---------+---------+---------+---------+--------+---------+
                   11111111 11111111111

22222222 22222   33333333 33 3333333      4444 44 44444    55555555
2222222 2222222  33333                    4444444444        55555555
222 222222       333333333333333333       4444              5
222222 2222 22   33333333333              44444444          5

6666 66666666    77777 777777777          888888888 88
66666            7777777 77777            888888 88   888 88888 88888
6666 666666      777777777777

99999999999      :::: :::::::::::          ;;;;;;;;;;   << << <<<<
99999999         ::::: ::::::::            ;;;; ;;;;;;;   <<<<
9999 9999999     ::::                      ;;;;;;;;;;    <<<<

======== =====   >>>>>> >> >>>>>>>         ?????????   @@@@@@@@@ @@@@
==== ======      >>>>>>>>>>>>               ?????       @@@@@

AAAAAA AAAA AAAA A                         BBBB BBBB     C
                 AAA AAAA                                CCC CCCCCCCC
                 AAA AAAAAAAAAAAAAAAAA                   CCC CCCCCCC
---------+---------+---------+---------+---------+---------+--------+---------+
```

```
Group  # Characters  Visual Angle      Group  # Characters  Visual Angle
1           19            6.0            ;          32            3.8
2           48            4.4            <          16            3.2
3           51            5.9            =          23            4.2
4           33            4.3            >          27            5.0
5           18            3.0            ?          14            2.7
6           27            3.8            @          19            4.2
7           38            4.4            A          42           10.9
8           32            7.8            B           8            2.4
9           30            3.8            C          23            3.8
:           32            4.4
```

Number of groups = 19

Maximum size   = 10.9 degrees (Group A)
Average size   =   5.1 degrees (weighted by # of characters in group)

Layout Analysis:

Starting position of character items (C) or decimal point of numeric items (N):
```
---------+---------+---------+---------+---------+---------+---------+---------+
                   C
C          C                              C          N
C              N                          C          N
C          C                              C          C
C          N                              C          C

C              NC                         C
C          C                              C      C   C                       N
C          N

C          C                              C          C
C          C                              C              N
C              N                          C              N

C          C                              C          C
C          •N                             C          C

C              N                          C              N
           C                                         C
           C                                         C
---------+---------+---------+---------+---------+---------+---------+---------+
```
Total number of items = 57

Number of different rows used   = 16   Vertical complexity   = 3.91 bits
Number of different columns used = 14   Horizontal complexity = 3.08 bits

Total Layout Complexity = 6.99 bits

SUMMARY:
```
              Overall   Local             Av. Visual          Layout
Filename      Density   Density   #Grps  Angle of Grps  #Items  Complexity
employ3        27.7%     44.7%     19        5.1 deg      57      6.99
```

Predicted Search Time =   3.21 sec
Predicted Subjective Rating = 1.66 (<2 is good; >4 is poor)

Figure 13. Output from Display Analysis Program (Version 4.0) for an improved version of the hypothetical employee information display shown in Figure 12.

sented search time data for realistic alphanumeric displays: Tullis (1981); Streveler and Wasserman (1984); Dodson and Shields (1978); Ringel and Hammer (1964); Callan, Curran, and Lane (1977); Burns, Warren, and Rudisill (1985); and Wolf (1986). That table shows the actual search times found in those studies, as well as the predicted search times from the Display Analysis Program.

Before considering each of these studies individually, a few points about the data as a whole should be made. For six of the seven studies, the search times predicted by the Display Analysis Program were lower than the actual search times. One obvious reason for this is the difference between the *semantics* of the displays used in Experiments 1 and 2 of the present study and that of the displays listed in Table 11. Experiments 1 and 2 involved relatively simple displays containing ordered lists of items that are familiar to the subjects. Most of the studies listed in Table 11 involved much more complex displays containing data in an order that may not be obvious to the subjects. For example, Tullis (1981) used displays of the results from diagnostic tests on a telephone line; Ringel and Hammer (1964) showed the status of battlefield units; and Burns et al. (1985) showed Space Shuttle displays.

Another reason for the difference in search times lies in the nature of the search tasks presented to the subjects. In Experiments 1 and 2, the subjects had to search for a single data item associated with a well defined target (e.g., the flight number of a plane arriving at a specified time). In many of the studies listed in Table 11, the task was not nearly so simple. For example, some of the questions asked by Tullis (1981) were very high-level, such as "Where is the trouble on this telephone line most likely to be?" This sort of question required the subjects to decide which items on the display were relevant, to encode their values, and then to integrate that information with their prior experience to make their best guess about the answer. In addition, some of the studies listed in Table 11 (such as Tullis, 1981, and Callan et al., 1977) included the time to type the answer in the search time, while Experiments 1 and 2 did not include typing time.

For those studies that involved more than two different display formats, Table 11 also shows the correlation between the actual search times reported in those studies and the predicted search times from the Display Analysis Program. The resulting correlations were quite high, ranging from .76 to .98. Thus, even though the absolute values of the predicted search times were generally too low, the relative values were quite accurate.

Table 11. Results of Applying the Display Analysis Program to Studies that Reported Search Times

Reference	Display Conditions		Actual	Predicted Real	Predicted Adj.	Comments
Tullis	Narrative		8.3	4.2	–	Same order
(1981)	Structured		5.0	3.2	–	
Streveler &	Patient Info 1		11.7	4.8	10.0	$r = .76$
Wasserman	Patient Info 2		8.0	4.4	9.0	
(1984)	Stewart 1		7.0	3.5	6.9	
	Stewart 2		3.8	3.2	6.2	
	NASA 1		5.5	2.9	5.4	
	NASA 2		6.0	3.0	5.5	
	Martin 1		7.8	3.?	6.1	
	Martin 2		7.0	3.3	6.3	
	Medical Info		6.4	3.3	6.2	
	Patient List		6.5	4.1	8.2	
Dodson &	"Density"					
Shields	30%		3.4	3.0	3.5	$r = .98$
(1978)	50%		3.9	3.1	3.8	
	70%		5.0	3.9	5.0	
Ringel &	"# Lines"	"Density"				
Hammer	10	low	18.7	4.8	17.1	$r = .79$
(1964)	18	low	17.7	5.9	19.2	
	25	low	22.3	6.8	21.0	
	10	medium	16.9	4.8	17.1	
	18	medium	21.1	5.9	19.2	
	25	medium	21.4	6.8	21.1	
	10	high	16.2	4.8	17.0	
	18	high	17.7	5.9	19.2	
	25	high	20.1	6.8	21.1	
	10	higher	–	3.5	14.5	
	18	higher	–	3.6	14.7	
	25	higher	–	3.6	14.8	
Callan,	"# Items"					
Curran,	6		4.2	2.9	4.6	$r = .91$
& Lane (1977)	10		4.5	2.8	4.5	
	19		5.0	3.2	4.8	
	24		5.2	3.3	5.0	
	33		5.2	3.6	5.3	
	40		5.5	3.8	5.6	
Burns,	Current Orbit					
Warren, &	Maneuver		9.6	3.6	10.1	$r = .79$
Rudisill	Reformatted					
(1985)	Orbit Mnvr.		6.1	3.2	7.4	
	Current Relative Navig.		10.2	3.5	9.1	
	Reformatted Rel. Navig.		7.6	3.2	6.9	
Wolf	HN1		2.3	3.5	2.6	$r = .86$
(1986)	HN3		2.9	4.0	3.0	
	HN4		2.9	3.5	2.5	
	HN5		3.7	4.6	3.6	

The regressions used to obtain those correlation coefficients can also be used to adjust the predicted search times to take into account the greater semantic complexity of the displays and search tasks used by the studies in Table 11. That adjustment simply involves, for each study, inserting the predicted times into the regression equation that fits the actual times using the predicted times. These adjusted search times are also shown in Table 11. Figure 14 shows a scatterplot of the actual search times and the predicted search times adjusted in this manner. The correlation associated with this scatterplot of 36 displays is .987.

Each of the studies listed in Table 11 will now be considered individually.

Tullis (1981). The Tullis (1981) study was really what started the entire line of research leading to the current experiments and the Display Analysis Program. In that study, the time that it took subjects

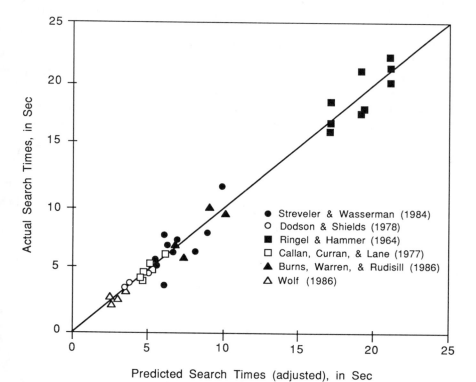

Figure 14.   Scatterplot of actual search times for 36 display formats from 6 studies in the literature and predicted search times from the Display Analysis Program, adjusted to take search task differences into account.

to interpret four different formats for results of diagnostic tests on a telephone was measured. Two of the formats were alphanumeric ("narrative," shown in Figure 15, and "structured," shown in Figure 16), while the other two formats made use of graphics and color. The key finding was that, with practice, subjects were able to interpret the information about 40% quicker with the structured format (5.0 s) than with the narrative format (8.3 s). In addition, there was no significant difference in interpretation time for the structured format in comparison to the color and graphic formats. These findings raised the issue of what characteristics of the structured display made it so much better than the narrative display.

Since only two alphanumeric formats were compared in that study, it is not meaningful to calculate a correlation between the actual and predicted search times for those displays. However, the order of the narrative and structured formats is the same for the predicted and actual times: Both show that the structured format is better. In addition, the ratio of structured to narrative is similar for the predicted (.76) and actual (.60) times.

Streveler and Wasserman (1984). Streveler and Wasserman (1984) described a system for quantitatively assessing screen formats that has many parallels with the Display Analysis Program. Neither of us was aware of the other's work until both systems were presented at the INTERACT '84 conference in London. The parallels between the two analysis systems will be described in Section 5, but for

```
TEST RESULTS    SUMMARY: GROUND

GROUND, FAULT T-G
3 TERMINAL DC RESISTANCE
  >  3500.00 K OHMS T-R
  =    14.21 K OHMS T-G
  >  3500.00 K OHMS R-G
3 TERMINAL DC VOLTAGE
  =     0.00 VOLTS  T-G
  =     0.00 VOLTS  R-G
VALID AC SIGNATURE
3 TERMINAL AC RESISTANCE
  =     8.82 K OHMS T-R
  =    14.17 K OHMS T-G
  =   628.52 K OHMS R-G
LONGITUDINAL BALANCE POOR
  =    39    DB
COULD NOT COUNT RINGERS DUE TO
  LOW RESISTANCE
VALID LINE CKT CONFIGURATION
CAN DRAW AND BREAK DIAL TONE
```

Figure 15. "Narrative" format studied by Tullis (1981).

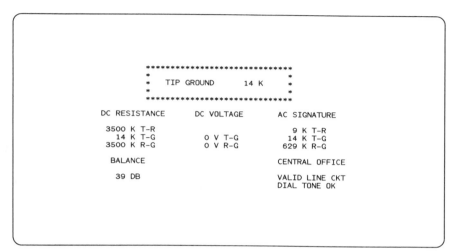

Figure 16. **"Structured" format studied by Tullis (1981).**

now let us consider the search time data that Streveler and Wasserman collected.[3]

Most of their search times were collected for pairs of displays, where the two members of each pair represented two different ways of presenting essentially the same data. The two displays called "Patient Info 1" and "Patient Info 2" in Table 11 are shown in Figures 17 and 18. These are two ways of presenting patient information from actual hospital systems. The subjects' task with these displays was to extract either the patient's age or occupation. Streveler and Wasserman found that the subjects took significantly less time to extract the information from "Patient Info 2" than "Patient Info 1" ($p < .001$). As Table 11 shows, the Display Analysis Program also shows that "Patient Info 2" is better.

The displays called "Stewart 1" and "Stewart 2" in Table 11 are shown in Figures 19 and 20. These are from Stewart (1976), who presented them as examples of displays for a hypothetical inventory system. "Stewart 2" was created by reformatting "Stewart 1" to adhere to certain principles of screen design. Stewart, however, did not present any empirical data to compare their effectiveness. Strev-

---

[3] The detailed search time data discussed here, and shown in Table 11, were not reported by Streveler and Wasserman (1984) in the proceedings of the INTERACT '84 conference, but were reported in the oral presentation at the conference. I am grateful to Dennis Streveler for providing me with a copy of the overhead transparencies he used in the presentation.

```
                 P R E - A D M I S S I O N - P E R S O N A L   D A T A
      PATIENT-ID PATIENT NAME              ADDITIONAL NAME  TTL   SEX AGE  ADM.DATE TIME
   >   403254<>BYERS MARTHA R              <>GRAYSON        <>MRS <>F<>24Y<>07-29---<>1400<
      PATIENT ADDRESS                                          CITY/STATE              ZIP
   >1901 SOUTH BOULEVARD              <>APT 3A            <>CHARLOTTE, N C         <>28209<
      HOME-PHONE     BIRTH-DATE  BIRTHPLACE               REL/CHURCH
   >704-555-4163<  >8-31-53 <  >WILMINGTON N C    <  >METHODIST                   <
      ROOM-BD   FC    CR  RACE  M/S NOTABLE    SVC   DR-CD  DOCTOR NAME
   >      < >02<  >  < > <    >M<  >4<        >SUR< >16025< BROWN J C
   HIST# >K36752     <   PREV-ADM  >03-75     <  SSN >841-00-3141 < SG-DTS
   EST-DAYS >      <  DIAGNOSIS >POSSIBLE CHOLECYSTOLITHIASIS                       <
   REMARKS>NOTIFY DR BROWN WHEN PATIENT ARRIVES                                    <
      OCCUPATION     EMPLOYER NAME/ADDRESS                             TELEPHONE
   >SECRETARY    < >APEX BUILDING SUPPLIES                         <>    643-1641<
      RESPONSIBLE PARTY           RELATION    TELEPHONE
   >BYERS MARTHA R            < >SELF     < >704-555-4163<
      RESPONSIBLE PARTY ADDRESS                          CITY/STATE              ZIP
   >1901 SOUTH BOULEVARD          <>APT 3A            <>CHARLOTTE, N C         <>28209<
   POSTN>SECRETARY    <EMP NM/ADDR>APEX BUILDING SUPPLIES                         <
      EMERGENCY CONTACT NAME      RELATION    EMERG CONT CITY/STATE       TELEPHONE
   >ROBERT E BYERS            < >HUSBAND  < >CHARLOTTE, N C          <>   555-6770<
   INS?
   >Y<
                                                                      Page 1
```

Figure 17. "Patient Info 1" format studied by Streveler and Wasserman (1984).

```
   FORMAT: INQPT1                          PRINTED: 04/16/83 15:55:16
   INQPT1
   =================================================================================
                       P a t i e n t   I n f o r m a t i o n
   =================================================================================
   Number:   40002407              Medical Record Number:   815 3609
   Name:     Amao, Remedios        Birthdate: 06/30/1920  Age: 63
   Other:                          Radiology Number:        428791-8
   Address:  4589 Lexington #4     District:
   City:     Los Angeles           State: CA      Zip: 90024
   Phone:    664-0597              Sex: F         Marital Status: M
   Soc Sec:  553-00-3672           Religion: RC   Racial Origin: F


   =================================================================================
                 P a t i e n t   E m p l o y e r   I n f o r m a t i o n
   =================================================================================
   Code:     PRI                        Occupation: clerk
   Name:     Medeiros Insurance Company  Length of Employment: 27 Y
   Address:  2227 Sunset Blvd           Phone: 555-8790
   City/St:  Hollywood CA 90021         Clock #:

                       TAB When Done: _

   Patient Name: Amao, Remedios             No: 40002407   Room: 216B
```

Figure 18. "Patient Info 2" format studied by Streveler and Wasserman (1984).

eler and Wasserman found that, when subjects were asked to extract the part number from these displays, they took significantly less time with "Stewart 2" ($p < .001$). Again, the Display Analysis Program also shows that "Stewart 2" is better, although the magnitude of the difference is clearly less.

The displays called "NASA 1" and "NASA 2," which are shown

```
PART NUMBER FILE    SUB-FILE MISC BKTS

SUPPLIER J.BLOGGS & SON, ROTHERHAM

PART 926431X  DESCRIPTION L11 BRONZE STUD BRACKET

SUB-ACCOUNT 92 BUDGET GROUP 2413

QUANTITY UNIT DOZENS DEPRECIATION PERIOD 15 ACTION

DATE OF ADDITION 12/1/75  ADDED BY F.BRIGGS

DATE LAST AMENDED 5/14/75  AMENDED BY PROC 11 R.SMITH

GROUP B CLASS R STATUS NOT YET ALLOCATED

DATE OF DELETION

COMPONENTS NONE

SUB ASSEMBLIES NONE
```

Figure 19. "Stewart 1" format studied by Streveler and Wasserman (1984), from Stewart (1976). (Adapted from *Applied Ergonomics, Vol. 7.3,* p. 142, with permission of the publisher, Butterworth Scientific Limited, Guildford, Surrey, U.K.).

```
PART NUMBER FILE:
PART:       7426181Z          LH BRONZE STUD BRACKET

GROUP:    J              BUDGET GROUP:        3612

CLASS:    Z              SUB-ACCOUNT:         45

UNITS:    DOZENS         DEPRECIATION PERIOD:  81

ACTION:   NONE           STATUS:         NOT YET ALLOCATED

ADDITION DATE:           3 DEC 76    F.BRIGGS DES 9

LAST AMMENDED            21 JUL 75   R.SMITH PROC 11

DELETION DATE:           NONE


MAIN SUPPLIER:           L.R. RICHARDSON, AMSTERDAM
```

Figure 20. "Stewart 2" format studied by Streveler and Wasserman (1984), from Stewart (1976). (Adapted from *Applied Ergonomics, Vol. 7.3,* p. 142, with permission of the publisher, Butterworth Scientific Limited, Guildford, Surrey, U.K.).

in Figures 21 and 22, are two very similar versions of a display used by NASA for presenting information about latitude and longitude, wind speeds, etc. The only significant difference between the displays is how well aligned the items in each column are. Streveler and Wasserman found a small, but reliable, advantage for "NASA 1" when subjects extracted values for latitude, drift, temperature, and gross weight. The ratio of actual search times for "NASA 1" to "NASA 2" was .93. The Display Analysis Program also indicated a very small advantage for "NASA 1," with the ratio for the predicted times being .97.

The displays called "Martin 1" and "Martin 2," shown in Figures 23 and 24, were based upon a display presented by Martin (1973, p. 110). The main difference between the two displays is how the items are grouped. When subjects were asked to locate the city that the order was being shipped to, they took an average of 7.83 s with "Martin 1" and 7.02 s with "Martin 2." However, the variance associated with these search times was high, and the difference in means was not statistically significant ($p = .38$). Interestingly, the Display Analysis Program predicts a slightly shorter search time for "Martin 1" (3.20 s) than for "Martin 2" (3.28 s).

The "Medical Info" display listed in Table 11 is shown in Figure 25. In this case, Streveler and Wasserman studied the effect of having subjects locate items that appeared in different quadrants of the display. However, by averaging the data across the four quad-

PRESENT SITUATION		GMT 1102:15
LAT		LONG
38 17' 42"N		94 52' 06"W
WIND	DRIFT	COURSE
292/146	6o L	281
G/S	TAS	TK ERROR
299	348	1o R
AVG WF		XTK ERROR
−100		0.5 L NM
OAT	TEMP D	A/C GROSS WT
−49	7+	408364 LBS

Figure 21. "NASA 1" format studied by Streveler and Wasserman (1984).

```
--PRESENT SITUATION--              GMT 1102:15

 LAT                                LONG

   61 07'31"N                         26 18'33"E

 WIND            DRIFT              COURSE

   187/116         3o R               021

 G/S             TAS               TK  ERROR

   487             530                4o  L

 AVG WF                            XTK ERROR

   -241                              0.5 L NM

 OAT             TEMP D            A/C GROSS WT

   -79             16+                717262 LBS
```

Figure 22. **"NASA 2" format studied by Streveler and Wasserman (1984).**

rants, it was possible to derive a single search time that could be used for comparison with the Display Analysis Program.

Finally, the "Patient List" display, shown in Figure 26, was actually one of two such displays studied by Streveler and Wasserman that were identical in format but different in semantics. The patients listed in Figure 26 are in alphabetical order (approximately); however, another version of the display listed the same names in a random order. Obviously, the random order made the search for the patient number associated with a particular patient more difficult. This kind of difference in semantics is beyond the scope of the Display Analysis Program, which can only detect differences in format. Thus, only the data for the alphabetical version are shown in Table 11.

The predictions from the Display Analysis Program corresponded well with Streveler and Wasserman's findings. The overall correlation between actual and predicted search times for all ten formats was .76. Likewise, in every case where they found a significant difference in search times for pairs of displays with different formats, the Display Analysis Program predicted a difference in the same direction.

Dodson and Shields (1978). Dodson and Shields (1978) manipulated

```
CUSTOMER NUMBER 758-003-49326

NAME   FLANAGAN CHEMICAL COMPANY

INVOICE TO:                    SHIP TO:

HADEN FLATS PLANT              WESTCHESTER PLAINS PLANT

P.O. BOX 783                   RTE 1

ENGLEWOOD CLIFFS               YONKERS

NJ 07632                       NY 11216


SALESMAN #53730  B. L. JONES


IS THE ABOVE INFORMATION CORRECT
* * * * * ANSWER YES OR NO
```

Figure 23. "Martin 1" format studied by Streveler and Wasserman (1984), adapted from Martin (1973, p. 110). Reprinted by permission of Prentice-Hall, Inc., Englewood Cliffs, New Jersey.

the overall density of displays for a Spacelab application using three levels: 30%, 50%, and 70%. An example of the 50% density format is shown in Figure 27. The three formats actually differed on other parameters in addition to overall density. For example, the number of groups varied from 4 to 10, while the average size of those groups varied from 16.8 deg to 4.9 deg.

The actual search times found by Dodson and Shields are plotted in Figure 28 by display density, as in the original study. The predicted search times from the Display Analysis Program, adjusted by the regression on the actual times, are also plotted in the figure. Dodson and Shields took their data as being evidence for an exponential function: "As can be seen from this figure, response time [search time] as a function of display density is an exponential function with times rapidly increasing as display density exceeds 60%" (Dodson & Shields, 1978, p. 2–7). This assertion has very little foundation, since it is based on only three data points, and since those three data points can be fit quite well by a *linear* function of display density ($r = .978$). Their finding, however, apparently led

```
CUSTOMER NUMBER 758-003049326
         NAME    DUPONT PAINT COMPANY


         INVOICE TO:                    SHIP TO:
         MARSHLAND MIXING FAC          DUPONT EXPORT COMPANY
         23 OAK PARK PLAZA             26 PARK AVENUE
         MARSHFIELD                    QUEENSTOWN
         WI 53520                      NY 10716



    SALESMAN #46231  R. K. HARRISON



    IS THE ABOVE INFORMATION CORRECT
    * * * * * ANSWER YES OR NO
```

Figure 24. "Martin 2" format studied by Streveler and Wasserman (1984), adapted from Martin (1973, p. 110). Reprinted by permission of Prentice-Hall, Inc., Englewood Cliffs, New Jersey.

```
    Anywhere in CMIT              Abbr   Name
                                   al     all

    Parts of Disease Descriptions

         Abbr   Name              Abbr   Name
          ds    disease            ss    signs or symptoms
          at    alternate terminology  cm   complications
          et    etiology           lb    laboratory
          sm    symptoms           rd    x-ray
          sg    signs              pa    pathology

    Categories (Body systems)

         Abbr   Name              Abbr   Name
          wb    whole body         gi    gastrointestinal
          sk    skin               ug    urogenital
          ms    musculoskeletal    en    endocrine
          lg    respiratory        nv    nervous
          cv    heart              mo    sense organs
          hl    hemic and lymphatic

    RECOGNIZED CONTEXTS                      Press <RETURN> to continue
```

Figure 25. "Medical Info" display studied by Streveler and Wasserman (1984).

```
799338-2   LADIA,FELECISIMA YABOT      08/12/1916  66  F
783472-1   LADD,GRACE BEULAH           06/21/1912  70  F
045682-9   LATO,ELVIRA VITTORIA        03/17/1960  23  F
697963-7   LEDAY,HAZEL                 04/14/1916  67  F
665817-2   LEDDY,ELIZABETH             11/25/1931  51  F
512186-8   LEDDY,GENEVIEVE V           12/21/1887  95  F
803531-8   LEETE,GLADYS                11/10/1904  79  F
574910-1   LEITE-AH YO,HARVELEE        07/03/1953  29  F
380706-5   LLOYD,EILEEN ISABELLE       08/01/1933  49  F
014018-0   LLOYD,EUGENIA               03/01/1930  53  F
213606-6   LLOYD,FERMER                12/12/1910  72  F
853664-3   LLOYD,FRANCEEN              01/03/1949  34  F
628806-2   LLOYD,FRANCES ELLSWORTH     02/24/1912  71  F
350935-4   LLOYD,GISELA RITA           07/04/1933  49  F
618304-2   LLOYD,GRACE V               08/20/1898  84  F
798330-1   LLOYD,GLORIA DEAN           01/28/1945  38  F
878846-4   LLOYD,GAIL LYNN             12/07/1951  31  F
429025-4   LLOYD,HAZEL                 04/22/1907  76  F
692202-3   LOTT,DOROTHY                08/07/1922  60  F
596394-0   LOTT,ELLA WEASE             07/03/1927  55  F
709939-4   LOYD,GWENDOLYN ANN          04/09/1948  35  F
594925-4   LUHT,EILEEN                 08/13/1915  67  F
726754-1   LUTHI,DEBORAH MAE           03/05/1948  35  F
```

Figure 26. "Patient List" display studied by Streveler and Wasserman (1984).

```
CMDS
1 FAULT CK=YES/NO        6 SRT=YES/NO
2 VAL CK=YES/NO          7 FC=YES/NO
3 START=YES/NO           8 TEST SELF=YES/NO
4 CAL=YES/NO             9 RESTART 1=YES/NO
5 STOP=YES/NO           10 POWER=YES/NO

FO SEQ       11 1A-870:16:14    14 2B-801:41:48
             12 1B-411:21:23    15 2C-958:46:50
             13 2A-582:49:10    16 O3-391:35:21
08 675:48:58
19 PAO=28       23 AMPER=12     27 SIGNL=YES/NO
20 PBO=40       24 HI VLT=2     28 FOV=7
21 PCO=26       25 LO VLT=4     29 MSG RELAY=61
                26 HOLD OFF=1
```

Figure 27. 50% density display studied by Dodson and Shields (1978).

NASA to adopt a guideline for their Spacelab displays stating that "display character density should not exceed 60% of the available character spaces" (NASA, 1980, p. x).

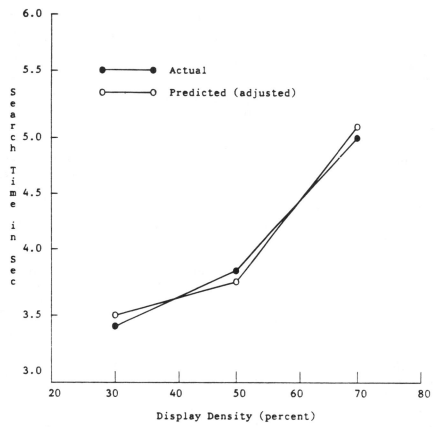

Figure 28. Plot of actual search times from Dodson and Shields (1978) and predicted (adjusted) search times from Display Analysis Program, as a function of display density.

The most interesting point about Figure 28 is that the predicted search times exhibit almost exactly the same exponential shape as a function of display density as the actual times. The critical point to remember is that these predicted times were derived from a *linear* combination of overall density, local density, number of groups, and size of groups. There is no need to postulate an exponential function.

Ringel and Hammer (1964). Ringel and Hammer (1964) studied tables of data describing the status of battlefield military units. An example of one of their displays is shown in Figure 29. They used nine different display formats, determined by the factorial combination of three levels of "Amount of Information" (10, 18, or 25 lines) and three levels of "Density" (low, medium, or high). "Density" was defined as the ratio of the height of a letter to the total space between lines: low = 1:4, medium = 1:3, and high = 1:2. Thus, their measure of "Amount of Information" correlates with overall density, and their measure of "Density" correlates with local density. The tasks performed with these displays were more complex than simple search, involving extraction of information from multiple columns (e.g., "Which unit has an armor equipment status of 95 and is combat experienced?").

Ringel and Hammer found a significant main effect of "Amount of Information," as illustrated in Figure 30, which also shows the predicted (adjusted) search times averaged across the three levels of density. Clearly, the same basic effect is exhibited by both the actual and predicted means.

Ringel and Hammer also found a very small, but significant, main effect of "Density" of lines, as illustrated in Figure 31. The corresponding predicted (adjusted) search times, averaged across the three levels of "Amount of Information," show essentially no effect, however. An interesting point is that, if the density of the lines had been increased even more—to a ratio of 1:1.5—then the predicted search time would decrease in the same manner that one would extrapolate for the actual search times based on the trend shown in Figure 31.

Callan, Curran, and Lane (1977). Callan, Curran, and Lane (1977) studied a variety of CRT display formats for presenting Navy tactical

TACTICAL UNITS STATUS

UNIT	LOCATION	DATE COMTD	EFFECT STRGTH	PT ART	STATUS TRN	CMB EFF	PRESENT ACTIVITY	REMARKS
25 INF DIV	XL 21	AUG 62	1400	80	75	95	DEFENDING	FIRST ACTION
29 INF DIV	TN 11	OCT 62	1300	85	90	95	SCREENING	COMBAT EXPER
26 INF DIV	LD 19	AUG 62	1400	75	85	90	SCREENING	HIGH MORALE
31 INF DIV	KR 14	SEPT 62	1500	90	75	85	ATTACKING	MOD RESISTNCE
28 INF DIV	TN 11	JULY 62	1100	90	90	75	ATTACKING	SWAMPY TERRN
33 INF DIV	PT 30	OCT 62	1500	85	85	85	ADVANCING	FIRST ACTION
32 INF DIV	PT 30	NOV 62	1200	85	95	95	ASSEMBLING	MOD RESISTNCE
36 INF DIV	XL 21	JULY 62	1200	90	80	75	ATTACKING	SWAMPY TERRN
17 INF DIV	XL 21	OCT 62	1400	90	95	85	ATTACKING	FIRST ACTION
35 INF DIV	LD 19	OCT 62	1000	80	80	90	ASSEMBLING	HIGH MORALE
23 INF DIV	XL 21	SEPT 62	1300	80	90	95	ADVANCING	SWAMPY TERRN
18 INF DIV	KR 14	NOV 62	1500	85	90	75	ASSEMBLING	HIGH MORALE
30 INF DIV	PT 30	AUG 62	1200	75	85	90	ADVANCING	COMBAT EXPER
16 INF DIV	PT 30	SEPT 62	1100	75	85	85	ASSEMBLING	SWAMPY TERRN
27 INF DIV	TN 11	JULY 62	1400	80	75	75	DEFENDING	COMBAT EXPER
34 INF DIV	KR 14	JULY 62	1100	90	85	75	DEFENDING	FIRST ACTION
45 INF DIV	KR 14	SEPT 62	1100	95	95	80	ASSEMBLING	COMBAT EXPER
43 INF DIV	TN 11	SEPT 62	1300	95	90	80	DEFENDING	FIRST ACTION
21 INF DIV	LD 19	OCT 62	1200	80	95	90	ADVANCING	MOD RESISTNCE
20 INF DIV	KR 14	NOV 62	1500	85	80	90	ADVANCING	MOD RESISTNCE
19 INF DIV	LD 19	NOV 62	1400	75	80	80	ATTACKING	HIGH MORALE
22 INF DIV	TN 11	NOV 62	1500	95	75	85	SCREENING	HIGH MORALE
42 INF DIV	XL 21	JULY 62	1200	95	95	80	DEFENDING	MOD RESISTNCE
41 INF DIV	LD 19	AUG 62	1300	75	80	80	SCREENING	SWAMPY TERRN
24 INF DIV	PT 30	AUG 62	1300	95	75	95	SCREENING	COMBAT EXPER

Figure 29. Example of display studied by Ringel and Hammer (1964).

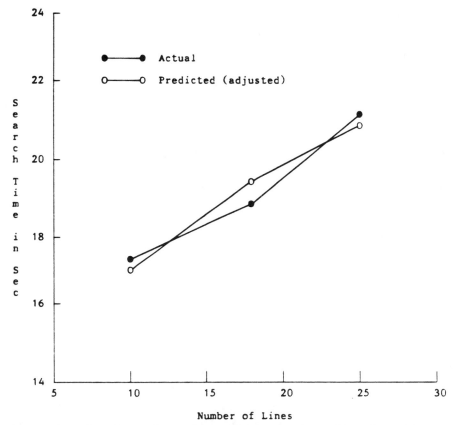

Figure 30.   Plot of actual search times for main effect of Number of Lines in Ringel and Hammer (1964) study and predicted (adjusted) search times from Display Analysis Program.

information. Specifically, six formats varying from 6 to 40 display items were studied. An example of a 19-item format is shown in Figure 32. A display item was defined as the pairing of a two- to five-character mnemonic code (e.g., TN) with a three-digit number. The subject's task was to search for a particular mnemonic code and then type the corresponding three-digit number on a keyboard.

As shown in Table 11, the predicted times are shorter than the actual times, but they are highly correlated ($r = .91$). The difference between the actual and predicted times might be attributable to the time that it took the subjects in the Callan et al. study to type the three-digit number. Both the actual search times and the predicted search times (adjusted by the regression) are plotted in Figure 33.

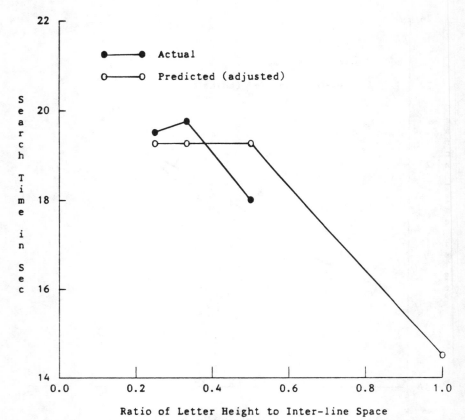

Figure 31. Plot of actual search times for main effect of Density in Ringel and Hammer (1964) study and predicted (adjusted) search times from Display Analysis Program.

Callan et al. reported that their search times could be fit by the following linear function of number of display items:

Search Time = .03458 × Number of Items + 4.203

(*r* = .946)

Interestingly, the predicted search times (not adjusted) are even better fit by such a function of number of display items:

Search Time = .02887 × Number of Items + 2.605

(*r* = .985)

```
ENGAGE

AIR  FRND  INT/FGTR  CAP
TN      392
PIF     977


MK76   685      MK54   829      LB11A   317      MK84   563      FUEL   498
MK44   244      FFAR   314      SU44A   822      MK58   164
MK46   201      HVAR   885      NAS     942
MK57   246      MK52   578      NPS     406
```

Figure 32.   Example of 19-display-item format studied by Callan, Curran, and Lane (1977).

The main difference between these equations lies in their intercepts (4.203 vs. 2.605) rather than their slopes (.03458 vs. .02887), reinforcing the idea that the difference between the actual and predicted times is due to a constant effect, such as typing the three-digit number.

Burns, Warren, and Rudisill (1985).[4] Burns, et al. (1985) studied two different displays currently being used on the Space Shuttle (the "Orbit Maneuver" and "Relative Navigation" formats), as well as two reformatted versions of those displays. Examples of the current and reformatted displays are shown in Figures 34 and 35. The same basic information was presented in the corresponding current and reformatted versions. They attempted to improve the usability of the reformatted versions by logically grouping data, using indentations, and adopting a consistent abbreviation scheme.

Burns et al. used two groups of subjects: experts, such as astronauts and flight controllers, who were familiar with the current displays; and nonexperts, such as technicians and clerks, who were not familiar with the displays. For the purposes of this discussion, only the results from the nonexperts will be considered, since the experts' familiarity with the current displays and lack of familiarity with the reformatted displays would tend to bias their data in favor of the current displays.

Burns et al. found a significant main effect of display type (current

---

[4] This study was also summarized in Burns, Warren, and Rudisill (1986).

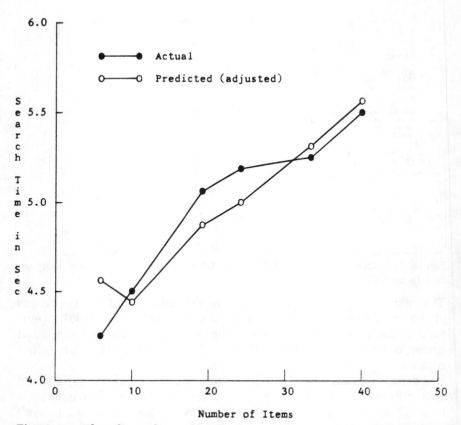

Figure 33.   Plot of actual search times from Callan, Curran, and Lane (1977) study and predicted (adjusted) search times from Display Analysis Program.

vs. reformatted), as illustrated in Figure 36. The reformatted displays yielded significantly shorter search times for the nonexpert subjects. (There was essentially no effect on search time for the expert subjects.) Figure 36 also shows the predicted search times from the Display Analysis Program, adjusted by regression on the actual times. Obviously, the predicted search times reflect a similar superiority of the reformatted displays.

Wolf (1986). Wolf (1986) studied five formats, called "HN1" through "HN5," for presenting the names of host computers that are accessible through a network. In "HN1," shown in Figure 37, the host names were alphabetized within each column. In "HN2," essentially the same format was used but with the names alphabetized across rows. In "HN3" through "HN5," shown in Figures 38 through 40, different methods of formatting the names into rows were tried. For

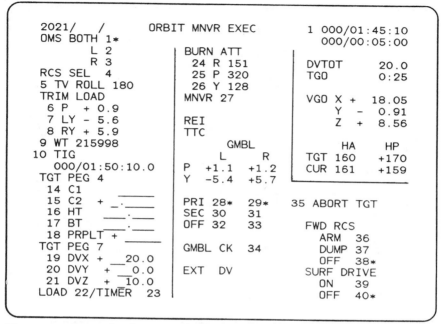

```
2021/    /        ORBIT MNVR EXEC        1 000/01:45:10
OMS BOTH 1*                               000/00:05:00
       L 2            BURN ATT
       R 3            24 R 151          DVTOT      20.0
RCS SEL   4           25 P 320          TGO         0:25
5 TV ROLL 180         26 Y 128
TRIM LOAD             MNVR 27           VGO X +    18.05
  6 P  + 0.9                                Y  -    0.91
  7 LY - 5.6         REI                    Z  +    8.56
  8 RY + 5.9         TTC
  9 WT 215998           GMBL                    HA      HP
 10 TIG                L       R         TGT 160    +170
   000/01:50:10.0    P  +1.1   +1.2      CUR 161    +159
TGT PEG 4            Y  -5.4   +5.7
   14 C1       _____
   15 C2  +  _._____  PRI 28*   29*     35 ABORT TGT
   16 HT     ____.___ SEC 30    31
   17 BT     ___.____ OFF 32    33      FWD RCS
   18 PRPLT + _____                       ARM   36
TGT PEG 7                               GMBL CK  34      DUMP  37
   19 DVX +  __20.0                         OFF  38*
   20 DVY   +  _0.0   EXT  DV            SURF DRIVE
   21 DVZ   + _10.0                         ON   39
LOAD 22/TIMER  23                          OFF  40*
```

Figure 34.   Example of current "Orbit Maneuver" format from Space Shuttle displays studied by Burns, Warren, and Rudisill (1985).

all formats, the subject's task was to locate nine different host names, one at a time, on the display.

For purposes of comparison with the Display Analysis Program, all of these formats except "HN2" will be considered. As with one of the displays studied by Streveler and Wasserman (1984), "HN2" represents a semantic manipulation that the Display Analysis Program is not intended to detect. In fact, Wolf's subjects had trouble detecting it as well. She reported that several of the subjects did not even realize that the host names were in alphabetical order on "HN2," so they approached the display as if the names were listed randomly.

Table 11 shows that the correspondence between actual and predicted search times for "HN1," "HN3," "HN4," and "HN5" was generally good ($r = .86$). Both the actual and predicted data show that "HN5" is clearly the worst format, since it yielded the longest search times. The actual times indicate that "HN1" is the best, followed closely by "HN3" and "HN4" with the same value. The predicted times, on the other hand, indicate that "HN1" and "HN4" are essentially the same, followed by "HN3."

```
  2021/    /      ORBIT MNVR EXEC  1    MET 001/03:10:00
                                        IGT 001/03:15:34.0
    SELECT ENGINE   BRN ATTITUDE        CDT 000/00:05:34
      BOTH OMS        ROLL    148       BRN LENGTH  1:10
  *  LF OMS           PITCH   332
     RT OMS           YAW     125       DV TOTAL      115.0
     RCS
                      SLP/INTRCPT GDC   VELOCITY TO GO
    ENGINE DRIVE      C1      _____       X      -  111.05
  *  PRMRY LF         C2    +_._____     Y      -    0.93
  *  PRMRY RT         HT     ___.___      Z      +    7.23
     SCNDY LF         DT       __.__
     SCNDY RT         PRPNT  +  ___                CUR  TGT
                                          APOGEE   161  163
    FWD RCS BRNOFF   EXT DV GDC           PERIGEE +159 + 95
      ARM             DVX   + 115.0
      DUMP            DVY   +   0.0      GIMBAL SETTINGS
                      DVZ   +   0.0                 CUR  TGT
    LOAD                                  PTCH LF +1.1 +0.4
    START CDT         TRJ VCTR RL 176     PTCH RT +1.1 +0.4
    START MNVR        WEIGHT    216008    YAW  LF -5.7 -5.6
    GIMBAL CHECK                          YAW  RT +5.3 +5.9
    SURFACE DRIVE     RNG TLS
                      TIME CRC            EXT DV
```

Figure 35. Example of reformatted "Orbit Maneuver" format from Space Shuttle displays studied by Burns, Warren, and Rudisill (1985).

Wolf also asked her subjects to rank order the displays based upon their preferences. By calculating the average ordinal position (1–5) for each format, it is possible to compare these subjective ratings with the predicted subjective ratings from the Display Analysis Program. Both sets of ratings are shown in Table 12.

The correlation between the actual and predicted ratings was quite high: $r = .98$. The order of the ratings was precisely the same for both the actual and predicted data. This higher correlation for subjective ratings than for search times is reminiscent of the results of Experiment 1 (described in the second section).

Application to "Good" and "Bad" Displays from the Literature

Several articles in the literature on display design have presented their authors' concept of "good" and "bad" versions of the same display. Predictions of search times and subjective ratings for such displays from four articles or documents (Marcus, 1982; Pakin & Wray, 1982; Galitz, 1981; Smith & Mosier, 1984) are summarized in Table 13. For each pair of "good" and "bad" formats, Table 13

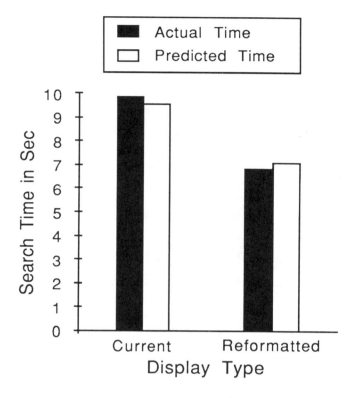

Figure 36. Plot of actual search times from Burns, Warren, and Rudisill (1985) for current and reformatted Space Shuttle displays, based on non-expert subjects; also predicted search times from the Display Analysis Program, adjusted by regression.

shows the predicted search times and subjective ratings, as well as the percentage improvement for both values.

Taken as a whole, the results shown in Table 13 indicate very good agreement between the authors of these articles and the predictions from the Display Analysis Program. The Display Analysis Program generally predicted that the authors' "good" versions of the displays were better than their "bad" versions.

The most interesting finding, however, is that, in every case, the improvements in predicted subjective ratings (an average of 49.1%) were larger than the improvements in predicted search times (an average of 16.2%). This is not particularly surprising when one considers the fact that these displays primarily represent their designer's subjective opinions about what constitutes a "good" or "bad"

```
            HN1                                      07:50 PM        MARC
Action: [                                                              ]
            HOme GO REturn COmnd + -               (Press SPCFY for Help)

Response returned at 07:50 PM:

   HOSTNAME: LF79AB
   USABLE BNA HOSTS ARE:
           CSSGAMPAC       LFA9E           SA79A
           CUMBENG         LF69AB          SSGB69
           DN59B           LF69E           TRENGA
           DN59B           MISSION         TRENGB
           DN79A           MV59E           TRENGC
           LFA10AB         MV68DE          TRENGD
           LFA3AJ          MV69G           TRPASA
           LFA3D           MV69K           TRPASB
           LFA3E           MV69L           TRPROGD
           LFA3F           MV79A           WHQDCB
           LFA3HI          SAA9A
           LFA9A           SAA9B
           LFA9C           SA59B

   HN
```

Figure 37. "HN1" format studied by Wolf (1986).

```
            HN3                                      07:50 PM        MARC
Action: [                                                              ]
            HOme GO REturn COmnd + -               (Press SPCFY for Help)

Response returned at 07:50 PM:

   HOSTNAME: LF79AB
   USABLE BNA HOSTS ARE:

       CSSGAMPAC, CUMBENG
       DN59A, DN59B, DN79A
       LFA10AB, LFA3AJ, LFA3D, LFA3E, LFA3F, LFA3HI, LFA9A, LFA9C, LFA9E,
            LF69AB, LF69E
       MISSION, MV59E, MV68DE, MV69K, MV69L, MV79A
       SAA9A, SAA9B, SA59B, SA79A, SSGB69
       TRENGA, TRENGB, TRENGC, TRENGD, TRPASA, TRPASB, TRPROGD




   HN
```

Figure 38. "HN3" format studied by Wolf (1986).

display. Most of these authors readily admit that much of what they say about display design is based upon an accumulated wisdom that has built up over the years, and not so much on empirical studies using criteria such as search time.

Each of the studies listed in Table 13 will now be considered individually.

Marcus (1982). Marcus (1982) provided three pairs of examples of actual "before" and "after" displays from the redesign of a large information management system. Two such displays are shown in

```
          HN4                                        07:50 PM        MARC
Action: [                                                               ]
             HOme GO REturn COmnd + -                (Press SPCFY for Help)
Response returned at 07:50 PM:

HOSTNAME: LF79AB
USABLE BNA HOSTS ARE:

        CSSGAMPAC, CUMBENG

        DN59A, DN59B, DN79A

        LFA10AB, LFA3AJ, LFA3D, LFA3E, LFA3F, LFA3HI, LFA9A, LFA9C, LFA9E,
           LF69AB, LF69E

        MISSION, MV59E, MV68DE, MV69K, MV69L, MV79A

        SAA9A, SAA9B, SA59B, SA79A, SSGB69

        TRENGA, TRENGB, TRENGC, TRENGD, TRPASA, TRPASB, TRPROGD

HN
```

Figure 39. "HN4" format studied by Wolf (1986).

```
          HN5                                        07:50 PM        MARC
Action: [                                                               ]
             HOme GO REturn COmnd + -                (Press SPCFY for Help)
Response returned at 07:50 PM:

HOSTNAME: LF79AB
USABLE BNA HOSTS ARE: CSSGAMPAC, CUMBENG, DN59A, DN59B, DN79A, LFA10AB,
        LFA3AJ, LFA3D, LFA3E, LFA3F, LFA3HI, LFA9A, LFA9C, LFA9E, LF69AB,
        LF69E, MISSION, MV59E, MV68DE, MV69G, MV69K, MV69L, MV79A, SAA9A,
        SAA9B, SA59B, SA79A, SSGB69, TRENGA, TRENGB, TRENGC, TRENGD, TRPASA,
        TRPASB, TRPROGD, WHQDCB




HN
```

Figure 40. "HN5" format studied by Wolf (1986).

Table 12. Actual and Predicted Subjective Ratings for Four Displays Studied by Wolf (1986)

Display	Actual Rating	Predicted Rating
HN1	1.2	2.5
HN3	3.4	3.3
HN4	1.8	2.6
HN5	4.2	3.9

Table 13. Predicted Search Times and Subjective Ratings from the Display
Analysis Program for "Bad" and "Good" Versions of Displays Published
in the Literature

Reference	Predictions for "Bad" Version		Predictions for "Good" Version		% Improvement ((Bad-Good)/Bad)	
	Search Time	Subject. Rating	Search Time	Subject. Rating	Search Time	Subject Rating
Marcus	4.32	2.10	4.24	1.05	1.8%	50.0%
(1982)	4.47	2.26	4.20	1.14	6.0%	49.6%
	4.17	2.17	4.30	0.94	-3.1%	56.7%
Pakin &	4.79	3.80	3.56	2.12	25.7%	44.2%
Wray (1982)			3.56	1.45	25.7%	61.8%
Galitz	4.79	3.50	3.25	1.72	32.2%	50.9%
(1981)			3.66	1.60	23.6%	54.3%
Smith &	4.12	4.12	3.38	3.08	18.0%	25.2%
Mosier (1984)						

Figures 41 and 42. As Table 13 shows, his redesigns had very little effect on the predicted search times. This is not particularly surprising, nor really a problem, since these are "help" displays that are intended to be *read* rather than searched like most of the other displays in this chapter. Linear text, like that used in much of Figures 41 and 42, tends to create relatively large groups of characters, thus causing the somewhat high values of search time shown in Table 13.

The more relevant finding from applying the Display Analysis Program to the Marcus displays is the substantial improvement in subjective ratings (49.6% to 56.7% improvement). These large improvements in predicted subjective ratings came about because Marcus focused the redesign on aligning data elements by using a small number of tab stops. This resulted in substantial reductions in the layout complexity measure (from 7.63 bits for Figure 41 to 5.24 bits for Figure 42), which is one of the most important factors in the prediction of subjective rating.

Pakin and Wray (1982). Pakin and Wray (1982) presented "good" and "bad" versions of a display for a hypothetical hotel reservation and billing system. The "bad" version is shown in Figure 43. They claimed that this display is too cluttered and should be broken into two separate displays: "It is better to have two neat, well-formatted screens with some unused space than one cluttered screen with no unused space" (Pakin & Wray, 1982, p. 37). The two new displays

```
READY
  MONITOR.SEEDIS.HELP.

                    INTRODUCTION TO SEEDIS

  The three major processes in SEEDIS are:

  AREA: define a geographic study area (composed of states,
        counties, or census tracts)

  DATA: select data appropriate to the geographic study area
        chosen.  For  example, for a study area consisting of a group
        of states, only state level data, and  not  county  or  tract
        level data, are appropriate.

  DISPLAY: manipulate and display the data in table, chart, graph,
        and/or map form.

  Normally  AREA,   DATA,  and  DISPLAY   are   performed in the order
  given. However, once the geographic study area is defined (AREA),
  one  may  alternate  between  DISPLAY  and  the  selection  and
  extraction of additional items in DATA.
  TYPE MORE TO SEE NEXT SCREENFULL
  TYPE ? FOR A LIST OF COMMANDS
```

Figure 41. One of three "before" formats presented by Marcus (1982). Reprinted with permission of the publisher, Association for Computing Machinery, New York.

```
                      SEEDIS: area, data, display, profile
  : help
                      USING SEEDIS
                      --------------------------------------------------------------
                      LBL's Seedis is an experimental information system that
                      includes integrated program modules for retrieving, analy-
                      zing, and displaying selected portions of geographically
                      linked databases. Program modules in Seedis include:

          area        select geographic area (level and scope of analysis)
          data        select, extract, enter, or transform data
          display     manipulate and display data in tables, maps, and charts
          profile     produce standard socio-economic reports for selected areas

                      Normally, Area, Data, and Display are used in the order
                      given. However, once the geographic study area is defined
                      in Area, you may alternate between Display and
                      the selection, extraction, or entering of additional items
                      in Data.

                      SEEDIS: area, data, display, profile
  :
```

Figure 42. One of three "after" formats presented by Marcus (1982). Reprinted with permission of the publisher, Association for Computing Machinery, New York.

are shown in Figures 44 and 45. Table 13 shows that each of the two new displays is, by itself, a substantial improvement over the old display, both in predicted search time (25.7% improvement in both cases) and predicted subjective rating (44.2% and 61.8% improvements).

The interesting question this raises is whether these predictions justify separating the one screen into two. These predictions by themselves cannot provide the answer to that question, but they can help. The predicted search time for each redesigned display was 1.23 s less than that for the original display. Since the data are now contained in two displays rather than one, however, one must consider the extra time that may be required for the user to decide

```
    Reservations
                        RESERVATION CREATION

    Name: ---------------    Company: ---------------    VIP Status: -
    Address 1: ---------------    Home telephone: ------------
    Address 2: ---------------    Business telephone: ------------
    City: -------------    Travel agent: --------    Tour group: --------
    State: --    Zip code: -----    Trip reason: ---    Guest status: -
    Bill to name: ------------    Payment type: --   Deposit required: ------
    Address 1: ---------------    Credit card number: ------------
    Address 2: ---------------    Expiration date: ---------
    City: -------------    Advice code: --    Credit limit: --------
    State: --    Zip code: -----    Reservation confirmation number: -------
    State: --    Zip code: -----    Reservation confirmation no.: ----------
    Arrival date: ----------    Departure date: ----------
    Number of nights: --    Number of guests: --    Number of rooms: --
    Room type: ----    Meal plan: --    Floor: ----    Room number: ----
    Room attributes: 1.----    2.----    3.----    4.----    5.----    6.----
    Guest status: -    Message code: ----
    Remarks: ------------------------------------------------------------
```

Figure 43. "Bad" version of display for a hypothetical hotel reservation and billing system from Pakin and Wray (1982). Reprinted with permission of the publisher, Data Processing Management Association, Park Ridge, IL.

```
    Reservations
                        RESERVATION CREATION

    Arrival date:        -----------   Name:            ------------
    Departure date:      -----------   Address 1:       ---------------
    Room type:           ----          Address 2:       ---------------
    Number of rooms:     --            City:            -------------
    Number of guests:    --            State:           --
    Meal plan:           --            Zip code:        -----
    Room rate:           ----          Telephone:       ----------
    Room number:         ----          Trip reason:     ---
    Floor number:        ----          Travel agent:    ----------
    Room attribute 1:    ----          Tour group:      ---------
                    2:   ----          Company:         -------------
                    3:   ----
                    4:   ----          VIP status:      -
                    5:   ----          Guest status:    -
                    6:   ----          Message code:    -
```

Figure 44. First of two new displays presented by Pakin and Wray (1982) to replace the one "bad" display. Reprinted with permission of the publisher, Data Processing Management Association, Park Ridge, IL.

```
 Reservations

                          BILLING INFORMATION

 Name:                                 ------------
 Reservation confirmation number:      ----------

 Direct billing                        Indirect billing

 Payment type:          --             Name:          ------------
 Credit card number:    ------------   Address 1:     --------------
 Expiration date:       --------       Address 2:     --------------
 Deposit required:      ------         City:          ------------
 Advice code:           --             State:         --
 Credit limit:          --------       Zip code:      -----
                                       Telephone:     ------------

 Remarks:  --------------------------------------------------------------
```

Figure 45. Second of two new displays presented by Pakin and Wray (1982) to replace the one "bad" display. Reprinted with permission of the publisher, Data Processing Management Association, Park Ridge, IL.

which display is needed and to retrieve that display. If that total extra time is greater than 1.23 s, then the split into two screens would not be justified, based on the predicted search times.

One can easily envision that these hotel reservation and billing screens would be just two of many screens in a complete hotel management system. It is quite likely that all of these screens would be selected from a single master menu. The comparison to make, then, is between the time it takes to choose a single menu item called "RESERVATION AND BILLING" and the time it takes to choose between two menu items called "RESERVATION" and "BILLING." In this particular case, it appears that the split into two screens is justified, since it certainly could not take more than 1.23 s longer to choose between the two items called "RESERVATION" and "BILLING" than to choose the one item "RESERVATION AND BILLING." In cases where the functional basis of the split is not so obvious, however, the split may not be justifiable. In any event, the Display Analysis Program can provide information that is useful in making that decision.

Galitz (1981). Another example of a display that was split into two screens when redesigned was provided by Galitz (1981). He presented the display shown in Figure 46 as an example of a data-entry screen that was patterned directly after a source document containing the data to be entered. As such, the primary goal in designing the display was compatibility with the source document. Galitz went on to propose that, if the data were not coming from an existing source document, the display could be improved by splitting it into two screens, shown in Figures 47 and 48.

The major difference between these screens lies in the grouping of characters: Figure 46 contains 5 groups with an average visual

```
                                                        *** PASUP ***
                  PERSONAL INFORMATION - SUPPLEMENT
APPLICANT INFORMATION
   AP-NM: -------------------------
                                                        POL#: -------------
DRIVER INFORMATION
   DR-NM: --------------------- BTH-DT: ------  SEX: -  OCC: ----------------
   MR-ST: - LIC#: ---------------- ST: -- YR-LIC: -- GD-ST: - DR-TR: - IMP: -
VEHICLE INFORMATION
   VEH-YR: -- N/U: - MAKE: -------------- ID: ------------- HP: - SYM: ----
      USE: -- MILE: -- AV/MI: -----        MOD: -  DRM: - CLS: ---- TER: --
LIENHOLDER INFORMATION
    VEH#: -
   LN-NM: ------------------------------
          ------------------------------
   ML-AD: ------------------------------
    CITY: --------------- ST: -- ZIP: -----
PAYOR INFORMATION:
   PY-NM: ------------------------------       ACCT#: ---------
          ------------------------------        TEL#: ----------
   PY-AD: ------------------------------
    CITY: --------------- ST: -- ZIP: -----
```

Figure 46. Sample data entry screen patterned after a source document, from Galitz (1981). Reprinted with permission of the publisher, QED Information Sciences, Wellesley, MA.

```
                                                       *** PASP01 ***
                  PERSONAL AUTOMOBILE - SUPPLEMENT

POLICY    POLICY #:        -------------

DRIVER    NAME:            ---------------------    SEX:             -
          BIRTH DATE:      ------                   MARITAL STATUS:  -
          OCCUPATION:      ----------------
          LICENSE #:       ----------------         STATE:           --
          YRS LICENSED:    --                       IMPAIRED:        -
          TRAINING:        -                        GOOD STUDENT:    -

VEHICLE   YEAR:            --                       NEW/USED:        -
          MAKE:            -------------            ID #:            ------------
          HP:              -                        SYMBOL:          ----

          USE:             --
          MILES:           --                       ANNUAL MILES:    ----
          MODIFIED:        -                        DAMAGE:          -
          CLASS:           ----                     TERRITORY:       --
```

Figure 47. First of two new data entry screens presented by Galitz (1981) to replace the one screen shown in Figure 46. Reprinted with permission of the publisher, QED Information Sciences, Wellesley, MA.

```
                                                              *** PASP02 ***

  LIENHOLDER     VEHICLE #:     -   .
                 NAME:          ------------------------------
                                ------------------------------
                 MAIL ADDRESS:  ------------------------------
                 CITY:          ---------------
                 STATE:         --
                 ZIP:           -----

  PAYOR          NAME:          ------------------------------
                                ------------------------------
                 MAIL ADDRESS:  ------------------------------
                 CITY:          ---------------
                 STATE:         --
                 ZIP:           -----

                 ACCOUNT  #:    ---------
                 TELEPHONE #:   ----------
```

Figure 48.   Second of two new data entry screens presented by Galitz (1981) to replace the one screen shown in Figure 46. Reprinted with permission of the publisher, QED Information Sciences, Wellesley, MA.

angle of 22.7 degrees, while Figures 47 and 48 contain 20 and 11 groups averaging 4.6 and 7.4 degrees, respectively. Consequently, the predicted search times and subjective ratings are substantially better for each of the two new screens than for the original screen.

As with the screens presented by Pakin and Wray (1982), one must consider whether this split of one screen into two is justified. That would appear to depend upon exactly how the screens are to be used. Galitz presented them as data-entry screens, but it should be clear that any data-entry task involves some amount of extraction of information from the display as well—either to locate the areas where data are to be entered or to review and/or correct data that have already been typed. In fact, a very common technique in system design is to use screens like this not only for the original entry of the data, but also for subsequently retrieving and modifying it.

It is reasonable to assume that each time someone uses these screens, they will have to locate a specific piece of information on the display at least once—perhaps to answer a customer's inquiry about their insurance. On the average it would take 4.79 s to extract that piece of information from the "old" version (Figure 46). The implication from Galitz's description of the redesigned screens is that the user would have to access the first screen (Figure 47) in order to get to the second screen (Figure 48). Examination of Figures

47 and 48 shows that the first screen contains 25 variable data items and the second screen contains 15, for a total of 40. Assuming that all data items are equally likely to be searched for, then the probability of needing to extract an item from the first screen is .625 (25/40), while the probability for the second screen is .375 (15/40). The average search time for these two screens, then, would be (.625 × 3.25) + (.375 × 3.66), or 3.40 s. This means that the average search time savings for the new version over the old is 1.39 s (4.79 − 3.40).

That search time savings, however, must be considered in light of certain penalties that are associated with splitting the information into two screens. One such penalty is the system response time in switching from the first to the second screen. That response time penalty would only be incurred 37.5% of the time, however. If the system response time is longer than 3.71 s (1.39/.375), then the total time to perform the task would be longer, on the average, with the new version.

Another possible penalty is the time that it takes the user to realize, upon viewing the first screen, that the required information is actually on the second screen. This time would depend upon the user's amount of experience with the system and how clearly defined the distinction is between what is on the first screen and what is on the second screen. With an experienced user and a clear distinction, that time should be very small.

Smith and Mosier (1984). The final example of "good" and "bad" versions of a display comes from Smith and Mosier (1984), who have compiled a comprehensive set of guidelines for the design of human–computer interfaces. In their section on "Data Display," they presented the format shown in Figure 49 as an example of a tabular display that violates several of their guidelines (e.g., justification of numeric data, row spacing, column spacing). They presented the format shown in Figure 50 as a better version of the same basic display.

Smith and Mosier stated that these displays would be used for finding the owner of a car with a particular license plate (e.g., an employee who has left headlights burning). That explains why the "good" version has the names listed in order by license plate, and why the bad version's alphabetical order by last name is inappropriate. This represents an interaction between the semantics of the displays and the tasks they are used for that the Display Analysis Program cannot possibly detect. However, there are also significant differences in format between the two versions. The major difference lies in the grouping of characters: Figure 49 has only 2 groups of

```
Automobile Owners
Sara Alwine                  2438 MA 929 448 103
Christopher Aranyi           2716 MA 797 AND 97
Maria Ashley                 3397 MA 375 NRC 34
Arlene Atchison              7672 NH 60731    28
Steven Bahr                  3272 MA 635 203 35
David Baldwin                3295 NH 63577    75
David Benkley                3581 MA 589 ADE 58
Marlin Boudreau              3413 MA 816 HER 93
Roger Cooksey                2144 MA 328 647 64
Joseph Curran                3167 RI 4693     83
Kent Delacy                  3619 MA 749 827 29
Susan Doucette               2797 MA 525 115 41
Joseph Drury                 7604 NH 42265    27
William Duvet                3898 MA 135 449 81
Samuel Everett               3619 MA 635 ASK 29
Jeanne Fiske                 7642 MA 614 CSU 10
Nancy Graham                 2358 MA 745 CKJ 10
Paul Greenbaum               3979 MA 846 BLN 103
Christopher Hesen            7544 MA 342 NCG 21
Joseph Hilsmith              2443 MA 286 PAM 100
```

Figure 49. "Bad" tabular display presented by Smith and Mosier (1984, p. 127).

characters, with an average visual angle of 13.2 degrees, while Figure 50 has 19 groups, with an average visual angle of 4.4 degrees. These differences, as well as a difference in local density, resulted in the substantial improvements in predicted search time and subjective rating shown in Table 13.

COMPARISON TO ANOTHER ANALYSIS SYSTEM

As mentioned earlier, Streveler and Wasserman (1984) described a system for quantitatively assessing screen formats that has many parallels with the Display Analysis Program. (Additional details of the system and its application, particularly to medical displays, have been provided by Streveler & Harrison, 1984, 1985). Streveler and Wasserman describe three basic techniques for analyzing screen formats: "boxing" analysis, "hot-spot" analysis, and "alignment" analysis.

```
                     AUTOMOBILE OWNERS              Page 1 of 4

     LICENSE          EMPLOYEE                EXT    DEPT

     MA 127 355       Michaels, Allison       7715    91
     MA 135 449       Duvet, William          3898    81
     MA 227 379       Smithson, Jill          2491    63
     MA 227 GBH       Zadrowski, Susan        2687    53
     MA 253 198       Jenskin, Erik           3687    31

     MA 286 PAM       Hilsmith, Joseph        2443   100
     MA 291 302       Leonard, John           7410    92
     MA 297 210       Toth, Kelley            7538    45
     MA 328 647       Cooksey, Roger          2144    64
     MA 342 NCG       Hesen, Christopher      7544    21

     MA 367 923       Maddox, Patrick         7070    66
     MA 375 NRC       Ashley, Maria           3397    34
     MA 376 386       Wheetley, Katherine     2638    58
     MA 385 248       Malone, Frank           2144    64
     MA 391 293       Lowman, Edward          8263    77

     n = Next page
```

Figure 50. "Good" tabular display presented by Smith and Mosier (1984, p. 126).

"Boxing" is their method for detecting groups. It involves finding groups of characters that are completely surrounded by white space and then drawing the smallest possible rectangular box around them. Although this algorithm is different from the algorithm used by the Display Analysis Program for detecting groups, the two techniques should have similar results. In fact, the three displays for which Streveler and Wasserman reported their screen measures yielded a high correlation ($r = .94$) between their number of boxes and the number of groups detected by the Display Analysis Program. In each case, the specific groups detected by the two systems differed slightly, however.

Streveler and Wasserman's "hot-spot" analysis involves calculating a moving average of "intensity" at each character position on the screen. To calculate intensity, each position is assigned a 0 or 1 depending upon whether or not it is occupied. Contributions of neighboring characters to the calculation of intensity are dampened by a factor of $\frac{1}{2}^d$, where d is the distance (in character positions) from the character of interest. Conceptually, this technique is very similar to the local density measurement used in the Display Anal-

ysis Program. However, the specific techniques used in the calculations are different. Since Streveler and Wasserman did not report
averages for the "hot spot" analyses, however, it is not possible to
correlate their values with the local density values.

Streveler and Wasserman's "alignment" analysis involves calculating the number of "alignment points" for each column of the
display. Alignment points are based upon the beginning and ending
points for strings of characters that contain no spaces (e.g., individual
words). This addresses the same concept as the layout complexity
measure used in the Display Analysis Program. However, the definitions of what constitutes an alignment point are different, as are
the computational techniques for manipulating the data concerning
the alignment points. Streveler and Wasserman reported values of
four different calculations based upon these alignment points for
three displays. Somewhat surprisingly, none correlated very well
with layout complexity (r's ranged from $-.10$ to $+.52$). On the other
hand, a measure of "balance" that Streveler and Wasserman proposed was highly correlated with layout complexity ($r = -.98$).
"Balance" was computed as the difference between the center of
mass of the array of characters and the physical center of the screen.

In short, there are many parallels between the measures discussed
by Streveler and his associates and those used in the Display Analysis
Program. In general, the two systems measure very similar qualities
about the layout of a screen, although the specific techniques used
are different. The major difference between the two approaches lies
in what the screen measures are used for. In the Display Analysis
Program, the major uses of the measures are to calculate a predicted
search time and subjective rating based upon regression equations.
However, Streveler and his associates have focused more on the
measures themselves and subjective interpretations of the displays.
They have not reported regression analyses that used their measures
to fit objective usability data for a large set of displays. It would
be interesting to use Streveler's measures to perform regression
analyses of the data from the 520 displays studied in Experiment
1 of the present studies.

CONCLUSIONS

The results of Experiments 1 and 2 and the results of applying the
Display Analysis Program to displays in the literature all support

the validity of the system. Given a set of alternative formats for presenting some alphanumeric data, the Display Analysis Program can quite accurately predict the relative search times and subjective ratings for the formats.

It is important to note, however, that this prediction system is intended to be used for making comparisons between alternative formats for presenting the same basic data. For example, it is not really meaningful to compare Pakin and Wray's (1982) redesigned hotel reservation display (Figure 44) to one of Marcus' (1982) redesigned displays (Figure 42). To say that Figure 44 is a better display than Figure 42 because of the difference in predicted search times is inappropriate because the displays were designed for quite different uses.

Given that the prediction system is valid for relative comparisons, it seems appropriate to examine it once more to see what can be gleaned about optimizing the design of alphanumeric displays. The following conclusions can be drawn:

A Display That Optimizes Search Times is Not Necessarily a Display That Optimizes Subjective Ratings, and Vice Versa.

This is based on the fact that different display parameters and coefficients are involved in the regression equations for predicting search times and subjective ratings. Thus, a system designer may need to decide which to optimize, or how to assign relative weights to the two predictions in deciding which of several alternative formats to use.

The Two Most Important Display Parameters in Determining Search Time are Those Associated With the Grouping of Characters.

This is based on the results of Experiment 1, which found that "number of groups" and "size of groups" provided the best-fitting two-variable regression equation for predicting search time ($R = .64$), and Experiment 2, which found that the same regression equation generalized well to a new set of displays ($r = .71$). Since both of these variables have positive coefficients in the regression equation, if either value increases then search time increases.

For example, consider the displays shown in Figures 51 through 53 and their corresponding characteristics shown in Table 14. Given that a fixed amount of data is to be presented (as in the case with these figures), there is generally a reciprocal relationship between number and size of groups: one can present the information in one large group as in Figure 51, many small groups as in Figure 52, or something in between as in Figure 53. The regression equation predicts that the best solution is one which minimizes *both* number of groups and size of groups. Thus, the predicted search times from the Display Analysis Program for Figures 51 through 53 are 4.87 sec, 6.74 sec, and 2.84 sec, respectively. In general, then, it is better to present data in an intermediate number of medium-sized groups (as in Figure 53) than either one large group or many small groups.

The exact relationship between the number of groups of char-

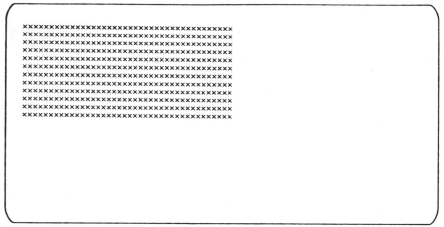

Figure 51.   Prototype display with one large group of characters.

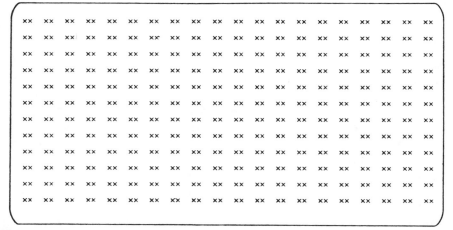

Figure 52.   Prototype display with 240 small groups of characters.

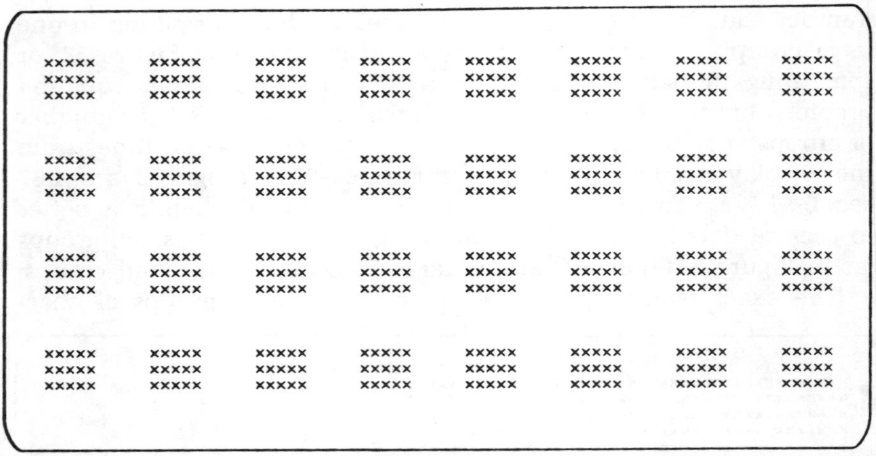

Figure 53. **Prototype display with 32 intermediate-size groups of characters.**

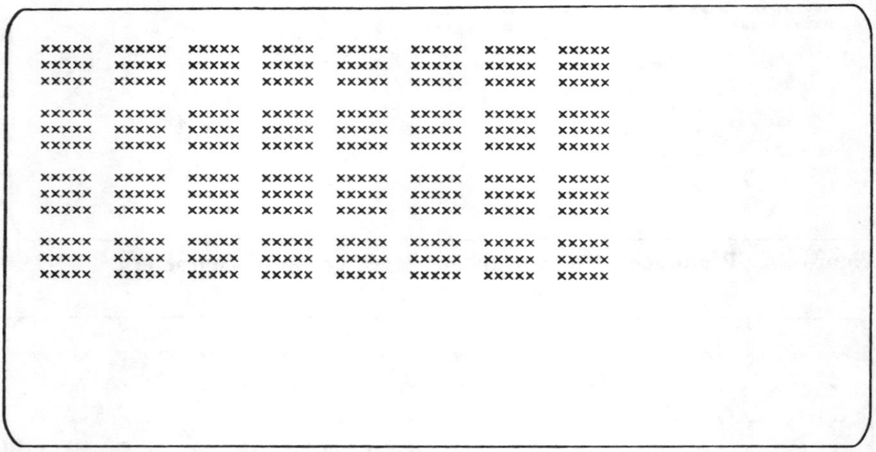

Figure 54. **Tightly packed version of Figure 53.**

acters on a display and the average size of those groups has been described in detail in Tullis (1986b). It was found that an inverse exponential function could be used to describe the relationship. By substituting that function into the regression equation that predicts search time using the two grouping measures, it was possible to identify the values for number of groups and size of groups that minimize search time. The results suggest that the upper limit of the optimum range for number of groups is about 40 and for size of groups is about 4.9 deg.

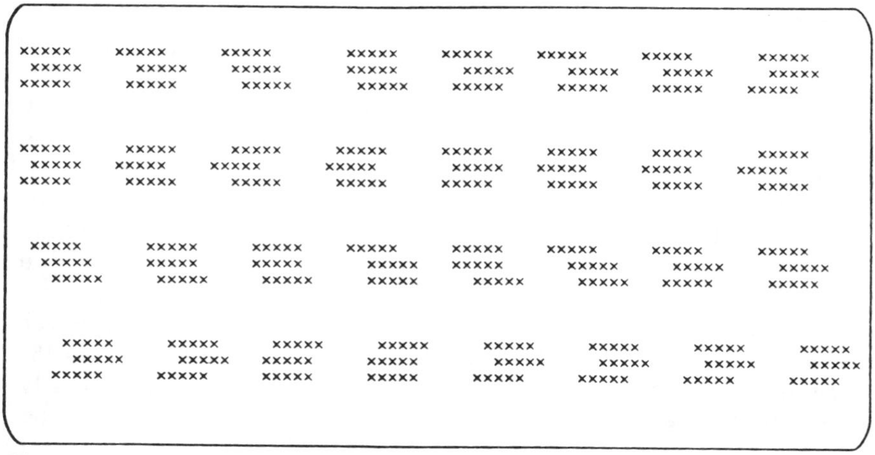

Figure 55.   Poorly aligned version of Figure 53.

Table 14.   Values of Six Display Measures, Predicted Search Time, and Predicted Subjective Rating for Five Prototypical Displays

							Predictions	
Display	Overall Dens.	Local Dens.	# Grps	Grp. Size	# Items	Layout Complex.	Search Time	Subj. Rating
Fig. 51	25.0%	84.7%	1	14.0	12	3.58	4.87	2.00
Fig. 52	25.0%	24.9%	240	0.6	240	7.91	6.74	8.51
Fig. 53	25.0%	31.4%	32	1.7	96	6.58	2.84	1.76
Fig. 54	25.0%	50.7%	32	1.7	96	6.58	3.40	2.77
Fig. 55	25.0%	30.9%	32	2.2	96	9.14	2.88	2.83

The Two Most Important Display Parameters in Determining the Subjective Rating of a Display are "Local Density" and "Layout Complexity."

This is based on Experiment 1, which found that those two variables provided the best-fitting two-variable regression equation ($R = .83$), and Experiment 2, which found that the same regression equation generalized well to a new set of displays ($r = .73$). As with the two grouping variables, both of these variables have positive coefficients in the regression equation, so if either value increases, the subjective rating increases (worsens). Unlike the grouping measure, however, local density and layout complexity are not clearly related to each other.

Local density is essentially a measure of how tightly packed the display is. For example, Figure 54 is a tightly packed version of Figure 53. As Table 14 shows, the only display variable that differs between the two figures is local density: 31.4% vs. 50.7%. As a result, the predicted subjective rating (using all six display variables) is worse for Figure 54 (2.77) than for Figure 53 (1.76)—a 57% increase. Note that the predicted search time is also worse, since local density plays a role in its prediction as well, but the increase is not as large (20%).

Layout complexity is a measure of how poorly aligned the items on the display are. For example, Figure 55 is a poorly aligned version of Figure 53. As Table 17 shows, the only display variable that differs significantly between the two figures is layout complexity: 6.58 bits vs. 9.14 bits. As a result, the predicted subjective rating is worse for Figure 55 (2.83) than for Figure 53 (1.76)—a 61% increase. (The small increase in search time is due to the slightly larger group sizes that resulted from the less-regular shapes of the groups.)

In conclusion, a computer-based tool for objectively evaluating the usability of any alphanumeric display format has been developed and validated. It is currently being used in a variety of settings, both as a tool for the design and evaluation of actual human–computer interfaces and as a tool for further research into screen design. In applied settings, the Display Analysis Program is well suited to an iterative approach: after a designer comes up with a preliminary design for a screen, the Display Analysis Program can analyze it and make suggestions for subsequent improvements. While nothing can ever fully replace empirical evaluations of human–computer interfaces, the Display Analysis Program can act as a valuable supplement.

REFERENCES

Burns, M.J., Warren, D.L., & Rudisill, M. (1985). *Expert and nonexpert search task performance with current and reformatted Space Shuttle displays* (Tech. Rep. JSC-20967). Houston, TX: NASA Johnson Space Center.

Burns, M.J., Warren, D.L., & Rudisill, M. (1986). Formatting space-related displays to optimize expert and nonexpert user performance. *Proceedings of CHI '86 Conference on Human Factors in Computing Systems* (Boston, April 13–17, pp. 274–280). New York: ACM.

Callan, J.R., Curran, L.E., & Lane, J.L. (1977). *Visual search times for Navy tactical information displays* (Report # NPRDC-TR-77-32). San Diego, CA: Navy Personnel Research and Development Center. (NTIS No. AD A040543).

Cohen, J., & Cohen, P. (1975). *Applied multiple regression/correlation analysis for the behavioral sciences.* Hillsdale, NJ: Erlbaum.

Dodson, D.W., & Shields, N.L., Jr. (1978). *Development of user guidelines for ECAS display design* (Vol. 1) (Report No. NASA-CR-150877). Huntsville, AL: Essex Corp.

Engel, S.E., & Granda, R.E. (1975). *Guidelines for man/display interfaces* (Technical Report TR 00.2720). Poughkeepsie, NY: IBM.

Furnival, G.M., & Wilson, R.W. (1974). Regressions by leaps and bounds. *Technometrics, 16,* 499–511.

Galitz, W.O. (1981). *Handbook of screen format design.* Wellesley, MA: QED Information Sciences.

Marcus, A. (1982). Typographic design for interfaces of information systems. *Proceedings: Human Factors in Computing Systems* (Gaithersburg, MD, March 15–17, pp. 26–30). New York: ACM.

Martin, J. (1973). *Design of man-computer dialogues.* Englewood Cliffs, NJ: Prentice-Hall.

NASA. (1980). *Spacelab display design and command usage guidelines* (Report MSFC-PROC-711A). Huntsville, AL: George C. Marshall Space Flight Center.

Pakin, S.E., & Wray, P. (1982). Designing screens for people to use easily. *Data Management,* July 1982, 36–41.

Ringel, S., and Hammer, C. (1964). *Information assimilation from alphanumeric displays: Amount and density of information presented* (Tech. Rep. TRN141). Washington, DC: US Army Personnel Research Office. (NTIS No. AD 601 973).

Smith, S.L., & Aucella, A.F. (1983). *Design guidelines for the user interface to computer-based information systems* (Tech. Rep. ESD-TR-83-122). Hanscom Air Force Base, MA: USAF Electronic Systems Division. (NTIS No. AD A127 345).

Smith, S.L., & Mosier, J.N. (1984). *Design guidelines for user-system interface software* (Tech. Rep. ESD-TR-84-190). Hanscom Air Force Base, MA: USAF Electronic Systems Division.

Stewart, T.F.M. (1976). Displays and the software interface. *Applied Ergonomics, 7*(3), 137–146.

Streveler, D.J., & Harrison, P.B. (1984). Measuring the "goodness" of screen designs. *Proceedings of the Seventeenth Annual Hawaii International Conference on System Sciences, 1,* 423–430.

Streveler, D.J., & Harrison, P.B. (1985). Judging visual displays of medical information. *M.D. Computing, 2*(2), 27–39.

Streveler, D.J., & Wasserman, A.I. (1984). Quantitative measures of the spatial properties of screen designs. *Proceedings of INTERACT '84 Conference on Human–Computer Interaction.* (London, Sept. 4–7, pp. 1.125–1.133). Amsterdam: Elsevier.

Tullis, T.S. (1981). An evaluation of alphanumeric, graphic, and color information displays. *Human Factors, 23,* 541–550.

Tullis, T.S. (1983). The formatting of alphanumeric displays: A review and analysis. *Human Factors, 25,* 657–682.

Tullis, T.S. (1984a). *Predicting the usability of alphanumeric displays* [Ph.D. Dissertation, Rice University]. Lawrence, KS: The Report Store.

Tullis, T.S. (1984b). A computer-based tool for evaluating alphanumeric displays. *Proceedings of INTERACT '84 Conference on Human–Computer Interaction.* (London, Sept. 4–7, pp. 2.123–2.127). Amsterdam: Elsevier.

Tullis, T.S. (1986a). *Display Analysis Program (Version 4.0).* Lawrence, KS: The Report Store.

Tullis, T.S. (1986b). Optimizing the usability of computer-generated displays. *Proceedings of HCI '86 Conference on People and Computers: Designing for Usability.* (York, England, Sept. 23–26, pp. 604–613). London: British Computer Society.

Tullis, T.S. (1986c). A system for evaluating screen formats. *Proceedings of the 1986 Annual Meeting of the Human Factors Society* (Dayton, OH, Sept. 29–Oct. 3, pp. 1216–1220). Santa Monica, CA: Human Factors Society.

Wolf, C.E. (1986). *BNA "HN" command display: Results of user evaluation.* (Unpublished technical report available from Cynthia Wolf Connally, Unisys Corporation, 3519 Warner Ave., Santa Ana, CA 92704.

CHAPTER 8

User Performance with Command, Menu, and Iconic Interfaces[1]

John Whiteside
Dennis Wixon
Sandy Jones

Digital Equipment Corporation
Nashua, New Hampshire

INTRODUCTION

Interface Styles and Conventional Wisdom

Recent research has described three general classes of interfaces for computers. These classes are not precisely defined but they are generally understood; one would have little difficulty placing most interfaces into a particular class. These classes of interfaces are:

- command,
- menu, and
- iconic or direct manipulation.

Command systems are the oldest; in these systems, the user interacts with the system via a specialized language, which requires that the users type commands in order to give the system instructions. The second oldest class is menu-oriented systems. In these systems, the users are presented a list of alternatives from which they may choose. Thus, presumably, there is no specialized language to learn and minimal typing is required. The newest class is the direct manipulation or iconic systems. (We use these terms interchangeably, since icons (output) and direct manipulation (input) are very often combined.) In these systems, users interact with the

---

[1] The views expressed in this paper are those of the authors and do not necessarily reflect the views of Digital Equipment Corporation.

system by using a pointing device such as a mouse and by manipulating objects on the screen, which is organized spatially.

Most researchers have presumed that the choice of a particular style of interface has a direct bearing on how easy that system is to use. For example, as early as 1973 James Martin hypothesized that a dialogue with photographic pictures could be learned in 30 minutes, and that, for APL, in contrast, some people "will simply never learn to use its (APL) more complex features" (p. 27).

Similarly, Ramsey and Atwood (1979) discussed a variety of interface styles and concluded that command languages are effective for experienced users, menus are easy for novices, and iconic systems show the greatest potential for improving interfaces. They have said that one of the most important choices facing a designer is the choice of interaction style.

More recently, Shneiderman (1983, p. 68) concluded that direct manipulation systems are promising and that tedious command languages will be replaced with "lively and enjoyable interactive systems that reduce learning time, speed performance, and increase satisfaction."

These perceptions have become conventional wisdom. An informal survey by Ledgard (personal communication, 1981) of prominent human factors researchers confirmed these beliefs. Most respondents thought that command systems were effective for experienced users. Menu systems were effective for new users. Iconic systems were most effective for everyone, and would be the wave of the future.

Part of this conventional wisdom assumes that initial difficulties with the learning of command systems may be overcome with experience. Accordingly, type of system is presumably less important for experts. Nonetheless, people assume that command systems are best for experts. This seems to be based on the belief that experts already know the commands, and can type more rapidly than most systems can present alternatives via menus. Predictions are less clear for iconic systems, but many designers seem to subscribe to an undifferentiated belief that the system that is good for experts is bad for novices, and, conversely, the system that is good for novices is bad for experts.

Roots of Conventional Wisdom

These general beliefs are held despite a lack of systematic empirical data to support them. They appear to stem from two basic sources. First, unsystematic but enthusiastic reports of designers lend support to these general expectations. Second, and more importantly, these beliefs are derived from apparently simple, straightforward, and unassailable premises about human behavior.

For example, recognition memory is better than recall memory. This principle seems to imply that any system in which the alternatives are explicitly presented to the user would be superior to those which require the user to recall the design choices. A reasonable conclusion in applying this principle to interface design is that iconic and menu systems which directly present their alternatives to users should be easier to use than command systems which impose heavy memory load. These differences would be reduced or eliminated for expert users of a system, since they have "over learned" the system and can recall commands easily.

A second seemingly unassailable principle is that an environment which incorporates familiar elements and operations is easier to learn than one which incorporates unfamiliar elements and operations. Thus, a system whose interface presents a pseudo-office environment, in which, for example, documents are transferred by moving them on the screen, should be easy for office workers to learn. Therefore, an iconic or direct manipulation system whose presentation attempts to mimic an office in its presentation and operation would be superior to the other types of systems. Again, this difference may be reduced for expert users.

A third principle has been most directly expressed with what might be called a rhetorical question: "How would you like to drive your car with commands?" It seems ridiculous to propose that one would steer a car by typing something like "turn right 30 degrees." By implication, command systems are ridiculous.

A fourth principle is colloquially stated as "What you see is what you get." In the limited context of document processing, it means that what is printed by the system looks like what you see on the screen. More generally, it means that the appearance of objects reflects the state of those objects.

A fifth principle is a common environment should apply to all aspects of the system. For example, a "delete" operation should apply to graphical objects, text objects, data record, and top level objects. By creating a small and generic command environment, the system is made easy to learn.

A sixth principle is that motor operations should be minimized. In practice, this often translates to eliminate or reduce typing. When comparing different styles of interfaces, this means that iconic or menu systems, where typing is minimized, would be more easily learned and used than command systems which require the user to type. Within command systems, those systems which minimize the number of keystrokes a user performs are best. It has been proposed that users be evaluated according to the extent to which they minimize keystrokes (Hammer & Rouse, 1982), and that they be trained to eliminate less efficient strategies.

Implications of Conventional Wisdom

These assumptions are widely held and appear to be reasonable. Some can even be related to experiments in the literature. In addition, designers seem to believe that, from these principles, they can directly derive a design for their system. That is, designers appear to assume that one need simply follow these principles, and an easy to use system will automatically result. According to this school of thought, extensive efforts such as empirical testing or prototyping are unnecessary. One finds the most extreme form of this doctrine in project plans and the popular press, and sales literature, where one reads statements such as "The system will use a mouse and icons and will have multiple windows; therefore, it will be easy to use." Although, as stated here, this doctrine may seem like a caricature, it does reflect a general ethos. It appears that this general ethos is determining major decisions made by corporations and is establishing a group of common beliefs for the relatively new discipline of human computer interaction.

There are at least two reasons why these beliefs are very important. First, manufacturers are spending millions of dollars to implement various styles of systems because these styles are presumed to be easy to use. Second this collection of assumptions is forming the basis for the new subdiscipline of human computer interaction. Before spending millions or building a discipline, one might be wise to test the derivations from some of these principles.

A Test of Systems Derived From Conventional Wisdom

We chose to test a wide range of systems, with a large number of users of various types, using a variety of tasks. Our purpose was not to upset the well-documented assumptions stated earlier. Rather, our purpose was to determine if the systems built using these assumptions would be easy to use. In some cases, the systems we tested reflected, not only the "conventional wisdom" we described above, but also a careful program of empirical testing of design alternatives.

However, the tests we conducted were designed to be tests of the whole system. Thus, we were not interested in contrasting specific alternatives related to some detail of the system. For many of the systems we tested, research of this type had already gone into the design. Instead, it was our intention to try to recreate an atmosphere in which a new system is delivered to a user, and he or she attempts to do some productive work on it.

In pursuing this research, we made a simple assumption: The systems which we tested represented the best efforts of excellent design teams. Thus, while it may be argued that the systems we tested contained flaws and did not reflect a true embodiment of these principles, our position is that any system is built with finite resources in finite time, and thus must be a compromise. Design always involves tradeoffs (Norman, 1983). In addition, when these systems are discussed in the literature, much attention is paid to the fact that they are derived from the first principles discussed earlier. These discussions may have led some more naive designers to assume that first principles are enough to build a successful system. In summary, while the systems we tested were not perfect, no system is, and every effort was made to test the best representatives of each class.

While we wanted to conduct a holistic and nonreductionistic test, we also attempted to be rigorous in our approach. We carefully designed three standard tasks, used standardized instruments to measure attitudes, developed a uniform metric for comparing performance, and tested a wide variety of systems in each class. This type of systematic approach is derived from the work of Roberts (Roberts, 1979; Roberts & Moran, 1983) on text editors. Roberts developed a standard task and a uniform way of scoring performance on text editors. Her benchmarks have provided a reliable basis (Borenstein, 1985; Good, 1984) on which editors can be compared.

Our research was thus motivated by a few simple questions:

- Are there large and uniform differences in the usability and evaluation of systems?
- Are any differences which exist related to class of interfaces (command, menu, iconic)?
- Are some types of systems more suitable for some types of users?

METHOD

Users Tested

A total of 165 users participated in this study. Ninety percent of these users were between the ages of 25 and 50, and had a bachelor's degree. Questionnaire data was analyzed for 146 of these.

Based on their previous computer experience, each user was classified. The classes were defined as follows:

- new users: little or no computer experience
- transfer users: use interactive computers daily, but have never used the system being tested
- system users: use interactive computers daily, and have used the system being tested for at least several months

Systems Tested

Eleven different interfaces were evaluated: six command systems, three menu systems, and two iconic systems. Five of these systems were all part of commercially developed, currently available, top-level interactive software systems. The other six interfaces were specially developed as "facade" interfaces, written for the purpose of conducting tests, and were not part of actual functioning systems. Descriptions of all the interfaces follow.

Command systems.

Command systems A and B. These systems were command line interfaces to general purpose operating systems. Both were developed and made commercially available in the mid-1970s, have been revised several times, and were tested in the early 1980s. The systems have been revised since these tests were conducted. At the time of testing, they differed in many details of philosophy, command syntax, and treatment of help.

A + restyled help. This system was Command System A, with a restyled help system incorporated. While the content of help was unchanged, the format and functionality of the help system were extensively revised. Specifically, the screen was split into two windows, one for help and one for commands. In addition, such functions as error message lookup, a glossary, and more effective navigation were provided. This system was never commercially available.

A + revised help. This was also Command System A, but the help and feedback components of the system had been extensively rewritten. The revised help system provided examples, was relatively jargon free, supported synonyms, suggested corrections for errors, was relatively brief, was limited to a subset of the system, included tutorial information, confirmed correct commands, was task oriented, and could be accessed by pressing a help key. In short, the designers attempted to include any feature which they thought would aid the user without changing the command semantics and syntax. This system was designed for research purposes only.

User-derived interface. This interface was derived from the commands of untutored participants, using a Wizard of Oz method to elicit participant input (Kelley, 1984). It was an easy to use interface for an electronic mail interface that provided synonyms for commands and a forgiving syntax. The user derived interface (UDI) is extensively discussed by Good, Whiteside, Wixon, and Jones (1984). This system was a facade system which did not actually manipulate mail, but gave the participants the appearance of doing so.

Windowing facade. The windowing facade was a command-line facade that used function keys and two windows. There were two versions of this system. One provided simultaneous display of the two windows; the other provided successive display of the two windows. One window always contained mail messages, and the other contained documents. The system provided brief online help. This was a facade system with a limited command set.

Menu systems.

Office menu system. This menu system provided a general set of office functions, including editing, electronic mail, scheduling, and the like. Each application provided its own environment, and most made extensive use of function keys. The system provided online help. This system was a production system which has since been revised.

Basic menu simulation. This interface simulated a simple menu interface in which each of the 25 interrelated menu frames had an identical format. Each menu presented navigation and selection instructions. Menu items could be selected either by pointing to the specific item or by typing a single number. In this system, no actual operations were performed.

Office menu simulation. This interface was derived from the basic menu simulation, but was more complete and complex. The interface split the CRT screen into two windows, one of which was a general work area and the other contained the menu items. As in the basic menu simulation, frames contained information about navigation and selection and were consistent in appearance. There were a total of about 50 interrelated menus in this system. This system was a facade of an office system, and was used for research purposes.

Iconic systems.

Iconic systems 1 and 2. Both these systems provided a top-level interface using icons on which the user operated directly using either function keys, a meta-key arrangement, menus, forms, or some combination of these. A number of applications such as text editing, graphics editing, and spread sheets were provided. Each of these applications had interfaces which were apparently consistent with the top-level interface. Both systems made extensive use of a mouse. The systems differed in terms of screen layout, input syntax, file organization and treatment of help and hardware. Both of these systems were commercially available, and have since been revised.

Tasks

Three benchmark tasks were designed to evaluate specific aspects of systems. The tasks were the:

- simple filing task,
- electronic mail task, and
- general office procedures task.

The simple filing task was originally developed by Magers (1983), and consisted of simple operations on text files, such as displaying, concatenating, and sending files to another user. Participants were provided with a copy of the task, and were allowed to make notes as they worked. To successfully complete some parts of the task, the user must have succeeded on some previous items. Users were provided with online help and documentation. A copy of the task is available in Magers (1983).

The electronic mail task design was based on a study of electronic mail systems and of procedures used by secretaries who deal with paper mail. It involved reading, sending, and throwing away mail. The participants were provided with a copy of the task and allowed to make notes. The users were not provided with system documentation or online help. A copy of this task is presented in Good et al. (1984).

The general office procedures task was designed to reflect frequency-of-use data and common office functions. In this task, no written instructions were provided, and the participants were not allowed to make notes. Users read a mail message containing an instruction, and had to remember the contents of the message while they used the system to complete the task. This memory load was deliberately imposed to measure "system overhead." The task alternated between electronic mail and the document filing system. The task required the users to read a document, forward a document, print a document, create and mail a short message, destroy a document, and find a document which was stored in a location other than the one where the user was working.

Manuals describing each of these tasks, instructing experimenters how to install them, and providing exact copies of associated documents were prepared for these experiments to insure that procedures were uniform.

Procedure

The purpose of the work was described to the participants. They were instructed with respect to their rights as participants as described by the American Psychological Association guidelines for research with humans. Additionally, we informed them that we were evaluating the system and not the user. They were asked to sign a general form describing their rights and a photographic release form. We gave each participant a prequestionnaire which asked a series of demographic questions. This questionnaire was used to classify users according to their experience.

Next, the experimenter gave users a 5- to 10-minute introduction which provided them with fundamental knowledge of the system being tested. For all systems, this included a description of how to get help, if available (task permitting). For command systems, it covered the concept of typing commands and pressing return to have the commands processed. For menu systems, it included the mechanism to select menu items. For iconic systems, the experimenter asked the participants what they thought the mouse would do. After noting their response, the experimenter illustrated the use of the mouse and allowed the participant to practice selection.

After receiving this introduction, the participants were left alone, but could contact the experimenter through an intercom or by phone. They were instructed to request help only if they were completely stuck or felt that the system had broken. In response to most of these requests, the experimenter was nondirective. If the system had crashed or the hardware had malfunctioned in some way, the experimenter intervened to reestablish the participant's environment.

All participants were allowed up to an hour to work on the system. When an hour had elapsed or the participant judged the task to be complete, the experimenter reentered the room and conducted a brief, nondirective interview with the participant. Participants were asked such questions such as what they liked about the system and what they did not like. Following this interview, the participants filled in a brief questionnaire dealing with an evaluation of the system. All participants were given a small gift. Participants who were not DEC employees were also paid $25.00.

RESULTS

Overview

We collected two general classes of data. The first type was quantitative. The performance data and the attitude data were of this type, and were analyzed using conventional statistical analysis. The videotape data, the experimenters' notes, and the interview data were examined systematically, but no statistical analysis was applied.

Quantitative Results

Performance analysis. We developed a general metric for measuring performance. This metric is a rate measure that expresses the percentage of the task completed per unit of time. The formula is:

$$S = \frac{1}{T} PC$$

where:

S = performance score
T = time spent in task
P = percentage of task completed
C = a constant (set to 5 minutes)

This score has the advantage of expressing time and amount of task completed as a single number. The higher the score, the better (more efficient) the performance.

For practical reasons, all possible combinations of participant type and system were not tested. As a result, a one-way analysis of variance was performed on the data, and planned comparisons were conducted to isolate differences. The planned comparisons were determined by the investigators' interests, and all were orthogonal.

Group differences. Collapsing across all conditions and simply testing the difference between levels of experience revealed highly significant differences [$F(2,162) = 54.17$, $p < .0001$]. For all the performance data we gathered, novice, transfer, and system users differ greatly. The mean performance scores were 7.9 for novice users, 21.9 for transfer users, and 50.2 for expert users (recall that a score of 100 on this scale would mean that users completed the entire task in 5 minutes). This finding is not particularly surprising, and suggests that the criteria used to classify users was reasonable.

To look at other differences, the data were transformed. Since variances in the groups were highly correlated with means, and since the large within group variance of the system users would "swamp" any differences for the novices, we computed Z-scores for each group using that group's overall mean and variance. For the rest of the analyses, we conducted contrasts within each group.

Simple filing task. Figure 1 depicts performance on the simple filing task. Novices using traditional systems (Command System A, Menu System, and Command System A with revised help) were more efficient than novices using the iconic systems (Icon System 1 and Icon System 2) $[F(1,128) = 4.55, p < .05]$. There was no significant difference between command (Command System A) and menu systems.

Transfer users using traditional systems (Command System A,

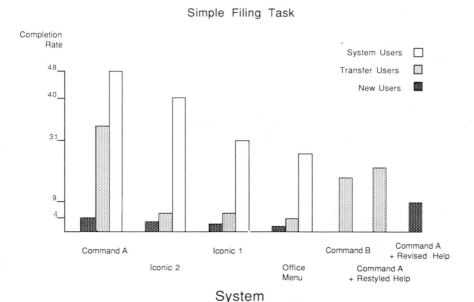

Figure 1. Performance on Simple Filing Task

Command System B, Menu System, and Command System A + restyled help) were more efficient than users of iconic systems (Icon System 1 and Icon System 2) [$F(1,128) = 14.53$, $p < .0005$]. These users were also more efficient with command systems (Command System A, Command System B, and Command System A + restyled help) than they were with menu systems [$F(1,128) = 14.34$ $p < .0005$]. We also examined one specific case of transfer; we found no significant differences in users who were transferred from one iconic system to another versus users who were transferred from a command system to an iconic system.

A somewhat different picture emerges for system users. Performance on iconic systems did not differ from performance on command systems [$F(1,128) = .11$ $p = .73$]. Performance on command systems was superior to performance on menu systems [$F(1,128) = 8.71$, $p < .005$].

Electronic mail task. The overall results for the electronic mail task are depicted in Figure 2. For both novice and transfer users, the UDI interface out performed the command interface, [$F(1,128) = 4.82$, $p < .05$, and $F(1,128) = 4.08$ $p < .05$, respectively]. Again, iconic interfaces were inferior to command interfaces (Command System A and UDI) for transfer users [$F(1,128) = 11.68$, $p < .001$].

General office procedures task. The results for this task are presented in Figure 3.

For both new and transfer users, the general result was that users of facade systems were more efficient than users of production systems [$F(1,128) = 10.87$, $p < .005$, and $F(1,128) = 30.89$, $p < .005$, respectively].

User evaluation. In addition to measuring performance, we also measured participants' evaluative reactions to the systems they used. To do this, participants indicated how strongly they felt about the system they used in terms of a set of positive–negative adjective pairs. In quantifying these data, we made the following numeric translation:

-3 extremely negative
-2 quite negative
-1 slightly negative
 0 neutral
 1 slightly positive
 2 quite positive
 3 extremely positive

These numbers provide the key for interpreting Figures 4, 5, and 6, which show the mean evaluative ratings for the various systems tested. Because our rating scales evolved as the study was conducted,

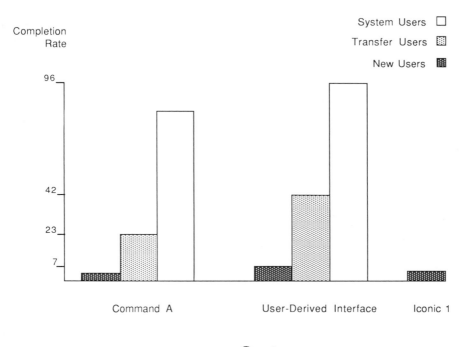

User Performance
Electronic Mail Task

Performance on Electronic Mail Task

Figure 2.

not all systems were rated using the same scale. Only systems which used the scale described above are included.

Simple filing task. Figure 4 shows the results of the user evaluations for those systems tested with the simple filing task.

The only significant difference for all groups was that new users of Icon System 2 evaluated the system significantly more positively than users of Icon System 1 [$F(1,128) = 9.05, p < .005$].

Electronic mail task. Figure 5 shows the results of the user evaluations for those systems tested with the electronic mail task.

The only significant difference was that transfer users preferred

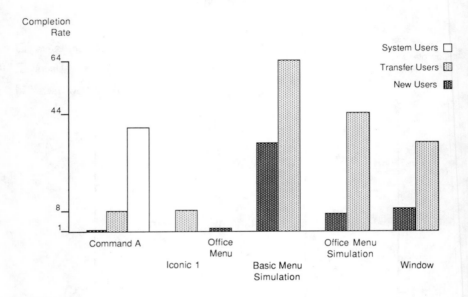

System

Performance on Office Procedures Task

Figure 3.

the command language interfaces over the iconic interface, [$F(1,128)$ = 18.81, p < .001].

General office procedures task. Figure 6 shows the results of the user evaluations for those systems tested with the general office procedures task.

For both new and transfer users, facade systems were preferred over production systems [$F(1,128)$ = 19.43, p < .001, and $F(1,128)$ = 10.32, p < .005 respectively].

Qualitative Results

In this section, the actual behaviors of the users on the various systems are analyzed and categorized. Specific problems were grouped into classes according to common themes. No attempt was made to derive a quantitative assessment of the relative impact of each of

User Evaluation
Simple Filing Task

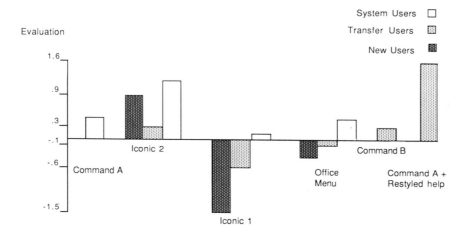

System
Evaluation Simple Filing Task

Figure 4.

these problems. Instead, a more descriptive and anecdotal approach was used.

System feedback. Problems surrounding feedback occurred on a number of systems. For example, new and transfer users who used the command system said that confirmation messages would have been helpful, especially when sending mail. As one transfer user put it,

> There are too many silent actions where an OK message would have been reassuring.

For one of the command systems, it was common to see new users execute a command twice because they were not sure that it had worked. Interestingly, this same behavior occurred on one iconic system in a very different context. One of the iconic systems saves and executes each mouse-button press, but does not immediately give feedback. A number of users impatiently pressed the

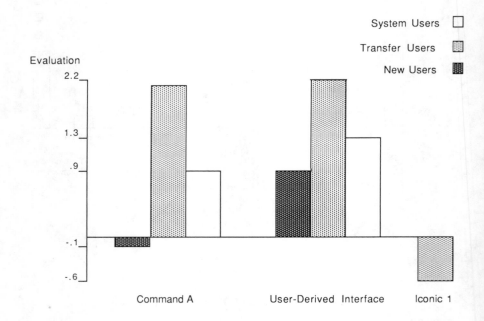

User Evaluation
Electronic Mail Task

Figure 5.

System

Evaluation Electronic Mail Task

mouse button several times, in effect issuing a whole series of commands before the first one was confirmed. This could have unpredictable and dangerous results.

Another feedback problem on the iconic systems involved using the shape of the cursor to provide status information. When the system was working, the cursor changed from an arrow, and a message was displayed in a corner of the screen. Unfortunately, many participants said that they noticed neither the changed cursor nor the message.

For the iconic system, there was a lack of effective feedback with respect to the interaction of the mouse and the keyboard.

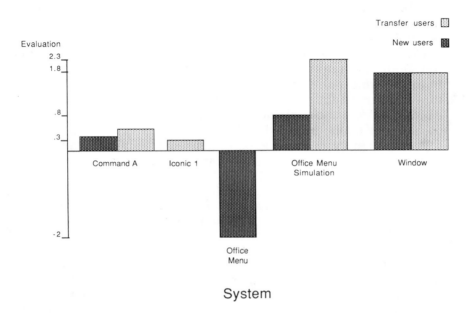

User Evaluation
General Office Procedures

Figure 6.

I found the mouse to be useful. However, the interdependencies between the keyboard and the mouse are very confusing and inconvenient.

In the menu system, lack of clear feedback concerning the effects of user actions posed problems for many new and transfer users. For example, messages were automatically moved to new locations after being read; this resulted in users believing all their messages had been deleted.

One of the iconic systems was very effective in presenting error messages. These occurred in the center of the screen and never escaped notice. In contrast, other systems often displayed messages in obscure locations or on a screen so crowded with information that the messages were missed. Frequently, the messages were in a virtually incomprehensible code and thus did the users no good even if they saw them.

In one case, in the menu system, a user performed an action

successfully, but the indicated change in status was presented on a very crowded screen and was preceded by a set of meaningless (to the user) numbers. In this case, the user continued to attempt the action (which had already been successfully completed) for the remaining 45 minutes of an hour session.

Consistency of input forms. For Command System A, new and transfer users were bothered by what seemed to them inconsistencies in input forms. For example, file names have a different form when they are the object of a deletion operation than in other contexts, and several users complained about this. Even system users were observed to make errors with the delete command.

A related problem surfaced on Command System B. The operation of the online help system seemed inconsistent. For example, one user noted:

> WOW! It works! . . . It's strange that when I typed HELP COPY it didn't know what I was talking about, but when I typed HELP MAIL, boom! There was the information.

Since COPY and MAIL are both commands in this system, this user expected that helpful information would be available about both commands, in response to similar request formats. Unbeknownst to him, the system at that time had several different help systems, each with their own properties. (Later versions of this system have integrated the various help systems; on these, the above example would now work.)

Inconsistent input forms caused all levels of user much difficulty on the menu interface. The key to return to the previous menu varied from application to application, as did the help key. If new users selected the NEW USER option prior to starting work, they would have seen information about this. But only one user thought to do so. The function keys also varied from application to application in this system, causing users extreme frustration. User comments about this aspect of the interface were extremely negative.

The pointing mechanism on Icon System 1 offered an interesting example of apparent inconsistency. It was very difficult for the majority of users to select with the arrow cursor. The tendency of all the new and transfer users was to select text and icons with the body of the arrow, and not with the tip. In fact, however, the arrow cursor would not select anything unless the tip of the arrow was on the object. Thus, it took most participants two to three tries before successfully selecting an object. This problem usually persisted for an entire session with users never realizing what the problem was, and forming a poor impression of the system's reliability as a result.

Usefulness of help systems. The quality of the help- and error-message systems was a problem on many of the interfaces. In the command systems, a major problem was the sheer amount of help available. Users were overwhelmed by the amount of information displayed as a result of the HELP command. One said,

> The HELP file is confusing. There's too much information on the screen.

Some transfer users thought the HELP information in the manuals contradicted the online HELP. They had difficulty locating command-specific information in the manuals. The large number of manuals was intimidating to most users, who rarely consulted them.

Transfer and new users also found fault with the error messages, saying,

> Error message did not convey what you did wrong.

> They were sometimes helpful, often misleading and confusing.

Although the help system for Command System B is considerably different from the help system for Command System A, users also had difficulty with it. Some typical comments were,

> poorly designed, misleading, and full of irrelevant information; uninformative and hard to use

> misleading and confusing

> Improve HELP

A specific problem was that participants could not find any actual examples of command-line syntax to use as models in forming their own commands. This was a major problem for both command systems (which has since been rectified). In fact, many users copied directly or mimicked the command forms that were presented to them. In the case of help for Command System A, the command forms tend to be presented as general-case, quasi-algebraic statements, not as working examples, so the very common user strategy of mimicry simply produced more error messages.

In many systems, the help information available did not correspond to what the user wanted information about. For example, in response to a query, one system identified which commands were legitimate, but did not provide what most users wanted, namely information about how the commands worked or what the syntax was.

In some cases, the HELP information was simply so poorly written as to be incomprehensible. This was a problem with the windowing facade, for example.

In the experiment as a whole, users had very little good to say about the online help on most systems. And yet, curiously, users seem to expect that help be available. One icon system has little online help available, and this surprised all of the transfer users and some of the new users. These people wanted immediate help on specific topics and were reluctant to look through documentation to find it. As one transfer user put it:

ADD HELP!

In the Icon System 1, a number of the problems with help were due to poor response time, which placed a very high cost on getting helpful information. However, users also complained about the help system independent of performance considerations. The online help system was written in a lengthy, tutorial style. Many users gave up looking for the information they needed. One transfer user remarked,

Getting help was impossible, finding out how to do things was near impossible, and waiting for the system was extremely frustrating.

One of the more interesting situations arose when the user needed help to get help. The menu system was particularly difficult in this regard. Users often found themselves trapped in a menu or application, with no idea of how to get out to get to the help frame that would tell them how to get out. This Catch-22 situation emerged from the study as one of the most demoralizing situations a user could encounter.

Command System A + extended help produced high performance for new users and also gathered some favorable reactions, such as,

The system was fantastic . . . I didn't need a book or anything!

The HELP frames in the Command System A + extended help were designed to include simple examples of commands and were written in everyday language. Some users pressed the HELP key and looked through the overview material before beginning; others typed HELP and then selected help on relevant topics. New users were insulated from commands that they would not immediately require. This kind of presentation made a significant difference to the interface. Users never saw the overwhelming list from a HELP command, and were guided in the use of supported commands by referral messages. In addition, synonyms were supported in the help system, and tutorial information was provided.

Naturalness of input forms. The choice of wording for commands, menu item, prompts, and instructions resulted in user problems for all three styles of interface. For example, on a command-line system, many new users assumed (not unreasonably) that the command READ could be used to read a file. In fact, the READ command has nothing to do with reading files. The result was pathetic interactions, such as the following, in which the user was trying to read the sales figures. The participant's entries are in lower case; the system responses are in upper case.

```
$ read
$_LOG NAME: sales.txt
$_SYMBOL: sales.txt
%DCL-W-UNDFIL, FILE NOT OPEN
```

But such problems were not confined to command-line systems. Users showed much confusion over the wording of items in the menu system. One user stated this explicitly:

The wording used was confusing and I was not sure what to look for or where to look.

For example, many users picked the READ item to read their mail. This did not work, however, since READ refers to messages already read, not to ones to read for the first time. This was completely counterintuitive to all the users.

Wording confusions were also found in iconic systems. For example, one aspect of an iconic systems that many users found confusing was the difference between "SET ASIDE" and "SAVE AND PUT AWAY." Choosing the wrong option made it much more difficult for users subsequently to retrieve their files.

Pushing a button carries with it the clear implication that something should happen as a result, much as issuing a command does. On Icon System 1, however, pointing at an icon and pushing the button did very little, from the user's point of view. In fact, that action "selected" an item, that is, made it available for further manipulation. In itself, however, selecting an object did nothing except turn the icon black. Many users selected icons by pushing the mouse button and then simply waited, encouraged in their faith that something would eventually happen by the generally slow response time of the system. Even system users did this from time to time.

In the user-derived mail system, the features that most accounted for the increased user performance were synonyms for all commands and flexibility of command syntax. For example, users accessed messages by typing in any or all identifying fields of a directory listing: message number, or sender, or title, or date.

Navigation through the system. All systems, whether command-line, menu, or iconic, presented the user with a conceptual space in which to navigate. Many problems were the result of users not understanding the structure of this space or the rules for moving in it. These difficulties cut across all interface styles and all levels of user.

In the menu interface, many participants (new, transfer, and system users) became so involved with maneuvering through the menu structure that, by the time they had done this successfully, they forgot what the task was. This happened to one of the system designers, among others. Other users simply got stuck for want of information about how to change states, as in the case of the user who said,

> The system is unfriendly in the sense that it did not give any clues on how to retrace steps, get out of a mode.

This problem was especially severe for new users, many of whom never saw the task documents simply because they could not get back to the main menu to find the document listing.

The iconic systems had their own navigation problems. For example, the online help system had a very deep hierarchical structure that dismayed some users, causing them to end up in entirely the wrong place in their search for helpful information. System users avoided the help system altogether, even when they didn't know how to do something.

Navigation problems frequently manifested themselves for new users in being confused about modes. For instance, new users often typed commands while in an editor, or tried to edit commands. Often users would get different help when in an application from that they received when they were at command level. Since users were usually unaware that they were running an application, the system appeared inconsistent to them.

It is possible for users to be successful with a system which has modes, even though they do not understand them. For example, when using the UDI interface, many users typed a mail message at command level. Instead of giving an error message and ignoring the command line, the UDI interface saved command lines longer than 75 characters and asked the user if he or she meant the command to be a message. This had the result of allowing several users who had no idea what an editor was successfully to use an editor.

DISCUSSION

Overview

Several general conclusions can be drawn from the findings presented here, some of which are counterintuitive and counter to current beliefs about interface development:

- There are large differences in the usability and evaluation of systems.
- These differences do not systematically relate to the class of interface.
- Systems which are most suitable for experts are also most suitable for novices.
- Traditional human factors problems were not solved simply by the adoption of new interface styles.
- Holistic testing is needed to uncover interface problems.
- Maturity of the product contributes strongly to its usability.

Each of these points is discussed below.

Large Differences in Usability of Systems

We found many significant differences in the usability and participant evaluation of systems. These differences suggest that the measures used were sensitive enough to detect differences. Many new users scored below the 5%-per-5-minute-interval on the performance measure. However, the quantitative measures do not fully convey how difficult some of these systems are to use. For some of the systems, novice users could accomplish almost no useful work in an hour. These sessions are difficult to watch and frustrating for the participants. In viewing such sessions, one is impressed by the intelligence, persistence, and resourcefulness of the participants.

Participants make valiant attempts to understand and work with these systems. Their efforts are rewarded by a series of cryptic error messages. The recalcitrance of these systems makes them appear almost belligerent.

In contrast, with other systems, novices can accomplish useful work in an hour session. While novices never attain the same level of performance on our task as experts, their work was on some systems quite smooth and efficient. Some of these systems were simulations or facades. These facades have often had limited command sets, provided clear feedback, and allowed for simple selection of items. For the UDI, the command set was empirically derived from the command constructions of novice users. Interestingly, this command set worked well for transfer users and did not impede the work of experts. In fact, experts were slightly more efficient using the UDI command system than their native command environment. Another easy system for novices to use system was Command System A + revised help. This system incorporated such features as synonym support, exposed users to a limited command set, provided tutorial information, and provided examples. Since the Command System A was itself unmodified, this result suggests that help systems can be effective even though most of the commercial help and training systems we have tested have had a negative impact on user performance.

Differences Unrelated to Interface Class

The fact that system type made little difference in usability was unexpected. Systems which supposedly were designed according to the best human factors principles, and for novice users, were neither easy to use or well liked. While these systems may have solved some interface problems, they presented new problems which rendered them ineffective. In some cases, the speed of the system not only slowed users down, but also made it difficult to learn the consequences of their actions. In some cases, feedback was presented in obscure locations. Many users found the presence of multiple mouse buttons and/or the syntax of using the buttons overly complex. Often, the feedback provided was misinterpreted.

A presumably easy-to-use menu system was one of the worst systems we tested. The system was fraught with problems. For example, menu items may minimize recall memory, but in many cases they were not only unrecognized but also misleading. In cases where the menu items themselves were correctly understood, a baroque series of required actions, combined with poor feedback and prompting, prevented the participants from understanding that they had successfully completed a step. Often, a series of menus had to be navigated to perform what was a single unitary action, from the participant's point of view.

The relationship between participant evaluation and productivity was not simple. In many cases, systems which performed best were liked best and systems which performed poorly were disliked. However, this generalization is not without exception. While performance differences on the two iconic systems were not different, evaluations were significantly different, with one system being one of the most negatively rated and the other system being one of the most positively rated.

Experts and Novices

Only a subset of our data is complete enough to compare experts performance with novice performance. The four systems shown on the left side of Figure 1 show a consistent picture. Those systems which are easy for experts are also easy for novices. This finding is consistent with Roberts and Moran's (1984) result for text editors. It is also consistent with informal tests we have conducted. Experts do not seem to be troubled by good feedback, straightforward command forms, flexible command syntax, help with examples, and support of synonyms.

Traditional Human Factors Problems Persist

The classification of user problems revealed that every type of problem was present in every style of interface. The problems simply appeared in different forms for different interfaces. All the types of problems—navigation problems, feedback issues, consistency issues, naturalness issues—all of these appeared in all styles of interface. Typing may be too difficult for some people, but a complex syntax of button presses on a mouse is also difficult. Command names may be counterintuitive, but menu items and icons are also subject to misinterpretation. Some systems may present no feedback, or cryptic feedback; other systems provide feedback in obscure places, or in the midst of a crowded screen.

Holistic Testing is Necessary to Uncover Interface Problems

These data contradict the implication of conventional wisdom, that adoption of an interface style alone can solve usability problems.

The data also raise questions about the strategy of settling on an interface style and then using testing to sort out the details. Frequently, the problems in a design were not related to isolated aspects of the design but to a complex interaction of problems. Such interactions might not be revealed in reductionist, carefully controlled, tests. For example, the problems with respect to the selection of items using a mouse were related to system speed, cursor shape, the buffering of mouse inputs, and overall syntax of the system.

In a larger sense, the design of human computer interfaces is quite complex, since it involves communication between two of the most complex entities known. This type of the design process is radically transformational (Carroll, Thomas, & Malhotra, 1979). Design is not simply top-down or bottom-up, but rather it may be top-up or bottom-down, or alternately proceed up and down. This type of design requires an open-ended, seemingly uncontrolled type of test in which the designer is not simply open to decide a preordained question, but rather is prepared to reevaluate the assumptions. Larry Tesler has spoken candidly on this point:

> And then we actually implemented two or three of the various ways and tested them on users, and that's how we made decisions. Sometimes we found that everybody was wrong. We had a couple of real beauties where the users couldn't use any of the versions that were given to them and they would immediately say, "Why don't you just do it this way?" and that was obviously the way to do it. So sometimes we got the ideas from our user tests and as soon as we heard the idea we all thought "Why didn't we think of that?" Then we did it that way. (Morgan, Williams, & Lemmons, 1983, p. 104)

By testing the whole system and being open to radical redesign, the designer can discover that either the overall approach was wrong or that problems are the result of the complex interaction of factors which heretofore may have been considered implementation details of no consequence.

Maturity of the Product

One factor which seems to relate to the usability of systems is their maturity. The systems which scored well in our testing tended to be mature products which had been through several revisions, based in part on customer input. As such, they showed a level of craftmanship and attention to detail not present in other systems. In contrast, systems which scored poorly were often early releases of

USER PERFORMANCE WITH INTERFACES 313

new styles of interfaces. As user feedback is incorporated into these newer interfaces, they will also improve substantially. This sort of improvement serves to reinforce the major point of this paper: Well designed systems require careful attention to detail based on user testing and feedback.

Conclusion

Our observations lead to the conclusion that craftsmanship is more important than interface style or design philosophy. In actual systems, "sweating the design details" exerts an enormous effect on usability.

We have not "proven" that one system is good and another is bad. Nor have we "proven" that one type of system is good and another type of system is bad. The results of this study point out the fallacy of even asking that sort of question. One might argue that a perfect menu system would necessarily be better than a perfect command system. However, since perfect systems are never built, such an argument is academic and irrelevant to the real world of designing and building products. The results also suggest that, at present and for the foreseeable future, effective designs require holistic and open ended testing. The results are consistent with design methodologies outlined by Gould and Lewis (1985), Bennett (1984), Gilb (1981), and Carroll and Rosson (1985) which stress clear interface goals, intimate knowledge of the users, empirical testing, and a flexible and holistic approach to usability. These methodologies can contribute much to the building of usable and enjoyable interfaces. Another implication of the results is that presumed trade-offs between learnability and usability are not necessary. All of these conclusions came as a surprise to us. At the beginning of this study, we expected to confirm conventional wisdom. The results proved us wrong and lead us to what we hope is a healthy skepticism.

ACKNOWLEDGEMENTS

This work took place over a period of 2 years and was a group effort by Software Human Engineering, managed by Bill Zimmer. John Whiteside proposed the original study and was project leader. The sponsorship of Jesse Lipcon of Digital's Research and Advanced Development committee is gratefully acknowledged. Many people contributed to the collection of the data, including Geoffrey Bock and Bob Crowling. Sandy Jones and Paula Levy ran many participants and collected the original descriptions of system problems. Mark Bramhall wrote the menu simulation software. Michael Good wrote the windowing facade. Michael Good and Jim Burrows were responsible for the programming of the UDI. Don Petersen wrote the software for styled help of Command System A. The early work of Celeste Magers is also acknowledged.

REFERENCES

Bennett, J.L. (1984). Managing to meet usability requirements: establishing meeting software development goals. In J. Bennett, D. Case, J. Sandelin, & M. Smith (Eds.), *Visual display terminals* (pp. 161–184). Englewood Cliffs, NJ: Prentice-Hall.

Borenstein, N.S. (1985). The evaluation of text editors: A critical review of Roberts and Moran methodology based on new experiments. *CHI 85 Proceedings of Human Factors in Computing Systems Meetings.* Baltimore, MD: ACM.

Carroll, J., & Rosson, M.B. (1985). Usability specification as a tool in iterative development. In H.R. Hartson (Ed.), *Advances in human–computer interaction* (Vol. 1, pp. 1–28). Norwood, NJ: Ablex Publishing Corp.

Carroll, J.M., Thomas, J.C., & Malhotra, A. (1979). Clinical-experimental analysis of design problem solving. *Design Studies, 1* 84–92.

Gilb, T. (1981). Design by objectives. Unpublished Manuscript. Available from the author at Box 102, N-1411, Kolbotn, Norway.

Good, M. (1985). The use of logging in the design of a new text editor. *CHI 84 Proceedings of Human Factors in Computing Systems Meetings.* Baltimore, MD: ACM.

Good, M.D., Whiteside, J.A., Wixon, D.R., & Jones, S.J. Building a user-derived interface. *Communications of the ACM, 27*(10), 1032–1043.

Gould, J.D., & Lewis, C. (1985). Designing for usability: key principles and what designers think. *Communications of the ACM, 28,* 300–311.

Hammer, J.M., & Rouse, W.B. (1982). The human as a constrained optimal editor. *IEEE Transactions on Systems, Man and Cybernetics, SMC-12,* 777–784.

Kelley, J.F. (1984). An interactive design methodology for user-friendly natural language office information applications. *ACM Transactions on Office Information Systems, 2,* 26–41.

Magers, C.S. (1983). An experimental evaluation of on-line help for non-programmers. *CHI 83 Proceedings of Human Factors in Computing Systems Meetings.* Baltimore, MD: ACM.

Morgan, C., Williams, G., & Lemmons, P. (1983). An interview with Wayne Rosing, Bruce Daniels, and Larry Tesler. *Byte, 8,* 90–113.

Martin, J. (1973). *Design of man–computer dialogues.* Englewood Cliffs, NJ: Prentice-Hall.

Norman, D. (1983). Design principles for human–computer interfaces. *CHI*

83 Proceedings of Human Factors in Computing Systems Meetings. Baltimore, MD: ACM.

Ramsey, H.R., & Atwood, M.E. (1979). *Human factors in computer systems: a Review of the Literature* (Tech. rep. No. SAI-79-111-DEN). Englewood, CO: Science Applications Incorporated.

Roberts, T. (1979). Evaluation of computer text editors (Report No. SSL-79-9). Palo Alto, CA: Xerox Park.

Roberts, T., & Moran, T.P. (1983). The evaluation of text editors: Methodology and empirical results. *Communications of the ACM, 26,* 265–283.

Schneiderman, B. (1983). Direct manipulation: A step beyond programming languages. *Computer, 16*(8), 57–69.

CHAPTER 9

An Examination of the Research Evidence for Computer-Based Instruction[1]

Theodore M. Shlechter

The US Army Research Institute, Fort Knox Field Unit

Computer-Based Instruction (CBI) proponents (e.g., Kearsley, Hunter & Seidel, 1983; Myers, 1984; Shavelson, Winkler, Stasz, Feibel, Robyn, & Shaha, 1984a; Wilson, 1984) have suggested that this technology's delivery capabilities make CBI superior to other instructional modes. As Shavelson et al. have stated:

> Federal and state policy makers all contend that recent technological innovations most notably the microcomputers hold particular promise not only for pulling education out of a rising tide of mediocrity, but also for reshaping education. (p. 1)

CBI denotes using computers in the instructional process. Computer-Assisted Instruction (CAI) and Computer-Managed Instruction (CMI) are considered to be components of CBI. In CAI, students receive instructions directly from the computer system. CMI involves using the computer for such instructional management issues as scoring, recording, and interpreting test results. Instructions for a CMI system, however, are provided offline, either by the teacher

[1] The opinions expressed in this paper are those of this author and do not necessarily reflect the views of the U.S. Army Research Institute, the U.S. Army, or the Department of Defense. Portions of this paper have appeared as: Shlechter, T.M. (1986). *An examination of the CBI research evidence for military training.* (ARI Technical Report 722). Alexandria, VA: U.S. Army Research Institute. I wish to thank Allen Avner, John Boldovici, Ronald Kramer, Donald Kristiansen, and Rae Shepherd-Shlechter for their insightful comments and help. A special thanks goes to Debra Hix for her help with the final draft of this paper.

or other instructional media. CMI is also used to help with scheduling the instructional program. Other uses of CMI will be discussed in the succeeding sections.

Claims about CBI's relative value as an instructional delivery system are based upon research studies which suggest advantages of CBI over conventional instruction. Several reviews of the CBI literature (e.g., Kearsley et al., 1983; Kemner-Richardson, Lamos, & West, 1984; Orlansky & String, 1981; Orlansky, 1983, 1985) have indicated that this instructional medium has led to: (a) reduced training time, and (b) reduced instructional costs. These reports have also indicated that students seemed to favor taking a course by means of CBI rather than receiving conventional instructions. The CBI literature also suggested that CBI training would be the most effective instructional mode for helping students to achieve a better mastery of the instructional content and for dealing with individual learning differences. The robustness of these findings about CBI will be analyzed in this chapter.

A major weakness in the CBI literature is that very few reviews have dealt with analyzing the possible methodological problems in this research area. This chapter will explore the extent to which previous research has confounded media effects with extraneous treatment effects. Avner (1978) and Clark (1985a) have noted that CBI is a medium rather than an instructional treatment, and, thus, that researchers must determine the unique educational contributions inherent in CBI as a delivery system. As Avner (1979), Director of Evaluation at the Computer-Based Educational Research Laboratory at the University of Illinois (CERL), has stated, "Computer-based education (CBI) is, despite its title, more a medium for communication of information than a coherent instructional plan or approach" (p. 136). Without a thorough analysis of the CBI literature, one is ill-equipped to make recommendations about using CBI over other instructional media, and to make decisions about future directions in designing CBI programs.

One must also carefully examine the CBI literature, because history has shown that educational innovations which were implemented without sufficient research and planning were always abandoned for still newer educational innovations (Montague & Wulfeck, 1984). Believing that CBI is immune to this historical progression is unrealistic and unhealthy, unrealistic because educators will only accept instructional technology which can withstand the passage of time and improve their teaching. And Ragsdale (1982) has suggested that the history of CBI may be following the same path as other recent educational innovations, from initial enthusiasm and excitement for the innovation to its eventual abandonment. A belief in CBI's immortality is unhealthy, because it may preclude advances in this technology.

This discussion of the CBI literature should then help CBI professionals to better understand: (a) the strengths and weaknesses of current programs, (b) the interaction between student variables and CBI, and (c) the complexities involved in evaluating this instructional medium. The conclusions drawn from this chapter should thus help in the development of future CBI programs. And the lessons learned from examining the CBI research literature should be applicable to research in the other arenas of human–computer interaction.

This review will then examine the state of CBI research on costs, learning increments, individual differences, and student attitudes. These four main areas of CBI research will be discussed in the next four sections, respectively. Methodological concerns in CBI research and implications for future research will also be addressed in these four sections.

COSTS

A major obstacle to widespread CBI implementation is the extensive capital investment associated with acquiring a system. Reed (1983) cited an EDUCOM Bulletin (1983) report which estimated that institutions of higher education should expect to invest between $1,000 and $6,000 per student for a current CBI system. Hofstetter (1983) noted that the per terminal hardware costs for a PLATO (Programmed Logic for Automatic Teaching Operations) system is $2,900. Avner (1986) has noted, however, that hardware costs are much lower in 1986 than they were in 1981, from a 1981 investment of $147,680 to a $30,000 investment in 1986 for the terminal hardware associated with a standard 32-terminal PLATO system. However, other costs associated with the PLATO system, e.g., communication costs, have doubled and tripled in the last 4 years. He indicated that an institution could expect a yearly investment of $135,000–$150,000 for an entire system. These costs reflect charges from a nonprofit organization (CERL) for the following items: (a) terminals, (b) power for terminals, (c) disk storage space, (d) system interface, (e) central computer, (f) system software, (g) central building, (h) service travel, (i) support personnel, (j) support equipment, (k) supplies and spare parts, and (l) communication system to host computer. Avner's figures do not reflect additional expenditures for such items as updating the instructional materials. Educators should expect to make similar financial investments for other CBI systems, e.g., MicroTICCIT (Microcomputer Network of the Time-Shared Interactive Computer-Controlled Information Television System).

Christensen (1985) observed, however, that the cost value of any product should be determined by its life cycle cost rather than by the costs of the initial outlay. As indicated in the introduction section, many CBI reports (e.g., Hofstetter, 1983; Kemner-Richardson el al., 1984; Orlansky, 1985; Orlansky & String, 1981; Seidel, 1980) have suggested, however, that such systems are cost effective (same effectiveness at reduced costs or more effective at same cost than alternative media) and would eventually lead to savings in education. Kemner-Richardson et al. noted, for example, that the PLATO system, as compared to conventional instruction, would lead to a $180,000-a-year savings for an average military educational program. Such analyses of life cycle cost savings attributable to a CBI system traditionally have involved estimating operating costs and personnel costs which would accompany implementation of new programs. Life cycle cost estimates for military systems have also involved calculating the dollars saved by reducing military training time.

Training Time

A most pervasive finding in the CBI military literature is that use of CBI leads to reduced training time. Orlansky (1985) noted that the median savings time for 19 military studies which compared CBI to conventional instruction was 30% with a time savings range of −31 to 89%. These studies have also failed to find any noticeable decrements in students' learning associated with spending less time in instruction.

Dallman, Deleo, Main, and Gillman (1977) reported that such a 30% time reduction would bring about a yearly savings of $23,000 for an Army course on vehicle repair which trains approximately 375 students per year. Orlansky (1985) believed that a 30% time savings could translate to a yearly financial savings as large as $10 million in FY 1977 money for training 50,000 Navy students. Both Dallman et al.'s and Orlansky's cost estimates are based upon calculating students' pay and allowances for the amounts of time saved in training.

Training time savings could further reduce military expenditures by allowing more students to complete a course without the military's having to hire additional instructors. A 3-week savings in a 10-week course would allow the military to teach the same course a few more times each year without hiring additional staff. Dallman et al.'s (1977) and Orlansky's (1985) cost savings estimates may then be conservative.

CBI and conventional instruction, however, are not equivalent media for measuring students' training time. Avner, Moore, and Smith's (1980) argument that CBI should be compared to other self-paced individualized instructional media, e.g., programmed texts, is especially relevant for training time data. CBI and other forms of individualized instruction allow the students to proceed at their own pace, while conventional instruction does not.

Mixed results have been found when CBI has been compared to programmed texts. Time savings of approximately 50% for both CBI and programmed texts as compared to conventional instruction have in fact been reported when all three media have simultaneously been tested (Orlansky, 1985). Dallman et al. (1977) cited a study conducted at the Aberdeen Proving Grounds which showed a 10% savings time for CBI when directly compared to programmed texts. Dallman et al. and Hemphill (1986), however, found that students took significantly longer to complete a CBI lesson than to complete an equivalent programmed text lesson. Time savings may then not be ascribable to CBI, but to self-pacing, which characterizes nearly all modern instructional innovations. And programmed texts are usually a fraction of CBI's costs for initial implementation.

Another problem with the CBI literature on time savings is that CMI has been compared to conventional instruction. These time savings effects can only be attributable to differences in instructional management techniques, e.g., time in scoring tests, rather than to instructional attributes inherent in CBI. Evaluators should then test the effects of CMI with other (perhaps less costly) administrative aids. Again, confounded comparisons have been made in measuring time savings associated with CBI.

A third problem with the time savings data is a lack of replicated findings. As stated by Longo (1972):

A paramount notion underlying any research is that of replication. In question, of course, is the matter of reliability of information across time, samples, and conditions. (p. 38)

Without replication and information on reliability, research data have little value. Orlansky's (1985) report on the time savings data does not include any description of studies which were replicated for the same instructional program using the same computer system. Also, inconsistent findings were reported by Orlansky when CBI and conventional instruction were compared for similar instructional situations. For example, time savings for electronic courses associated with CBI were found for Army personnel at the Signal Training School, but not for Navy personnel at San Diego.

Operating Costs

Determining life cycle costs also includes estimating the hidden costs associated with operating a CBI system. Kopstein and Seidel (1969) have identified maintenance and courseware production costs as the major variables in estimating hidden costs.

Hofstetter (1983) noted that the maintenance costs of the PLATO system would be minimal. He estimated the hourly maintenance cost per PLATO system to be 21 cents. This figure is based upon dividing the number of terminals into the money included in the contract for maintenance costs. His calculations do not consider the system's actual reliability.

System reliability is important to measure, because repairing malfunctions will cost additional money in repairing the problem area and in training time losses. Holmes (1982) has indicated that an unreliable system may result in severe loss of instructional time, as faulty equipment may have to be shipped to outside repair centers. A system reliability index—(failures per hour × terminals affected) / (working days by terminals affected) × 100—has been developed by Francis, Welling, and Levy (1983).

Such reliability data for a CBI system must be compared to similar data found for alternative programs (Boldovici & Scott, 1984); otherwise, the data are meaningless. Evaluators should obtain information about delays in conventional instruction due to waiting for teachers. Seidel (1980) has suggested that such information for non-CBI programs has rarely been ascertained.

Seidel (1980) has also suggested that cost comparisons between prototype CBI systems and fully operational educational systems are not a fair test of CBI's potential cost value. CBI evaluations are usually conducted for a prototype or a newly implemented system, such as Francis et al.'s (1983) evaluation. Such evaluations may then not be an accurate assessment of a fully fielded system's reliability and corresponding costs. Evaluations are needed in which reliability data are collected during the initial assessment period and after a few years of operation. Information from these evaluations would help CBI professionals to more clearly understand the discrepancies found in a system's reliability between initial evaluation and actual use.

A related question to system reliability is how long a system can last. Avner's yearly projections for the PLATO system cited at the beginning of the costs section were based upon a 12-year life span. Except for Avner's data, little is known about the average life span for a CBI system. Accurate information about a system's potential life span is needed to better understand the life cycle costs associated with CBI.

Another important consideration in determining cost efficiency is the hourly cost associated with using the instructional medium. Tremendous variation exists in the hourly cost of CBI service. Avner (1982) has noted that PLATO terminal costs can vary, depending on terminal use, software use, and distance from the central computer, from $1.76 per terminal to $10.94 per terminal. Okey and Majer (1976) have noted that CAI costs per student contact hour are $2.07. The $1.76 and $2.07 figures represent nearly continuous and daily use of the system, while the $10.94 figure represents sporadic CBI use. Unfortunately, these figures have no value, because comparisons of hourly costs for using CBI have not been made with those for other media.

Production cost differences between CBI and other instructional media have also rarely been systematically analyzed. Several CBI proponents (e.g., Avner, 1982; Burnside, 1985; Dallman et al., 1977) suggested that long-term production costs might be cheaper for CBI than for other instructional media. Their claims were based on the assumption that updating CBI courseware is relatively easy and inexpensive. Dallman et al. have argued, for example, that PLATO's editing features help to reduce sharply the costs involved in updating and modifying CBI lessons. According to Avner, up-dating PLATO lessons is a function of the quality of the original work and the volatility of the subject matter, with some PLATO lessons needing little modifications after 8 years of continuous use. Another reason for reduced long-term production costs is that the CBI system would allow the same instructional materials to be repeatedly presented throughout the system's lifetime, while some separate programmed texts might have to be created for each student. Very few CBI evaluations have examined the differences in actual expenses and problems with updating the instructional materials for CBI and for other instructional media (Orlansky, 1985).

Initial development costs for a CBI program might be quite expensive. Walker (1984) reported that the developmental costs for a CBI program might range between $2,000 and $100,000 per contract hour. Johnson and Plake (1980) noted that it would have cost the University of Nebraska library over $30,000 to present a 1-hour program to 4,000 students. By contrast, similiar text materials cost a few hundred dollars to produce (Walker, 1984). These expenditures associated with initial courseware development might then negate the previously discussed savings associated with CBI for other production costs.

Himwich (1977) and Stone (1985) have detailed the financial costs involved in developing in-house courseware. Himwich noted that military courseware developers must be formally trained in computer procedures and educational practices. He also found that it took around 230 hours to complete 1 student contact hour of courseware. Stone's developmental team consisted of five Army captains, civilian educational specialists, and outside consultants. These Army personnel also had to take a computer course in order to design this courseware. Himwich's project was aborted because of financial problems, and Stone's team did not meet its goal of completing 100 hours of instructional time by the following year.

Several instructional specialists (e.g., Holmes, 1982; Montague, Wulfeck, & Ellis, 1983) believe that in-house courseware can be developed rapidly and successfully. Holmes has argued that a template system would allow instructors to design CBI courseware in a relatively short space of time and with little knowledge of computer programming. Montague et al. have argued that computer aids can help reduce the time and thus costs involved in producing in-house courseware. The cost effectiveness of such templates and computer aids has rarely been studied.

Avner (Avner, Smith, and Tenczar, 1984) did complete a longitudinal observation of 143 independent production groups. He found that production efficiency was best predicted by: (a) deadline time, (b) using software authoring tools, (c) subject matter expertise, and (d) experience with media and individualized instruction methods. The use of software authoring tools, which can be difficult for the inexperienced programmer, provides the most cost-effective method of improving both production efficiency and quality. Avner et al. gave as an example the use of EnBASIC to meet the needs of most courseware programmers working with the Apple II series computers and those compatible with this series. Other systems, e.g., MICRO-TICCIT, however, dictate that a special authoring language is used. Thus, a successful courseware programmer might have to know several authoring languages or programs for just one type of system.

Avner (1979, 1982) also emphasized the importance of the courseware designers' having previous experience with the medium and the authoring language. Avner (1979) noted that an inexperienced team of courseware designers (less than a year of experience) took between 165 to 610 hours per student contact hour, while highly experienced designers (greater than 2 years of experience) took between 27 to 180 hours per contact hour. He then concluded that:

> Much of the published data (e.g., Stone's) on production costs for CBE, for example, are based on groups with only about a year of working experience with the medium. Such data may grossly overestimate production costs possible in steady-state operations by experienced design teams and underestimate start-up costs (for inexperienced designers). (p. 176)

CBI production costs must then be figured for both "steady-state" and "start-up" costs and be compared with the same costs involved in developing courseware for other media, e.g., device simulators.

Avner (1982) has noted that 430 hours of experience with the TUTOR (PLATO) authoring language is needed for most experienced college teachers to produce their own administrative and pedagogical structures. He also has noted that $1000 is the average cost with a range of $600–$8,000 for an experienced university staff to program an hour's worth of CBI material. This figure may be reduced when authoring tools and computer aids are further refined.

Personnel Costs

Personnel costs usually are determined by estimating the increases and decreases in the number of educational personnel who would accompany implementation of new programs. As previously argued, training time savings could allow the military to train more students without hiring more teachers. Assuming that the yearly expenditures for civilian and military instructors, including benefits, range between $20,000 to $30,000, the resulting cost savings for not hiring teachers could be in the millions of dollars. Also, if CBI is indeed more effective than conventional instruction, then, ultimately, teachers may not need to be the primary instructional medium. Teachers would then only be necessary to tutor poor learners and to monitor operations of the computer system. Again, more students could be taught by fewer teachers.

Burnside (1985) has argued that CBI can reduce the educational support staff. His argument is based upon the expectation made by computer experts (e.g., Baker, 1978) that CBI, especially CMI, can accomplish the administrative tasks usually done by the clerical staff. Dallman et al. (1977) also projected that support staff needs would require minimal expenditures. They estimated spending only

$7,200 a year for support personnel's operational maintenance tasks. This figure was based upon three civilians—a GS-9, GS-7, and GS-5—spending 20% of their time on such problems. Dallman et al.'s projection may be conservative, as maintenance tasks may occupy more of these people's time than anticipated. Also, neither Burnside nor Dallman et al. made any mention of the costs involved in hiring support staff to operate and update the system. Burnside's and Dallman et al.'s estimates may then not reflect all support staff costs. Avner (1982) has noted that the total overhead for support personnel for a civilian 32-terminal PLATO system at an institution is $989 (at 1982 prices) per terminal. (An institution shares their system with a larger 1000 network terminal system.) This figure includes a share of 5 full-time administration positions, 9 full-time maintenance positions, 7 full-time operating positions, and 15 full-time user service positions. Burnside's and Dallman et al.'s position may then not reflect all support staff costs, while Avner's data may be a gross overestimation for a military CBI implementation. Unfortunately, this author could not find any study which provided information about support staff expenditures for implemented CBI systems at a military training site. Nor was any study found which compared differences in support staff needs for CBI with those of other media.

Several sources (e.g., Bellinger, 1986; Shavelson, Winkler, Stasz, Feibel, Robyn & Shaha, 1984a, b; Walker, 1984; Wisher & O'Hara, 1981) have indicated that CBI may not reduce personnel expenditures. Wisher and O'Hara reported that the offline instructor task elements of PREST (Performance-Related Enabling Skills Training) CBI program increased rather than decreased instructor dependence. They also failed to find any significant performance differences between PREST subjects and those who were instructed by conventional courseware. They then concluded that PREST was not as cost efficient as was the conventional system. However, as discussed in the learning achievements section, this study's data may be problematic.

Bellinger (1986), Shavelson et al. (1984a), and Walker (1984) have suggested that personnel costs should also include expenses associated with training teachers to be "computer experts." Shavelson et al. observed that using a CBI system in a typical school necessitated a staff development program which trained teachers to be thoroughly knowledgeable about computers. Walker noted that experience at the Microcomputer Institute for Educators at Stanford University demonstrated that 180 hours of study (8 hours a day for a month) was needed for teachers to use microcomputers properly in the classroom. He has also noted that schools do not have the resources to provide additional in-service training for ever changing computer systems. Clearly, such hidden costs as these teacher training programs must be included in any analyses of CBI's life cycle costs. Of course, possible hidden costs in personnel expenditures for conventional instruction must also be examined.

Conclusions

Any claims about the comparative costs of CBI and other educational media are premature. As discussed, current estimates for CBI expenditures may be too high or too low, and very few studies have actually compared the cost effectiveness of a CBI system with other media. Claims about the cost savings associated with using a CBI system may also be premature. Training time savings may not be attributable to this medium, but to self-pacing, which characterizes any individualized instructional program. Conclusions about training time reductions and CBI are also problematic, because information is not readily available about the reliability of these data. Also, the cost savings in personnel expenditures associated with CBI have not been demonstrated.

The following methodological concerns must then be incorporated in future cost comparisons. If training time is the important criterion measure, then CBI must be compared with other self-paced instructional systems. Also, information about costs must be gathered for implemented systems. Seidel (1980) has noted that reliable and meaningful cost information will only be obtained when the innovation is in a stable, operational state. All potential costs for CBI and the alternative medium must also be identified and examined. Cost analyses must be done for each CBI implementation. As Avner (1978) stated, "Just because 20 prestigious researchers found CBE to be cost-effective in their application does not mean it will automatically be cost-effective in yours" (p. 25).

LEARNING ACHIEVEMENTS

As previously indicated, a major assumption behind implementing CBI is this medium's positive impact upon students' learning processes. Many CBI professionals (e.g., Bangert-Drowns, Kulik, & Kulik, 1985; Eberts & Brock, 1984; Fletcher & Rockway, 1986; Kearsley et al., 1983; Kulik, Kulik, & Cohen, 1980; Robinson & Kirk, 1984; Suppes & Morningstar, 1969) have indicated that CBI has led or will lead to the development of superior instructional materials. Kearsley et al. stated that "we (CBI professionals) have ample evidence that computers can be used to make instruction more effective or efficient in a variety of ways" (p. 14).

Critics of CBI research (e.g., Clark, 1985a, b; Reinking, 1985) have questioned the evidence of CBI's instructional superiority. Reinking noted that comparisons between CBI and alternative media have produced inconsistent findings. These critics have also questioned the implied assumption that CBI is an inherently superior instructional medium.

An examination of the CBI training studies is thus needed to help resolve this dispute. Existent training studies have usually compared differences between CBI students and conventional instruction students with regard to test performance and course completion. This latter measure concerns the number of students completing the course. Such studies have been referred to as outcome studies (Kulik, Kulik, & Bangert-Drowns, 1985). Analysis is also needed of CBI's relative efficiency for facilitating students' transfer. Finally, specific CBI features affecting students' learning will also be discussed.

Outcome Studies

Fletcher and Rockway (1986) have suggested that CBI is an efficient instructional medium for military training purposes. They cited evaluations conducted by each service demonstrating CBI's potential effectiveness. An evaluation of a CBI program for an Army Signal Training Course showed that the CBI group achieved higher test scores and less attrition than did the control group (Longo, 1972).

Orlansky (1985) and Orlansky and String (1981) have provided evidence challenging CBI's instructional effectiveness for military training. Learning achievement was found to be about the same for the CBI and conventional instruction students in 32 of the 48 military cases reviewed by Orlansky and String. Fifteen of these studies reported a slightly superior learning achievement for the CBI programs, while one study reported a slightly poorer achievement for the CBI group.

Francis et al. (1983) provided another example of the inconsistency found in CBI results. They conducted two studies of CBI's effectiveness for training at the U.S. Army Missile and Munitions Center and School. PLATO simulators were found to be an effective and efficient instrucitonal medium for the TOW (missile) Field Test Site Training Course. Data analyses failed, however, to find any differences between PLATO students' and non-PLATO students' test results for the HAWK Continuous Wave Radar Repair Training Course.

Montague (1984) and Orlansky (1983) claimed that consistent evidence has been found in the civilian training literature for CBI's effectiveness. This conclusion is based upon a series of meta-analyses (Banger-Drowns et al., 1985; Kulik, Bangert, & Williams, 1983; Kulik et al., 1980) showing noticeable effects for CBI upon students' test scores. Bangert-Drowns et al. found that exam scores for secondary school students in a CBI program were .4 standard deviations higher than were the scores reported for the conventional instruction students. This finding suggested that CBI was moderately more effective than were the conventional instruction programs.

Inconsistent data for CBI's effectiveness are also found in the civilian training literature. A close examination of Kulik et al.'s (1980) data has indicated that only one quarter of the 54 studies sited found large or medium positive effects for CBI upon college students' exam performance. Alderman, Appel, and Murphy's (1978) often cited evaluation of PLATO's and TICCIT's effectiveness for community college students also found inconsistent results. The TICCIT programs had a significantly positive impact upon students' math achievement. However, significantly fewer students completed the math course for the TICCIT program than completed the conventional instruction program. No significant differences were found between PLATO and conventional instruction students' test scores and completion rates. These inconsistent findings may be due to several factors, such as courseware differences or problematic research practices.

Methodological Criticisms

Clark and his associates (Clark, 1983, 1985a,b; Clark & Leonard, 1985; Clark & Salomon, 1985) have suggested that the cited inconsistent findings in the CBI literature are due to problematic research practices. They have suggested that CBI has only been shown to be more effective than conventional instructional programs when confounded comparisons have been made between CBI and other media. They have also indicated that such confounded comparisons are prevalent in the CBI effectiveness literature. Clark and Leonard noted that 75% of the studies which were randomly selected for their review had serious design flaws. And Clark (1985b) has noted that the most probable source of confounding in CBI research has been that different instructional treatments were employed in the computer and control conditions.

Failure to match instructional content is a common problem in the CBI literature. Alderman's (1974) plans for these evaluations of TICCIT and PLATO described methods for comparing students' achievement for dissimilar instructional materials. He has claimed that such comparisons can be made when substantial overlap exists between objectives for the different courses. Some CBI studies, e.g., Wisher and O'Hara (1981) and those cited by Fletcher and Rockway (1986) may have indeed compared similar objectives with substantially different instructional content. The CBI and conventional instruction programs in Wisher and O'Hara's study were designed to remedy reading problems. The CBI program consisted of 11 reading modules within the Basic Skills Learning System devised by the Control Data Corporation, while the conventional classroom instruction included reading materials created by Memphis State University. The similarity of the instructional content for these two reading programs was never discussed. Wisher and O'Hara's inability to find significant differences between programs might be due to differences in instructional content. Conversely, the effects for CBI reported by Alderman et al. (1978) and Fletcher and Rockway might have been attributed to presenting different content and not to any features inherent in the CBI program.

Morrison and Witmer's (1983) comparative evalution of computer-based and print-based job aids for a military maintenance task is one of the few CBI studies which have matched instructional content. They made a special effort to make the wording and format of the two programs identical. These two programs did differ in that the computer-based program used a branching instructional format while the print-based program used a linear model. Given these differences, the positive effects found for the computer-based program might be due either to the medium or the branching sequence.

Comparing similar instructional materials also requires that identical efforts be made in designing the courseware. Clark (1984, 1985a) discussed the possible confounding in CBI research due to differences in designing the courseware for CBI and conventional instruction. The most powerful extraneous factor which CBI studies rarely control for is that a greater effort has been made to design the CBI presentation than that required for the comparative media involved (Clark, 1984). Clark does not, however, provide any evidence that instructional effort differences do exist or effect CBI research.

Evidence does exist that some CBI program development has involved considerable design effort. As previously stated, developing CBI courseware involves considerable time and effort. Also, some CBI programs (e.g., PLATO's and TICCIT's) were designed by some of the finest educational specialists. Bunderson (1981) noted that the prototype TICCIT courseware was primarily a function of the analytical theorems and artistic talents of the courseware development team at Brigham Young University, with some help from the community college teachers. The Brigham Young staff did not help with the development of any of the conventional instruction courseware used in this evaluation. One would expect that efforts associated with the classroom instruction design did not approach the efforts involved in the TICCIT courseware development.

Several CBI professionals (e.g., Gray, Pliske, & Psotka, 1985; Montague & Wulfeck, 1984; Walker, 1984) challenged the assumption that considerable effort was spent developing most current CBI courseware. In fact, Gray et al. have suggested that most current CBI courseware is underdeveloped. Walker has contended that there is a lack of quality CBI courseware. Furthermore, Stone's (1985) and Himwich's (1977) developmental teams may have spent the majority of their time on programming and not on courseware designing. Clark's (1984, 1985a) claims about confounding due to instructional efforts differences may not be totally valid, but this potential confounding must be examined in future CBI studies.

Clark and Leonard (1985) described another type of confounding associated with not matching instructional content. After reviewing 42 randomly selected civilian CBI programs, they found that CBI subjects received more instruction in completing the lessons than did the control subjects. One example provided by Clark and Leonard is a study in which CBI groups have received as much as 8 minutes more of drill-and-practice time than have the conventional instruction groups. Practice effects, rather than the medium, may have influenced the achievement gains found for the CBI students. The extent to which such additional instructional time is a problem depends, of course, on the amount of instruction observed to the amount intended by a system's designer. But the need for special instructor prompting undermines CBI's promise to reduce costs by reducing instructional personnel. Unwarranted instruction, such as additional prompting, should then be another variable measured in CBI research.

Using CBI to supplement the instructional program is another issue associated with additional instruction. Several studies (e.g., Dengler, 1983; Jelden, 1985; Mevarech & Rich, 1985) have indicated that CBI is effective when used with a conventional instruction program. Most of these studies, however, did not include a comparative group receiving either a similar amount of conventional instructional time or conventional instruction with another educational medium.

Clark (1983, 1985a) and Clark & Salomon (1985) have argued that "novelty effects" may also confound CBI research findings. They claimed that the positive instructional effects found for CBI in the previously cited meta-analyses were due to students' initial motivation and enthusiasm to learn novel courseware, rather than to any characteristics inherent in the CBI system. Clark (1985a) has shown that CBI effectiveness may be very different for long- and short-term studies. Clark noted from Kulik et al.'s (1983) data that secondary school students' achievement scores were .56 standard deviations higher for CBI groups than for conventional instruction groups when the studies lasted 4 weeks or less. Differences between groups' performance reduced to .30 for studies lasting 5 to 8 weeks, and to .20 for studies lasting more than 8 weeks.

Kulik et al. (1985) argued that "novelty effects" were not pervasive in CBI research. They reported that CBI raised students' achievement scores by .26 standard deviations in the typical long-term evaluation study, and by .34 standard deviations in the typical short-term study. These differences in standard deviations are not statistically significant. Another problem with Kulik et al.'s findings was that short- and long-term evaluations were not defined by Kulik et al. Using Kulik et al.'s data to refute the notion of "novelty effects" may then not be valid. Clark (1985b) conceded, however, that "novelty effects," were not significant detractors from the validity of CBI studies. The issue of novelty effects will be further explored in the section on student attitudes.

Duration problems may exist for military training studies. Orlansky (1985) and Orlansky and String (1983) both noted that half of all CBI military courses lasted 1 week or less. Some studies (e.g., Francis et al.'s, 1983) involved limited comparisons only for particular course segments. Since most military training lasts for a few months, evalutions of less than a week's duration or evaluations of only a few instructional segments are not sufficient for making equivalent comparisons between CBI and other modes of instruction. These limited durations for CBI military studies may work against the possibility of finding significant differences between CBI groups and control groups.

Other criticisms of outcome studies include points made about the cost studies. For one thing, existent outcome studies rarely involved an implemented system. Several CBI researchers (e.g., Montague & Wulfeck, 1984; Gray, 1986) have argued that quality CBI programs involve quality implementation. And Bunderson (1981) noted that the TICCIT courseware used in the Alderman et al. (1978) evaluation was not completely debugged. Outcome studies using prototype systems may then provide inaccurate estimates of CBI's instructional impact.

Outcome studies have also rarely been replicated and have rarely involved comparisons with other individualized instructional media. Questions then exist about the stability of these studies' results. Any effects found for CBI may, then, not be due to the media but rather to attributes inherent in individualized instruction.

Transfer Studies

Evaluating CBI's instructional value also involves determining whether a system is being used correctly. Avner (1978) has observed that the correct usage of the medium is more important than the fact that it works. Correct usage of any educational system involves helping students make the necessary transfer of information to the appropriate environmental situations.

Controversy exists in the CBI literature regarding this medium's effectiveness for facilitating transfer. Many CBI researchers and developers (e.g., Gleason, 1981; Kern, 1985; McLaughlin, 1985; Montague, 1984; Reigeluth & Garfield, 1984; Salomon, 1979) have suggested that CBI would help develop the learning processes needed for successful transfer. For one thing, McLaughlin has indicated that the computer is ideally suited for developing both procedural and declarative level knowledge. Procedural level knowledge is a basic understanding of the steps involved in completing a task, while declarative level knowledge involves an understanding of the principles and concepts associated with that task (Clark & Voogel, 1985). According to McLaughlin, CBI courseware should then augment the students' ability to make basic procedural level transfer—e.g., following a technical manual to troubleshoot an armor system. CBI will also help students with cognitive transfer—e.g., understanding the principles behind the repair.

CBI proponents also believe that this medium would help students to develop the memory skills needed for long-term transfer. One reason for this belief is that drill-and-practice programs would enable students to rehearse the information continuously. Continuous rehearsal is a primary way of storing information into memory (Landhauer, 1982). Also, many computer professionals and behavioral scientists (e.g., Bunderson, 1981; Kosslyn, 1981; Merrill, Schneider, & Fletcher, 1980; Olson & Bruner, 1974; Salomon & Gardner, 1986) have suggested that active learning and dual-modality processing are associated with computer instruction. Active learning and dual-modality processing can help facilitate deep cognitive processing of information. And information processed into deep cognitive levels is resistant to forgetting (Craik & Lockhart, 1972). These elements of drill-and-practice, active learning, and dual-modality processing often found in CBI programs would then seem to facilitate a more permanent transfer of information than would be offered by other instructional media.

Clark and his associates (Clark & Salomon, 1985; Clark & Voogel, 1985) challenged the assumption that CBI would augment students' transfer abilities. Clark and Voogel have suggested that current CBI courseware is geared toward helping students to make procedural-level transfer but not cognitive-level transfer. Bialo and Erickson (1984), after evaluating the courseware for 163 microcomputer programs, found that 70% of the courseware dealt solely with procedural-level objectives. Clark and associates correspondingly have indicated that CBI has minimal influence upon students' long-term transfer and memory processes. Cognitive effects cited to be associated with CBI, e.g., deeper processing of information, are not necessarily unique to this medium (Clark & Salomon, 1985).

Limited research evidence has been collected about CBI's potential effectiveness for facilitating either cognitive processes or transfer. Gleason (1981), McDonald and Crawford (1983), and Tatsuoka and Misselt (1978) have suggested that retention following CBI training is substantial. As stated by Gleason: "retention following CAI is at least as good if not superior to retention following conventional instruction" (p. 16). Nevertheless, Gleason does not provide any data to verify this claim. Furthermore, McDonald and Crawford failed to compare the retention obtained by CBI's subjects with a control group's retention performance, and Tatsuoka and Misselt's findings seem to be an artifact of the lesson's being inadvertently repeated because of hardware problems.

Several other reports (e.g., Swezey, Criswell, Huggins, Hays, & Allen, in press; Swezey, Huggins, & Perez, in press; Pagliaro, 1983) failed to find any significant effects for CBI upon either subjects' transfer or retention performance. Pagliaro found that pharmacology students' retention performance was the same for both CBI and conventional instruction training. Swezey, Criswell et al. found that practice on a 3-D module component was more instrumental than were the instructional media (CAI, CRT, or videotape) in facilitating military students' transfer on a simple engine repair procedural task. The same results were replicated by Swezey, Huggins, and Perez (in press) for a complex procedural task.

Personal experience has indicated that incidental learning is an important part of conventional instruction. Students, for instance, in an educational psychology class may incidentally learn from the teacher's mannerisms and class discussions teaching techniques which may last a lifetime. Incidental learning is another aspect of transfer which has rarely been examined. Such incidental learning may indeed not be possible with CBI because of programming limitations. In this case, the spontaneity and richness found in classroom environments may not be completely duplicated. Limitations in this medium may then be limiting the courseware, and the courseware not limiting the medium as previously indicated. However, some important incidental learning may be occurring in CBI which evaluators are not measuring. For instance, a CBI military training course on maintenance may also help the students to become better readers. Even though measuring incidental learning is difficult, information is needed about CBI's impact upon such learning. As noted by Reeves and Lent (1982), "The sponsors and consumers of CBI should be informed as much as possible about the ultimate effects of this medium when they make decisions about continuance, expansion, or selection" (p. 13).

Human Factors and Effectiveness

Sawyer (1985) noted the importance of examining human factors issues in CBI evaluations. According to Sawyer, evaluating human factors issues involves examining the effects of a system's hardware and documentation upon students' performance.

Kearsley et al. (1983) have claimed that a CBI system's response time and downtime are important factors in the success of a CBI project. These dimensions may affect users' mastery of the instructional information. Tatsuoka and Misselt (1978) noted that mechanical failures with the PLATO system had negatively affected U.S. Air Force students' learning efficiency. Also, noted educational experts not in the CBI field have stressed the importance of measuring the relationship between educational productivity and a medium's downtime. Gump (1985) suggested, for example, that a downtime of 10% in a conventional instruction program could equal an instructional efficiency loss of 10% or more. Comparisons between CBI and other instructional media should examine potential instructional loss due to "downtime" problems.

The civilian computer literature (e.g., Chapanis, 1985; Card, English, & Burr, 1978; Phillips et al., 1984; Reigeluth & Garfield, 1984) has discussed the impact that certain computer hardware features have upon users' performance. Card et al. found significant differences in subjects' abilities to use four common computer responding mechanisms—a mouse, a joystick, step keys, and text keys—with the mouse leading in the best results (see Card et al. for a description of these devices). Chapanis noted that people were normally able to read materials presented on a hard copy 30% more efficiently then when they were presented on a CRT. Phillips et al. reported that problems with screen visibility on CRT's impeded the educational performance of secondary school students. They also found that awkwardly designed keyboards and terminals poorly placed in classrooms led to educational problems.

Documentation problems may also adversely affect CBI's educational potential. One cannot fully understand nor use any instructional program without adequate source materials. Bialo and Erickson (1984) found the documentation to be barely adequate for most of the 163 microcomputer systems reviewed, and information about instructional materials was absent or inadequate for 62% of these programs. Chapanis (1965, 1985) also found documentation materials for computers to be inadequate. He has also shown that reading a system's documentation requires the reader to be familiar with normal computer jargon and the particular system's jargon.

Conclusions

Inconsistent findings have been obtained about CBI's potential impact upon students' learning, and positive instructional effects found for CBI might be traceable to factors other than the medium. Most pronounced among these nonmedium effects were practice differences and instructional content differences between the CBI treatment and that of the comparative medium. Assumptions about computers making instruction more effective have thus not been validated. Human factors and courseware problems, however, may limit the computer's potential effectiveness, especially for facilitating cognitive skills. A basic unresolved question in CBI research is whether possible problems with CBI are due to such courseware and human factors limitations or to the limitations of the medium.

Also, CBI researchers need to obtain more conclusive data on the long-term effects of CBI. A primary function of any educational program is to insure that long-term changes occur within the students.

CBI AND INDIVIDUAL DIFFERENCES

Handling individual learning differences has long been a difficult problem for educators. Many CBI professionals (e.g., Avner et al., 1980; Carrier, 1979; Kearsley et al., 1983; Merrill et al., 1980; Steinberg, 1984) believe that this medium is ideally suited to handle individual learning differences. As stated by Carrier, "To many educators, the computer represents the ultimate individual difference machine" (p. 25).

CBI's superiority over other media would then be most pronounced for meeting the educational needs of all students. Arguments supporting this position have come from CBI reports on learner control mechanisms and cognitive differences. Reports by Carroll (1984), Hess and Miura (1985), and Wood and Pitz (1985) have suggested, however, that some students may have problems learning from a CBI program.

Learner Control Mechanisms

A basic belief held by many educators is that students should be encouraged to make educational choices for themselves (Carrier, Davidson, Higgson, & Williams, 1984). Such choices would enable students to process the instructional material more actively. As previously indicated, such active learning would lead to superior learning. Learner control is also expected to help educators deal with individual learning differences. Gay (1985) has noted that:

> It is commonly assumed that individual differences in abilities and aptitudes will be accommodated if learners have more control over the pace, amount of practice, or style of instructions they receive. (p. 1)

CBI designers have developed learner control mechanisms which provide students with some degree of freedom in selecting the instructional materials to study. TICCIT students, for example, can select through a special keyboard the display best suited to their educational needs (Merrill et al., 1980). Merrill et al. have also claimed that this learner control mechanism differentiates TICCIT from other instructional media, including PLATO and some other CBI systems.

Some research evidence (e.g., Collier, Poynor, O'Neill, & Judd, 1973; Fishman, 1985; Hansen, 1972) exists supporting the use of learner control mechanisms for accommodating individual learning differences. Hansen found that subjects who used learner control mechanisms exhibited less state anxiety than did control subjects. Collier et al. also found reduced anxiety levels to be associated with using learner control mechanisms. Increased learning usually occurs when extreme anxiety toward the instructional material is reduced. And Fishman observed that learner control mechanisms allowed students to have the additional practice needed to most effectively master the material. She found that learner control students outperformed students who received instruction from lecture and video presentations. Perhaps then, learner control mechanisms can make CBI a unique and superior instructional medium.

Several reports (e.g., Ford, Slough, & Hurlock, 1972; Gay, 1985; Judd, Daubek, & O'Neil, 1975; Snow, 1980; Steinberg, 1977; Tennyson & Buttrey, 1980), however, have challenged the previously cited research about the instructional effectiveness of learner control features. Steinberg, in a comprehensive review of this literature, concluded that students given complete control over course flow (experimental students) took longer to complete the course than did control students. Also, experimental and control students scored equally well on achievement tests. Ford et al. did not find any improvements in Navy students' learning in the Basic Electricity and Electronics School associated with using learner control mechanisms. Tennyson and Buttrey noted that, when students controlled the instructional process, they often terminated the process too early and did not effectively learn the materials. Judd et al. furthermore concluded that a complex interaction existed between subjects' abilities to use learner control mechanisms and the subjects' personalities. Students with high Achievement-Independence scores— as measured by the California Psychological Inventory—were the students most able to use the learner control features.

Gay (1985) found that learner control mechanisms did not accommodate individual background differences. Subjects with high prior conceptual understanding of the material made significantly better use of these control options than did subjects with poor prior understanding. Reinking (1983) and Carrier et al. (1984) also found that control options did not accommodate individual learning differences. Reinking found that the use of learner control options did not improve poor readers' level of reading. All students may then not be able to use and benefit from learner control options.

Cognitive Differences

If CBI's instructional impact was not found for the learner control issue, it might then be discovered by examining the literature on cognitive differences. Many reports (Allen & Merrill, 1985; Bangert-

Drowns et al., 1985; Farr, 1985; Gray et al., 1985; Neimiec & Walberg, 1985; Zemke, 1984) have suggested that the main reason for selecting a CBI system is to better deal with differences in cognitive abilities and styles.

Most studies concerning disadvantaged learners have used highly structured drill-and-practice programs (see such projects as Cleveland Public Schools, 1981; Mevarech & Rich, 1985). Such courseware seemed to provide slow students with the needed additional structure of and practice with the materials. As Bangert-Drowns et al. discovered, CBI has a greater effect upon increasing low ability students' test scores than for any other usage. The meta-analysis comparison between CBI and conventional instruction revealed an effect size of .46 in favor of CBI for teaching low ability subjects. Zemke (1984) also observed that low achievers seemed to gain a great deal from CBI.

Problems do exist with selecting a CBI program based on this literature. Mevarech and Rich (1985), Bass, Ries, and Sharpe (1986) and Zemke (1984) noted that CBI programs were most effective when used to supplement classroom instruction. As stated in the learning achievements section, many of these supplemental studies did not include a comparative control group. Improvements in disadvantaged students' learning could have been produced by using any instructional medium to supplement the conventional instruction program.

Drill-and-practice programs might not be useful for all subjects. Such courseware might be too structured and limited for most students, especially gifted students. B. Clark (1983) has concluded that gifted students need tasks which allow them the freedom to proceed beyond a rudimentary rehashing of the materials. Since drill-and-practice programs dominate the market, most current CBI programs may have limited value for gifted students.

Data from a study conducted by Barsam and Simutis (1984) provided some insight into courseware which might be geared toward certain kinds of gifted students. This study explored the relationships between individual differences in spatial abilities and soldiers' performance on a CBI terrain visualization task consisting of three-dimensional graphics. This study also examined differences in soldiers' abilities to benefit from courseware which utilized active (subjects select the graphic for viewing) vs. passive (computer selects the graphic for the subjects' viewing) training procedures. They found that the high spatial ability subjects were better able to complete the lesson successfully and benefit from the active training procedures than were soldiers with normal or low spatial abilities.

The high spatial ability students seemed to have learner characteristics similar to "field-independent" students (Witkin, Goodenough, & Karp, 1967), who are usually the high achievers in math and science courses. (See Witkin, Moore, Goodenough, & Cox, 1977), for a further description of the relationship between field independence and math/science aptitudes). Field-independent students are also quite analytical in viewing three-dimensional objects, and can also benefit from self-structuring the instructional environment. Correspondingly, then, students with mathematical and scientific aptitudes would be the most likely to handle successfully CBI lessons, e.g., simulation programs, with numerous complex graphics. These last few paragraphs thus suggest that: (a) the basic drill-and-practice CBI programs favor the more problematic learners, while (b) the advanced CBI simulation courseware is geared toward the more "gifted students," especially in mathematics and science.

Variability in students' abilities to use different types of CBI programs should then relate to cognitive style differences. Witkin et al. (1977) claimed that individual differences among the field independence/dependence continuum reflected basic differences in people's characteristic styles of dealing with the environment. This continuum does not differentiate students with different I.Q. levels— but it does differentiate students with different modes of handling instructional materials. Field-dependent people rely on external sources, e.g., teachers, to structure and help them understand the complex perceptual and abstract stimuli, e.g., computer graphics, while field-independent people do not need such external aids. And, as previously indicated, field-independent people are better able to more effectively use the information inherent in such situations. Witkin et al. have also observed that instructional situations with explicit instructions, a concrete presentation of stimuli, and explicit information about performance outcome favor field-dependent students. Field-independent students are better able to perform more abstract and less structured tasks. One would then expect that drill-and-practice CBI programs with structured instructional sequencing and continuous performance feedback would be the most appropriate for field-dependent people. CBI programs with complex graphics and learner control features—as described in the previous paragraphs—would be more geared toward field-independent people.

Limited and contradictory evidence exists about the actual relationship between current CBI programs and cognitive styles. Carrier et al. (1984) and Park and Roberts (1985) found data which indicated differences—as expected—in CBI performance associated with cognitive style differences. Park and Roberts found that field-dependent people did need more guided instruction to complete a set of CBI lessons than did field-independent people. Carrier et al., however, did not find differences between field-independent and field-dependent subjects in their use of control options. Burger (1985) did not find any significant relationships between students' cognitive styles and CBI preference and performance.

The instructional system's adaptability to students' cognitive styles is a major issue addressed by Witkin et al. Indeed, they emphasized the need for the educational medium to match the learners' cognitive styles. Several CBI professionals (e.g., Kearsley et al., 1983; Olsem, personal communication, October, 1985; Tennyson, Christensen, & Park, 1984) have suggested that the new generations of CBI systems with intelligent programs (ICBI) can make the instructional system adaptable to students' learning styles. Olsem has claimed that these ICBIs have the capacity to modify the instructional mode to best meet the students' learning profiles. These learning profiles are determined by cognitive tests embedded in the first phase of the ICBI's instructional program.

ICBIs can also be used for accommodating students with different cognitive abilities (Allen & Merrill, 1985; Gray et al., 1985). Intelligent programs involve interactions between students and the computer so that the type of feedback and instructional materials provided fit the student's level of knowledge (Gray et al., 1985). They have also claimed that the promise of this technology is that each student's unique cognitive needs will be met.

Adaptive control programs have also been shown to be effective for dealing with learning differences (Ross, 1984; Tennyson & Buttrey, 1980). Adaptive control occurs when the amount of instruction is managed by the CAI program based upon students' achievement level, aptitude, or cognitive style (Carrier et al., 1984). Ross has shown that such a program can accommodate individual learning differences. Furthermore, Avner et al. (1980) have claimed that adaptive control programs represent the real basis for CBI's superiority. CMI is another adaptive control mechanism which is seemingly suitable for accommodating individual differences (Baker, 1978; Federico, 1983; Kearsley et al., 1983). CMI can be used to advise students and teachers about the most appropriate instructional sequence for each student. Federico showed that, for Navy trainees, CMI programs reduced the learning variability usually associated with cognitive differences. ICBIs with adaptive control mechanisms may be the most effective ways of using this medium to accommodate individual learning differences.

The supportive research for ICBIs and adaptive control mechanisms may be problematic. Research on ICBIs has involved experiments of short duration which have rarely compared CBI to other media. These studies have also mainly investigated ICBI programs in laboratory-type settings. Questions thus remain about the relative effectiveness of ICBI programs for educational settings. And Ross (1984) has demonstrated only limited advantages for CMI over other media for dealing with learning differences. CMI was only found to be advantageous for complicated and lengthy lessons.

Individual Differences and CBI Limitations

As discussed previously, CBI may not be beneficial to all students. Several investigators (e.g., Cambre & Cook, 1985; Jay, 1981; Loyd & Gressard, 1984a,b; Maurer, 1983; Wood and Pitz, 1985) have found that computer anxiety can inhibit a person's ability to master computer skills successfully; consequently, such anxiety may inhibit a student's mastery of information from a CBI system. As discussed by Cambre and Cook (1985), the following four behaviors are associated with computer anxiety (p. 52):

1. Avoidance of the computer and general area where the computer is located.
2. Excessive caution with the computer.
3. Negative remarks about the computer.
4. Attempts to cut the computer session short.

The existence of and problems associated with computer anxiety have not been systematically investigated. Loyd and Gressard (1984b) have attempted to rectify this problem in the CBI literature by devising a self-report questionnaire which measures these cited dimensions of computer anxiety. They have claimed that this questionnaire provides an effective, reliable, and convenient measure of students' computer anxiety. Wood and Pitz (1985), however, have suggested that any self-report questionnaire on computer anxiety (e.g., Loyd and Gressard's) without scales for lying and social desirability may not be a valid measure, because subjects' stated expectations about using a computer are not always congruent with their actual computer behaviors. Personal experience has also demonstrated that people may be reluctant to state their fears of using a computer.

A reliable and valid questionnaire on computer anxiety would be beneficial to both educators and researchers. Such a questionnaire would provide additional insights into explaining possible variability in students' abilities to use CBI materials. This scale would also, then, help educators to pinpoint those students who need additional support and guidance in using this medium. Schubert (1985), for example, found that computer-anxious females had to go through a formal desensitization process before they were able to deal with the CBI materials. Consequently, the educational, temporal, and financial costs associated with helping such computer-anxious students should also be included in any evaluation of a CBI system.

Differences in computer experience may also differentially affect students' use of CBI materials. Carroll and his associates (e.g., Carroll, 1984; Carroll & Mazur, 1984; Carroll & Thomas, 1982) have noted that infrequent computer users often have difficulty in learning to use a computer system. They also suggested that embedded instructions for using a computer must relate to students' prior computer use and knowledge. CBI professionals must then consider both novice and experienced computer populations when designing and evaluating a CBI system. If the system cannot accommodate all levels of users, then a segment of students, especially the infrequent users, will not be able to use and benefit from the CBI system. There also may be extreme variability in subjects' training time on a CBI system, with infrequent users proceeding much more slowly than regular and frequent users. Such variability may then negate CBI's previously cited potential for reducing instructional time.

Computer experience may also relate to computer anxiety (Loyd & Gressard 1984a; King, 1975). Even though the data may be problematic, Loyd & Gressard did find a significant relationship between infrequent computer use and computer anxiety. If this is so, then computer-experienced users would likely be excited and motivated to use a novel CBI program, while nonexperienced users might be apprehensive about using such a program. This novelty issue will be further discussed in the section on student attitudes.

Hess and his associates (e.g., Hess & Miura, 1985; Hess & Tenezakis, 1973; Miura & Hess, 1983; Schubert, 1985) have indicated that there are sex differences associated with students' use of computers. Miura and Hess have found that middle-school boys, more than girls, (a) owned and used home computers, and (b) enrolled in computer camps and summer classes. They also asked these students to rate a number of randomly selected courseware titles as being either male or female-oriented. These students rated a significantly larger number of courseware titles to be primarily suited for male audiences and not for female audiences. Other studies, e.g., Loyd and Gressard (1984a), however, did not find gender differences to be significantly related to computer use or anxiety.

Conclusions

CBI's potential as the "ultimate individual difference machine" has not been substantiated. Even though this potential may become more evident for future CBI generations, research on current CBI programs and individual differences is problematic, with confounded and contradictory findings. Finally, the educational and financial costs associated with helping students, especially computer-anxious students, to use a CBI program successfully must also be included in a system's cost analysis.

CBI AND STUDENT ATTITUDES

The most seemingly pervasive finding in the CBI literature is that students favor taking a course by this medium. Many reports (e.g., Clement, 1981; Merrill, et al., 1980; Meyers, 1984) have urged implementation of CBI because of such student attitudes. Meyers noted that PLATO has been enthusiastically accepted by students and teachers. Also, advertisements on CBI products have claimed that a particular CBI product would facilitate a learner's motivation because this system was easy and fun to use. The implied assumption, then, is that students will be more motivated to learn from a CBI system than from any other instructional system.

As the research on students' CBI attitudinal data has rarely been examined, the robustness of the data about students' attitudes toward CBI as compared to their attitudes toward other media must then be analyzed. This analysis must also include examining the psychometric attributes of the different attitudinal measures used in these studies. In this section, factors influencing students' CBI views will also be discussed.

Attitudinal Studies

Comparisons of students' attitudes toward CBI and other media have been included in some of the previously cited military studies (e.g., Dallman et al., 1977; Ford et al., 1972; Longo, 1972; Tatsuoka & Misselt, 1978). These studies indicated that students favored taking a course by CBI than by other media. Longo, for example, found in two separate studies more positive ratings being exhibited by the CBI group than by the conventional instruction group.

Dallman et al. (1977) also reported that students tended to favor taking a CBI course rather than a conventional instruction course.

They noted, however, that the conventional instruction course was taught by newly trained teachers. They also found that a conventional instruction course taught by a popular teacher was more favorably received than was CBI. In a second study, they failed to find any significant differences between students' attitudes toward CBI and toward programmed instruction.

Mixed results about students' preference for CBI over other instructional media were the pattern for the civilian literature. Avner and associates (Avner, 1981; Jones, Kane, Sherwood, & Avner, 1983), in a series of course evaluations, found that University of Illinois students favored PLATO over other instructional media. For two semesters, Chemistry 100 students were asked to rate several different media with regard to helpfulness in learning the class materials. These media were PLATO, textbook, lecture, labs, and quiz sections. The main professor for this course had received several outstanding teaching honors. For both semesters, the PLATO system received the highest rating—4.5 on a 5-point scale. Differences between ratings for CBI and conventional instruction were substantial—over a point difference on a 5-point scale. Differences in students' ratings of CBI and Quiz section were .9 and .4 for the Fall 1977 and Spring 1978 semesters, respectively. These course evaluations and Dallman et al.'s study are some of the few studies in which students' attitudes toward CBI were compared with their attitudes toward other nonconventional modes of instruction.

Bangert-Drowns et al. (1985) and Kulik et al. (1980) demonstrated limited support for the assumption that students preferred CBI. Both meta-analyses could only find a few studies—11 for the Bangert et al. analysis, and 5 for the Kulik et al. analysis—which compared attitudes toward CBI with attitudes toward conventional instruction. Bangert et al. found an average effect of .09 for CBI upon secondary students' attitudes, and Kulik et al. discovered an effect of .18 favoring CBI for college instruction.

Problems with concluding that students prefer to take a CBI rather than a conventional instruction course are vividly demonstrated by Alderman et al.'s (1978) findings. A large percentage of PLATO students indicated positive feelings toward this courseware, as manifested by their desire to take another course using this system. They also disagreed that using PLATO was dehumanizing or boring. Attitudinal comparisons between PLATO and conventional instruction students, however, failed to reveal any noticeable differences in these students' feelings toward their classes. Alderman et al. also found that student reaction to TICCIT was favorable; however, the attitudinal results for the TICCIT program were usually less positive than those for the conventional instruction program. Interestingly enough, this study has been widely cited as providing evidence that CBI has a positive impact upon students' attitudes.

Magidson's (1978) study is also widely cited as demonstrating that students prefer to take a CBI course. Magidson's results about PLATO users' views parallel those found by Alderman et al. Over 90% of these students enjoyed using PLATO and would recommend that their friends take a PLATO-based course. He also reported that less than 10% of these students found PLATO to be boring and dehumanizing. Attitudinal comparisons between PLATO and conventional instruction students were not made.

Conclusions cannot then be made about students' preference for CBI over other instructional media based upon Alderman et al.'s and Magidson's studies. As indicated, the previously discussed assumptions about students' desires for CBI courseware have been based on these two studies with problematic data and others (e.g., Dengler, 1983; Jenkins & Dankert, 1981) which obtained parallel results using similar methodologies. Nonetheless, these studies do suggest that students would accept taking a course by CBI.

Alderman et al.'s (1978) and Magidson's (1978) findings have also suggested that students do not believe that CBI is dehumanizing as an educational experience. King (1975) provided more substantial evidence for this point about CBI and the possible dehumanization threat. After thoroughly reviewing the military and civilian CBI literature on student attitudes, King concluded that CBI was not a dehumanizing instructional experience.

King (1975) also examined the data on the relationships between student attitudes and individual differences. She concluded that learner control has not been shown to significantly influence student attitudes. However, some limited evidence was found showing that computers motivated underachievers, slower students, and potential dropouts. Mevarech and Rich (1985) also demonstrated that CBI could improve disadvantaged students' perceptions of school life. Again, these studies did not systematically compare the relative effects of CBI and conventional instruction on the attitudes of poor students.

Psychometric Attributes of Attitudinal Measures

Attitudinal data may be inconsistent because of problems with some of the instruments used in measuring these data. Knerr and Nawrocki (1978) have noted that most attitudinal instruments are designed ad hoc, with neither the items nor the metric properties of the scales described. As stated by King (1975):

> Most (attitudinal) studies are experimenter constructed tests which have unknown or unreported reliabilities. (p. 7)

For example, Jenkins and Dankert (1981) indicated that reliable data were collected; however, descriptions of their items and the test-retest reliabilities were not provided. And Bangert-Drowns et al. (1985) and Kulik et al. (1980) failed to describe the reliabilities of the different attitudinal measures reviewed in their reports.

Several of the previously cited studies (e.g., Avner, 1981; Dallman et al., 1977; Knerr & Nawrocki, 1978; Longo, 1972; Loyd & Gressard, 1984b; Mevarech & Rich, 1985) have developed or used attitudinal measures with apparently sufficient reliabilities. Mevarech and Rich measured students' perceptions of the instructional environment with a questionnaire developed by Epstein and McPartland (1976). This questionnaire had a known internal consistency coefficient of .84. Longo reported nearly identical attitudinal scores on the same items for two separate studies, which indicates that the measures were reliable. Perhaps then, potential reliability problems with attitudinal measures can be eliminated by using established questionnaires or by replicating the results. Other than the few studies cited in this report (e.g., Dallman et al., 1977; Longo, 1972), a lack of replicated findings comparing CBI to other media exists in this research literature.

Avner (1972) argued that reliability for attitudinal measures should not be determined by using a large number of items selected for internal consistency. Rather, a highly reliable single item should be used for each attitude to be measured. He has claimed that reducing the number of items allows the researcher to sample student opinions more frequently without encroaching on the students' good will or the limited class time available. And reliabilty measures which are based upon internal consistency can be a misleading indication of the questionnaire's value, because such a group of items can only be vaguely interpreted. Except for a few studies conducted by Avner and associates, the reliability of single item attitudinal measures has rarely been determined.

Problems may also exist with the validity of the attitudinal measures used in CBI research. Discrepancies between students' responses to questionnaires and more objective data have been found by Knerr and Nawrocki (1978), Shlechter (1985), and Wood and Pitz (1985). Shlechter, for example, noticed that soldiers reported that using a light pen was relatively easy, when in fact many of their errors related to problems with using this responding mechanism. Additional efforts to compare self-reports with objective performance measures seem warranted. As stated by Avner (1972):

> While the questionnaire provides a convenient and useful method of gathering student data in certain situations (e.g., students' learning to use a system) there is no alternative to direct observation of student behavior. (p. 5)

And Bessemer (personal communication, October 31, 1985) has suggested that attitudinal data must be validated by students' actual use of an implemented system.

Another threat to CBI attitudinal measures is that items regarding social desirability are not included. This problem is especially important for studies (e.g., Dallman et al., 1977; Tatsuoka & Misselt, 1978) in which instructors have been part of the evaluation process. Reasons for including a social desirability measure will be elaborated upon in the next few pages.

Problematic attitudinal measures are frequently found in the CBI literature. As indicated, psychometric problems with these measures were observed in both studies with favorable outcomes and in those with neutral outcomes about students' preference for CBI. These measurement problems tend to further limit conclusions about CBI and student attitudes.

Factors Affecting Student Attitudes

The main factor affecting students' attitudes should be the CBI program's instructional value. Gleason (1981) has claimed that students do react very positively to good CBI programs, and reject poor programs. Clement (1981) has also noted that CBI lesson materials which reduce student error rates may be beneficial to maintaining and producing positive attitudes. Clement and Gleason however, do not provide any data supporting their positions.

Limited evidence exists about the effects of performance upon student attitudes, King (1975) reported only one study (Mitzel & Wodtke, 1965), which examined the relationship between attitudes and performance. Mitzel and Wodtke found that a significant positive correlation existed between these variables. On the other hand, Tatsuoka and Misselt (1978) could not find any substantial relationships between military students' gain scores on a CBI training program and attitudinal measures. This study investigated students'

CBI use and their attitudes toward four different courses at the Chanute Air Force Base. Correlations between students' gain scores and attitudinal indexes of instructional effectiveness and positive affect were not significant at levels of .19 and .21, respectively. Significant correlations ($p < .05$) of .32 and $-.29$ for the instructional effectiveness and positive affect variables, respectively, were found when a multiple regression technique was used to determine the correlational coefficients. The .19 and .32 correlations dealt with students' perceptions of PLATO's effectiveness and performance, while the other two correlations involved students' positive feelings toward CBI and performance. Tatsuoka and Misselt never explained the reason for the directional shift in the second set of correlations. Also, as reported, Alderman et al. (1978) found that students had less favorable attitudes toward TICCIT than toward conventional instruction, but TICCIT was found to be more effective for some educational measures. A link has not then been found between attitudes and instructional quality.

A link does seem to exist between users' attitudes and human factors issues (Avner, 1986; King, 1975; Magidson, 1978; McVey, Clauer, & Taylor, 1984, Shlechter, 1985; Tatsuoka & Misselt, 1978). Avner found correlations of .80 between users' (28 instructors) ratings and system reliability. He also found a significant point-biserial correlation of .593 between instructors ratings and the decision to continue/discontinue using the PLATO system. Tatsuoka and Misselt found correlations of $-.43$ and $-.45$ between students' perceptions of mechanical failures and students' attitudes toward the system's acceptability and instructional effectiveness, respectively. McVey et al. discussed the possibility that hardware features might affect users' comfort. As stated by McVey et al.:

> A thorough review paper by Campbell and Durden (1983) suggests that there are many overlooked factors contributing to the humorous accusation that VDT (CRT) means "Visual Discomfort Terminals." (p. 1)

Other reports from the human factors literature (e.g., Dainoff, Happ, & Crane, 1981; IBM, 1984; Helander & Rupp, 1984; Rupp, 1981) have also discussed problems with CRTs. Dainoff et al. found that visual fatigue was more pronounced among typists using CRTs than among typists using print-based terminals. They also noted that these differences in visual fatigue were not related to the amount of work or other job pressures.

Different CRT standards have been recently developed by different countries and agencies, e.g., Department of the Defense (DoD), to control for possible problems with the design of these terminals (Helander & Rupp, 1981). Unfortunately, as noted by Helander and Rupp, the DoD standards have emphasized productivity over operator comfort and convenience. Possible instructional inefficiency, however, may be associated with "visual discomfort terminals," as students may not be able to use these problematic terminals for an extended period of time. Reliable attitudinal data are thus needed for ascertaining specific problems that students may have with the CBI system.

Useful information about CBI programs has been obtained when attitudinal measures have been used to ascertain specific issues. Tatsuoka and Misselt (1978) found that students' responses to open-ended attitudinal questions were helpful in revising problematic CBI lessons. Avner (personal communication, November 5, 1985) discovered through such open-ended responses, positive attributes of CBI, such as scheduling flexibility for students, which would not have been discovered through other procedures. And Shlechter (1985) found, through students' interview responses, that a particular system might be best used as a supplement to the conventional instructional program. Attitudinal measures, especially open-ended questions, may then be most useful for providing formative feedback on students' perceptions of a system's strengths and weaknesses.

Factors other than the CBI system may unduly influence students' attitudes. Abrami and Mizener (1982) noted that teacher attitudes had a substantial effect upon students' attitudes in conventional instruction courses. Avner (1985) demonstrated that teachers' attitudes toward CBI did effect students' attitudes toward the system. Avner used exemplary and mediocre CBI courseware, as judged by a panel of CBI professionals. He found that students initially judged both courseware to be either positive or negative, depending upon the teachers' positive or negative feelings toward the system. The data also indicated that students who had teachers with positive attitudes toward CBI still—after a month's period—maintained positive attitudes toward the mediocre program. And, these students had slightly more positive attitudes toward CBI than did the students in the exemplary CBI materials—hostile teacher condition. Teachers' attitudes could then confound students' CBI attitudinal data.

Because of the unique relationship between military instructors and their students, evaluations of military CBI programs would be especially prone to problems associated with instructor attitudes. Military instructors need to be involved in the evaluation process. Draxl and Aggen (1981) and Gray (1986) have described the need to give briefings to enlist military instructors interest in and support of, new instructional systems. Military instructors' attitudes—like civilian instructors' attitudes—may also be influenced by their superiors' beliefs. Indeed, it is hard to imagine how these instructors can remain neutral toward CBI when their superiors have indicated that this medium will be an integral part of all future Army training. Such briefings by CBI evaluators and Army staff may engender positive attitudes in instructors while militating against obtaining unbiased reports from students. Military students may be more reluctant than civilian students to state their dislike of a CBI system, because military instructors have much more power over their students than do civilian teachers. This possible difference between military and civilian students can explain why more favorable comments toward CBI would be found in the military training literature than in the civilian literature.

Another possible confounding in attitudinal research is novelty effects. As previously reported, Clark (1983, 1985a) has claimed that students are initially motivated and enthusiastic to learn from a new CBI program. Questions, though, remain about a system's ability to sustain students' interest and motivation. Pagliaro (1983), in a year-long study of a CBI program for pharmacology students, found that these students reported the system to be significantly less interesting across testing periods. The magnitude of the decrements in students' ratings, however, were not great.

Other CBI reports (e.g., Avner, 1985; Ford et al., 1972; King, 1975; Magidson, 1978) also have not been able to find any substantial effects for CBI experience upon attitudinal data. Ford et al. found that long term CBI users' attitudes toward CBI were more positive than the attitudes of first time users. The long time users were 50 students out of more than 200 sampled who had prior experience with CBI. Avner showed that subjects across the different experimental conditions reported more positive attitudes toward the CBI system with increased usage. Thus, novelty effects as defined by length of CBI experience do not seem to have a major influence upon students' attitudes.

Clark and his associates (e.g., Clark & Salomon, 1985) also suggested that students would prefer any newer instructional technologies over the established ones—"program novelty effects." Support for "program novelty effects" comes from Simonson's (1980) extensive review of the research on student attitudes. Simonson has concluded that students seemingly prefer to learn from any new instructional mode, e.g., instructional T.V. or programmed instruction, over conventional instruction. Shlechter (1985) reported that students preferred a CBI system to conventional instruction because of the individualized instruction associated with this system. These students would then seemingly prefer any individualized mode of instruction over conventional instruction. As has been argued previously, individualized instruction characterizes nearly all modern instructional innovations.

Juola (1977) reported findings which conflicted with those previously cited about new media and student attitudes. Seven hundred freshman at Michigan State University found instructional television and programmed instruction to be undesirable instructional media. Juola's study, however, is not typical of this research literature. Future research is needed in which students' CBI attitudes are compared with attitudes for other (a) equivalent instructional media, and (b) new instructional modes.

Conclusions

Inconsistent and confounded findings predominate the CBI attitudinal findings. Furthermore, these problematic findings seem to relate to factors other than courseware differences. Recommendations have also been made about using attitudinal data primarily for formative feedback, making attitudinal comparisons with other new and equivalent instructional technologies, using objective measures to validate the subjective attitudinal measures, and conducting more naturalistic attitudinal studies. Such naturalistic studies would ultimately provide CBI professionals with the most useful data about CBI and student motivation.

SUMMARY AND IMPLICATIONS

Robust empirical support does not exist for the claimed advantages of CBI over other instructional media for: (a) reducing life cycle costs, (b) facilitating students' mastery of the instructional materials, (c) accommodating individual learning differences, and (d) motivating students' learning. And some previously claimed benefits of CBI, e.g., reduced training time, appear to be attributable to instructional features which are inherent in any individualized instructional medium. CBI's relative value as a primary instructional medium has thus not been established. Unsubstantiated claims about this medium's instructional effectiveness may hurt the computer industry, as instructors who are expecting too much from CBI may become disillusioned with this medium.

A major reason for this inability to find clear empirical support for CBI is that problematic research practices pervade this literature. For the most part, media effects have been confounded with extraneous treatment effects. The most noticeable of these extraneous treatment effects involve:

1. having instructional treatment differences between the computer and control conditions.
2. making comparisons with nonequivalent media.
3. having teacher attitudes unduly influence student attitudes and performance.

Program novelty effects, insufficient testing durations, and nonreplicated findings also plague this research area. These problematic research practices would seemingly hamper advances in CBI, because questions remain whether possible problems with CBI are due to courseware limitations or due to limitations of this medium. These research problems also preclude developing future CBI systems based upon "good" systems and learning from the problems with "bad" systems.

The research reviewed here did provide some insights into human–computer interactions which will help the CBI designer. CBI programs must be designed to accommodate naive, occasional, experienced, and anxious computer users. ICBIs with adaptive control mechanisms may accommodate individual learning differences. Students' abilities to use a CBI system may be negatively affected by a system's reliability, CRT display, and responding mechanism. For example, students may commonly experience learning fatigue and reading problems with certain types of CRT displays. And different types of courseware may differentially effect different types of students with drill-and-practice courseware holding great promise for slow learners.

Evaluators and researchers are also beginning to provide help for designers in other ways. The cognitive revolution in psychology has demonstrated that the designer of instructional materials must be concerned with the interface between the learners' cognitive strategies and the structure of the task/materials to be learned (Montague & Wulfeck, 1984). As discussed by many recent works (e.g., Carroll, 1984; Carroll & Thomas, 1982; Gray & Orasanu, in press; Montague & Wulfeck, 1984), discoveries in cognitive science have led to dramatic changes in instructional theory which must be incorporated into any new instructional program. Unfortunately, most of the CBI programs reviewed in this chapter were based upon noncognitive instructional approaches. This medium could then possibly be improved by instructional designers' using the latest information from the cognitive science laboratories. Several excellent reviews of the cognitive science literature (e.g., Gardner, 1985; Shlechter & Toglia, 1985) can help the CBI designer more fully understand the importance of this field. The CBI design team must then be aware of the most current developments in basic psychological research.

The CBI design team must also be aware of teachers' needs and objectives. My review of the CBI literature has indicated that teachers' input into the CBI program usually comes after the design process. For example, Walker (1984) has suggested that educators can influence the design process by being discriminating buyers of CBI courseware and software. Teachers' roles in the CBI development, however, must change, and their influence must precede the developmental phase. As stated by Shavelson et al. (1984b):

> Courseware with greater pedagogical value can result if teachers play an expanded role in its design and development. (p. XV)

Evaluators must then provide information to designers about teachers' needs and objectives. Information is especially needed about specific instructional situations for which teachers would use CBI. For example, Gorrell, Haas, Pearson, Cuevas, and Higginebotham (1985), have claimed that CBI is most useful for enabling students to have training experiences which are difficult to arrange and monitor in classroom situations. Gorrell et al. then discuss devising a CBI program to simulate the implementation of a behavior modification program. Information about teachers' needs for CBI, of course, is more easily obtained for small educational systems, e.g., corporations and military schools, than for different public school systems. However, input is needed from as many educators as possible if the computer designers are to meet the needs of their users. Input from a variety of teachers is also necessary so that the CBI program can accommodate many different teachers. Evaluators, rather than designers, should survey educators and classrooms, because that is their specialty. Also, evaluators should be able to obtain objective teacher reports without overselling the product.

Data do exist about the current use of computers in the classroom which provide insights into teachers' computer needs (see Becker, 1983; Wright, Melmed, & Farris, 1982). Wright et al. have found that computers are mainly used for compensatory, remedial, and basic skills instruction by elementary school teachers, and for computer science instruction by secondary school teachers. These usages may be a function of the types of programs available. Also, the current reports on computer use do not differentiate CBI use from general computer use.

The military training research literature (e.g., Montague, 1984; Shlechter, 1986) has also provided some information about the instructional situations most appropriate for CBI. Shlechter has suggested, for example, that CBI is appropriate for providing National Guard soldiers with needed sustainment training. My argument is based on the fact that National Guard armories cannot purchase sufficient military equipment, e.g., M1 tanks, for training purposes. Researchers and educators can then help CBI designers understand the type of training most suitable for this medium. And researchers should thus spend more time on providing designers with such information.

Evaluators should also spend more time on determining the quality of the developed CBI program. Inconsistencies in the quality of CBI programs may have contributed to the inconsistencies found in the CBI research literature. Information about the quality of the CBI program and the comparative media, however, is very rarely provided. Poorly developed CBI may have been compared to well developed conventional instruction programs, and vice versa.

Determining the quality of any instructional program is problematic. Outcome studies have been primarily used to provide a basic assessment of a program's worth to train students. Outcome studies involve using a pretest—posttest evaluation design to measure changes in students' performance on representative achievement measure(s). Even though the instructional program may train students, it may not be at an optimal level of efficiency. Important instructional objectives and content may be missing from the courseware, or students may not understand certain segments. As previously recommended, feedback from educators and students on possible instructional problems should then be collected. The evaluation team should also examine any possible problems that the instructor(s) may have with implementing the courseware. All potential problems found in this evaluational phase must be carefully examined and reported to the design team. Of course, the design team should eliminate potential courseware problems, especially content errors, with a thorough quality check before releasing the program for outside evaluation. There may be a need for several cycles of in-house quality checks and independent outside evaluations.

Several recent reports (e.g., Gray, 1986; Linn & Fisher, 1984; Montague et al., 1983) have also stressed a need for researchers to provide information about the most efficient methods for quality

CBI implementation(s). As stated in the title of Montague et al.'s paper, "Quality CBI depends on Quality Instructional Design and Quality Implementation" (p. 90). Shlechter (1987) has collected data which shows that group presentation of CBI materials would enable the Army to implement the courseware conveniently and economically.

Gray (1986) has suggested that the evaluator should observe the implementation of training programs until the program either fails or becomes obsolete. Comparisons should then be made between successful and unsuccessful implementations. Such comparisons would help designers and researchers to better understand the variables involved in quality CBI implementations and programs. Data from implemented systems are also needed to provide information about the relationship between projected and actual life cycle costs, and more precise information on CBI and student motivation.

Successful CBI programs should eventually be compared with successful alternative media. The methodological considerations discussed throughout this chapter should be incorporated in these comparisons. Also, these studies should assess differences in students' long-term retention of the materials, transfer abilities, and incidental learning associated with the different media presentations. Such studies would provide clearer insights into CBI's relative educational value.

Information about CBI's relative educational value is vital to educators and CBI designers. Educators demand and need to be assured that the CBI system is the most appropriate and cost-efficient instructional medium for their intended purposes. And CBI designers need to know whether this medium has advanced the educational process.

The CBI design process should be built on the continuous work done by researchers and evaluators. Presently, communication problems in the CBI field present an obstacle to this building process. Many previous reports on CBI systems and related research are not easily available. Bangert-Drowns et al.'s (1985) meta-analysis of the CBI literature included only 6 published studies of more than 40 studies examined. This author also found that many CBI reports could only be found through corporation and military archives. And many military and corporation reports were not available for general distribution.

A CBI "data base" or handbook, e.g., *Buros' Mental Measurement Yearbooks,* could help solve this communication problem by providing a common information source for educators, designers, and researchers. This "data base" must include a description of the CBI program and synopsis of the corresponding evaluation and research. The research synopsis must include descriptions of the subjects, research procedures, and findings. Civilian and military agencies have previously tried to establish such CBI libraries, with varying degrees of success. However, these libraries, e.g., TRIADS (see Dallman et al., 1983, for a description of this program), have usually included a description of CBI programs or media selection procedures, with little description of the corresponding research or evaluation data. Creating this proposed "data base" may not be practical, but we must find some method of improving the communication among the different types of professionals involved in developing a successful CBI system and program.

In closing, the major lessons learned from the CBI literature are that research and evaluation on student–computer interactions require the utmost care, involve many issues and variables, and are required at every phase of the development and implementation process. Without such research and evaluation, significant advances in CBI will not occur. These lessons learned should be applicable to other areas in the study of human–computer interaction. The research problems and issues discussed in this chapter reflect the complexities associated with studying human–computer interaction. And advancements in developing any interactive system require the interface among researchers, developers, and users.

REFERENCES

Abrami, P.C., & Mizener, D.A. (1982, August). *Student/instructor attitude similarity, course ratings and student achievement* (Document No. HE–015–572). Paper presented at the Annual Meeting of the American Psychological Association, Washington, DC.

Alderman, D.L. (1974, April). *Planning for the evaluation of the PLATO and TICCIT computer-based instructional systems: The comparison of performance for community college students.* Paper presented at the Annual Meeting of the American Educational Research Association, Chicago.

Alderman, D.L., Appel, L.R., & Murphy, R.T. (1978, April). PLATO and TICCIT: An evaluation of CAI in the community college. *Educational Technology, 18,* 40–46.

Allen, B.S., & Merrill, M.D. (1985). System-assigned strategies and CBI. *Journal of Educational Computing Research, 1,* 3–21.

Avner, R.A. (1972). *Student attitudes toward PLATO, survey results.* Unpublished evaluation report. Urbana, IL: University of Illinois.

Avner, R.A. (1978). Cost-effectiveness of CBE. *Educational Technology, 17*(4), 24–26.

Avner, R.A. (1979). Production of computer-based instructional materials. In H.F. O'Neil Jr. (Ed.), *Issues in instructional systems development* (ch. 7, pp. 133–180). New York: Academic Press, Inc.

Avner, R.A. (1981, February). (Update on PLATO-based physics teaching). Unpublished data. Urbana, IL: University of Illinois.

Avner, R.A. (1982, February). *Cost and Planning Estimates for PLATO CBE Operations* (CERL Report). Urbana, IL: University of Illinois Computer-Education Research Laboratory.

Avner, R.A. (1985). (Effects of teachers' CBI attitudes upon student attitudes). Unpublished data. Urbana, IL: University of Illinois.

Avner, R.A. (1986). (Reliability of CBI and user attitudes). Unpublished data. Urbana, IL: University of Illinois.

Avner, R.A., Moore, C., & Smith, S. (1980). Active external control: A basis for the superiority of CBI. *Journal of Computer-Based Instructions, 6*(4), 115–118.

Avner, R.A., Smith, S., & Tenczar, P. (1984). CBI authoring tools: Effects on productivity and quality. *Journal of Computer-Based Instruction, 11*(3), 85–89.

Baker, F.B. (1978). *Computer-Managed Instruction: Theory and practice.* Englewood Cliffs, NJ: Educational Technology Publications.

Bangert-Drowns, R.C., Kulik, J.A., & Kulik, C–L., C. (1985). Effectiveness of computer-based education in secondary schools. *Journal of Computer-Based Instruction, 12*(3), 59–68.

Barsam, H.F., & Simutis, Z.M. (1984). Computer-based graphics for terrain visualizations training. *Human Factors, 26*(4), 659–665.

Bass, G., Ries, R., & Sharpe, W. (1986). Teaching basic skills through microcomputer assisted instruction. *Journal of Educational Computing Research, 2*(2), 207–219.

Becker, H.J. (1983). *School uses of microcomputers: Reports from a national survey* (nos. 1 and 3). Baltimore: Johns Hopkins' Center for Social Organization of Schools.

Bellinger, K. (1986, February). *CAI as part of the total faculty development package.* Paper presented at the Twenty-Seventh International Association for the Development of Computer-Based Instructional Systems, New Orleans.

Bialo, E.R., & Erickson, L.B. (1984, April). *Microcomputer courseware: Characteristics and trends.* Paper presented at the Annual Meeting of the American Educational Research Association, New Orleans.

Boldovici, J.A., & Scott, T. (1984). *The Hewlett-Packard HP-41CV Hand-Held Computer as a medium for teaching mathematics to fire control systems repairers.* (ARI Research Report 1408). Alexandria, VA: Army Research Institute.

Bunderson, C.V. (1981). Courseware. In H.F. O'Neil, Jr., (Ed.), *Computer-*

based instruction: A state-of-the-art assessment (ch. 4, pp. 91–125. New York: Academic Press.

Burger, K. (1985). Computer-assisted instruction: Learning style and academic achievement. *Journal of Computer-Based Instruction, 12*(1), 21–25.

Burnside, B. (1985, July-August). Using technology to train the TC (tank commander). *Armor: The magazine of mobile warfare, 94*(4), 42–45.

Cambre, M.A., & Cook, D.L. (1985). Computer anxiety: Definition, measurement and correlates. *Journal of Educational Computing Research, 1*(1), 23–36.

Campbell, F., & Durden, E. (1983). The visual display terminal issue: A consideration of its physiological, psychological, and clinical background. *Ophthalmology and Physiological Optics, 3,* 175–192.

Card, S.K., English, W.K., & Burr, B.J. (1978). Evaluation of mouse, rate-controlled isometric joystick, step keys, and text keys for text selection on a CRT. *Ergonomics, 21*(8), 601–613

Carrier, C.A. (1979). The role of learner characteristics in computer-based instruction. *National Society for Programmed Journal, 18*(5), 25, 22.

Carrier, C., Davidson, G., Higgson, V., & Williams, M. (1984). Selection of options by field independent and dependent children in a computer-based concept lesson. *Journal of Computer-Based Instruction, 11*(2), 49–54.

Carroll, J.M. (1984, May). *Mental models and software factors* (RC 10616)(#47016)). Yorktown Heights, NY: IBM Watson Research Center.

Carroll, J.M., & Mazur, S.A. (1984). *Learning to use an office system with an on-line tutorial* (RC 106445(#47740)). Yorktown Heights, NY: IBM Watson Research Center.

Carroll, J.M., & Thomas, J.C. (1982). Metaphor and the cognitive representation system, *IEEE Transactions on Systems, Man, and Cybernetics. 12*(2), 107–116.

Chapanis, A. (1965). Words, words, words. *Human Factors, 7*(1), 1–17.

Chapanis, A. (1985). Human factors methodology. In R.W. Pew & P. Green (Eds.), *Human factors engineering short course* (26th ed.), (Lecture 4). Ann Arbor, MI: University of Michigan, Chrysler Center for Continuing Engineering Education.

Christiansen, J.M. (1985). Human factors considerations in reliability and maintainability. In R.W. Pew and P. Green (Eds.), *Human factors engineering short course notes* (26th ed.), (Lecture 9). Ann Arbor, MI: University of Michigan, Continuing Engineering Education, Engineering Summer Conferences.

Clark, B. (1983). *Growing up gifted* (2nd ed.). Columbus, OH: E. Merrill Publishing Company.

Clark, R.E. (1983). Reconsidering research on learning from media. *Review of Educational Research, 53*(4), 445–459.

Clark, R.E. (1984). Research on student thought processes during computer-based instruction. *Journal of Instructional Development, 7*(3), 2–5.

Clark, R.E. (1985a). Confounding in educational computing research. *Journal of Educational Computing Research, 1,* 389–394.

Clark, R.E. (1985b). The importance of treatment explication: A reply to J. Kulik, C-L. Kulik and R. Bangert-Drowns. *Journal of Educational Computing Research, 1,* 389–394.

Clark, R.E. & Leonard, S. (1985, March). *Computer research confounding.* Paper presented at the annual meeting of the American Educational Research Association, Chicago.

Clark, R.E., & Salomon, G. (1985). Media in teaching. In M.C. Wittrock (Ed.), *Third handbook of research on teaching,* (Vol. 3, pp. 464–477). New York: McMillian.

Clark, R.E., & Voogel, A. (1985). Transfer of training principles for instructional design. *Educational Communication and Technology Journal, 33* 113–123.

Clement, F.J. (1981). Affective considerations in computer-based education. *Educational Technology, 21*(4), 28–32.

Cleveland Public Schools (1981). *Disadvantaged public program fund evaluation.* Final Report. (ERIC Document Reproduction Service No. ED 211–637).

Collier, R.R., Poyner, L., O'Neil Jr., H.F., & Judd, W.A. (1973, February). *Effects of learner control on performance and state anxiety in a computerized concept learning task.* Paper presented at the Annual Meeting of the American Educational Research Association, New Orleans.

Craik, F.I.M., & Lockhart, R.S. (1972). Levels of processing: A framework for memory research. *Journal of Verbal Learning and Verbal Behavior, 11,* 671–684.

Dainoff, M.J., Happ, A., & Crane, P. (1981). Visual fatigue and occupational stress in VDT operators, *Human Factors, 23*(4), 421–438.

Dallman, B.E., DeLeo, P.J., Main, P.S. & Gillman, D.C. (1977). *Evaluation of PLATO IV in vehicle maintenance training* (Report No. AFHRL-TR-77–59). Chanute Air Force Base, IL: USAF School of Applied Aerospace Sciences, Training Research Applications Branch.

Dallman, B., Pohlman, D., Psotka, J., Wisher, R., McLachlan, J., Wulfeck, W., Ahlers, R., & Cronholm, J. (1983). TRIADS: A foundation for military computer-based instruction. *Journal of Computer-Based Instruction, 10*(3–4), 59–61.

Dengler, P.E. (1983). Computer-assisted instruction and its use in occupational therapy education (automated instruction, PLATO, self-study, tutorial). *The American Journal of Occupational Therapy, 37,* 255–259.

Draxl, M., & Aggen, W. (1981). *Computer-based instruction project: Final report* (Contract No. DAJA 37-79-C-0483). College Park, MD: University of Maryland, European Division.

Eberts, R., & Brock, J.F. (1984). Computer applications to instruction. In F.A. Muckler (Eds.), *Human Factors Review 1984* (pp. 239–284). Santa Monica, CA: The Human Factors Society.

EDUCOM Bulletin, Summer 1983, p. 29.

Epstein, J.L., & McPartland, J.M. (1976). The concept and measurement of quality of school life. *American Educational Research Journal, 50,* 13–30.

Farr, B.J. (1985, March). *The Job-Skills Education Program (JSEP): Systems for Army education.* Paper presented at the International Conference of the Association for the Development of Computer-based Instructional Systems, Philadelphia.

Federico, P-A. (1983). Changes in the cognitive components of achievement as students proceed through computer-managed instruction. *Journal of Computer-Based Instruction, 9*(4), 156–168.

Fishman, D.J. (1985). Interactive video: The next frontier. *Proceedings of the Twenty-Sixth International Association for the Development of Computer-Based Instructional Systems* (pp. 144–148). Bellingham, WA: Western Washington University.

Fletcher, J.D., & Rockway, M.R. (1986). Computer-based training in the military. In J.A. Ellis (Ed.), *Military contributions to instructional technology* (pp. 171–213). New York: Praeger.

Ford, J.D., Jr., Slough, D.A., & Hurlock, R.E. (1972). *Computer assisted instruction in Navy technical training using a small dedicated computer system: Final report* (Research Report SRR 72–13). San Diego, CA.: Naval Personnel and Training Research Laboratory.

Francis, L.D., Welling, L.G., & Levy, G.W. (1983). *An evaluation of the CAI (Computer-Assisted Instruction) segments of the TOW Field Test Site and the HAWK CW Radar Repair Course* (TDI-TR-83-3). Fort Monroe, VA: US Army Training and Doctrine Command.

Gardner, H. (1985). *The mind's new science: A history of the cognitive revolution.* New York: Basic Books.

Gay, G. (1985, April). *Interaction of learner control and prior conceptual understanding in computer-assisted video instructions.* Paper presented at the Annual Meeting of the American Educational Research Association, Chicago.

Gleason, G.T. (1981, March). Microcomputers in education: The state of the art. *Educational Technology 21,*(3), 7–18.

Gorrell, J., Haas, D., Pearson, K., Cuevas, T., & Higginbotham, T. (1985, November). *Interactive simulation of classroom behavior for educational psychology.* Paper presented to the Annual Meeting of the South Central Association for Computing Machinery, Houston.

Gray, W.D. (1986). A role for evaluators in helping new programs succeed. In J.S. Wholey, M.A. Abramson, & C. Bellavita (Eds.), *Performance and credibility: Developing excellence in public and nonprofit organizations* (pp. 149–163). Lexington, MA: D.C. Heath and Company.

Gray, W.D., & Orasanu, J.M. (in press). Transfer of Cognitive Skills. In S.M. Cormier & D.J. Hagman (Eds.), *Transfer of learning.* New York: Academic Press.

Gray, W.D., Pliske, D.J., & Psotka, J. (1985). *Smart technology for training:*

Promise and current status (Research Report No. ARI-RR-85-1412). Alexandria, VA: Army Research Institute.

Gump, P. (1985, April). *An environmental perspective on classroom order.* Paper presented at the Annual Meeting of the American Educational Research Association, Chicago.

Hansen, J.B. (1972). *An investigation of cognitive abilities, state anxiety, and performance in a CAI task under conditions of no feedback, feedback, and learner control* (Document No. EM 010–722). Austin, TX: Texas University, Computer-Assisted Instruction Laboratory.

Helander, M.G., & Rupp, B. (1984). An overview of standards and guidelines for visual display terminals. *Applied Ergonomics, 15*(3), 185–195.

Hemphill, M.R. (1986, February). *The impact of computer technology on self-instructional materials in speech communication.* Paper presented at the Twenty-Seventh International Association for the Development of Computer-Based Instructional Systems, New Orleans.

Hess, R.D., & Miura, I.T. (1985). *Gender differences in enrollment in computer camps and classes.* Unpublished Manuscript. Palo Alto, CA: Stanford University.

Hess, R.D., & Tenezakis, M.D. (1973). Selected findings from "the computer as socializing agent: Some socio-affective outcomes of CAI." *AV Communication Review, 21*(3), 311–325.

Himwich, H.A. (1977). *A comparison of the TICCIT and PLATO systems in a military setting* (Contract No. DAHC 15-73-C-0077). Urbana, IL: University of Illinois, Computer-Based Research Laboratory.

Hofstetter, F.T. (1983). The cost of PLATO in a university environment. *Journal of Computer-Based Instruction, 9,*148–155.

Holmes, G. (1982). Computer-assisted instruction: A discussion of some issues for would-be implementors. *Educational Technology,* 7–12.

IBM (1984). *Human factors of workstations with visual displays.* San Jose, CA: IBM Human Factors Center.

Jay, T.B. (1981). Computerphobia: What to do about it. *Educational Technology, 21,* 47–48.

Jacobs, R.L., Byrd, D.M., & High, W.R. (1985). Computerized testing: The hidden figures test. *The Journal of Educational Computing Research, 1*(2), 173–178.

Jelden, D.L. (1985, March). Effectiveness of Phoenix as a computer-based education system. *Proceedings of the Twenty-Sixth International Association for the Development of Computer-Based Instructional Systems* (pp. 50–55). Bellinghan, WA: Western Washington University.

Jenkins, T.M., & Dankert, E.J. (1981, March). Results of a three-month PLATO trial in terms of utilizations and student attitudes. *Educational Technology, 21*(3), 44–47.

Johnson, K., & Plake, B. (1980). Evaluation of PLATO library instructional lessons: Another view. *Journal of Academic Librarianship, 6,* 154–158.

Jones, L.M., Kane, D., Sherwood, B.A., & Avner, R.A. (1983). A final-exam comparison involving computer-based instruction. *American Journal of Physics, 51*(6), 533–538.

Judd, W.A., Daubek, K., & O'Neil Jr., H.F. (1975, April). *Individual Differences in learner controlled CAI.* Paper presented at the Annual Meeting of the American Educational Research Association, Washington, D.C.

Juola, A.E. (1977). *Student influence and higher education* (Document No. HE-013-030). East Lansing, MI: Michigan State University, Learning and Evaluation Service.

Kearsley, G., Hunter, B., & Seidel, R.J. (1983). *Two decades of CBI research: What have we learned* (Professional Paper 3–83). Alexandria, VA: Human Resources Research Organization.

Kemner-Richardson, S., Lamos, J.P., & West, A.S. (1984). *The CAI decision handbook.* Lowry AFB, CO: US Air Force Human Resources Laboratory.

Kern, R.P. (1985, April). *Design of computer-based tutorials: Training students to apply cognitive processing skills in the context of tactical training.* Paper presented at the Air Force Conference on Technology in Training and Education, Colorado Springs.

King, A.T. (1975). *Impact of computer-based instruction on attitudes of students and instructors: A review* (AFHRL-TR-75-4). Brooks AFB, TX: US Air Force Systems Command.

Knerr, B.W., & Nawrocki, L.H. (1978). *The measurement of military student attitudes toward computer-assisted instruction* (ARI-78-18). Alexandria, VA: US Army Research Institute.

Kopstein, F., & Seidel, R.J. (1969). Computer-administered instruction versus traditionally administered instruction: Economics. In R.C. Atkinson & H.A. Wilson (Eds.), *Computer-assisted instruction* (pp. 327–359). New York: Academic Press.

Kosslyn, S.M. (1981). The medium and the message in mental imagery: A theory. *Psychological Review, 88,* 46–66.

Kulik, J.A., Bangert, R.L., & Williams, G.W. (1983). Effects of computer-based teaching on secondary school students. *Journal of Educational Psychology, 75*(1), 19–26.

Kulik, J.A., Kulik, C-L. C., & Bangert-Drowns, R.L. (1985). The importance of outcome studies: A reply to Clark. *Journal of Educational Computing Research, 1,* 381–387.

Kulik, J.A., Kulik, C-L. C., and Cohen, P.A. (1980). Effectiveness of computer-based college teaching: A meta-analysis of findings. *Review of Educational Research, 50*(4), 525–544.

Landhauer, T.K. (1982). Discussant comments on trends in everyday memory research. In T.M. Shlechter, D.J. Herrman, & M.P. Toglia (Chairs), *Current trends in everyday memory research.* Symposium conducted at the Annual Meeting of the American Psychological Association, Washington, D.C.

Linn, M.C., & Fisher, C.W. (1984, June). *The gap between promise and reality in computer education: Planning a response.* (ERIC Document Reproduction Service No. ED 249–598).

Longo, A.A. (1972). *A summative evaluation of computer assisted instruction in U.S. Army Basic Electronics Training* (Technical Report No. 72–1). Fort Monmouth, NJ: U.S. Army Signal Center & School, Computer Assisted Instruction Division.

Loyd, B.H., & Gressard, C. (1984a, February) *The effects of sex, age and computer experience on computer attitudes.* Paper presented at the Annual Meeting of the Eastern Educational Research Association, West Palm Beach, FL.

Loyd, B.H., & Gressard, C. (1984b). Reliability and factorial validity of computer attitude scales. *Educational and Psychological Measurement, 44*(2), 501–506.

Magidson, E.M. (1978). Students' assessment of PLATO: What students like and dislike about CAI, *Educational Technology, 18,* 15–18.

Maurer, M.M. (1983). *Development of validation of a measure of computer anxiety.* Unpublished master's thesis. Ames, IA: Iowa State University.

McDonald, B.A., & Crawford, A.M. (1983). Remote site training using microprocessors. *Journal of Computer-Based Instruction, 10,* 83–86.

McLaughlin, D.H. (1985, April). *Computers and teaching thinking skills.* Paper presented at the Annual Meeting of the American Educational Research Association, Chicago.

McVey, B.W., Clauer, C.K., & Taylor, S.E. (1984). *A comparison of antiglare filters for positive and negative image displays* (HFL-50). San Jose, CA: IBM Human Factors Center.

Merrill, M.D., Schneider, E.W., & Fletcher, K.A. (1980). *The instructional design library (vol. 40): TICCIT* (pp. 3–15, 117–127). Englewood Cliffs, NJ: Educational Technology Publications.

Mevarech, Z.R., & Rich, Y. (1985). Effects of computer-assisted instruction on disadvantaged pupils' cognitive and affective development. *Journal of Educational Research, 79*(1), 5–11.

Meyers, R. (1984). PLATO: Historical roots, current applications and future prospects. *Training Technology Journal, 1*(2), 33–37.

Mitzel, H.E., & Wodtke, K.H. (1965). *Development and presentation of four different college courses by computer teleprocessing* (Report R-1). State College, PA: Pennsylvania State University, CAI Laboratory.

Miura, I.T., & Hess, R.D. (1983, August). *Sex-differences in computer access, interest, and usage.* Paper presented at the Annual Meeting of the American Psychological Association, Anaheim.

Montague, W.E. (1984). *Computer-based systems for Navy classroom training* (Report No. NPRDC TR85-11). San Diego, CA: Navy Personnel Research and Development Center.

Montague, W.E., & Wulfeck II, W.H. (1984). Computer-based instruction: Will it improve instructional quality? *Training Technology Journal, 1*(2), 4–19.

Montague, W.E., Wulfeck, W.H. II, Ellis, J.A. (1983). Quality CBI instruction depends on quality instructional design and quality implementation. *Journal of Computer-Based Instruction, 10,* 90–93.

Morrison, J.E., & Witmer, B.G., (1983, Autumn). A comparative evaluation of computer-based and print-based job performance aids. *Journal of Computer-Based Instruction, 10*(3 & 4), 73–75.

Niemiec, R.P., & Walberg, H.J. (1985). Computers and achievement in the elementary schools. *Journal of Educational Computing Research, 1,* 435–550.

Okey, J.R., & Majer, K. (1976). Individual and small group-learning with computer-assisted instruction. *AV Communication Review, 24*(1), 79–86.

Olson, D., & Bruner, J. (1974). Learning through experience and learning through media. In D. Olson (Ed.), *Media and symbols: The forms of expression, communication and education* (73rd yearbook of the National Society for the Study of Education). Chicago, IL: University of Chicago Press.

Orlansky, J. (1983). Effectiveness of CBI: A different finding. *Electronic Learning, 6,* 59–60.

Orlansky, J. (1985). The cost-effectiveness of military training. *Proceedings of the symposium on the military value and cost-effectiveness of training* (pp. 1–17). Brussels, Belgium: NATO.

Orlansky, J., & String, J. (1981). Computer-based instruction for military training. *Defense Management Journal, 18*(2), 46–54.

Pagliaro, L.A. (1983). CAI in pharmacology: Students academic performance and instructional interactions. *Journal of Computer-Based Instruction, 9*(4), 131–144.

Park, O., & Roberts, F.C. (1985, April). *Effects of guided instructional strategies in computer-based instruction.* Paper presented at the Annual Meeting of American Educational Research Association, Chicago.

Phillips, R.J., Burkhardt, H.M., Coupland, J., Fraser, R., Pimm, D., & Ridgway, J. (1984). Computer-aided teaching. *Ergonomics, 27*(3), 243–258.

Ragsdale, R.G. (1982, May). *The computer threat to educational technology.* (Document No. IR 010-482). Dallas, TX: Paper presented at the Annual Meeting of the Association for Educational Communications and Technology, Research and Theory Division, Dallas.

Reed, D.D. (1983). *Information paper on computer-assisted instruction in higher education and industry (a literature search).* Unpublished paper. Maxwell Air Force Base, AL: Air University.

Reeves, T.C., & Lent, R.M. (1982, March). *Levels of evaluation for computer-based instruction.* Paper presented at the Annual Meeting of the American Educational Research Association, New York.

Reigeluth, C.M., & Garfield, J.M. (1984). Using videodiscs in instruction: Realizing their potential through instructional design. *Using Videodiscs in Instruction, 4*(3), 199–214.

Reinking, D. (1983). *The effects of computer-mediated text and reader study behavior on measures of reading comprehension.* Unpublished doctoral dissertation, University of Minnesota, Minneapolis.

Reinking, D. (1985). On conceptualizing research methodologies for computer-based instruction. *Proceedings of the Twenty-Sixth International Association for the Development of Computer-Based Instructional Systems* (pp. 241–245). Bellingham, WA: Western Washington University.

Robinson, E.R.N., & Kirk, F.G. (1984). Interfacing learning strategies and instructional strategies in computer training programs. In F.A. Muckler (Ed.), *Human Factors Review 1984* (pp. 209–238). Santa Monica, CA: Human Factors Society.

Ross, S.M. (1984). Matching the lesson to the student: Alternative adaptive designs for individualized learning systems. *Journal of Computer-Based Instruction, 11,* 42–48.

Rupp, B.A. (1981). Visual display standards: A review of issues. *Proceedings of the SID, 22*(1), 63–72.

Salomon, G. (1979). *Interaction of media, cognition and learning.* San Francisco, CA: Jossey-Bass.

Salomon, G., & Gardner, H. (1986). The computer as educator: Lessons from television research. *Educational Researchers, 15,* 13–19.

Sawyer, T.A. (1985). Human factors consideration in computer-assisted instruction. *Journal of Computer-Based Instruction, 12*(1), 17–20.

Schubert, J.G. (1985, April). *Cooperative learning, equity, and computer learning.* Paper presented at the Annual Meeting of the American Educational Research Association, Chicago.

Seidel, R.J. (1980, March). *It's 1980: Do you know where your computer is?* (Document No. IR-008-536). Alexandria, VA: Human Resources Research Organization. (ERIC Document Reproduction Service NO. ED 190 059).

Shavelson, R.J., Winkler, J.D., Stasz, C., Feibel, W., Robyn, A.E., & Shaha, S. (1984a). *Teaching mathematics and science: Patterns of microcomputer use.* Santa Monica, CA: Rand Corporation.

Shavelson, R.J., Winkler, J.D., Stasz, C., Feibel, W., Robyn, A.E., & Shea, S. (1984b). *"Successful" teachers patterns of microcomputer-based mathematics and science instruction.* (N-2770-NIE/RC). Washington, DC: The National Institute of Education.

Shlechter, T.M. (1985, November). *CBI and students' attitudes.* Paper presented at the Annual Meeting of the Mid-South Educational Research Association, Biloxi, MS.

Shlechter, T.M. (1986). *An examination of the research evidence for computer-based instruction in military training* (ARI Technical Report 722). Alexandria, VA: Army Research Institute.

Shlechter, T.M. (1987, April). *Group vs. individualized computer-based Instruction.* Paper presented at the annual meeting of the American Educational Research Association, Washington, D.C.

Shlechter, T.M., & Toglia, M.P. (Eds.). (1985). *New directions in cognitive science.* Norwood, NJ: Ablex Publishing Corporation.

Simonson, M.R. (1980). *Instructional media, attitude formation and change.*

Paper presented at the Annual Meeting of the Association for Educational Communication and Technology, Denver.

Snow, R.E. (1980). Aptitude, learner control and adaptive instruction. *Educational Psychologists, 15*(3), 151–158.

Steinberg, E.R. (1977). Review of student control in computer-assisted instruction. *Journal of Computer-Based Instruction, 3*(3), 84–90.

Steinberg, E.R., (1984). *Teaching computers to teach* (pp. 1–14). Hillsdale, NJ: Erlbaum.

Stone, C.S. (1985, March). *Instruction at the US Army Engineer School: Evolution and management of an in-house coding team.* Paper presented at the International Meeting of the Association for the Development of Computer-Based Instructional Systems, Philadelphia.

Suppes, P., & Morningstar, M. (1969, October). Computer-assisted instruction: Two computer-assisted instruction programs are evaluated. *Science, 166,* 343–350.

Swezey, R.W., Criswell, E.L., Huggins, R.S., Hays, R.T. & Allen, J.A. (in press). *Training effects of hands-on practice and three instructional methods on a simple procedural task* (ARI Technical Report). Alexandria, VA: Army Research Institute.

Swezey, R.W., Huggins, R.S., & Perez, R.S. (in press). *Effects of three instructional delivery methods and hands-on practice on a procedural maintenance task* (ARI-Technical Report). Alexandria, VA: Army Research Institute Technical report.

Tatsuoka, K.K., & Misselt, A.L. (1978). *Attitude and performance of military students and instructor attitudes in computer-based technical training* (Contract No. DAHC 15-73-C-0077). Urbana, IL: University of Illinois, Computer-Based Research Laboratory.

Tennyson, R.D. & Buttrey, T. (1980, Fall). Advisement and management strategies as design variables in computer-assisted instruction. *Educational Communication & Technology, 28*(3), 169–176.

Tennyson, R.D., Christiansen, D.L., & Park, S.I. (1984). The Minnesota Adaptive Instructional System: An intelligent CBI system. *Journal of Computer-Based Instruction, 11,* 2–13.

Walker, D.F. (1984). *Computers in schools, I: Potential and limitations, II: The software problem* (Document No. IR–011–114). San Francisco, CA: Far West Laboratory for Educational Research and Development. (ERIC Document Reproduction Service No. Ed 244 593).

Wilson, L.S. (1984). Presenting TICCIT: State of the art computer-based instruction. *Training Technology Journal, 1*(2), 26–32.

Wisher, R.A., & O'Hara, J.W. (1981, May). *Computer-based approach to the Navy's Remedial Training Project (PREST): A cost-effectiveness evaluation* (NPRDC Special Report 81–18). San Diego, CA: Navy Personnel Research and Development Center.

Witkin, H.A., Goodenough, D.R., & Karp, S.A. (1967). Stability of cognitive style from childhood to young adulthood. *Journal of Personality and Social Psychology, 7,* 291–300.

Witkin, H.A., Moore, C.A., Goodenough, D.R., & Cox, P.W. (1977). Field-dependent and field-independent cognitive styles and their educational implications. *Review of Educational Research, 47*(1), 1–64.

Wood, J.A., & Pitz, G.F. (1985, October). *Computer aversion as source of bias in computerized testing.* Paper presented at the Annual Meeting of the Military Testing Association, San Diego.

Wright, D.A., Melmed, A. & Farris, E. (1982). *Instructional use of computers in public schools Spring 1982* (FRSS Report No. 14). Washington, D.C.: National Center for Education Statistics.

Zemke, R. (1984, May). Evaluating computer-assisted instruction: the good, the bad and the why. *Training Technology Journal, 21*(5) 22–47.

Author Index

Subject Index

QUEEN MARY
COLLEGE
LIBRARY